Second Edition

Interactive GROUP WORK

Jane E. Atieno Okech
Deborah J. Rubel
William B. Kline

American Counseling Association
2461 Eisenhower Avenue, Suite 300 | Alexandria, VA 22314 | counseling.org

American Counseling Association
2461 Eisenhower Avenue, Suite 300
Alexandria, VA 22314

Publisher | Carolyn C. Baker

Digital and Print Development Editor | Nancy Driver

Senior Production Manager | Bonny E. Gaston

Copy Editor | Joan Flynn

Cover and text design by Bonny E. Gaston

Library of Congress Cataloging-in-Publication Data

Names: Atieno Okech, Jane E., author. | Rubel, Deborah J., author. | Kline, William B., author.
Title: Interactive group work / Jane E. Atieno Okech, Deborah J. Rubel, William B. Kline.
Description: Second edition. | Alexandria, VA : American Counseling Association, [2023] | Includes bibliographical references and index. |
Identifiers: LCCN 2023008774 | ISBN 9781556203978 (paperback)
Subjects: LCSH: Group counseling. | Group psychotherapy.
Classification: LCC BF636.7.G76 A76 2023 | DDC 158.3/5—dc23/eng/20230503
LC record available at https://lccn.loc.gov/2023008774

Dedication

We dedicate this book to our current and former students who continue to inspire us to learn and grow from their education, supervision, and practice of group work.

For our practitioner readers, we hope that our book will stimulate your ongoing growth and development as group leaders.

Lastly, we hope that our book will encourage counselor educators and supervisors to broaden their perspectives about conceptualizing group process and the roles of group leaders.

Table of Contents

Preface

Over 20 years ago, we (Jane Okech and Deborah Rubel) had front row seats for the creation of a seminal book on group counseling and therapy. Our major professor, William ("Bill") Kline, had not only taken on the formidable task of launching our careers as researchers and counselor educators but also signed a contract to create a book that would expand and improve upon prior texts used in training group counselors and therapists. We watched, listened, and learned as Bill guided us through our own group training and also as he labored to communicate his distinct, pure, disciplined, and incredibly useful vision of the potential and reality of groups and group leadership to us, to the other students, and to the reading audience. We were privileged to experience leading groups and receiving supervision for these groups in a way that was thoroughly consistent with Bill's teaching and writing and authentic to Bill as a person, group leader, and scholar. For both of us, this experience was life changing and instilled a lifelong belief in the potential of groups and how they should be structured and led.

As we (Jane Okech and Deborah Rubel) moved on to our own counselor education careers we used Bill's book in both our beginning and advanced group classes. Sometimes it was difficult to fit the content into our institutions' existing group counseling course structures because the book was so direct and focused on group-specific conceptualization and intervention. Often, we chose to add separate readings to address areas commonly overlooked in group coursework. At times, we toyed with using other texts but always found them filled with information that was not useful or systematic and lacking in information that assisted in the conceptualization of groups and group interventions.

When we used Bill's text, we found that our courses, once liberated from old structures, became highly effective as the foundation for budding group counselors. As I (Deborah Rubel) taught advanced group counseling to doctoral students who had already learned about group work, I received feedback that the book revolutionized the way they thought about groups and assisted them in integrating the bits of disparate information from past learning into a useful approach across group types. As time wore on, we and our master's- and doctoral-level students continued to find the text useful, unique, and substantial.

After a few years, Bill's book went out of print. We and our students still had access to the book in the form of used copies and PDF files, but we pondered why the book had not been used more often and how we could potentially update it and reintroduce it to a larger audience. Thoughts, meetings, plans, plan revisions, outlines, jobs, kids, aging parents, and COVID-19 all happened. Some of these challenges (or "delays") became opportunities as the world of helping and helping in groups shifted in unimaginably dramatic ways, even as it stayed, at its core, essentially the same. This book, in collaboration with Bill and the American Counseling Association, is the culmination of these experiences over time.

Like the first edition, this second edition presents principles, theories, and procedures to help readers develop their understanding of group interaction and begin their practice of group work. Experienced leaders will learn about new ideas that can invigorate and improve their practice, as well as be challenged to "try on" new perspectives and procedures. Novice leaders and students will be challenged to view group work as a distinct and uniquely powerful evidence-based mode of counseling and therapy that stands apart from individual counseling. Both experienced and novice group leaders will find that the perspectives and procedures offered are different from, and offer additional benefits over, what they have learned in their training in individual counseling and therapy.

The perspectives on group work that have guided the preparation of this second edition vary from the perspectives present in most group counseling and therapy texts. First, the principles, theory, and procedures presented here place the group process at the center of group work. This perspective views the quality of group members' interactions within the group process as the most critical determinant of member change. The centrality of group process and quality of member interactions have several critical implications for group leaders' roles, responsibilities, and actions (which lead to the second set of differences). The centrality of group process and quality member interactions is emphasized most often in counseling and therapy groups but is also significant to psychoeducational and work groups.

Second, although this text positions group leaders as important to group members' learning, change, and therapeutic success, the group leader's impact is characterized throughout as a less direct change and therapeutic agent. The role of a leader is characterized more as a builder and steward of optimal group conditions for change than as a purveyor of group techniques. This differs from most texts. It means that group leaders are responsible for creating and maintaining a learning, change-promoting, and therapeutic environment. This environment supports teaching members communication skills and other tools necessary for interpersonal learning and structures and supports interactions so that members learn from one another and change as desired. This perspective holds that members' interactions, not the individual therapeutic technique of the group leader, provide the medium for learning, change, and growth.

Another set of beliefs that inform this text is a systems perspective and the view that helping groups are social systems. From this perspective, the environment in which the group exists, the composition of the group, the group's goals, the internal and external communication boundaries of the group, and members' issues are all intertwined. As part of the environment within which all groups operate, the sociopolitical realities of power and differences in culture, race, gender, sexual orientation, socioeconomic class, religion, primary language of communication, national origin, immigration status, and age, among others, affect leadership and member interactions. The implications of systemic interrelatedness include the replication and display of individual, familial, societal, and cultural dynamics within the group and the potential for growth or harm to result.

Finally, this text is grounded in the belief that the principles of group dynamics and theories specific to group should inform leaders' actions. This belief implies that leader actions and interventions are severely limited when they are not informed by theoretically based conceptualizations of group interaction. Principles of group dynamics and theories specific to group offer new and experienced group leaders information about group-as-a-whole functioning, when to intervene, which intervention to use, and why an intervention may not have been effective. Surprisingly, this emphasis on group-specific theory is relatively uncommon.

This second edition differs from the first edition in several ways. Updated perspectives on diversity and social justice, current research on group efficacy and process, and updated professional frameworks are included and integrated into all aspects of the text. In particular, attention to accreditation standards will enable training programs to utilize this text as a comprehensive resource for entry-level and advanced group coursework. Additionally, extra care is taken in this text to apply the systemic perspective, foundational concepts of group dynamics, and group-specific theory to a variety of settings and group types, including online settings and populations of relevance to counselors.

Organization and How to Use This Book

This updated text includes four parts with several chapters in each part. Each chapter is relevant to both novices and more experienced group leaders. If you are just learning, use the learning outcomes for novice leaders outlined at the start of each chapter to guide your reading and learning efforts. If you are more advanced, use the advanced leaders' learning outcomes to deepen your learning and application of concepts.

The information in Part I helps new and experienced leaders understand groups as human phenomena that occur naturally in a social context, have shared interactive and environmental characteristics, and develop over time. Learning can be directly supported by reflection, discussion, and writing about current group membership and leadership experiences. Learning can also be enriched through reflection, discussion, and writing on recalled past informal and formal group experiences, on group interaction in movies or training videos, or on written group interaction scenarios.

Part II explains three group-specific theories—focal conflict, group general systems, and interpersonal—that each contribute to a comprehensive, integrated, and useful framework for understanding groups and group leadership. The chapters emphasize the types of understanding that are critical to counseling and therapy groups but are also useful to understanding psychoeducation and task groups. Learning for novice group leaders can be best extended through applying the concepts to group interaction in training videos that use facilitated groups. Learning for more advanced group leaders may be facilitated by viewing video recordings of their own groups and applying the concepts, preferably in the context of supervision.

In Part III, this theoretical framework is translated into concrete leadership and membership skills, ongoing leadership tasks, and intervention strategies for moving groups and group members forward through common challenges. Again, these skills, tasks, and intervention strategies are directly applicable to counseling and therapy groups but also adaptable to psychoeducation and task groups. Novice and advanced group leaders will benefit from extending their learning of these skills, tasks, and interventions by applying the concepts to group interaction in video recordings.

The first two chapters in Part IV integrate all of the foundational learning into the "real world" of groups through a discussion of professional ethical issues. Novice group leaders can support their learning by analyzing group work cases to identify potential ethical dilemmas and apply ethical decision-making models. More advanced group leaders should regularly process the concepts of ethical group work during group planning and supervision.

Part IV also summarizes current research on the effectiveness of groups, introduces readers to common types of groups and settings, describes how groups should be organized and operated, and discusses the importance of leadership personal development and style to the function of the group. It may be helpful to read Chapter 14 on group types and settings earlier in learning—for example, after reading Part I—to become familiar with the broad, real-life world of groups before revisiting it later to deepen understanding of how interactive group leadership is used across group types and settings.

Acknowledgments

We want to express our gratitude to Maya Jamaleddine for her careful literature review and for reviewing all book chapters during the early stages of this project. We also thank Carolyn Baker for her support, patience, and dedication to our success in publishing our second American Counseling Association book. We extend our sincerest congratulations and well wishes to her as she embarks on her retirement journey. Lastly, we thank all the peer reviewers and the staff at ACA Publications for their dedication in helping us publish a book that we are proud of.

About the Authors

Jane E. Atieno Okech, PhD, is a professor of counselor education and supervision and vice provost for faculty affairs at the University of Vermont. Professor Okech's scholarship primarily focuses on the advancement of proficiencies in the practice of group psychotherapy and clinical supervision with diverse populations. Her scholarly publications in group work and counselor education in general have received multiple professional accolades, including the 2015 Outstanding Article and 2017 Article of the Year awards by the Association for Specialists in Group Work for her collaborations with Drs. Rachel Vannatta, Asher Pimpleton-Gray, and Julia Champe. Professor Okech also received the 2019 *Counselor Education and Supervision* Publication of the Year award from the Association for Counselor Education and Supervision for her collaboration with Dr. Rubel. She was designated a fellow by the Association for Specialists in Group Work in 2018 and is executive editor of *The Journal for Specialists in Group Work.*

Deborah J. Rubel, PhD, is a professor of counselor education and supervision at Oregon State University. Dr. Rubel's recent scholarship focuses on examining and critiquing qualitative approaches to research, describing mental health stigma and bias in counseling/counselor education, and promoting group work. She received the 2019 *Counselor Education and Supervision* Publication of the Year award from the Association for Counselor Education and Supervision (ACES) for her collaboration with Dr. Okech. She was designated a fellow by the Association for Specialists in Group Work in 2017. Currently, she serves as the chair of the ACES Social Justice and Human Rights Committee.

William "Bill" Kline, PhD, is a retired counselor educator and counselor. During his career, he focused on group work and qualitative research, publishing in both areas. His professional service included numerous terms on the editorial boards of *Counselor Education and Supervision* (*CES*) and *The Journal for Specialists in Group Work*. He also served as editor and then as associate editor for qualitative research for *CES*. He received the Eminent Career Award and was later designated a fellow by the Association for Specialists in Group Work.

Part I

The Interactive NATURE of GROUPS

Chapter 1

The Social Context of Group Counseling

Outcomes

Level 1 Outcomes

After reading this chapter, entry-level students and practitioners should be able to:

1. Describe how human reliance on relationships is connected to the value of group work.
2. Communicate how change occurs in group work and how these changes can impact individuals' lives.
3. Recount the origins and evolution of group counseling and therapy.
4. Identify the core values of group counseling and therapy in a socioculturally and sociopolitically diverse world.
5. Articulate the importance of group work in a socioculturally and sociopolitically diverse world.

Level 2 Outcomes

After reading this chapter, advanced-level students and practitioners should also be able to:

1. Explain a theoretical basis that connects human reliance on relationships to the value of group work.
2. Compare and contrast how change occurs in group work and how change occurs in individual helping relationships.
3. Critique the origins and evolution of group work in light of our changing society.
4. Justify the shift in the core values of group work in light of our rapidly changing world.
5. Explain the connection between the needs of a socioculturally and sociopolitically diverse world and the potential of group work.

Group membership defines our lives as humans. The instant we are born we gain membership in groups, starting with membership in the family group that consists of our primary caregivers and siblings. These group memberships evolve and multiply over time to include those associated with friends, school, community, and work or profession, among others. We are also born into a society where our positionality with respect to a multitude of social identities, such as race, ethnicity/culture, gender, age, sexual orientation, ability status, and religion, is defined and nurtured from birth. Potentially, we may become members or leaders of helping groups, such as task, psychoeducational, counseling, and therapy groups. Our intersecting identities and these multiple memberships shape the roles we play in our lives and sculpt our relationships with other individuals and groups. We often refer to ourselves in terms of the roles we play. We may identify as someone's child or sibling, partner, spouse, parent, or friend or as a counselor or therapist, a researcher, a fan of a sports team, a member of a political party, or an advocate for a social cause. We, the authors of this book, are human beings, too—an Asian American biracial woman, a Black woman, and a White man. We are multifaceted human beings with several intersecting identities. Because we are human beings, we are a part of many groups—for example, a race, a gender, a sexuality, a family, an extended family, friendship groups, a profession, and groups of people who share similar passions and problems. We are connected in some way to all who live in the world with us, all who have preceded us, and all who will follow.

Interpersonal Relationships, Social Connectedness, and Mental Health

The social connectedness that results from effective communication and mutual relationships forms a foundation for mental health. Social connection includes a sense of closeness and belonging, and this develops in relationships ranging from acquaintanceship to intimate relationships (R. M. Lee & Robbins, 2000). If we are able to interact effectively with others, we are likely to get our social needs met and to develop a satisfactory social connection to our primary groups and to the world. Effective interactions with others contribute to our sense of personal value, self-esteem, and belonging. When we are not able to interact effectively, we may become lonely, we may lose our sense of social connection or belonging, and our identity may suffer. Ineffective interactions with others may also lead to very real difficulties in educational environments and the workplace, to a diminished view of our own personal worth, and to lowered self-esteem.

Many theorists representing a broad range of views (e.g., Bugental, 1965; Freud, 1921/1948; Fulmer, 2018; Maslow, 1970; Rogers, 1961; Schutz, 1966; N. Thomas et al., 2015) have described relationships as essential in meeting core human needs. Bugental (1965) discussed rootedness and relatedness as core existential needs and suggested that individuals are motivated to develop a sense that they are a part of humankind and involved in authentic relationships with others. Freud (1921/1948) held that individuals have a basic psychological need for affiliation. Maslow (1970) maintained that individuals need to experience a sense of belonging as well as have a need for love and intimate relationships. Rogers (1961) held that individuals develop a sense of self-worth in the context of their relationships and strive to gain acceptance from others. Rogers also stressed that, as individuals age, their "need for positive regard from others increases. Such needs include being loved by others, being emotionally and/or physically touched, and being valued and cared for" (Sharf, 1996, p. 220). Finally, Schutz (1966) identified three essential interpersonal needs—inclusion, control, and affection—that can be satisfied only in relationships with others. All these theorists supported the essential need of individuals to be in connected relationships in which they feel valued and accepted.

The literature affirms that an individual's ability to effectively self-disclose in relationships plays a significant role in the effectiveness of their social functioning and sense of well-being (Davis & Franzoi, 1987). Effective self-disclosure leads to connectedness, which leads to a sense of well-being and mental health (Davis & Franzoi, 1987; Jourard, 1964). Neuroscientists such as Matthew Lieberman (2013) also have contended that human brains are wired for connection, which serves as the core foundation for modern neurobiology studies. Without a sense of connectedness, individuals may become lonely, may lack a clearly defined sense of identity, and may not feel they belong in society (Lieberman, 2013).

Although the ability to self-disclose effectively is important in developing essential connections with others, effectively communicating one's experiences to others is challenging. For some, this is complicated by a variety of barriers, the development of which can also be traced to relationships. Fears that may originate from inadequate or damaging relationships with families of origin or peers may limit what individuals feel safe to disclose. Even when self-disclosure and connection are desired, patterns of behavior established over time in unhealthy environments—for example, avoidance or aggression—may prevent or limit connections. Similarly, lack of modeling and reinforcement in formative relationships may result in a lack of communication skills. These limitations to appropriate and effective self-disclosure restrict the capacity of an individual for intimate involvement with others. Individuals who hear messages from significant authorities in their lives (e.g., teachers, priests, counselors, caregivers, political leaders) that they are inferior or do not have value in society may begin to internalize such messages or develop anger and resentment toward those who harbor such values and beliefs.

Individuals who have not witnessed effective self-disclosure or listening skills may become discouraged if their attempts at connecting are ineffective. Thus, to build authentic and healthy relationships, acquire a sense of social connectedness, and develop a clear sense of identity, individuals must resolve those interpersonal issues that influence how they communicate and respond to the communications of others. Individuals may also need to acknowledge the impact of sociocultural factors and systemic oppression on how they experience themselves and their relationships with people in general, with their own primary identity groups, and with groups that have contributed to their marginalization. The resolution of interpersonal issues in all these contexts is a crucial prerequisite for mental health, and adequately resolving interpersonal issues is a critical part of improving mental health.

Interpersonal Relationships

Historical and contemporary research both support the idea that individuals learn how to view themselves and others, and how to act in relationships, from interactions in their families as well as in social, educational, and occupational groups. Foundational theorists such as Sullivan (1953), Bowen (1966), and Kernberg (1976), despite their varied perspectives, contended that family-of-origin experiences shape the roles that individuals assume and the way in which they fill those roles. From the perspective of these theorists, experiences with significant others shape how individuals interact with others and influence their choices about forming relationships and interacting with others throughout their lives.

Relationship patterns formed in their family of origin define the behaviors and roles that individuals perform in all their relationships. This means that individuals' interactions, with some variation, are relatively consistent between home, work, school, and other social-cultural contexts. For example, an individual who suppresses the expression of their anger at home probably suppresses it at work and with their friends. An individual who believes they need to please others to be acceptable in their family is likely to work hard to please their friends, their peers at work or at school, and their employers or teachers.

Learning how to be in a relationship is a result of the experiences individuals have in their family of origin or in their primary family grouping. At times, the "rules" families have about how to be appropriate, acceptable, and noticed create self-perceptions and relationship behaviors that cause pain and limit the extent to which individuals are able to be fulfilled in their relationships. Family rules that forbid the expression of painful emotions severely limit how openly family members can share their feelings to gain support from other family members. Later in life, individuals who have grown up operating by these rules are not likely to know how to ask for or receive the support offered in more fulfilling relationships. Conversely, many families have rules that lead to self-perceptions and relationship behaviors that are fulfilling and allow individuals to develop and prosper. These families provide a nurturing environment in which it is safe to be vulnerable, share emotions, openly seek support, and experience acceptance.

Individuals who experience problems in their relationships are often dissatisfied with their lives and less mentally healthy than individuals who do not experience relationship problems. When individuals who experience relationship problems become members of counseling or therapy groups, they have an opportunity to identify their relationship problems, to identify the origins and impact of these on their current relationships, and also to gain insight into self-perceptions that lead to unfulfilling relationships. The primary goals of group counseling and therapy are to help group members learn effective ways to make fulfilling interpersonal connections, change their limiting self-perceptions, and acquire the interpersonal skills and behaviors necessary to develop healthy relationships.

Group Interaction as a Reflection of Social-Cultural Context

The social issues present in the social-cultural context of counseling and therapy groups invariably appear in group interaction. Most commonly, these issues emerge when members treat each other according to stereotypes (Miles et al., 2021; Okech et al., 2016). Examples include a female member accusing a male member of not valuing the expression of emotions, a male member accusing a female member of not being able to make rational decisions, a cisgender group member telling a member who identifies as gender nonbinary to choose a "side," or a member suggesting that another member has limited intelligence because of race. Other occasions in which stereotyping occurs are less blatant but just as demeaning. For example, group members may treat another member very carefully (e.g., making sure a member understands what is going on or does not have hurt feelings) or patronize a member because of assumptions about how to get along with "that kind of person." Such careful or patronizing treatment is a subtle demonstration of stereotyping that limits member participation and learning and stymies the relationships the targeted member can develop with other group members. Members are often unaware that their long-held stereotypes of others limit the choices they make about their treatment of others. Many members are unaware that they inadvertently cause others pain (Okech et al., 2015). Perhaps most tragically, these members are totally unaware of how their stereotypes severely limit their opportunities for satisfying relationships and what they can learn from those whom they stereotype.

The clearest manifestation of social-cultural issues emerging in the group context occurs when there is an open expression of bigotry or intolerance. Although the open expression of prejudice is appalling and immediately damaging to the group, it is only a more blatant expression of the same limiting beliefs usually expressed more subtly (Miles et al., 2021). In all cases, members bring the biases they acquire in their social environments into the counseling and therapy groups they attend. Regardless of how they are expressed, biases disrupt interpersonal interactions within the group and delay the group's progression toward cohesion as overt and covert conflicts (Okech et al., 2016). Assuming counseling or therapy groups will be "cultural islands" free of intolerance and bigotry is an enormous mistake.

Social Issues and Social Responsibility

Leaders who understand that groups are social microcosms, inevitably reflecting the dynamics of the social-cultural contexts within which they exist, should expect that sociocultural issues will emerge within their groups. Leaders who witness social and cultural issues emerging in their counseling and therapy groups are responsible for identifying and confronting these issues. Confronting social issues is a fundamental aspect of a leader's role and social responsibility. At a minimum, leaders who are sincere about helping members make productive changes in their lives are concerned about the social issues that cause members pain and limit their potential for growth. Such leaders are also invested in creating a group culture that encourages members to directly address sociocultural concerns and to work on understanding each other and resolving conflict.

Leaders must recognize that group members live in environments where there are devastating social issues, such as religious and cultural bigotry, intolerance of differences, racism, ageism, and sexism. These socially exhibited attitudes and beliefs significantly influence what individuals can be and limit their opportunities to have social relationships that could contribute to their well-being. These realizations have three important implications for the work of group counselors and therapists. First, the leaders' responsibility to proactively identify and confront these issues during group interaction is critical. Second, leaders must help members learn not only how to confront and cope with the tyranny of social issues but also how to help others outside the group confront these issues.

Finally, group counselors and therapists must find a meaningful way to confront social and cultural issues in their own lives.

The Critical Need for a Multicultural Perspective

Individuals from diverse cultures, races, religious practices, and worldviews populate the earth we live on. These diverse perspectives enrich us all because they offer alternative perspectives and variety; each of us becomes richer in our experiences when we embrace and respect diversity. Treating others with respect, and valuing the development of common understanding and acceptance, completes a cycle of relationships that increases the possibility that social systems will come nearer to nurturing all individuals and their potential. The entire world is interconnected through global economies and political movements; impacted by global pandemics and sociopolitical changes; and intractably influenced by social media, international education, and cultural movements. Developing a multicultural perspective in one's work is therefore imperative.

Multicultural Group Counseling and Therapy

In a sense, all group counseling and therapy is multicultural and requires the engagement of diverse perspectives. Each group member represents diverse communities and the diverse qualities, identities, histories, experiences, and circumstances of their families. Later discussion will describe various ways to compose groups and the advantages and disadvantages of composing groups of people who are alike or different in some way (see Chapter 14). At this point, prospective leaders should understand that there is diversity in even the most homogeneous groups. Leaders who assume the presence of diversity even when members appear and behave similarly are most likely to develop an effective group environment.

Assuming diversity means that leaders presume that each member differs from the others in meaningful ways. Leaders who assume diversity always strive to help members confront and answer the question "How can we work together in a way that benefits us all?" Confronting this question means acknowledging members' differences and finding a common ground for members working together in the group. Confronting and acknowledging diversity means members' differing histories, identities, experiences, and perspectives can benefit all group members. For example, men and women can gain insight into their own relationships by listening to others' perspectives on intimacy and gender roles. Individuals who struggle with emotions and those who are comfortable with emotions can learn to empathize with those who are different and to respect the ways in which others express themselves. Spontaneous members and members who are more measured in their interactions can learn ways to interact with each other. Cisgender, heterosexual group members can learn about the dynamics of cisgender gay and lesbian relationships or those of nonbinary, gender-nonconforming, or transgender group members. In each of these examples, members learn tolerance and respect for different perspectives and identities, experience alternative ways to interact, and broaden their perspectives about others.

Change

From a group counseling and therapy perspective, three fundamental beliefs are useful guides for counselors and therapists. These pertain to how individuals develop relationship problems, how they maintain those relationship problems, and how they can best change how they relate to others. The first belief is that individuals form and enact their personalities in relationship to others. The second is that because of their relationships, individuals develop a pattern of "acceptable" interpersonal behaviors that they believe are appropriate to use in their relationships. The third belief is that because individuals form self-perceptions and interpersonal behaviors in relation to others, they are more likely to change how they interact with others and in relation to their self-perceptions. This is what makes group work such a powerful tool for interpersonal change.

Interpersonal Learning and Group Interaction

From as early as 1905, literature on group membership has described the powerful impact of group members on one another and of group dynamics within the group (I. D. Yalom & Leszcz, 2020), allowing members to learn from their here-and-now interactions. Bloch and Crouch (1985) analyzed factors previously identified by research as crucial for achieving therapeutic goals in therapy groups. One of these factors, interacting with one another, was found to be the most crucial in helping members achieve therapeutic success. In other words, members profited most from their interactions with each other, not from their interactions with the group leader. The idea of members profiting from their interactions with other members may be foreign to group counselors and therapists who have been trained in traditional, individual-oriented approaches to counseling and psychotherapy. As a result of their clinical training, they may perceive themselves to be the primary agent of change in their work with clients.

From our perspective as authors, effective group leaders are those who can successfully create environments that promote effective member interaction. When members interact effectively, they experience the profound power of group interaction to influence their interpersonal behavior. When leaders recognize that their goal is to establish and maintain conditions that allow interpersonal learning, the way they lead groups often changes dramatically. Members who participate in groups that demonstrate necessary conditions and emphasize interpersonal learning become intensely engaged and acutely aware of their relationships with each other. This awareness can often lead to significant changes in how members relate to each other and to people outside their groups.

The Relevance of Change in Group Interaction to Real Life

Because members participate in counseling and therapy groups to deal with relationship problems, they eventually enact their relationship issues in the here and now of group interaction. Ultimately, group members realize the way they interact with others in group is very similar to how they interact in relationships outside group. Additionally, the social-cultural context of the group has a significant impact on the interpersonal dynamics and interpersonal issues with which a group may grapple. Group members' beliefs and values regarding, for example, their socioeconomic status, racial identity, gender identity, political views, and sexual orientation are likely to emerge in group in both overt and covert ways. Inevitably, members will also see how their perceptions of others and their interactions in their group relationships are related to early experiences in their family of origin and their social-cultural context.

When members become aware of the behaviors and perceptions that create problems in their relationships with others in group, change is possible. Group members who become aware of what they do to cause relationship problems are then able to make different choices about interacting with other group members. A reflective and introspective process allows group members to examine the personal beliefs and values underlying their behaviors and interpersonal patterns. Eventually, members can apply those changes they make to improve their relationships with other group members to improving their relationships outside group.

Issues can arise, however, when members do not transfer what they learn in group to their out-of-group relationships or when members believe that their interpersonal patterns within the group are untransferable and unrelated to how they engage outside the group. Leaders who are sensitive to this transfer of learning involve members in fine-tuning their behavior changes in group and in making thoughtful decisions about when and how to use their new interpersonal behaviors outside group. When considering the relevance of group interaction to "real life," new leaders and members must recognize that relationship behaviors in group correspond with relationship behaviors outside group. Group leaders also should recognize the need for and value of a conscious decision-making process for transferring what members have learned in group to their out-of-group relationships, so members have no doubt about the relevance of in-group changes to real-life situations.

Essential Values for Group Work

Helping people become more satisfied in their relationships with others is the core objective for group counseling and therapy. This objective can be translated, if necessary, into such terms as promoting mental health, increasing the effectiveness of interpersonal behaviors, improving boundary functioning, bettering social adjustment, changing limiting cognition, developing congruence, increasing self-acceptance, or ameliorating developmental issues. Counselors and therapists can also express the foundational value of group work, which is that effective and fulfilling relationships are necessary for optimal functioning and mental health.

Leaders who understand that group interaction mirrors interaction occurring in the social and cultural environment outside the boundaries of their groups also see the relevance of group work to improving society as a whole. Among the things members should learn in groups are how to be sensitive to the needs of others, how to accept and live with differences, how to communicate to ensure more complete understanding, and how to deal productively with conflict. Thus, each member who leaves a group with these learnings can contribute to the quality of their social and cultural environment. Similarly, issues in the broader society/culture have a powerful impact on individuals' lives, both limiting and defining possibilities for interpersonal connection, personal development, and life satisfaction. Leaders who are concerned about members leading satisfying lives cannot ignore the social and cultural conditions that limit the possibilities for group members outside counseling and therapy groups.

The Efficacy of Group Counseling and Therapy

The first description of group counseling and therapy as a formal practice appeared in an article by Joseph Pratt in 1906. This article described the powerful influence that group interaction had on group members. Pratt's ideas have evolved continuously since the publication of his accounts. At present, there continues to be overwhelming support for group counseling and therapy and an ever-growing need for group interventions.

The Accounts of Pratt, Trigant Burrow, and Lewis Wender

The pioneers of group therapy learned about the power of group interaction to improve individuals' lives through happenstance, challenging circumstances, and inquisitiveness. As mentioned, Pratt (1906) was the first to write about the curative effects of group interaction. He used groups due to overwhelming practical demands and stumbled on the discovery that group interaction had a powerful influence on those who participated. Another pioneer, Trigant Burrow (1928), was curious how loneliness affected individuals and so explored how relationships with others influenced a person's psychiatric issues. Lewis Wender (1936), by contrast, faced the practical issues of applying individually focused psychoanalytic therapeutic interventions to hospitalized psychiatric patients. He discovered that group interaction was productive because of some essential dynamics present in group interactions.

On July 1, 1905, as a result of being overwhelmed with a constant stream of new patients, Pratt began treating tuberculosis patients in groups (MacKenzie, 1992; Pratt, 1906). Pratt's Emmanuel Church Tuberculosis Class was a group of 25 members who met weekly at Massachusetts General Hospital for socializing and education. Members of the class represented many racial identities and religious sects. Pratt noted that the members, although different in many ways, shared the common bond of their disease. Of the tuberculosis patients in Pratt's classes, many of whom had been given no hope, 75% recovered.

On April 30, 1928, Burrow presented a paper at the Phipps Psychiatric Clinic at Johns Hopkins Hospital (MacKenzie, 1992). Burrow initiated his work with groups because of his interest in exploring the effects of isolation. He believed that many psychiatric problems were related to how individuals interacted with others in their communities. To study problems in community living, Burrow examined the here-and-now interactions of individuals in groups. He concluded that interventions designed to address "mental disorder and insanity, in industrial disorders and crime" (Burrow, 1928, p. 206) should focus extensively on how individuals relate to each other. He also reached the conclusion that interpersonal relationships play a critical role in the development and enactment of psychopathology.

In 1936, Wender published a paper that described the practical realities of making efficient psychotherapeutic interventions with an inpatient population. Using a psychoanalytic frame of reference, Wender faced the issues of time, cost, patients' unsuitability for analytic procedures, and the difficulties he perceived in establishing productive transference relations. Wender determined that analytic procedures were unsuitable for his situation and that he needed to devise a therapeutic program that could overcome the limitations of analytic procedures. After extensively applying group therapeutic interventions in his setting, Wender identified several essential "dynamics" that operated in group psychotherapy: intellectualization, patient-to-patient transference, and catharsis in the family. Essentially, Wender was the first to articulate what are now called *group therapeutic factors*.

The contributions of Pratt (1906), Burrow (1928), and Wender (1936) were the products of accidental discovery, curiosity, and practical demands. Pratt accidentally discovered the powerful effects of group interaction. Burrow advanced concepts that describe the role of group interaction in the development and amelioration of psychopathology. Wender was the first to identify some of the critical group therapeutic factors. Each of these contributions plays a significant role in current conceptualizations of the purposes and applications of group counseling and therapy.

The Evolution of Group Work

The practice of group work dramatically expanded in the 1940s in response to the overwhelming needs of military personnel after World War II (Rutan, 1993; Scheidlinger, 1993). During the mid-1940s, group therapy grew dramatically in terms of theory and practice. "The group therapists of those days did the best they could through trial and error and by incorporating their dyadic psychotherapy skills in a group setting" (Rutan, 1993, p. xvii). Although the group therapists during this time were relatively unsophisticated, they recognized that something powerful was taking place in their groups (Rutan, 1993; Scheidlinger, 1993).

In the 1950s, therapists continued to recognize the power of their groups to heal members; however, numerous debates emerged. One of the first, which occurred between individually oriented therapists and group therapists, focused on the relative efficacy of individual versus group therapy. Individual therapists, most of whom were analytically oriented, argued that group therapy offered only superficial treatment (Rutan, 1993). They argued in particular that group therapy diluted transference and that group therapy patients could thus make only superficial changes. This argument ended when group therapy consistently demonstrated that group interaction actually enhanced transference (Rutan, 1993). Subsequent debates occurred between group therapists over theory and the most effective group therapy techniques (Rutan, 1993; Scheidlinger, 1993). Despite these debates, by the end of the 1950s, the literature recognized group therapy as a powerfully effective and versatile form of treatment.

In the 1960s and 1970s, major advances occurred in the applications of psychoanalytic theory and object relations theory to group therapy (Scheidlinger, 1993). Also, during this period, Whitaker and Lieberman (1964) presented a new theory that continues to contribute significantly to the practice of group counseling and therapy. At the same time, various applications of group therapy developed and became highly popular. In particular, encounter groups and variants such as T-groups and sensitivity training groups emerged as vehicles for personal growth.

One of the foremost advocates of encounter groups was Carl Rogers (1970), who stated, "For more than thirty-five years, individual counseling and psychotherapy were the main focus of my professional life. But nearly thirty-five years ago I also experienced the potency of the changes in attitudes and behavior which could be achieved in group. This has been an interest of mine ever since" (p. v). Many authors echoed Rogers's enthusiasm during the 1970s (Schutz, 1973).

Unfortunately, many practitioners of encounter and related "growth" groups were insufficiently trained and incautious about using provocative group interventions and activities, which often led to members having adverse experiences in their groups. These groups "challenged and embarrassed the professional group work field because many people began to equate those controversial and at times even harmful group enterprises with group therapy" (Scheidlinger, 1993, p. 5). To clarify the difference between the abuses of group work and competent practice, practitioners recognized the need to professionalize group work.

Group work practitioners in 1973 formed the Association for Specialists in Group Work (ASGW). Like the American Group Psychotherapy Association (AGPA), which was founded in 1942, ASGW seeks to advance professionalism in group work. Both organizations contribute to group work knowledge and practice through their journals: the *International Journal of Group Psychotherapy*, published by AGPA, and *The Journal for Specialists in Group Work*, published by ASGW.

In 1994, AGPA, which has developed standards for clinical membership and ethical practice, supported certification for group therapists who meet stringent standards for training and experience. Certification and recertification of group psychotherapists is currently managed by the International Board for Certification of Group Psychotherapists.

ASGW, now a division of the American Counseling Association (ACA), has made substantial contributions to the professionalization of group workers in the fields of counseling and psychotherapy. For example, it has defined standards for training, practice, and multiculturalism in group work. Guiding documents include Multicultural and Social Justice Competence Principles for Group Workers (ASGW, 2012), Professional Standards for Training Group Workers (ASGW, 2000), and Best Practice Guidelines (R. V. Thomas & Pender, 2008).

In the field of psychology, the recognition of group work was slower to develop. In 1991, the American Psychological Association formed the Group Psychology and Group Psychotherapy division, which in 1996 began publication of the journal *Group Dynamics* (Gladding, 1999).

Since the 1970s, group therapy has seen continued growth and development. Dies (1993) pointed out that new group paradigms, such as time-limited therapy groups and self-help groups, have replaced the encounter movement of the 1970s. Scheidlinger (1993) described the growth of the group therapy movement since the 1970s as "an unprecedented growth spurt" (p. 9). Evidence of the continued growth in group work includes the increasing presence of group research in psychotherapy and counseling literature (I. D. Yalom & Leszcz, 2020) and the increased presence of group treatments in inpatient, outpatient, community, school, and "virtually all human service facilities" (Scheidlinger, 1993, p. 9). The substantial evidence of the effectiveness of group work interventions fuels the ongoing rapid expansion of group work.

Since 2000, group work has expanded exponentially with an increasing emphasis on practices that are effective across diverse racial and cultural groups (Kivlighan et al., 2019, 2021; Okech & Rubel, 2007; Rubel & Okech, 2018). For years group work has been criticized for not keeping up with the needs of racial minority groups (Bemak & Chung, 2004; Rubel, 2006). The practice has also expanded in its provision of treatment to specialized groups of clients who present with specific concerns, such as anger management or addictions, or who are in sexual offender treatment programs and the like. Treatment programs have expanded from unstructured counseling groups to structured and manualized psychoeducational groups (M. J. Galinsky et al., 2008). Even more recently, the trend toward evidence-based group work has influenced how practitioners in counseling and allied fields think about their work and the field (Muskat et al., 2010; Pollio & Macgowan, 2010). The call for evidence-based counseling has resulted in more focus on assessment of interventions and group outcomes, as well as how group work is taught and supervised in academic programs preparing counselors and therapists for practice (Hollenbaugh & Goodrich, 2021). Diversity-focused and evidence-based group practice are at the front lines of the continuing evolution of group counseling and therapy training and practice. In fact, the proliferation of manualized treatment is directly linked to the call for evidence-based group counseling practices (Burlingame et al., 2013; Miles & Paquin, 2013).

Research on the Efficacy of Group Counseling and Therapy

H. S. Bernard and MacKenzie (1994), in describing the 15 years of psychotherapy research prior to 1994, reported that approximately 85% of individuals involved in group psychotherapy did better than individuals in control groups. They went on to state that the results were "essentially the same whether the psychotherapy [was] delivered in an individual or group format" (H. S. Bernard & MacKenzie, 1994, p. viii). I. D. Yalom (1995) and I. D. Yalom & Leszcz (2005, 2020) concurred that a significant amount of evidence supports the efficacy of group therapy. Piper (1993) also made the point that reviews of the outcome literature during the past decade have confirmed the general effectiveness of group therapy and its similar efficacy to that of individual therapy.

In 1993, Dies summarized 40 years of research in group psychotherapy, finding that the literature showed continued growth in the confidence that group treatments were effective. This confidence followed from meta-analytic studies of group research, surveys, comprehensive reviews of outcome studies, and studies that demonstrated the effectiveness of group interventions with specific client groups (e.g., depressed, bulimic, or sexually abused clients; Dies, 1993). Authors generally have agreed that group treatment is both effective and cost-efficient (H. S. Bernard & MacKenzie, 1994; Dies, 1993; Piper, 1993; Scheidlinger, 1993; I. D. Yalom & Leszcz, 2020).

By the 2000s, the question of whether group work is effective was noncontentious. Evidence gathered over the last century has consistently shown group work is effective (Kline, 2003). Consequently, the field has expanded to focus on refining its approaches to meeting the needs of members with diverse backgrounds and identities, to assess group work practice to develop evidence-based practice approaches, and to improve pedagogical and clinical approaches to training and supervising group workers. The prevalence and popularity of group work has grown dramatically in the last century. The dramatic growth of group work and the ever-increasing professionalization of group counseling and therapy have continued through the 2000s. Currently, group work has a solid grounding in research that supports its effectiveness. Group work is a primary treatment modality practiced in a wide array of settings. Now, as the demand for cost-effective and efficient treatment intensifies, group work will continue its explosive growth. The environment demands it. The COVID-19 pandemic can be credited with boosting a fledgling online group counseling practice (see Chapter 14) and pushing it into the mainstream of clinical practice of a medium long thought to be incompatible with online services. See Chapter 13 for a discussion of research findings on online group counseling.

Conclusion

At present, the demands of managed health care and the need to provide cost-effective psychotherapy are mounting (Namburi & Tadi, 2021). In addition to economic demands, practitioners in human service settings—colleges, universities, and schools, in particular—face diminishing resources and increased demand for services. These environmental realities forecast a continuously increasing need for group work. This bodes well for the practice to expand and reach more clients than formerly thought possible—especially through online approaches, which are the new frontier of psychotherapy (Weinberg, 2021).

The Interactive Group Environment

Outcomes

Level 1 Outcomes

After reading this chapter, entry-level students and practitioners should be able to:

1. Define and differentiate between group content, group process, and group structure.
2. Describe the concept of group norms and identify norms that promote effective, culturally responsive group functioning.
3. Articulate the concept of group member roles and describe facilitative and hindering roles and the factors contributing to their formation.
4. Outline the influence of the "supersystem" and sociocultural environment on group dynamics and how group leaders must use their power to shape group interactions that are effective, fair, and inclusive.
5. Restate the importance of the relationship between group environment and member attitudes.

Level 2 Outcomes

After reading this chapter, advanced-level students and practitioners should also be able to:

1. Identify group process in a group scenario and explain its relationship to group structure.
2. Analyze group interaction, identify norms, and determine whether these are beneficial or detrimental to culturally responsive group interaction.
3. Identify group members' roles in a group case and explain how the roles developed.
4. Evaluate group interaction and describe how norms and roles may influence member attitudes.
5. Analyze group interaction and identify how power and sociocultural and personal contexts affect individual group members and the group as a whole.

One of the crucial goals for group leaders is to codevelop with members an environment in which attitudes are conducive to the collaboration and growth of all group members. This environment must provide diverse group members access to and influence in the group process to meet their individual goals while promoting the overall function of the group. To accomplish this, leaders must understand the essential group properties (i.e., norms, roles, and attitudes) that influence the group environment and, thereby, group effectiveness. Once leaders learn to recognize these properties, they can further distinguish obstructive and facilitative forces in their groups and intervene to optimize the environment, help members develop beneficial attitudes, and support interpersonal learning. This chapter describes key concepts, or dynamics, through which the group leader assesses and intervenes in the functioning of the group. The first of these to be discussed is the concept of group process. Next are power and group as a social microcosm, two often-mentioned concepts that are rarely integrated but are crucial to a culturally inclusive and fair group process. Last to be described are group norms and group roles, two useful and historically significant concepts.

Group Process

Numerous disciplines that require an understanding of group interaction have used the term *group dynamics* (Vander Kolk,

1985). These disciplines, with their diverse perspectives, define group dynamics in varied ways. Our purpose in Part I is to define group dynamics in a way that helps leaders observe and conceptualize group interaction to benefit all group members. Group dynamics describes the purposes of group interaction (group process) and the interactive patterns (group structure) that emerge from these interactions.

It is essential for group leaders to understand what group process is and to be able to distinguish it from group content and group structure as a component of group dynamics. *Group process* is fluid and refers to the overt and covert interactions between group members, including the leader and subgroups within the group. It is the "how" of group interaction. *Group content*, conversely, is the "what" of group interaction. It is the covert and overt topics introduced by group leaders and members as well as the deeper collective and individual meanings those topics may have. *Group structure* refers to relatively stable characteristics of the group that affect group process. Group structures include aspects the group leader can easily plan, such as group size and session length, as well as aspects the leader must actively respond to and develop via the group process with members, such as group norms and roles.

For the purposes of group work in the helping professions, group process consists of interactions that "promote behavioral and attitudinal conformity with the group's emerging culture" (Wheelan, 1994, pp. 60–61). In other words, group process involves members negotiating how to communicate, participate, and perceive group involvement to meet their covert and overt individual and collective purposes in the group. Group process includes negotiations about the immediate and long-term focus of the group, how intimately members should interact, whether and how members should acknowledge differences and handle conflict, the acceptable level of honesty, what to expect from each member, and how to respond to each other's concerns. The questions "What is the purpose of this interaction?" and "What are members negotiating?" will assist group leaders as they attempt to identify and make sense of the group process. Once they identify group process negotiations, leaders can intervene to shape the development of the group environment. These interventions are discussed in the chapters of Part III.

The following example of a common negotiation during a first group meeting depicts a group process of directly negotiating the importance of sharing emotions:

Francis: "I'm not sure why you keep asking me about my feelings. It just makes me feel worse."
Angel: "I'm with you, Francis. If we talk about our problems and get ideas, that should be enough to help."
Francis: "I know, right? I want your help; I don't want to spend this time crying."
Shell: "What you're saying makes me feel like my hands are tied, though. What if I'm sad and want to talk about it? What then?"

Group process also includes more subtle, indirect negotiations. Indirect negotiations occur as members observe the outcomes of others' interactions. These observed outcomes shape what members regard as safe or acceptable group behavior. Interactions that appear to have productive or nonthreatening outcomes are more likely to be repeated, and those that seem to have negative outcomes are less likely to recur. Thus, both direct and indirect negotiations affect group interaction. For example, if sharing emotions seems productive, members are more likely to share emotions. If, on the other hand, sharing emotions seems damaging, members will attempt to avoid sharing emotions.

A more specific example of an indirect negotiation occurred in the third meeting of a group. During this meeting, Brian was 30 minutes late to the group, and Erin expressed anger about Brian's participation. Rob, another group member, reacted strongly: "Whoa! Whoa! Can't you see Brian is really having a hard time?" The other group members looked on in stunned silence until Brian said, "Erin, I did my best to get here. Your anger seems really out of line; I didn't come here to be judged!" With that, the group attempted to move back to the discussion they were engaged in prior to Brian's entrance. In this example, a powerful indirect negotiation took place. All group members experienced anger as hurtful and as something to be avoided.

Although direct and indirect negotiations in group processes can result in effective group interactions, these negotiations frequently have the purpose of avoiding interactions that challenge old ways of being and feel risky. When avoidant negotiations are successful, members are unlikely to share honest reactions, to participate spontaneously, or to share a full spectrum of emotions. Consequently, leaders should be alert to members negotiating "rules" for interaction that limit what can be shared. Members use negotiations to add certainty and safety to interaction and to avoid the uncertainty of group membership and change. Because these negotiations can block interchanges that can help members learn, they should be the target of leader attention and intervention.

The result of ongoing group process negotiations is usually relatively stable group interaction patterns. These interaction patterns include consistencies in member attitudes toward participation and interaction with each other. These stable patterns are referred to as group structure (Forsyth, 1999). Historically, the most significant of these patterns are norms and roles. Norms describe consistent patterns in the behaviors of all group members. Roles describe unique behaviors consistently performed by individual group members. However, a pair of related dynamics—power and group as a social microcosm—can affect group process, norms, and roles in ways that are often detrimental to group members who have marginalized identities and can limit the effectiveness of groups for all members.

Power and Group as a Social Microcosm

Chapter 1 emphasized the significance of culture and experiences in society to how individuals may experience group helping processes. It also introduced the idea that, via the attitudes of group leaders and group members, group dynamics will parallel societal dynamics. This parallel is called *group as a social microcosm*. The group as a social microcosm may pose a hindrance to therapeutic factors that benefit all group members and an opportunity for learning, growth, and healing. It can also pose a specific threat to the safety and well-being of group members, particularly those with marginalized identities. Group leaders must be aware of how the social microcosm is represented in the group and intervene to keep group members safe, counteract unproductive aspects of the group as a microcosm, and utilize this powerful dynamic to the advantage of group members. Not only should the methods of group leadership be responsive to the culture of group members, but the group leader should facilitate development of a group environment that makes space for, invites the participation of, and validates the experiences of group members with marginalized identities and perspectives.

One particularly important aspect of the group as a social microcosm is how it is structured around social power. *Social power* is a person's potential to exert influence over another and to enact social influence. Social power is the potential to change behavior in others, while social influence actually contributes to change in behavior. Social power and social influence can shape group interaction in both constructive and destructive ways. Ideally, group leaders and group members use their power in beneficial ways—for example, to promote group member autonomy, connection, support, learning, and growth toward member-selected goals. Power that is wielded by the group leader and members to promote unnecessary conformity, to silence uncomfortable perspectives and experiences, and to promote an unfair or damaging status quo consciously or unconsciously is destructive and counter to the values of group work.

This misuse of power can include "sins of omission" whereby powerful leaders and members—that is, those who have largely privileged social identities or highly valued characteristics—do not understand the added vulnerability and burden experienced by those with marginalized identities and perspectives. Without this understanding, leaders and privileged members may negatively misjudge the silence or frustration of marginalized group members or simply not understand that marginalized group members are not benefiting at the same level as other group members. Such group leaders and, to a lesser degree, privileged members have not used their power to invite participation, actively elicit and listen to diverse perspectives, and equitably balance the disparate needs of group members.

Group leaders are often admonished to be aware of their own power and to understand who is powerful or not in their groups, without being provided with specific guidance on the nature of power. However, several frameworks describing types of power and their sources exist, and these can provide group leaders with insight into their own power as well as the power or lack of power of their group members. One of the most common frameworks, often used in organizational psychology, is Raven and French's (1965) six bases of power. These six bases are as follows:

- *Informational power,* which involves the agent using information and logic to influence the target.
- *Expert power,* which involves the agent having influence on the target based on trust and respect, often built over time. Expert power is related to informational power but is more connected to the specific agent using it.
- *Referent power,* which is based on the target both identifying with and liking the agent. The target's affiliation with the agent causes them to comply with the agent's requests.

- *Coercive power*, which involves the agent having the ability to threaten the target, overtly or covertly, with punishment or consequences of some kind. The consequences can be mild (personal disapproval) or severe (being banned from a group).
- *Reward power*, which is the opposite of coercive power. It occurs when the influencing agent can grant some kind of reward to the target. Similarly, this reward can be either personal or impersonal.
- *Legitimate power*, which is based on common social norms, such as having the right to ask for something based on position or job title, expecting reciprocal behavior from others, being expected to support others in getting what they deserve, or being socially responsible or obligated to help others who are dependent.

The literature on group counseling also describes common dynamics that occur at the interface of the social microcosm of groups and their inherent power imbalances. According to Helms and Cook (1999), three main diversity themes typically occur within the dynamics of groups:

1. Power within the group is associated with each person's role. Thus, group leaders and group members with powerful roles will tend to have more influence in the group.
2. Power may be distributed based on the quantitative representation of social identities within the group.
3. Members with agent or majority social identity typically have more power than members with target or minority status.

Agent groups are social identity groups that tend to hold power, whereas target groups are social identity groups that are oppressed (Griffin, 1997). Drawing from the work of various group and social justice education authors (e.g., Griffin, 1997; Han & Vasquez, 2000; Helms & Cook, 1999; Sue & Sue, 2003), Rubel and Okech (2010) identified oppressive conditions that can occur with agent and target groups as follows:

- Group leaders who have cultural biases or blind spots will perpetuate their biases in the group. Without intervention, agent group members will dominate group interaction, prescribe group norms and processes, and determine group topics.
- Group members with invisible target identities may hide those identities in the group for safety reasons, much as they

do outside the group. This may result in a sense of invisibility and powerlessness that parallels their experience in society.

- Group members with target identities may be unwilling to discuss their feelings or experiences associated with their status because they feel unsafe or ashamed. Honest sharing of feelings and experiences by target group members may be challenged or denied by agent group members who are uncomfortable with their status. Agent group members may scapegoat target group members for expressing oppression-related anger, mistrust, and pain or for resisting dominant group norms. Group leaders may compound the damage by labeling a target member "resistant" for having legitimate fear.
- Agent group leaders and members may pressure target group members into roles responsible for representing their identity group or educating other group members. These roles depersonalize target members and remove agent group members' and leaders' responsibility for oppressive dynamics in the group.

Norms

As people interact within the groups to which they belong, whether the groups are social or therapeutic, they will demonstrate verbally or behaviorally that some behaviors are supported by the group and other behaviors are not. These behaviors and interactions may signify the norms that operate in those groups. *Norms* are the rules that dictate the ways in which a group interacts (I. D. Yalom & Leszcz, 2020). Because norms strongly influence how members interact, they strongly influence a group's safety, fairness, and effectiveness.

Leaders should be aware that the behaviors necessary for effective group interaction become norms only when the behaviors become a pattern in group interaction. This point is critical. It means that behavioral guidelines suggested by the leader or agreed upon by group members do not meaningfully affect group interaction until they become norms. For example, a group leader may suggest that members restate feedback they have received to ensure that they understand. Afterward, some members may restate feedback they receive, but others may immediately accept feedback or quickly defend themselves. At this point, restating feedback is not a norm. It will be a norm and have a meaningful effect on group interaction when most members regularly restate feedback, notice a lack of restatement, and actively encourage each other to use the behavior.

Norm and role development happen either consecutively or simultaneously, and they take time to occur. The development of social and cultural norms also follows the same pattern, which affects the social and cultural identity of group members (see Figure 2.1).

Norms prescribe a range of productive or ineffective group interactions and indicate the attitudes that members share about participation. When a group's norms are counter to meaningful interaction, then group members must, to some extent, share attitudes that bias them toward avoiding those meaningful interactions. For example, in a group that changes subjects or minimizes individual differences whenever conflict surfaces, members likely share an attitude that conflict is too difficult and dangerous to address. Likewise, in a group where, despite persistent direction by the leader, group members insist on talking about their relationships outside the group rather than their relationships within the group, group members must largely share the attitude that focusing on their relationships within the group is unfamiliar and scary. When leaders can identify norms that hinder group interaction and are aware of the attitudes that shape these ineffective norms, they can plan interventions that will move the group to establish better norms and better functioning.

Because norms develop largely through indirect negotiation, new norms may evolve before leaders are aware of them. Group members rarely directly discuss norms. Fortunately, alert group leaders can identify a norm when it is broken through a set of common behaviors that occur when this happens. Most often,

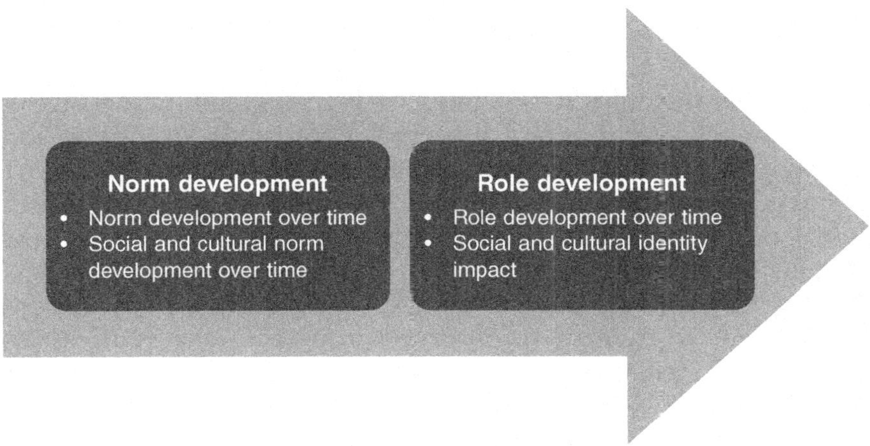

FIGURE 2.1
Dynamics of Norm and Role Development

when leaders observe members correcting each other's behavior directly (e.g., "Sophia, please use 'I' language.") or indirectly (e.g., "I wish people would not generalize what they feel to everyone."), it indicates that a group norm has been broken. Other ways that group members may respond to a member breaking a norm include challenges (e.g., "Gerald, you can give better feedback than that."), criticism (e.g., "That's so insensitive. You really don't care about getting along."), angry or anxious reactions (e.g., "Shut up, you jerk! You don't belong here!" or "I'm stunned. I don't know how to react to what you've said."), or simply ignoring the person and their behavior.

Leaders can judge the importance of a norm by observing the strength of the group's reaction to that norm being violated. The following situation demonstrates how members might react to the breaking of an important group norm:

Abi: "Hunter, what the . . .? You said that? Really? Not the place, not the place."

Skylar: "I'm really offended by that, too. I hope you never attack me like that."

Hunter: "Wow! I really feel like I've broken some kind of rule in here, and you all want to punish me. I was only being honest!"

Riley: "Hunter, you should know how we're supposed to get along. I'm not sure I ever want you to talk with me like that."

Jayden: "I'm not sure this group is for you. Have you thought about taking care of your problem somewhere else?"

A strong reaction to a norm violation indicates that members believe that the behaviors defined by the norm are important. By observing which norms and norm violations elicit a strong reaction from group members, leaders can gain insight into members' fears about participation. Once identified, these fears should be explored. For example, when the norm "anger will not be expressed" is stringently enforced, members will vigorously correct, challenge, or criticize those who express anger or who attempt to discuss sharing anger. Leaders who observe a group enforcing rigid norms about expressing anger can assume that members have fears about expressing anger and should explore those fears.

When leaders observe members working hard to maintain a norm, they should also expect members to resist changing that norm. This is because members attempt to maintain norms that will protect them from the anxiety that is associated with new and risky but potentially helpful behaviors. In general, the harder members fight to maintain a norm, the more difficult it will be to change that norm. Intervention strategies can be used to address norms that block group progress and to instead form productive norms (see Chapter 11).

The Formation of Norms

Norms are formed via negotiations where members influence one another covertly and overtly. When members are uncomfortable with a particular behavior, their shared reactions and responses to each other's reactions can define that behavior either as inappropriate (more likely) or as a behavior that is worth the risk they assume it brings (less likely without intervention). For example, a group member may appropriately express anger toward another member. In response, some group members may express their discomfort or fear, some may relate how such strong "negative" feelings have hurt them, and others may remain conspicuously silent. Thus, the development of a norm commences without specific discussion of or intent of shaping group rules. The following interaction depicts this process:

London: "Harper, I'm very angry that you're late. It feels disrespectful to me."
Elijah: "Ugh, London, that sounds so judgmental. Not really your place."
River: "That reminds me of my ex-partner. He was always angry at me for little things."
Liza: "It upsets me too, River. I don't think this is the place for that kind of emotion."
Harper: "You really hurt my feelings. That kind of talk is not helpful for me!"
Elijah: "Yeah, I thought we were going to be here to help each other. I'm really upset."

These reactions begin to establish the norm that expressing anger is unacceptable. Conversely, when members understand and admire a behavior, their reactions will establish the acceptability of that behavior. For example, after a member shares fears about giving feedback to another member, the others share how impressed they are by this sharing. Consequently, the norm that expressing fears is appropriate begins to be established:

Elijah: (*Tears in his eyes*) "River, I really want to give you the feedback you asked for, but I can't. I'm so scared you'll hate me. I really like the connection we've made, and I don't want to lose it."

Liza: "Wow, just wow, Elijah. I've never heard you share this way, and I can so relate. That took a lot of courage."

River: "Elijah, what I hear is that you value our connection. So do I, even more so now. I trust that connection, and you, even if the feedback stings."

Elijah: "This is really new for me. I guess I was scared because I thought I was going to get hurt, but I'm so relieved."

Harper: "This is so weird but good. I've really been holding back, but at least I feel like I can talk about my fear of wrecking my relationships in here with honesty."

These examples illustrate how indirect negotiation forms group norms. Norms form when members' negotiations result in a consistent pattern of group behavior. This process is most notable in a newly formed group where norms are unclear, members have differing personal or cultural ways of communicating, or members are uncertain how to behave. Sherif (1936) described the reciprocal influence process of norm development as a *funnel* pattern. When a new group begins and members are unsure of what is expected, they use behaviors that are familiar from their familial, social, educational, and professional settings. Over time, as members react to each other and to the interventions of the leader, their interactive behaviors become less variable. After a while, members' behaviors begin to conform. At the point where "members align their behaviors until they match certain standards" (Forsyth, 1999, p. 121), norms have developed.

The following case example illustrates a common process of norm development during a group's first two sessions:

Early in the first session, members engage in a discussion about their families, their job situations, and the current weather conditions. Members interact spontaneously and shift from topic to topic. Often, several members talk at once and laugh nervously. The group leader intervenes and shares a few ideas about how the group can interact effectively. These suggestions include listening to each other and staying with a topic for as long as it is productive. Some members use these suggestions, whereas others continue to interact as they had earlier. By the end of the session, after several leader interventions, members begin to be more attentive, talking one at a time and staying with a topic for longer periods.

> The second session begins with the same interaction patterns as the first meeting, but this does not last long. Without the leader saying anything, members stop their customary social interactions and focus on being in the group; a period of silence ensues. After a moment, a member talks without interruption about a relationship problem, while others listen attentively. At the end of the member's sharing, other members take turns offering their ideas on how to solve the problem. Eventually, discussion drifts as others share experiences with relationship problems. Occasionally, a member interrupts, but others remind that member to wait until the current speaker has finished.

In this example, group behaviors became less variable. The group rapidly established the norm of one speaker at a time. Interaction began to conform to a standard of behavior, and the group committed to enforcing the standard. In addition, it appears that the group made progress in developing a "staying on the topic" norm. Although the member did not resolve the problem, the group stayed focused on relationship concerns.

By being aware of how and why norms are formed, leaders can encourage the inclusion of effective group behaviors and the exclusion of counterproductive behaviors. Clearly, the development of productive norms is most easily accomplished during the process of norm formation. To change a norm, the leader must identify the norm, obstruct its use, and replace it with a more productive norm (see Chapter 9).

Obstructing Norms

Obstructing norms support behaviors that are inconsistent with group objectives. Obstructing norms include behaviors such as criticizing, denying feelings, overreliance on talking about events external to the group, avoiding responsibility for personal reactions, assuming motivations behind others' behaviors, demanding conformity, and engaging in competitive interactions. These obstructing norms tend to emerge during early phases of group interaction because members fear being hurt. For example, members might negotiate norms that support withholding emotions, changing topics when conflict emerges, or discussing events external to the group to lower their sense of being vulnerable.

When this occurs, however, members limit their ability to address real concerns that arise in the group or in their lives. Counter to effective group interaction, when a group is dominated by obstructing norms, members who share feelings and concerns risk the criticism of others for breaking the group's norms. Consequently, obstructing norms discourage openness, honesty, creativity, risk-taking, and experimentation with new behaviors. A group that operates with obstructing norms is unlikely to provide members with productive experiences.

In the dialogues that follow, Example 1 demonstrates the presence of two obstructing norms: "criticize those who do not conform to group norms" and "do not disclose negative feelings." In Example 2, members use the norms "topic changing" and "avoid responsibility for personal opinions." Continuation of the norms in both examples paints a grim picture for the future of these groups. The first example involves a scenario where an obstructing norm is broken; the second demonstrates a group conforming to its obstructing norms:

Example 1

Ursula: "Linda, why can't you just get along and stop being so nasty! You're so defensive and hostile!"

Liz: "Yeah, Linda, when you're angry like that, it doesn't work for me. You seem to have some real problems!"

Jeff: "If you were more agreeable, the group would be better for all of us."

Linda: "I'm really upset that I'm angry and can't share it."

Ursula: "Listen, Linda, if you want to get along, you'll need to stay positive. Why can't you understand that?"

Example 2

Jesse: "You just can't imagine how I was treated in that store."

Phil: "We are really getting somewhere in here. This is great."

Sue: "Phil, you know how important it is that we continue to progress the way we have."

Jesse: "Did you all see the news last night?"

Phil: "I'm really tired of how they cover the same story over and over again."

Lucille: "It's supposed to be warm tomorrow."

Helping Norms

Helping norms encourage members to use behaviors that help members meet their group counseling and therapy objectives. Generally, helping norms contribute to a facilitative group environment in which members can self-disclose without fear of criticism, trust others to act in their best interest, and be confident that their concerns and feelings will be heard and respected.

Behaviors largely seen as helping norms include sharing and exploring emotions, working with a member's concern for as long as it is productive, interacting in the here and now, being responsible for personal opinions and reactions, checking for understanding, accepting negative feelings, openly addressing conflict, and observing and discussing group process. These behaviors, along with the shared attitudes of respect and acceptance, result in a group environment that promotes the growth and change of members.

Even though helping norms reduce many of the anxieties that are associated with group membership, groups often have trouble establishing them. This is because helping norms are inconsistent with the way individuals customarily interact. To develop helping norms, leaders ask members to exchange customary social behaviors for more risky modes of interaction. For example, customary social interaction does not involve giving feedback or confronting or sharing immediate feelings and reactions. In addition, what is accepted as customary social interaction is heavily dependent on culture. Leaders should be aware that members need to be convinced that the behaviors associated with helping norms actually work before they can become norms.

The following dialogue examples demonstrate the presence of helping norms. In Example 1, members are reacting to a member breaking the valued helping norm "use responsible language." In Example 2, members are conforming to two helping norms: "paraphrase for understanding" and "stay in the here and now." These norms suggest that both groups are becoming productive learning environments:

Example 1

John: "You just get so angry when you don't get your way."

Jesse: "Are you saying that's your reaction to me?"

John: "I'm not going to talk to you about it."

Richard: "John, it seems to me that you are the angry one here, but you won't admit it!"

Linda: "I'm experiencing you as really hard to get to know. I don't know how you feel or what you think. I feel shut out by you!"

Richard: "Why don't you just say how you feel for a change? I tried it, and it worked for me."

John: "OK, I get your point. I am angry. I'm angry that none of you seem to be getting to know me. I'm sorry, Jesse, what you said really hit home! It's what I've been struggling with in here and at home and work."

Example 2

Diane: "I'm reacting to what you just said to me, Rick. Are you saying that I put you off because of the way I look at you and that you perceive me as angry?"

Rick: "I'm scared now. But, yes, I feel intimidated right now. I feel like you'll hurt me. Your brow is furrowed, your voice is raised, your fists are clenched, and you're staring at me."

Julie: "Diane, I agree with Rick. I'm perceiving you as angry, and I'm feeling like I want to back away from you. I'm scared now, too. Most of it has to do with the way you're looking and the volume of your voice."

Nancy: "Diane, I'd find you easier to approach if you would relax your face and hands and talk in a softer voice."

Diane: "So I'm putting all of you off, scaring you, because of the loudness of my voice and the expression on my face?"

All: "Yes!"

Norms and Differences in Culture

Although the preceding narrative is written as if the negotiation of norms within groups is a uniform and culture-neutral process, nothing could be further from the truth. Within individual groups, the prevailing norms are determined by many factors, including (a) the individual behavioral preferences of the members and leaders, (b) the power dynamics between members and leaders, (c) the purpose of the group, and (d) the needs of the group members with respect to the purpose of the group. Culture and social identity play a role in three of these four factors. Members' and leaders' behavioral preferences are heavily influenced by culture. Power dynamics, especially those related to whoever's preferences prevail in the group, are heavily influenced by culture and social identity. Finally, what group members need to benefit from the group's purpose may vary greatly depending on their socialization and experiences in society (i.e., their culture and social identity).

Responsibility for evaluating the purpose of the group, goals of interactions, responses of group members, and resultant norms belongs to group leaders. Thus, it is also their responsibility to evaluate and have some understanding of how culture, cultural differences, and group members' social identities impact the development of facilitative norms. This includes determining whether traditionally defined helping norms—those based on Western helping professions and group work culture—are ideal for the composition of the group. The process of negotiating norms that meet both individual needs and group needs in a culturally and socially diverse group may take additional time, intentionality, and adaptation. This requires that group leaders have insight into their own culture and social identities and what that means in terms of their behavioral preferences, power in the group, and attitudes toward group members who may not easily relate to traditional helping norms.

To summarize, norms are a significant determinant of a group's therapeutic effectiveness. Most norms are established covertly through indirect negotiation. The norms that emerge in a group reflect members' shared attitudes about participation. Members, especially during early group meetings, usually consider the norms necessary for effective interaction very risky and will attempt to develop norms that provide safety. Once group members experience the value of effective group interaction and begin to associate interpersonal anxiety with potential learning opportunities, the behaviors associated with helping norms will be established.

Roles

Roles, like norms, are a group structural property. Whereas norms are the behaviors expected of all group members, *roles* are the unique behaviors group members expect from an individual member. As groups form, they become social systems composed of member roles. Member roles develop so that the group can meet the needs of its members, meaning that each member will behave differently to perform necessary functions. This is important to remember, as members do not always appear to be acting in a way that helps them meet their needs when in fact they are. It is also important to remember that like norms, role development and function in groups are impacted by individuals' socialization and life experiences, which are tied closely to culture.

Role Development

Groups become social systems very rapidly. Even as members form initial impressions of each other, they establish expectations for the roles each other will fill. Wheelan (1994) discussed how members' roles develop during the initial stages of a group:

> Role assignment . . . is not entirely the product of rational assessment of each member's skills and talents. Rather, it is based on first impressions, external status, and initial self-presentation as well as the group's needs at the moment. Members may or may not secure a role that will facilitate group goal achievement. Or an individual

> level, a member may find him- or herself in a role that is comfortable and allows for positive contribution to group effort. On the other hand, the member may find his or her assigned role inhibiting and unfamiliar. (p. 57)

Wheelan (1994) made several other key points group leaders need to understand. First, roles form covertly. Members seldom discuss which member will fill a particular role. Second, members are not initially aware that they are assuming a role assigned to them by other group members. Finally, roles develop early in the life of the group and are difficult to change.

When groups form, members are concerned about what they and others will be doing in the group. Members ponder questions related to roles, such as "What do others want from me?" "What can I expect from others?" and "What am I supposed to do?" Ultimately, the roles that members assume depend on how other members react to their behaviors; it is an indirect negotiation process. Although members tend to seek and desire roles that meet their needs and are acceptable to them, they ultimately will enact roles based on expectations communicated by others in the group. Even members who enact roles involving behaviors that receive negative responses from others in the group are meeting the expectations of other members. Wheelan (1994) stated,

> The power of social roles to influence the behavior and attitudes of both the role occupant and others viewing the role should not be underestimated. Roles shape attitudes and behavior. Once a person assumes a role, the role creates a new mental perspective in the individual. (p. 56)

Direct negotiation of roles occurs only when group members and leaders openly discuss a role's relationship to group function or when leaders intervene to modify member roles that are not facilitative. Examples of direct negotiation include members agreeing on who will be responsible for keeping the group on task or for making sure that members are seated and ready to start the group on time. Another example is the leader asking a particular member to monitor the expression of emotions in feedback exchange or asking a member to refrain from minimizing sad feelings in the group.

Role Types

The literature on group roles contains descriptions of different role types. The classification of roles is defined in terms of specific member behaviors (e.g., Benne & Sheats, 1948; MacKenzie, 1990). MacKenzie (1990) offered a typology based on the belief that roles play an integral part in the group's social system. This typology holds that members must perform four complementary roles for a group to be therapeutically viable: sociable, structural, divergent, and cautionary. Any number of group members can fill any of these roles. How each of these roles is performed determines whether the role facilitates or inhibits group effectiveness—that is, each type of role can contribute to effectiveness, but if overemphasized each type of role can detract from effectiveness.

Sociable roles (MacKenzie, 1990) are filled by group members who share emotions, demonstrate caring toward others, encourage others to become involved, and develop positive interpersonal relationships. Sociable roles assist in developing safe and facilitative group climates. Group members who fill sociable roles act to ensure that all members have positive relationships. However, an overabundance of members in sociable roles, very powerful members filling sociable roles, or extreme forms of sociable role behaviors can block the expression of anger or other strong feelings as well as necessary confrontation and conflict.

Structural roles (MacKenzie, 1990) are filled by members who attend to group organization so that the group can provide effective learning experiences and meet group goals. These group members are concerned with meeting goals and achieving positive outcomes. Structural role behaviors, such as asking for guidelines or clarifying procedures, help group members understand the group process and help reduce the anxiety produced by the ambiguity of group interaction. Members who fill this role tend to be cognitive in orientation and push for structure and consistency. When extreme or supported by many group members or particularly powerful group members, structural role behaviors inhibit spontaneity and block the expression of emotion.

MacKenzie (1990) described members who fill divergent roles as persistently challenging others and as energetically expressing their differences from others. Members often perceive those who fill divergent roles as hostile and critical. Because of the seemingly antagonistic attitudes displayed by members filling divergent roles, others must clarify their own perspectives and learn how to accept divergent points of view. In addition, divergent role behaviors make the positive contribution of introducing the expression of anger into group interaction. However, extreme divergent role behaviors may have harmful effects on group interaction—namely, polarization around differences and unresolved hostile feelings.

Cautionary roles (MacKenzie, 1990) are demonstrated by members who withhold personal information and involvement. When cautionary members join groups, they are apprehensive and tend to withdraw from interaction. Cautionary members' reluctant involvement leads to other members examining and questioning their commitment to the group and their willingness to self-disclose. Members who fill cautionary roles may resist other members' efforts to involve them in group interaction. Cautionary members' reluctance also encourages other group members to examine their own concerns about being unacceptable. In extreme cases, however, cautionary role behaviors increase other group members' anxiety about self-disclosing in the group. If left unaddressed, extreme or dominating cautionary role behaviors threaten group cohesion.

MacKenzie (1990) held that these four social roles, each with constructive and destructive manifestations, are essential. Leaders must remember that all roles, no matter how pleasantly or unpleasantly they are perceived, can contribute to an effective group. A group social system that includes all of these roles has a structure that allows it to confront the essential interpersonal issues associated with these roles. It is the unchecked presence of extreme role behaviors that negatively impacts groups.

Role Performance

How a social role is performed influences its impact on group interaction. Members who perform roles that encourage involvement, improve interpersonal communication, and foster the development of helping norms are necessary for an effective group learning environment. The following examples of facilitative role performance for each of MacKenzie's (1990) role types show how each role can make an important contribution to group effectiveness:

- Facilitative sociable role: "Danae, when you shared your fears with Alex, I could really relate. I really appreciate you."
- Facilitative structural role: "Char, I'm confused about what you're trying to tell me. Try using the feedback model Bill taught us."
- Facilitative divergent role: "I don't buy all this peace and love stuff right now. I'm not going to agree just to smooth things over, like you all are!"
- Facilitative cautionary role: "I know other people have been sharing a lot, but I just don't feel that safe right now. I'll tell my story when I know I can trust you."

Roles may also hinder group progress. Role performance that hinders serves individual members at the group's expense. The performance of hindering roles typically includes ineffective behaviors developed to satisfy interpersonal needs in family-of-origin and social environments. Hindering role performance has the consequence of diverting other members from productive interactions. The following examples of role performance for each of MacKenzie's (1990) role types show the enactment of roles that hinder group effectiveness:

- Hindering sociable role: "There seem to be a lot of negative feelings in here. We need to stop this and focus on the good things that are going on in the group."
- Hindering structural role: "As the leader of the group, aren't you supposed to tell us what to do now? Some people have shared emotions, and that doesn't work! What exactly is the procedure?"
- Hindering divergent role: "It's all your fault; you've just succeeded in getting us all upset. Where did you learn how to lead groups?"
- Hindering cautionary role: Silence.

Some members play roles that help other group members meet their needs for safety, and this can threaten group effectiveness. Avoidant role performance helps group members avoid confronting their shared apprehensions. Individuals in sociable, structural, cautionary, and divergent roles can all enact their roles as avoidant role performers. For example, when a member performs an avoidant divergent role, they are likely to be the only member who shares anger. This member performs a role that helps others in the group who have difficulty expressing anger avoid having to express it. The following dialogue demonstrates this process

Wally: "Ryan, I'm really angry! How dare you!"

Hayden: "Wally, I'm sure you're not really angry; it's just a misunderstanding. Anger doesn't help."

Laura: "That's right, Wally. I'm sure if you would just listen to what Ryan is saying, you wouldn't be angry. Your anger is not useful."

Ron: "Wally, I'm really uncomfortable with how you continue to be angry. It's like you're ready to throw a chair or something. You just don't know how to get along!"

Laura: "If you would just try to understand what Ryan is saying, you wouldn't have to be angry. You always seem angry!"
Bob: "Wally, what's your problem? Can't you control yourself?"

This illustration shows how group members deal with their fears about anger by confronting an individual whose role involves expressing anger. Instead of talking about their own fears, group members use an avoidant role performer to escape dealing directly with their concerns. This process involves members criticizing the member in the avoidant role for unacceptable behavior instead of directly discussing their fears. If this process continues, it has the effect of establishing norms that preclude the enactment or discussion of the behaviors that members fear. When these norms are established, members avoid confronting the fears that led them to become group members.

Filling any role as an avoidant role performer can be difficult because no matter what a member does, they will continue to represent the fears that other members want to avoid. When members persist in labeling a member as a problem, that member's behaviors and the group's avoidance of a shared fear will continue. Leaders should be aware that a member who fills any role as an avoidant role performer is in danger of becoming a scapegoat and intervention may be warranted (see Chapter 11).

Leaders can differentiate hindering from avoidant role performance by examining how a role affects the group. If members are dealing with interpersonal fears and a member diverts the group's attention from those fears, that member is performing a hindering role. If the group has a strong reaction to a member's behavior, avoids dealing with their own reactions to the issues that member presents, and criticizes that member for the behavior, that member is performing an avoidant role. By differentiating avoidant and hindering roles, leaders can intervene more effectively.

Role Problems

When a group member does not perform the behaviors expected of their role, others in the group will respond by exerting pressure on the member to perform the expected behaviors. The pressure to perform a role can cause a member to struggle with participating in a personally congruent manner. The following are some common scenarios:

- Martha is expected to offer spontaneous opinions. She has the latitude to offer opinions in a personally congruent way as long as she offers opinions quickly. When she decides not to offer opinions because she wants to experiment with being more reflective, other group members pressure her to offer opinions. Some members ask her for her opinions, and others confront her, saying that they feel rejected by her because she is withholding her ideas.

- When the group begins, John tries to act according to how he perceives himself—caring and emotionally sensitive. Ideally, others would support his acting this way, but this is not the case. Other members persistently try to influence him to angrily confront those members who break the group's norms.
- The group has been meeting for several months. Recently, Scott has become progressively annoyed about other members' reactions to him. He shares his anger: "I thought we were supposed to be honest and care about each other! But every time I'm honest and show I care, I get criticized. Some of you seem to want me to go away."
- During the group's third session, Sally makes an emotionally charged statement: "What the h— am I supposed to do! I can't figure it out. All I know is that whatever I do, it's not what I'm supposed to do!"

These scenarios are representative of how group members may experience pressure as they find and fill their roles. When these pressures are vague or conflicting, they create role problems. Forsyth (1999) described these problems as *role stress* in two basic categories: (a) role ambiguity, which is the outcome of ambiguous role expectations; and (b) role conflict, which is the product of conflicting expectations for a role or conflicts between the various roles a member may fill in and outside of the group.

Role Ambiguity

Role ambiguity occurs when members are uncertain what they are supposed to do or doubt whether they can do what is expected of them (Forsyth, 1999). They may experience pressure from others in the form of subtle dissatisfaction or frustration with their behavior but without a clear desired alternative behavior. Role ambiguity is also related to Gladding's (1995) description of *role confusion*, which depicts members who do not understand what they are supposed to do. Role ambiguity and role confusion often occur in newly formed groups or when new members enter an ongoing group. These role issues are common in the early stages of group development.

Role Conflict

Role conflict occurs when members experience incompatible role expectations (Forsyth, 1999). *Intrarole* conflict arises when members are expected to perform a role that involves seemingly incompatible behaviors—for example, a member who is expected to provide support and at the same time confront others is experiencing an intrarole conflict. Intrarole conflicts also emerge when different members expect different behaviors from a particular member.

Interrole conflict emerges when members struggle with roles that are inconsistent with their self-image and the roles they normally perform. Gladding (1995) used the term *role incompatibility* to describe this aspect of role conflict, stating that "in role incompatibility a person is given a role within the group . . . that he or she neither wants nor is comfortable exercising" (p. 38). Members who are influenced to act in unfamiliar ways commonly experience interrole conflict. In some cases, members experiencing interrole conflicts are making productive changes in their interpersonal behaviors. For example, a member who fills the role of the listener in the group and never listens at home experiences interrole conflict. Occasionally, however, interrole conflict involves members filling roles that do not include productive behaviors (e.g., interrupting those who express emotions or taking on a persistent educative role when it is counter to their own well-being). The group leader needs to decide when it is necessary to support or challenge the roles performed by members experiencing interrole conflicts.

Leaders who understand the significance of roles and role problems have a means to conceptualize the behavior patterns of each group member in the context of the group social system. It is important to remember that members are always responding in some way to the expectations of other members and that how they respond to these expectations may be indicative of useful or harmful life patterns. In addition, roles are structures that arise from a group's social system as a product of negotiation and then influence that social system. Clearly, leaders should consider these dynamics when they intervene to help members change their roles.

Roles in Effectively Functioning Groups

In general, group members must be able to enact a variety of roles to bring essential group issues to the surface. Groups in which all members perform sociable roles will not be as effective as a group in which members also enact structural, cautionary, and divergent roles

(MacKenzie, 1990). The presence of all role types within a group provides a checks and balances system for the group process. Additionally, groups that do not have members who create interactive issues will have a less effective environment within which to examine personal and relational issues. This is because the interactions of "difficult" members cause other members to address their own concerns.

In a productive group experience, members develop the flexibility to enact a range of roles that will work effectively in a wide range of relationships. To do so, members need to develop comfort and competence with a range of relationship skills. Groups that encourage experimentation with new behaviors have norms that allow members to experiment with alternative roles and value different roles.

Summary

Each member's role is necessary for the continuation of the group's social system. Persistence of the social system does not mean that the group operates effectively. Rather, it means that the social system created through group members' negotiations is maintained. This implies that the roles that form the structure of the group's social system can support or block the group's purposes.

When members chastise a member for acting "inappropriately," the leader should carefully examine what is occurring. A member who does not perform according to role expectations threatens the continuation of the group's social system. When observing a group's attempt to force a role on a member, leaders should ask themselves, "What purpose does this role serve for the group?" A member's inappropriate behavior is likely consistent with a concern that the other members want to avoid.

Leaders should understand that a group that keeps a member in a particular role might hinder the progress of the member and the group. The leader must intervene if the expectations of members are keeping a member in a role that does not allow growth. At the same time, the leader should be cognizant that a group that keeps a member in a role sustains the status quo in the group social system. Defining this status quo is an important diagnostic step in understanding a group's functioning.

Membership Attitudes

The norms and roles members negotiate and attempt to sustain represent their attitudes about participation. These attitudes bring about opportunities for learning and changing and shape the social structure and effectiveness of group environments. Leaders should understand that a recursive relationship exists between effective participation attitudes and facilitative norms and roles. Norms and roles influence members' attitudes, and members' attitudes influence group norms and roles through their negotiation. A group will be effective when it develops norms and roles that support essential member attitudes and when members' attitudes support facilitative norms and roles.

Members value participation when they experience a group structure that supports meaningful interaction that leads to productive change. Once developed, attitudes that reflect the valuing of participation can guide members to become more actively involved and more committed to group participation. Conversely, members who have not had productive experiences interacting in groups will display attitudes that question the value of participation. This skepticism is usually associated with the promotion of norms and roles that do not support interactions that allow interpersonal learning. The longer the group structure is counter to interpersonal learning, the more likely it is that members will regard the group as a waste of time and honest participation as too risky. To reverse this skepticism, members must experience what it is like to have productive group interactions.

Group leaders should also be aware of how the social microcosm phenomenon affects members' attitudes toward participation. Group interaction may seem especially risky for individuals who have been historically marginalized or threatened because of their social identities. To develop essential member attitudes, these individuals must also experience productive interactions in the group. However, productive interactions may take support and persistent action by leaders to create an environment that acknowledges the added vulnerability, to foster listening to and validating hard-to-hear experiences, and to carefully counteract marginalizing dynamics within the group.

As leaders work to develop a social structure that creates an effective group environment, they should be cognizant of several essential member attitudes. Leaders who can help members develop these attitudes are more likely to develop an effective interactive group environment. These attitudes include members' beliefs about the potential outcomes of participation, personal responsibility for learning, the usefulness of risk-taking, and commitment to learning from one another. It is also important that the attitudes leaders demonstrate are consistent with the attitudes they attempt to develop in members.

Participation

Participation that is based on a shared commitment to personal learning and the learning of others is a hallmark of an effective group environment. Participation attitudes describe members' beliefs about the potential benefits of participation. Members will believe in the benefits of participation when they observe or personally experience productive learning. Because of these observations and experiences, members develop participation attitudes that lead to greater investment in group participation. For instance, when members observe another member learning to communicate more effectively, the entire group observes productive learning. Consequently, members experience the group as an effective learning environment and understand the value of participation.

Members will be successful when they believe that participation will benefit them, and they act on this attitude. The emerging attitude that participation is worthwhile eventually develops group norms and roles that support the importance of participation. In turn, norms and roles that support the importance of participation further develop attitudes that the group is meaningful and important for its members. On the other hand, when members question the value of participation, they create an environment that is less likely to develop norms and roles that support productive learning experiences. If most of a group's membership shares this attitude, the group becomes boring and unproductive.

Personal Responsibility

Members who act on the attitude that they are personally responsible for their own learning will have productive group experiences. Initially, most members balk at the prospect of being personally responsible for their own learning, wanting the leader to be in charge. During the initial stages of a group, however, members are unclear regarding how to learn and may also have no idea what to do to be responsible for their learning. Because they are anxious and may not yet know how to engage in a beneficial way, members often expect the leader to provide inappropriately specific instructions or the answers to their concerns. Group leaders are, of course, responsible for monitoring, analyzing, and intervening to create a group predominated by beneficial norms and roles. But without group members' realization of their choices about participation, and the positive and negative consequences of those choices, a truly facilitative group environment is unlikely. Once members understand that learning depends on the choices they make about their participation, they comprehend what it means to be responsible for their own learning. Members who comprehend this actively self-disclose, participate in feedback exchange, and experiment with new behaviors. Members who persist in the fantasy that the leader knows what each member needs to learn are not likely to benefit from their experience in an interactive group.

Risk-Taking

As group members develop attitudes that value participation and personal responsibility for learning, risk-taking increases. Risk-taking means that members choose to participate despite their anxiety. Members who take risks choose to disclose, offer feedback, or experiment with behaviors in ways that challenge what they believe they need to do to be safe or accepted by others.

Members' uncertainty about the way others might respond, and their need for acceptance when taking a risk, both influence the amount of anxiety they experience. Members who are very uncertain about the outcome of the risk they take, and who believe that their participation could lead to rejection, take a major risk. Conversely, people who are more certain that the risk they take will have a positive outcome face a less threatening risk and less anxiety. The greater the uncertainty, the greater the anxiety.

Groups that have norms and roles that support risk-taking as an essential aspect of participation become exciting environments for learning and change. Because members must first learn to tolerate the anxiety that is associated with taking risks, the belief that risk-taking is desirable is not easily developed. As members confront their fears and learn that risk-taking can lead to important learning, they reframe the anxiety associated with risk-taking as excitement.

Commitment to Others' Learning

Members of groups that are especially productive share the attitude that being committed to the learning of others is extremely important. This shared commitment is the outcome of observing and experiencing interpersonal learning. When members learn productively from each other and understand that they rely on each other for learning, they develop norms and roles that support collaborative learning.

Leader and Member Attitudes

The development of essential member attitudes is necessary if a group is to be an effective learning environment. Achieving these attitudes is unlikely when leaders' attitudes are inconsistent with the attitudes they attempt to develop. Leaders who act congruently on the beliefs that participation leads to learning, that personal responsibility for learning is essential, that risk-taking leads to growth, and that collaborative learning is critical will communicate attitudes that lead to the development of a powerful learning environment. Leaders who have not experienced the impact of this form of interpersonal learning or who doubt members can learn from each other will not communicate these attitudes effectively.

Conclusion

An effective interactive group environment is one in which members interact openly and honestly. For this to happen, a group must have a social structure that encourages interpersonal learning. Groups that have norms and roles that encourage members to accept personal responsibility, to believe in active participation, to commit to collaborative learning, and to value risk-taking are powerful learning environments. Group leaders who wish to facilitate the formation of an effective interactive group environment must be able to differentiate facilitative norms and roles from nonfacilitative norms and roles. They must be able to distinguish group process from content and be aware of the various types of power they and group members may hold in the group. Finally, they must be aware of the potential for oppressive societal dynamics to operate within their groups and be able to recognize the common ways this appears.

Chapter 3

Group Development Theory

Outcomes

Level 1 Outcomes

After reading this chapter, entry-level students and practitioners should be able to:

1. Discuss the usefulness of group development theory for group leaders.
2. Describe the various group development theory models and the essential components of a practical group development theory.
3. Discuss how group member characteristics influence group development and the issues that emerge during group interaction.
4. Outline essential themes in group development theories.
5. Explain the core tenets of the four classic group development theories and the interactive group development theory.

Level 2 Outcomes

After reading this chapter, advanced-level students and practitioners should also be able to:

1. Discuss each group development theory and provide an illustrative narrative that emphasizes interpersonal issues and the circumstances that lead to the recycling of these issues.
2. Explain how the recycling of interpersonal issues influences group development and members' interactions.
3. Discuss how variations in members' personalities and unresolved interpersonal issues influence group development.
4. Discuss how variations in members' social and cultural identities and identity development issues influence group development and member interactions.
5. Provide an explanation of how a model that considers member personalities, recycling concerns, and a culturally responsive life-cycle approach can be used to depict group development.
6. Describe leader responsibility in facilitating the transition of the group from one stage of the classic theories to the next.

Group development theory helps leaders anticipate events that occur regularly during a group's life span. Group development theories describe "patterns of growth and change that occur in groups throughout their life cycle, from formation to dissolution" (Forsyth, 1999, p. 76). Similarly, group development theory presents phases of interpersonal activity organized around the resolution of specific interpersonal concerns.

Group counselors and therapists need to understand group development theory for several important reasons. First, all groups encounter similar phases of development, each of which addresses a significant interpersonal issue. Because group development theory suggests a sequence in which interpersonal issues arise, leaders can plan initial and concluding sessions, anticipate the emergence of interpersonal issues, consider relevant social and cultural factors, and understand surfacing issues as naturally occurring phenomena. Second, group development theory provides a framework that organizes and contextualizes the observation of process and structure. This framework describes how interpersonal concerns influence the nature of interaction and evolving group structure. Finally, group development theory offers leaders a means to understand and predict dominant group issues and patterns of group interaction on the basis of the social and cultural context of the group as well as the interpersonal styles of group members. Leaders who do not address the social-cultural influences of their groups and the impact of diverse group membership may find that their groups do not develop beyond the initial phases of group development (Fenster & Fenster, 1998; Rubel & Okech, 2018).

Following the discussion of developmental models that are relevant to group theory, this chapter is divided into two sections. The first presents four classic group development theories, whereas the second section presents coauthor William Kline's (2003) contemporary interactive group development theory.

Models

Group development theories have been formulated from a variety of theoretical and research perspectives. These theories have been structured using different developmental models that are important to understand because they provide a system for evaluating and applying group development theory. Gibbard et al. (1974) categorized these models and described their strengths and limitations.

The *linear-progressive model* links group development with movement toward a goal. This model sees groups moving from an initial stage of tentative interaction to the resolution of interactive problems and, finally, to a stage of productivity. It ignores the presence of recurring group issues and group termination, which can be considered the final stage of group development.

The *life-cycle model* addresses the omission of the final stage of group development by describing the experiences members have as they adjust to group termination. However, this is also a linear model that suggests that once group problems are resolved, they never recur.

The *recurring-cycle model* describes cycles of recurring themes in group interaction. These themes represent critical issues that emerge and reemerge during group interaction. According to Gibbard et al. (1974), the recurring-cycle model focuses on how group members attempt to manage anxiety in order to maintain equilibrium, deal with interpersonal boundaries, and resolve their individual concerns. Although the recurring-cycle model addresses the limitations of the linear models, it is not the only model to consider. Perhaps the best approach would be a synthesis of these models that does not oversimplify the complexity of group development (Gibbard et al., 1974).

To be useful, a group development theory must meet certain criteria from an interactive perspective. It must account for issues that occur as groups begin, conclude, and recycle as groups progress. At the same time, a useful group development theory must address how the social and cultural context of a group and the interactive styles of group members influence the emergence of initial, concluding, and recycling issues.

Section 1: Classic Group Development Theories

The classic group development theories of Bion (1961), Bennis and Shepard (1956), Schutz (1966), Tuckman (1965), and Tuckman and Jensen (1977) are the most widely cited and researched with respect to group development. More recent presentations of group development theories, for the most part, have included similar components and the same developmental stages (Forsyth, 1999). Other recent presentations of group development have included stage models with similar stages that are used to organize the presentation of group counseling texts (M. S. Corey et al., 2017; Gladding, 1999). These models are also based on classic group development theory and are not intended to be construed as formal group development theories.

The classic theories presented in this chapter have diverse origins. Bion's (1961) theory emerged from his clinical experience in Great Britain, Bennis and Shepard's (1956) was developed from research on unstructured groups of American college students, Schutz's (1966) initially emerged from research on work groups in the U.S. Navy, and Tuckman's (1965) and Tuckman and Jensen's (1977) were the product of meta-analyses of existing group therapy literature. Despite their diverse origins, a number of consistent themes have emerged that are important to understand.

Bion

Bion (1961) viewed group interaction as members' attempts to deal with the anxiety created by recurring interpersonal issues. Although these issues are dealt with as they occur, groups can reach only a temporary resolution. These essential interpersonal issues inevitably resurface. Bion's theory was the initial recurring-cycle model of group development. Rioch (1975) credited Bion with initiating a paradigm shift from thinking about group interaction as an indication of individual members' concerns to thinking about group interaction as a demonstration of the concerns of a social system. Bion extended this premise to maintain that the concerns members experience in groups mirror the problems they experience in society. Bion's work constituted a major theoretical shift by originating the *group-as-a-whole* perspective (MacKenzie, 1990) and emphasizing a here-and-now focus (I. D. Yalom & Leszcz, 2020). Bion's fundamental premise was that every group behaves "as if" there are two groups present: the work group and the basic assumption group. Thus, a group will act at times as if it is a work group and at other times as if it is a basic assumption group.

The Work Group

The *work group* functions on a rational level to accomplish its objectives; it was characterized by Rioch (1975) as follows:

> The work group takes cognizance of its purpose and can define its task. The structure of the group is there to further the attainment of the task. The members of the work group cooperate as separate and discrete individuals. Each member of the group belongs to it because it is his will and his choice to see that the purpose of the group is fulfilled. He is therefore at one with the task of the group and his own interest is identified with its interest. The work group constantly tests its conclusions in a scientific spirit. It seeks for knowledge, learns from experience, and constantly questions how it may best achieve its goal. (p. 23)

Groups that act as if they are a work group are rare, although many groups, for limited periods, occasionally act this way (Rioch, 1975). Most of Bion's (1961) theory described why groups do not act as if they are work groups.

Basic Assumption Groups

The term *basic assumption* refers to the irrational assumptions that serve as the basis for group members' interactions; that is, members act as if their assumptions about the conditions that exist in the group are true. These assumptions are not often shared verbally. However, by observing consistency in member behavior, leaders can identify the assumption that the group is acting on. Bion believed that group members experience three primary emotional states: dependency, fight/flight, and pairing. These emotional states categorize the basic assumptions.

Dependency assumption group members act as if they must have someone protect and reassure them. Members often assign leaders the ability to understand what they need without having to share their concerns and expect leaders to supply solutions. These members "de-skill" themselves by acting as if they are unable to deal with their own concerns. These members are often passive and expect leaders to make their groups anxiety free. Because leaders cannot possibly meet these expectations, members become angry and disappointed. Eventually, members become angry that they have depended on the leader to take care of them.

Fight/flight assumption group members

> cluster together as if threatened by a dangerous force. The language of the group centers around the themes of threat and the need to defend itself or escape. Such groups may experience rapid alternations between themes of fear and themes of revenge. (MacKenzie, 1990, p. 9)

When members act on fight/flight assumptions, leaders come under direct attack because members believe they have not adequately taken care of them. Sometimes members' attacks are indirect. Such attacks take the form of being late or absent, storytelling, having "social" conversations, or trying to sidestep the purposes of the group (Rioch, 1975).

The *pairing* assumption group focuses on pairs of members. This focus can take several forms. First, the group can focus on improving the relationship of a pair of members. This attention indicates that if this member pair could get along better, it would have some critically important effect on the group. Second, pairs can develop intimate relationships, which occasionally can take on a sexual overtone. This pattern of behavior distracts members from focusing on the work and vulnerability required to build a group-as-a-whole relationship; instead, members focus on the familiar medium of intimacy, which tends to be in pairs. However, the benefit is that this models a level of intimacy that is possible between the group members. Third, the group develops a hopeful atmosphere, and positive feelings shared in dyads permeate interactions. If the pairings are successful, members have more confidence in the possibility that the group-as-a-whole relationship can be as meaningful.

Bion's (1961) work served as the transition from conceptualizing interaction in terms of individual dynamics to thinking about the group as a social system. His thinking also initiated a transition from practicing individual treatment techniques in a group setting to using interventions that focus on the entire group. Although Bion's work tends to be somewhat obscure and limited in addressing social-cultural factors and their influence on group dynamics and outcomes, his perspectives are helpful for understanding the dynamics of the group as a whole and the issues that recur in groups.

It is important to remember that the concerns that characterize the basic assumptions will recur regardless of the effectiveness of the leader or the intentions of the group members. Bion's (1961) most important idea was that consistency in members' interactions is related to shared, erroneous, and usually unspoken assumptions about group interaction.

Bennis and Shepard

Bennis and Shepard's (1956) theory describes the effects of subgroups and personalities on group interaction and development. This theory uses a linear-progressive model. It suggests that once issues are handled, they are forever resolved. It does not account for members' experiences as the group approaches termination.

Bennis and Shepard (1956) contended that communication is the most essential concern of all groups. Without effective communication, a group cannot adequately address its conflicts, members are unlikely to benefit from participation, and members cannot overcome the issues that prevent effective group functioning. Bennis and Shepard described two essential areas of interpersonal concern as obstacles to effective communication: dependency and interdependence.

Dependency describes members' attitudes toward authority, beliefs about the use and distribution of power, and how responsibility should be assigned. Interactions indicating the presence of dependency issues include discussions about norms and ground rules, why the group should or should not be structured, members' responsibilities, conflict over the leader's role, and direct challenges to leaders. During interaction about dependency concerns, members can be withdrawn, aggressive, or submissive. Group development is demonstrated when members move from being concerned about authority to addressing concerns related to intimacy.

Interdependency describes members' attitudes and feelings about relationships. Intimacy, or how emotionally and psychologically open members are to one another, forms the basis of interdependency issues. Interaction that depicts interdependency concerns focuses on members' relationships.

During group development, members' personal styles of interaction, and the extent to which they have resolved personal issues with authority and intimacy, play a significant role. Bennis and Shepard (1956) described three personality types that emerge during dependence and interdependence (see Table 3.1).

The personality types that emerge during the *dependence phase* are dependent, counterdependent, and independent. Dependents seek out authority relations. Leaders who provide structure and clear rules comfort them. In effect, dependents want leaders to take care of them. Counterdependents, on the other hand, resent authority. They challenge leaders because they do not trust authority. Outspoken counterdependents often challenge the group's usefulness and have conflicts with assertive dependents. Independents have successfully resolved authority issues. These members are flexible in their authority relations, being submissive or rebellious as circumstances dictate. They tend to be objective in their relationships with the leaders.

During the *interdependence phase* of group development, overpersonal, counterpersonal, and independent personalities emerge. Overpersonals will not rest until they have achieved a high level of intimacy with others. Counterpersonals, conversely, are not interested in intimate relationships and try to avoid them. Independents have successfully resolved intimacy issues and do not compulsively seek out or avoid close relationships with other members.

These personalities have a profound influence on group development because their shared issues become themes in group interaction. Groups composed of an outspoken majority of one personality type will develop very slowly and may stall in a phase

TABLE 3.1

Bennis and Shepard's (1956) Group Development Model

Phase	Subphase	Dominant Personality
Dependent	• Dependence-flight • Counterdependence-fight • Resolution-catharsis	• Dependent • Dependent and counterdependent • Independent
Interdependent	• Enchantment-flight • Disenchantment-fight • Consensual validation	• Overpersonal • Overpersonal and counterpersonal • Independent

of development. For example, a group composed of individuals who have not successfully dealt with their authority concerns (counterdependents) is not likely to progress beyond authority issues. Conversely, a group with a balanced distribution of member personalities is much more likely to have interactions that can move it forward.

Phase I: Dependence

During the initial phase of development, members encounter issues related to authority. Members begin group either having successfully resolved authority issues, distrusting authority, or needing the security offered by an authority who offers specific instructions on how to behave (Bennis & Shepard, 1956). The interplay of these personalities is the basis of interaction occurring during this phase. Bennis and Shepard (1956) described three subphases of the dependence phase.

Subphase 1: Dependence-flight. During the subphase of *dependence-flight*, members struggle with the anxiety involved in a new and uncertain experience. Interactions tend to be social exchanges, whereby members attempt to find similarities or common experiences. Usually, members look to the leaders to offer instructions on how to interact and for specific information about the goals they should have for the group. If leaders are unable to provide answers that reduce members' anxiety, the members have a dilemma. They face the ambiguity of not knowing exactly what they need to do and of having leaders who are either incapable or unwilling to tell them what to do. Dependent members try harder to get directions from the leaders. At the same time, counterdependents look for excuses to stage a rebellion, and independents observe—waiting to see what transpires. This subphase ends as members exhaust ways to acquire direction and approval from the leaders. Members become increasingly uncomfortable with their anxiety.

Subphase 2: Counterdependence-fight. Because group leaders have failed to reduce anxiety and dependents' attempts to get direction have not succeeded, counterdependents become more outspoken. Consequently, two subgroups emerge, and the anger that was avoided during the dependence-flight subphase surfaces as dependents and counterdependents battle for control. In *counterdependence-fight*, dependents attempt to find a way to structure the group and reduce anxiety, whereas counterdependents oppose any attempt to structure the group. This battle is accompanied by disenchantment with the leaders. Because leaders have not met their needs, members on both sides view them as ineffective or incompetent. Input from leaders is ignored or discounted as the conflict over control of the group continues. During this time, independents present compromise solutions to group issues and urge finding a middle ground. These attempts are fruitless, and the conflict continues.

Subphase 3: Resolution-catharsis. Conflict reaches its peak, but interaction begins to change. *Resolution-catharsis* begins when independents, who are less affected by dependency concerns, begin to be heard. Independents who have been unsuccessful in introducing compromise solutions now become successful mediators. Independents are heard because dependents and counterdependents realize they cannot resolve their disputes and because the conflict has become excessively uncomfortable.

The independents' mediation initiates a transition in group interaction that allows members to look at the group's potential usefulness. When group members make this transition, they address norms, members' responsibilities, and the importance of group membership. The outcome of conflict over group control is the emergence of group cohesion. Members become aware that they are not helpless or isolated, that they are able to solve problems, and that they can successfully communicate their apprehensions.

Phase II: Interdependence

As the interdependence phase begins, members have endured conflict and resolved issues. Members now share a commitment to the group. Members enjoy "the end" of conflict and the positive feelings experienced in the group. Interaction stresses maintaining these feelings, and members begin to face their concerns about intimate relationships.

Members are in various stages of resolution over the emerging intimacy concerns. Overpersonal members feel a desperate need to establish and maintain intimacy, counterpersonals fear intimacy and wish to avoid it, and independents are comfortable with varying levels of interpersonal intimacy. During this phase, the interactions of these personalities shape group development.

Subphase 4: Enchantment-flight. *Enchantment-flight* begins with members enjoying the relaxed atmosphere that has emerged after a difficult period of group conflict. Many members share the attitude that everyone must be happy. This shared attitude produces norms that insist that conflict be avoided at any cost and that decisions be unanimous. Bennis and Shepard (1956) characterized the beginning of this subphase as "sweetness and light" (p. 429), recognizing, however, that as this phase continues, "the myth of mutual acceptance and universal harmony must be recognized for what it is" (p. 429).

Eventually, the pressure to conform to the group's norms begins to meet resistance. Members subgroup into two camps: one that urges the maintenance of harmony and the other that rebels against the demands of forced agreement. Counterpersonals challenge the "fake attempt to resolve interpersonal problems by denying their reality" (Bennis & Shepard, 1956, p. 430). As this subphase closes, conflict over norms that demand harmony builds.

Subphase 5: Disenchantment-fight. At the beginning of *disenchantment-fight*, two subgroups represent opposing views on how intimate interaction should be. Overpersonals urge complete openness and present "a demand for unconditional love" (Bennis & Shepard, 1956, p. 430). Counterpersonals oppose intimacy and argue for more closed interpersonal boundaries.

The members of these opposing subgroups share a common apprehension about maintaining self-esteem. Counterpersonals believe they can maintain self-esteem by avoiding intimacy, and overpersonals believe that by establishing very intimate relationships, they can gain acceptance and maintain self-esteem. As members interact during this subphase, a theme emerges: "If others really knew me, they would reject me" (Bennis & Shepard, 1956, p. 431). Overpersonals believe that by requiring intimacy, they will be safe: "If we know each other completely, we couldn't possibly hurt each other." Counterpersonals believe that by avoiding intimacy, they will be safe: "If I don't let you know me, you can't reject me."

As intimacy issues are confronted, anxiety increases. In response, members use defensive behaviors to avoid facing their fears of intimacy. These defenses include absenteeism, intellectualization, questioning the value of the group, and boredom. At the conclusion of this subphase, overpersonals and counterpersonals are involved in sustained conflict over the acceptable level of intimacy in the group.

Subphase 6: Consensual validation. *Consensual validation* often begins when members become aware that the conclusion of the group is approaching. Independents believe that the resolution of conflict is necessary, express confidence in the value of the group, and begin to look earnestly at their roles. The actions of the independents encourage members to confront their fears by disclosing emotions and personal reactions. The disclosing members discover that others, because of their disclosures, do not reject them as they had anticipated. Members speak about the assumptions they have made about themselves and others and how these assumptions influence their perceptions and understanding of their behaviors and those of others.

During this subphase, numerous values surface that are consistent with highly effective group functioning:

- Members accept each other and do not attach a value to others' characteristics.
- Conflict over emotional issues ceases, yet conflict over tangible group issues (e.g., logistical problems, norms) is tolerated.
- Although consensus is important, agreement is not forced. Instead, hearing divergent views is valued and encouraged.
- Members discuss group process and personal involvement in the group without alarm.
- Communication explores thinking, emotions, and behaviors. Effective communication that involves members exploring their thoughts, emotions, and behaviors is a rare achievement for most groups, owing to their composition.

The contributions of Bennis and Shepard's (1956) theory are in the areas of group composition, crucial interpersonal concerns, and communication. The personalities described by Bennis and Shepard offer group leaders guidelines for making group composition decisions during recruitment and pregroup screening. The personality characteristics of potential members in the areas of dependency and interdependence allow leaders to anticipate the communication problems a group will encounter as it deals with developmental concerns. Bennis and Shepard suggested that groups are neither good nor bad, but that some groups are more effectively composed than others. When a group is poorly composed, the leader can do little to help it achieve optimal functioning.

Bennis and Shepard (1956) do not account for how members experience group termination or for recycling group issues. Neither do they address social-cultural and identity factors and their critical role in emerging group issues. Despite these limitations, this theory offers leaders valuable information.

Schutz

Schutz's (1966) theory of group development and interpersonal behaviors was based on extensive empirical research. The cornerstone of his theory was his conceptualizations of interpersonal needs. These concepts describe patterns of interpersonal behaviors and essential relationship variables. Although Schutz later modified his theory, his initial conceptualizations are relevant to understanding group development.

Schutz (1966) maintained that interpersonal behaviors are directed toward meeting interpersonal needs. These needs "may be satisfied only through the attainment of a satisfactory relation with other people" (Schutz, 1966, p. 15). These needs were for inclusion, control, and affection. Schutz (1966) contended that "inclusion, control, and affection constitute a sufficient set of areas of interpersonal behavior for the prediction and explanation of interpersonal phenomena" (p. 13).

As adults, individuals have deficient, excessive, or ideal levels of need fulfillment, because as children, they had varied degrees of success in learning how to meet these needs. People who have deficient, excessive, or ideal fulfillment in one need can demonstrate a different level of need fulfillment in the other areas. For example, people can have an ideal level of affection needs, a deficient level of control needs, and an excessive level of inclusion needs.

Inclusion: Needs and Personalities

Inclusion involves establishing and maintaining satisfactory relationships. A satisfactory relationship involves experiencing a mutual interest between self and others and believing in the worth and significance of the self within the relationship. Inclusion needs are related to being attended to, acknowledged, and recognized. The interpersonal behaviors directed toward satisfying this need include participation, interaction, and involvement. Inclusion needs also define a desire to have an identity that separates an individual from others and to be recognized. Schutz (1966) characterized the interpersonal behaviors of inclusion as seeking "prominence rather than dominance" (p. 189). Each individual, depending on their experience as a child, has varying inclusion needs and associated fears. Individuals who have deficient inclusion needs are undersocial, those who have excessive inclusion needs are oversocial, and those who have ideal inclusion needs are social.

Undersocials tend to be withdrawn and avoid participation. They attempt to maintain distance from others and guard their privacy.

Schutz (1966) contended that undersocials experience the inclusion needs of wanting to be attended to and of being regarded as significant. However, because they fear rejection, not being paid attention to, or being seen as insignificant, they choose to not be involved with others. They avoid interactions that could help them meet their needs in order to prevent their fears from becoming a reality. Schutz (1966) depicted the underpersonal's attitude as "No one is interested in me, so I'm not going to risk being ignored. I'll stay away from people and get along by myself" (p. 26).

Oversocials experience the same fears and needs as undersocials. Instead of avoiding interaction, however, oversocials relentlessly seek it out. Oversocials confront their fears of being ignored by doing everything in their power to gain others' attention. Schutz (1966) characterized the attitude of oversocials as "Although no one is interested in me, I'll make people pay attention to me in any way I can" (p. 26). Oversocials seek opportunities to prove their worth by being involved with others. These efforts include intensive and occasionally exhibitionistic group participation.

Socials do not experience the fears of oversocials and undersocials. Socials perceive themselves as significant persons with unique identities who are worthy of attention. Consequently, interactions with others do not cause socials to experience significant anxiety. Socials feel comfortable being involved with others or spending time alone. Their group participation varies because they are comfortable participating frequently or infrequently. Socials experience the freedom of having a wide range of choices in interpersonal behaviors because their self-worth does not depend on how others respond to them.

Control: Needs and Personalities

Control needs surface in interactions that involve influencing or being influenced by others (Schutz, 1966). Control describes individuals' needs for authority and power in relationships. Control refers to the need to influence others, whereas inclusion reflects the need to be involved with others. Control depicts needs for dominance, whereas inclusion describes needs for prominence. Individuals satisfy inclusion needs by being noticed and involved, and they satisfy control needs by winning. Schutz (1966) believed that control issues are most effectively resolved when individuals share a mutual respect for each other's competence. The extent of individuals' control needs reflects the intensity of their fears. The fears relevant to control needs have to do with being regarded as incompetent, irresponsible, stupid, or unreliable. The more concerned individuals are about others perceiving them as such, the more control issues will surface in their relationships. Schutz (1966) classified individuals with deficient control needs as abdicrats, those with excessive control needs as autocrats, and those with ideal control needs as democrats.

Abdicrats avoid situations that require them to act responsibly or participate in decision-making with others. Schutz (1966) described abdicrats as being submissive, gravitating toward being subordinates, wanting to be relieved of obligations, and regarding themselves as untrustworthy. Abdicrats fear that they cannot competently manage their responsibilities and that others will not help them when they need help, and they believe that others are aware of this. Because of these beliefs, abdicrats avoid circumstances that could demonstrate their incompetence. Abdicrats are passive-aggressive in interpersonal interactions because they are too fearful to confront or disagree with decisions made by others.

Autocrats also fear that they are not capable of responsible adult behaviors and that others know this. Autocrats, however, use behaviors designed to take charge and establish themselves as the most powerful persons in their relationships. Autocrats deal with their fears by seeking out every possible opportunity to prove their competence. Autocrats make decisions for others because they do not trust others to make decisions that are in their best interest. Schutz (1966) described the autocrat's attitude as "No one thinks I can make decisions for myself, but I'll show them. I'm going to make all the decisions for everyone always" (p. 29).

Democrats have resolved power and authority issues in their relationships. Consequently, democrats believe that they are capable, responsible, and trustworthy. Democrats are not concerned about others perceiving them as helpless, stupid, or incapable. Democrats believe in their own competence and trust themselves. They perceive that others respect and trust them and believe that they are capable of making effective decisions.

Affection: Needs and Personalities

Affection needs involve developing satisfactory intimate interpersonal relationships that include liking, affection, and love. These needs can be met only in intimate interactions that express fondness and attraction and that lead to close relationships. Schutz (1966) contrasted affection needs with inclusion and control needs by using polarities to describe how these needs surface in relationships.

Inclusion needs have to do with "in or out," control needs with "top or bottom," and affection needs with "near or far."

To develop close emotional relationships, individuals must confront their innermost fears about revealing themselves to others: "If I reveal my private thoughts to another person, will that person find me acceptable, or will I be rejected?" To meet affection needs, individuals confront their apprehensions about others, perceiving them as deserving affection: "Will this person care enough about me to return my affection?"

The extent to which individuals fulfill affection needs and perform affection behaviors depends on their fears. Those who expect rejection will experience intense fear when they attempt to meet affection needs. Conversely, individuals who believe that they are lovable and do not fear rejection will not be apprehensive about meeting affection needs. Schutz (1966) classified individuals with deficient affection needs as underpersonals, those with excessive affection needs as overpersonals, and those with ideal affection needs as personals.

Underpersonals believe that they are unlovable and unlikable and that they do not deserve the affection of others. Consequently, underpersonals avoid close emotional connections and stay emotionally distant. Because they perceive themselves as unlovable and unlikable, they do not trust others' expressions of positive feelings toward them. Schutz (1966) described the underpersonal's attitude as "I find the affection area very painful since I have been rejected; therefore, I shall avoid close personal relations in the future" (p. 30). Underpersonals maintain distance by avoiding opportunities for close relationships and actively attempting to keep people away. These behaviors include being overtly antagonistic and having superficial relationships with many people so that they will not have to get uncomfortably close to any one person. Underpersonals fear that allowing people to know them intimately would be devastating because others would discover what makes them so unlovable. Schutz (1966) stated, "As opposed to the inclusion anxiety that the self is of no value, worthless, and empty, and the control anxiety that the self is stupid and irresponsible, the affection anxiety is that the self is nasty and bad" (p. 31).

Overpersonals work tirelessly to develop intimate relationships to confront the interpersonal fears of being unlovable, unlikable, and rejected. Their goal is to develop relationships that have a very personal quality. They want to be very close to as many people as possible. Schutz (1966) characterized the overpersonal's attitude as "My first experiences with affection were painful, but perhaps if I try again they will turn out to be better" (p. 31). The incessant efforts of overpersonals to be liked and loved include making blatant attempts to secure others' approval and making overly personal self-disclosures. Other overpersonal behaviors include manipulating others to sustain close, enmeshed relationships. As Schutz (1966) put it, overpersonals "devour friends and subtly punish any attempts by [others] to establish other friendships" (p. 31). Overpersonals are clingy and jealous.

Personals are comfortable in intimate relationships and in those that require emotional distance. They are not concerned with rejection, and they feel free to be emotionally and psychologically intimate whenever it feels right. Personals perceive themselves as lovable and as able to give and receive affection and are not excessively concerned with being liked. When others do not want to be involved in a personal relationship with them, it is not because they are unlovable. Rather, failed relationships are the consequence of incompatibility. Personals are self-accepting and can give and receive affection freely because they are not emotionally needy.

Theory and Phases of Group Development

Schutz's (1966) group development theory was formulated on the premise that individuals are motivated to meet inclusion, control, and affection needs in the group context. To meet these needs, group members use necessary interpersonal behaviors. When members attempt to meet a particular need, the behaviors they use characterize group interaction and define the group's stage of development. Thus, when group members are attempting to meet inclusion needs, their inclusion behaviors characterize group interaction, and the group is in the inclusion phase.

Group development follows a predictable course that is dictated by the interpersonal needs of group members. Schutz's (1966) principle of group integration described the initial progression of development. This principle stated that group members' initial interpersonal behaviors are inclusion behaviors meant to meet basic inclusion needs. Then, as group members meet inclusion needs, they begin to use control behaviors to meet control needs. Once members meet control needs, affection behaviors emerge in order to meet affection needs. Schutz (1966) proposed that interaction related to meeting inclusion, control, and affection needs recycles repeatedly over the life span of a group.

As groups conclude, the process of group integration is reversed. Schutz's (1966) principle of group resolution described how groups confront termination, stating that prior to a group's anticipated termination, group development follows the opposite sequence, "in that the predominate area of interpersonal behavior is first affection, then control, and finally inclusion" (p. 168). As members of a group in the affection phase become aware of the group's ending, they again confront control and inclusion needs—that is, members struggle first with deciding how to finish being a group and then with what it means to no longer be involved with each other.

Inclusion phase. During initial meetings, individuals are concerned about becoming group members. To address this concern, members make decisions about the extent of their involvement. These decisions range from choosing to be highly engaged in the group to leaving the group. In the process of making involvement decisions, members confront their personal concerns about their identity and importance. Group interaction during this *inclusion phase* concerns boundary issues (Schutz, 1973)—that is, members decide whether they want to belong to the group and whether belonging to the group is safe. To reach this decision, members try to determine whether leaders are committed to their welfare and whether other members will pay attention to them and regard them as unique individuals.

Inclusion interaction is tentative and includes discussion of safe social topics. Although these discussions are irrelevant to the purposes of the group, they help members get to know each other and are unavoidable. Schutz (1973) stated, "Groups not permitted this type of testing will search for some other method of obtaining the same information" (p. 52). Although all members experience some degree of inclusion concerns, oversocial and undersocial members are especially concerned with inclusion issues.

Control phase. Once members are comfortable with inclusion concerns and begin to think of themselves as a group, control issues surface. When members confront control issues, they face concerns related to their ability to influence others and to assume responsibility. Autocrats and abdicrats, in particular, confront issues that involve their fears about competence.

Once the group enters the *control phase,* interaction becomes more confrontational. Interaction involves conflict over issues that include how feedback should be exchanged, whether anger is appropriate, how the group should be structured, rules for attendance and interaction, the leaders' roles, responsibility for learning, and so on. Interaction with leaders involves similar issues. Abdicrats want the leaders to have all the power and responsibility for how the group proceeds, whereas autocrats want the leaders to have none. Interaction has the purpose of sorting out how much influence, power, and responsibility members will have in the group. The control phase involves each member's attempt to find a comfortable way to participate in interactions regarding power, responsibility, and influence (Schutz, 1966).

Affection phase. After members become comfortable with control issues, they face intimacy issues. Members decide how close or distant they will be with each other, especially with one other member. Overpersonals and underpersonals are especially concerned about how lovable others perceive them to be. Group interaction becomes progressively more emotional during the *affection phase*. Affection behaviors involve expressing positive feelings. This phase can also contain expressions of anger and jealousy Members also direct affection behaviors toward leaders to determine whether the leaders like or approve of them. The prevalence of emotional expressions between pairs of members is the key to identifying this phase. Affection interactions have the objective of establishing a comfortable level of expressing and receiving emotional intimacy.

Schutz (1966) did not suggest a linear progression of developmental stages. Rather, group development characterizes members' greatest concern at any given moment. Inclusion, control, and affection issues always exist. This suggests that as members conclude one phase or subphase and enter the next, they can return to a previous one. For example, members of a group have decided that membership in the group is desirable and look forward to being together. However, as they deal with control issues, interaction becomes heated, and they become frightened by the intensity of emotion in the group. In response, members reconsider inclusion in a group where intense emotions are expressed. The recurrence of inclusion, control, and affection concerns can be confusing if group leaders expect a linear progression of developmental phases.

Group development is also heavily influenced by the interpersonal orientations of members and the assertiveness with which they try to meet their needs. For example, a group composed of assertive autocrats will be overly concerned with control issues. Therefore, control issues will reappear over and over again, and the group will not enter the affection phase.

Group development is influenced by a group's duration. Groups meeting for extended periods are more likely to cycle and recycle through group development phases. Groups meeting for limited periods may not progress through the phases. Thus, a group composed of undersocials meeting for a brief time may never leave the inclusion phase.

Schutz's (1966) theory can assist leaders in a number of ways. First, group composition decisions can be made with an awareness of how potential members' personalities and interpersonal behaviors will influence group effectiveness. Second, knowing the combination of members' personalities allows leaders to anticipate how the group will confront developmental issues. Third, when members' interactions are conceptualized in terms of interpersonal needs, leaders have insight into issues that influence interpersonal behaviors in the group. Schutz's (1966) theory sensitizes leaders to the early needs of group members regarding inclusion, to the factors that contribute to control issues that may result in leadership challenges, to the way in which affection concerns play out during the course of the group, and to the way termination issues will appear as the group nears conclusion. The core limitation of the theory is its approach to groups from a monocultural perspective and the lack of consideration of the role that social and cultural factors play in groups' inclusion and exclusion practices.

Tuckman

Tuckman (1965) derived his linear-progressive group development model from a meta-analysis of group development research. His model defined group development concepts and the dominant themes in group development studies. Later, Tuckman and Jensen (1977) converted Tuckman's initial formulation to a life-cycle model by adding a termination stage.

Tuckman (1965) concluded that group members engage in activities, or task behaviors, designed to accomplish the purposes for which the group was convened. To accomplish a group's purposes, members interact. As a result of this interaction, patterns of interpersonal relationships emerge and change as the group progresses. Tuckman used the term *group structure* to define these relationship patterns.

Tuckman's (1965) initial model had four developmental stages: forming, storming, norming, and performing. Later, adjourning was added as a fifth stage (Tuckman & Jensen, 1977). Tuckman (1965) maintained that these stages "hold up under widely varied conditions of group composition, duration of group life, and specific group task" (p. 397).

Forming

The first stage of group development, *forming*, witnesses members involved in testing and dependency as they acclimate to a new group. During this stage, members participate hesitantly, attempting to discover what behaviors are acceptable and what their relationships with other members and leaders will be like. Members engage in a lot of discussion regarding group norms, their expectations, and their hopes for the group. Members also share their assumptions about what the group will be like, as well as expected group dynamics and outcomes.

Structure (testing and dependency). Initially, members attempt to establish relationships with the leaders and other members in a new and unfamiliar situation. This process involves testing out interpersonal boundaries. As this stage unfolds, members learn what behaviors are appropriate by judging the reactions of leaders and other members to their behaviors. This testing-out process is accompanied by dependency. Members often want the leaders or "some powerful group member" (Tuckman, 1965, p. 386) to offer direction and support in order to lower anxiety. Group members may become angry or even withdraw when their expectations are not met at this stage.

Task behaviors (orientation to the task). As group interactions begin, members try to achieve certainty about what they will be expected to do and how these behaviors will accomplish the goals of the group. They also struggle to discover what information they will be required to share. During this stage, the members seek to understand the rules for group interaction. Group leaders must be attentive to the pattern of group members discussing group rules, as it may stagnate the group's development if they are unable to move beyond discussing and seeking an understanding of the expectations of the group.

Storming

During the second stage, *storming*, members engage in conflict with the leaders and with one another. This conflict involves members challenging each other and the leaders, withdrawing from interaction, questioning the usefulness of the group's structure and task activities, and occasionally attacking the leaders directly. Members resist the demands of group involvement and want to maintain their individuality. Storming emerges from the realization that group members cannot discuss group expectations indefinitely. They have to begin to work on those expectations. The intersections of those expectations and the fears that accompany them result in the storming phase.

Structure (intragroup conflict). Group interactions during the storming phase are characterized by competition and defensiveness. Members become polarized around issues related to the anxiety involved in developing closer relationships with each other. Tuckman (1965) observed, "There are characteristic key issues that . . . boil down to the conflict over progression into the 'unknown' of interpersonal relations or regression to the security of earlier dependence" (p. 386). Although Tuckman's theory does not consider cultural and social factors, studies suggest that groups with diverse memberships representing traditionally conflicting or oppressed groups face additional challenges in building trust and relationships among members. For example, Indigenous people may have a difficult time trusting White group members and cisgender heterosexuals may have difficulty trusting transgender group members because of their social and cultural backgrounds (Rubel & Okech, 2010, 2018).

Task behaviors (emotional response to task demands). During the storming stage, members resist performing the behaviors required to accomplish group objectives. Members challenge the need to disclose personal information, the usefulness of group interactions, and the techniques and procedures used by the leaders. Some may even challenge the purpose and utility of the group. These challenges reflect members' concerns about the discrepancy between their customary interpersonal behaviors and the demands of the group's task activities. Members have emotional reactions to group demands that require making changes in their interpersonal behaviors. Commonly, leaders are the target of members' challenges and animosity resulting from these emotional reactions. Interactions have the goal of avoiding involvement and exposure. A leader's ability to address anger and comfort with anger being directed at them is important at this stage. Additionally, leaders' confidence in their competence as a leader and their comfort with their competence being questioned play a major role. Finally, a leader's ability to confront avoidant behavior is key to helping groups transition from the storming phase to the norming phase.

Norming

At the beginning of the third stage, *norming*, members accept the usefulness of the group's structure and task activities. Members have more confidence in the leader's ability to facilitate and guide their experience in the group. Despite personality differences, members increasingly accept each other and regard group membership as important. Members commit to the group and to maintaining the interpersonal harmony that marks the initiation of this stage.

Structure (development of group cohesion and functional role relatedness). During the norming stage, the group becomes more cohesive because it has become increasingly important to its members. Members view minor disagreements as a threat to the harmony that has followed a period of conflict. Norms emerge that suppress conflict, instead encourage conformity and agreement, and are vigorously enforced. Group leaders must be prepared to confront these emerging norms to avoid having them become entrenched in the group and impede the group's growth and development.

Task behaviors (discussing oneself and other group members). The overall theme of interaction in the norming stage is "probing and revealing by group members at a highly intimate level" (Tuckman, 1965, p. 390). Other related themes emerging during this stage are "confiding . . . discussing personal problems in depth . . . exploring the dynamics at work within the individual . . . and exploring the dynamics at work within the group" (Tuckman, 1965, p. 390). Members become increasingly intimate yet careful not to confront each other. A leader's ability to address these emerging norms and their skill at supporting members at their most vulnerable is important at this stage. In this stage, it is valuable for group leaders to assist members in setting appropriate boundaries around what they choose to share or not share. They should also demonstrate critical consciousness by openly addressing social and cultural factors that may influence group members' interactions with each other. Additionally, leaders' confidence in the purpose of the group and their ability to challenge group members to confront their fears, to trust in the group's support, and to act in spite of their fears are key to helping groups transition from the norming phase to the performing phase.

Performing

In the fourth stage, *performing*, the group achieves its greatest effectiveness. Members' task behaviors are highly productive in terms of reaching group goals. The roles that members assume promote therapeutic progress and constructive action in the group. Group norms and culture promote openness, authentic engagement, trust, and risk-taking in all members' interactions.

Structure (functional role relatedness). The performing stage marks the time when members typically gain self-understanding and insight into their interpersonal and intrapersonal patterns. Group goals are achieved, and members' roles achieve greater flexibility. The group becomes a therapeutic environment, with members demonstrating investment in the work of the group and not resisting the therapeutic process.

Task behaviors (emergence of insight). During the performing stage, members achieve understanding of their personal and interpersonal issues. Members develop insight into personal concerns, achieve understanding of their interactions, and initiate therapeutic change. Members willingly exchange feedback, self-disclose, confront one another, take risks, and participate in therapeutic interactions. A leader's ability to highlight group-as-a-whole accomplishments and individual successes is critical at this stage. Group leaders can actively help members apply the skills learned in the group to their lives outside the group so that they can be prepared for the forthcoming termination phase of the group. Group members can also actively encourage members to take advantage of the culture of the group to address any concerns they might have been holding, to repair relationships that were bruised in the early stages of the group, and to report back on the benefits of the group being witnessed in their life outside the group. The efforts invested in the group and the challenges confronted in the previous stages pay off in the performing stage for both group members and leaders.

Adjourning

In the adjourning stage, members experience separation from and termination of the group as a significant event. By the conclusion of counseling and therapy groups, members usually have developed close emotional connections. When termination nears, members have significant emotional reactions to the end of the group and experience it as a significant loss. A group leader's ability to facilitate the group members' grief as they prepare for termination is crucial to helping members transition positively into their lives outside the group. Effective leader facilitation includes helping members understand that the grief is tied to the value of the group, to the work that they have done in the group, to the relationships they have created, and to the fears they might have about not being able to sustain the group relationships and group processes in their personal life outside the group. Helping members develop confidence in their group accomplishments and the efforts they demonstrated in the group is key to a successful termination phase.

Tuckman's (1965) paradigm described themes in group development research prior to 1977. The model has two crucial limitations. First, it does not account for recurring issues. Second, it does not include a description of the effects of the interpersonal styles of group members on group development. Perhaps its greatest weakness, however, is that it does not acknowledge the influence of cultural and social forces at play in group and its implications for group members and leaders.

Essential Group Development Concepts

The group development theories presented in this chapter evolved from the study of various groups in a variety of settings over a time span of nearly 50 years. Despite the diversity, however, these theories share concepts, developmental themes, and limitations in addressing the impact of social and cultural contexts in the dynamics of groups and their emergent concerns.

Group development theories offer some important foundational concepts that help leaders comprehend group interaction. These concepts include the following:

- Counseling and therapy groups are social and cultural systems.
- Groups address variations of core interpersonal issues.
- Anxiety related to core interpersonal issues is always present.
- Conflict is inevitable, indispensable, and productive.
- Members have had varying degrees of success in dealing with core interpersonal issues.

Counseling and Therapy Groups Are Social Systems

As members of groups interact with each other, relationship patterns develop (Tuckman, 1965). Over time, these relationship patterns define a group as a distinct social system, a critical aspect of which is the group's *normative structure*. This structure expresses members' tolerance for the anxiety produced by shared interpersonal concerns (Bennis & Shepard, 1956; Bion, 1961; Schutz, 1966). This means that leaders can judge the strength and nature of members' apprehensions by observing how intensely members negotiate norms and apply their sanctions. For example, when members are very intense in negotiating norms that prohibit the expression of "negative emotions" or "anger," leaders can conclude that members are especially concerned about safety or very fearful of the expression of anger.

A group's emerging social structure also establishes interpersonal boundaries that define the behaviors required for membership. These negotiated boundaries define how openly members should interact and the issues they should discuss. Consequently, interpersonal boundaries reflect members' decisions about becoming included in the group. Thus, when members avoid discussing emotions, a leader can conclude that members are reluctant to be fully involved in the group.

An especially significant social systems concept is that the issues members encounter in groups are not separate from the issues members experience outside groups (Bennis & Shepard, 1956; Bion, 1961; Schutz, 1966; I. D. Yalom & Leszcz, 2020). They are isomorphic. *Isomorphy* occurs when the interpersonal dynamics and behaviors of members in group are identical to those they demonstrate outside group. The concerns experienced by each member are shared, to some extent, by other members. Thus, when one member struggles with intimacy, other members also struggle, and all members (even the leader) indirectly confront their intimacy concerns outside the group. More broadly, in isomorphy, counseling and therapy groups confront the same issues as larger social systems and society in general (Bion, 1961).

Groups Address Core Interpersonal Issues

Group development theory (Bennis & Shepard, 1956; Bion, 1961; Kline, 2003; Schutz, 1966; Tuckman, 1965) describes how members struggle to deal with core interpersonal issues: involvement, dependency, authority, individuation, intimacy, and loss and loneliness. Variations of these core interpersonal issues emerge and recycle as long as groups remain intact (Bion, 1961; Schutz, 1966).

Two common factors influence the emergence of core interpersonal issues: how effectively members have resolved these core issues before coming to group, and apprehensions related to intimacy. In groups composed of individuals who have unsuccessfully resolved a particular core issue, members will have an intense reaction when the issue emerges. Usually, the issue emerges only to be avoided. When members avoid a core issue, it surfaces over and over again with no indication of progress. Conversely, in groups where most individuals have had some success in dealing with a core issue, the issue will reemerge but will be addressed successfully and the group progresses (Bennis & Shepard, 1956; Schutz, 1966).

When group interaction becomes more intimate, variations of issues that were successfully addressed during earlier, less intimate interactions resurface. For example, when involvement is addressed during initial group meetings, members might readily accept what is required to be a group member. Later, when sharing increasingly personal information becomes a part of group interaction, members will reconsider involvement (Bion, 1961; Schutz, 1966).

Anxiety Is Always Present

Anxiety is a persistent element of group interaction. Bion (1961) stressed that group interaction seeks to maintain a homeostasis that keeps anxiety at a level members can tolerate. Even when members successfully confront a concern that creates anxiety, apprehensions remain. These apprehensions are related to the fear that subsequent interaction may demand greater intimacy or that other, riskier issues may surface. Anxiety related to core interpersonal issues is commonly related to fear associated with intimacy—that is, rejection, abandonment, incompetence, and significance (Schutz, 1966).

Conflict and Anger Are Inevitable, Indispensable, and Productive

Conflict is associated with members' failed attempts to avoid anxiety. Direct and indirect expressions of anger aimed at group leaders may occur when members react to leaders' failing to provide freedom from anxiety or a group structure that provides total safety (Bennis & Shepard, 1956; Bion, 1961; Schutz, 1966; Tuckman, 1965). At the same time, members can conflict and become angry with each other when they disagree over how to best avoid anxiety (Bennis & Shepard, 1956; Schutz, 1966).

Conflict and anger are indispensable if groups are to become highly productive. Conflict is productive because it exposes members' interpersonal concerns. For example, when members conflict over the expectations of group membership, leaders can direct members to explore their inclusion needs. This intervention directs members to confront the concerns they are experiencing in the here and now. Leaders who understand that the potential for change exists whenever conflict emerges are more likely to look for opportunities to identify conflict.

Members Have Had Varying Degrees of Success Resolving Core Interpersonal Issues

Individuals who enter counseling and therapy groups have had varying degrees of success resolving core interpersonal issues (Bennis & Shepard, 1956; Schutz, 1966). Very few new members are likely to have achieved the resolution depicted by Schutz's (1966) socials, democrats, and personals or by Bennis and Shepard's (1956) independents. It is more likely that members have developed personality patterns that reflect varying degrees of success in meeting interpersonal needs and confronting core issues in their relationships. This means that when core interpersonal issues emerge, members will react with various degrees of intensity. These reactions will have a definite impact on group functioning.

Counseling and therapy groups function effectively when members develop insight and a deeper understanding of their interactions with others (Tuckman, 1965). These outcomes are likely to occur when members communicate effectively (Bennis & Shepard, 1956).

Unfortunately, groups encounter barriers to effective communication that are closely related to members' shared core interpersonal concerns. A group composed of individuals who share the same interpersonal issue has a prearranged dominant issue and is likely to stall when that issue emerges (Bennis & Shepard, 1956; Schutz, 1966). If a group is to function effectively, it requires the presence of individuals who have, to some degree, resolved the interpersonal issue being addressed.

Section 1: Conclusion

Group development can be described in several different ways. Despite their different descriptions, however, group development theories display common themes. Understanding these theories and their common themes is important for leaders because it allows them to anticipate and conceptualize surfacing concerns and group events. In addition, by understanding how the interactions of individual members influence group development, leaders can make informed decisions about group composition and anticipate more specific developmental issues. Also, by understanding the role of social and cultural factors, as well as the play of historical events in influencing issues that are likely to emerge in groups, leaders can be prepared with effective process-oriented interventions to facilitate effective communication and interpersonal connections. Finally, by having a clear understanding of the interpersonal dynamics that are likely to emerge in groups when addressing contextual social, cultural, and historical factors, leaders can run groups that do not cause further harm or trauma by encouraging group interactions that are based on oppressive and marginalizing histories of social interactions. Making decisions about group composition and dealing with the impact of individual members on group social and cultural systems are addressed in Chapter 10.

Section 2: Interactive Group Development Theory

The first section of this chapter described classic group development theories and the essential concepts they share. This second section presents a discussion of the core interpersonal issues that are emphasized in Kline's (2003) theory of group development. This theory recognizes as group development realities the essential concepts of group development theory explained in Section 1 (i.e., counseling and therapy groups are social and cultural systems; groups address core interpersonal issues; anxiety related to core interpersonal issues is always present; conflict is inevitable, indispensable, and productive; and members join groups having had varying degrees of success in dealing with core interpersonal issues).

Core Interpersonal Concerns

As discussed briefly in Section 1, one of the themes in classic group development theory is the way in which groups address six core interpersonal issues: involvement, dependency, authority, individuation, intimacy, and loss and loneliness. Groups address these issues in the context of group interaction that becomes increasingly intimate as the group progresses. The issue a group confronts at any particular time during its interaction denotes its stage of development.

Involvement

When groups begin, members confront the same concerns they have experienced whenever they have become initially involved in any relationship. In the group setting, however, these concerns are magnified because members are asked to interact in a way that is more self-revealing and intimate than customary interaction. Accordingly, members confront their fears about being rejected and ignored (Schutz, 1966) and react emotionally (Tuckman, 1965). From the start, members experience anxiety. This is the *involvement* stage.

Most members try to establish certainty to lower their anxiety, testing each other to discover what their relationship will be like (Schutz, 1966; Tuckman, 1965). In doing so, members are attempting to ensure that other members will acknowledge their presence, uniqueness, and importance and to learn whether they share mutual interests (Schutz, 1966). Members also test the leaders to ensure that they care about them. Ultimately, members examine what is required to participate and face the decision to engage or disengage. Members who decide to be involved in the group begin to engage each other more honestly, whereas those who remain uncertain assume a more disengaged stance. All share a common experience: anxiety. Anxiety about participation demands increasingly personal interaction and operates in the background throughout the life of most counseling and therapy groups.

Dependency

Once members become uncomfortably anxious, they act as if they need leaders to take care of them and protect them (Bennis & Shepard, 1956; Bion, 1961; Kline, 2003; Schutz, 1966; Tuckman, 1965). This is the *dependency* stage. To avoid excessive anxiety, members want guarantees that the group will not be too scary. However, if the group is to have any real impact on its members, anxiety cannot be avoided. The efforts of leaders who believe they can create an anxiety-free environment will be futile. This theory also acknowledges that, depending on the social-cultural context of a group and the historical context of the group and the membership composition, some anxiety beyond the basic anxiety about forming new relationships is warranted or justified (Rubel & Okech, 2018). For example, during the rise of the Black Lives Matter movement and the 2020 racial unrest in the United States, anxiety about conversations about race was heightened. It was particularly high in interracial groups, which were not immune to the dynamics and impacts of the events of the time.

Authority

During the *authority* stage, members react angrily when they learn that leaders cannot or are not willing to remove anxiety from their interactions (Bion, 1961). Members blame leaders for their anxiety, challenge leaders' competence, question the need for self-disclosure, and debate the structure and usefulness of the group (Bennis & Shepard, 1956; Bion, 1961; Kline, 2003; Schutz, 1966; Tuckman, 1965). Members may express their anger directly through verbal attacks or indirectly by ignoring or refusing to respond to leaders' interventions, being late, refusing to act according to the group's ground rules, and so on (Bennis & Shepard, 1956; Bion, 1961; Schutz, 1966; Tuckman, 1965). During this stage, conflict over control of the group emerges between those members who distrust authority and those who cling to the belief that leaders can rescue them from anxiety (Bennis & Shepard, 1956; Bion, 1961; Schutz, 1966). Depending on the group's composition, this conflict can become heated and anger can surface between members. Even though members' opposing points of view might be far apart, all members struggle with the question of how to interact in a way that guarantees safety from anger and anxiety (Bennis & Shepard, 1956; Bion, 1961; Schutz, 1966; Tuckman, 1965). Attempts to find a useful solution to the problem of anxiety inevitably fail.

As anxiety and anger continue to build, members air their apprehensions about group interaction, their responsibility for learning, and the role of the leader. Eventually, members become aware that airing their apprehensions, although it creates anxiety, helps them to confront important issues. Group cohesion emerges when members discover that they are able to solve problems and survive intense expressions of emotion (Bennis & Shepard, 1956; Schutz, 1966; Tuckman, 1965). At this point, a palpable sense of relief occurs in the group. Whenever interaction becomes excessively threatening, authority issues can recur. This happens because members, rather than confronting their fears, turn to their leaders for a rescue (Schutz, 1966). Leaders should be prepared for such critical events in the group. Leaders who have not addressed their own fears of conflict and anxiety may quash the group's anxiety by temporarily helping members avoid addressing their concerns. Leaders who understand the importance of this process in group development, and its value in enhancing members' trust and sense of cohesion in the group, are more patient during this stage of the group; they encourage members to share their fears with each other, collectively address concerns that inhibit trust, and take more risks in the group. This means that conversations about topics such as race and gender may need to be broached much earlier in the group's life span (from recruitment to informed consent and the process of preparation for sessions) so that issues associated with members' identities and other general interpersonal fears can be addressed in the group (Rubel & Okech, 2018).

Individuation

The *individuation* stage begins as members experience the relief of having reached a conclusion to their conflict. Members enjoy the harmony and the unquestioned endorsement of the group's importance that follow the intense conflict (Bennis & Shepard, 1956; Schutz, 1966; Tuckman, 1965). So that these feelings of well-being can be sustained, norms emerge that forbid the expression of "negative" emotions. These norms also demand that members ignore conflict and maintain the status quo (Bennis & Shepard, 1956; Schutz, 1966; Tuckman, 1965). After a time, members become disgusted with the phoniness and contrived nature of group interaction (Bennis & Shepard, 1956; Schutz, 1966). Anger builds, and a new battle begins.

Members conflict over norms that maintain contrived harmony. Those who value diverse points of view and want to confront interpersonal issues are eventually the most persuasive. Ultimately, members come to value the expression of individual perspectives and sincere emotions. They develop increased tolerance for conflict and see it as productive. As a result, the valuing of differences becomes a norm. Leaders have a responsibility to nurture this dynamic among members and to encourage interactions that are productive for the group. This stage closes when members express themselves and accept others as unique individuals. The pressure to conform has transformed into valuing individuality and encouraging members to express a full range of perceptions and feelings. As long as the group atmosphere is one of acceptance, anxiety about intimacy will build.

Intimacy

When group acceptance norms support individuation, members openly express their emotions, values, beliefs, and perceptions. In this *intimacy* stage, questions about intimacy come into intense focus. Members share their fears about vulnerability to rejection, their own acceptability, maintaining self-esteem, and how deserving they are of affection (Bennis & Shepard, 1956; Bion, 1961; Kline, 2003; Schutz, 1966; Tuckman, 1965). Conflict at the onset of this stage concerns how intimately members should interact (Bennis & Shepard, 1956; Schutz, 1966; Tuckman, 1965). Members confront the issues they experience in their intimate relationships during this stage (Bennis & Shepard, 1956; Bion, 1961; Schutz, 1966). Although in previous stages members have addressed interpersonal concerns, in this stage the work can be the most intense and productive (Kline 2003; Tuckman, 1965).

As this stage progresses, members are increasingly open and develop intimate relationships (Bennis & Shepard, 1956; Bion, 1961; Schutz, 1966). Intimacy and the open expression of emotions, perceptions, and ideas permeate this stage. For many members, this is the most personally open and connected they have ever been, and the group leader's role in facilitating this level and kind of group interaction is key to the group's success. Leaders who have confronted their own fear of engaging in intimate relationships, and who have experienced the value and depth of meaningful intimacy, are more likely to help group members stay the course in navigating their way through and their anxiety and fears of rejection. As termination nears, members confront what it will mean to lose these relationships.

Loss and Loneliness

At the termination of a group, members who have stayed the course and confronted their interpersonal fear and anxiety have learned to overcome isolation by openly sharing their emotions and perceptions. They have interacted meaningfully and have developed close emotional relationships (Kline, 2003; Schutz, 1966; Tuckman

& Jensen, 1977). These experiences make termination an emotionally and symbolically significant event. Members confront the prospective loss of significant relationships and the loneliness of being disconnected from those who have had a profound effect on their lives. At termination, members leave with an understanding of how to confront loss and loneliness in their lives.

Interactive Group Development Model

A useful model of group development describes the core interpersonal issues that emerge and recycle during the life of a group. It explains interaction among members by identifying the influences of members' personalities and describes stages in terms of their interactive dynamics, the influence of group social-cultural contexts, and the events and emotional climate that accompany transitions to preceding or ensuing stages. Finally, this model describes the experiences that members face as their group reaches termination. The following model builds on the concepts and themes that appear in classic group development theory and attempts to meet the demands of a useful group development model.

Additionally, the emotions and the energy members generate serve as stage transitions—that is, intense emotions shared by group members often serve as the end of one stage and the initiation of the next. Groups can occasionally stagnate as concerns recycle with no outlet. For example, when members struggle with intimacy concerns, they may either look to the leader to take care of them (i.e., intimacy recycling to dependency) or reconsider their involvement in the group (i.e., intimacy recycling to involvement). Although the issues members encounter during the intimacy and the loss and loneliness stages are the most common initiators of recycling, any stage except involvement can result in recycling to a previous stage.

The following narrative describes the interactive content occurring during the various stages of group development and the events that lead to the transitions between stages. An ongoing group dialogue illustrates typical group interaction and the effects of members' personalities. Recall from Section 1 that members' personalities reflect varied levels of resolution in the areas of inclusion, control and authority, and intimacy and affection (Bennis & Shepard, 1956; Schutz, 1973). For simplicity, the narrative describes experiences that are likely to occur in a closed, time-limited group. As you read the interactive content of each stage, the stage transitions, and the dialogue, reflect on how and when recycling might occur and on how other group compositions could affect development.

Involvement

Interactive Content

In the involvement phase, group members are facing the prospect of establishing new relationships. Because they are there to discuss sensitive topics, and leaders have directed them to interact in a more personal way, they become anxious. Initial interaction is superficial as they try to get to know each other and cope with their anxiety. Members are making several decisions at this point, considering questions such as "Will I be safe in here?" "Can I trust my fellow group members?" "What does it take to be a member of this group?" and "How involved do I want to be?" As members decide whether to become involved, their self-disclosures become more revealing.

Stage Transition

As members begin revealing more personal information to the group, their anxiety increases. Along with having initial concerns about acceptance, members are now approaching the discussion of material that has the potential to result in embarrassment, ridicule, and rejection. This stage concludes when members experience what they perceive as excessively uncomfortable anxiety.

Dialogue

Seven members of a diverse and multiracial group have convened for its second meeting. The first session was characterized by questions and mistrust about the potential for group success. All group members identified as cisgender and heterosexual, except for Wanda, who identified as a lesbian. With two African American female members of the group (Atieno and Wanda), one Asian American female member (Parminder), two White male members (Dave and George), and two White female members (Susie and Tracy), issues of race, gender, sexual orientation, and their intersection with the trust and risk-taking required for the group to succeed emerged during the first session. The leader, Terry, who identifies as cisgender, White, female, and heterosexual, greets the members and briefly reminds them of a few ground rules. She then asks the members to share what being back in the group is like for them. Wanda, Parminder, Dave, Atieno, Tracy, Susie, and George take turns offering comments. Terry asks the members to describe their reactions to what they have heard others say.

Wanda: "I'm not sure what you're asking us to do. What are we supposed to say? I want to belong to a group where I know other people care about me. It's kind of scary to say stuff before you know what they want to hear."

Terry: "You all listened carefully to what others had to say. I'd like to hear you share your impressions with each other—you know, the emotions you experienced, the connections you may have made with others. Maybe you found that you have some things in common, or maybe you had a negative reaction to something you heard."

Atieno: " You are not really telling me what I need to do. I think Wanda is right; I don't want everyone to think I'm a real jerk by telling them something they don't want or need to hear. I want to be part of a group where others like me."

Dave: "Atieno, I'm like you. I need more specific instructions before I make a fool of myself."

Parminder: "I'm having a reaction to what you folks are saying. Sure, I'd like to be friends with everybody, but if I just say what you want to hear, you wouldn't learn anything. I want to hear what your real reactions are to me."

George: "Me too. Let's be real in here."

Susie: "Hold the phone you two! This is making me real nervous. I don't know if I'm ready to hear everything people think about me. I don't want to get hurt."

Wanda and *Atieno*: (*In unison*) "Right!"

Terry: "Tracy, you haven't said anything. What's going on?"

Tracy: "I'm kind of agreeing with Wanda, Atieno, Dave, and Susie. I don't want to get hurt. I came here to feel better about myself, not get slammed. Anyway, I've already said too much."

Dependency

Interactive Content

As the dependency phase begins, members' anxiety about participation in group reaches a peak. Anxiety about self-disclosure and safety is extremely uncomfortable for most members. Members turn to the leader, asking for a guarantee that they will not be hurt, a "silver bullet" that will quell their anxiety. Some members want the leader to offer specific guidelines for how they should interact. Others are less active, watching and occasionally commenting. An observer would characterize members' nonverbal communication as anxious and their interactions as cautious.

Stage Transition

After repeated attempts to get the leader to remove their anxiety, members realize that the leader is not able or willing to provide them with the comfort they desire. This stage concludes as members continue to experience intense anxiety about participation. At this point, they also become angry with the leader for what they perceive as abandonment and incompetence. It is critical that a leader not attempt to rescue members from experiencing these feelings. This emotional process is key to members feeling compelled to make different choices about how they engage with other group members in order to form meaningful and fulfilling relationships.

Dialogue

Tonight is the group's fifth meeting. Wanda, Atieno, Dave, Susie, and Tracy are becoming increasingly agitated. They appear anxious, shifting in their chairs and looking intently at the footwear of other members. Meanwhile, Parminder and George seem excited to begin.

Parminder: "This has been great for me, being able to share what's going on with me. I don't do that enough."

Atieno: (*Sarcastically*) "I'm glad you've been having such a wonderful time."

George: "Whew, Atieno, what's your problem?"

Atieno: "George, I'd like to get into this with you, but this is not the time. I'm at loose ends. I need more information about how this group thing is supposed to work."

Wanda: "Terry, can't you have us do an activity or something?"

Dave: "I really don't want to get involved in pointing fingers, but I need to say something. Terry, it really seems that you could do something to make this easier."

Tracy: "I'm with Dave, I'm going to hold back until I know what to expect. I've been hurt enough."

Parminder: "I think this group is getting out of hand."

Terry: "I can see that all of you are at least a little scared, and some of you are very scared. I'm also getting the impression that I'm the one who's responsible for how uncomfortable you are. I wonder what would happen if you started to talk about what's scaring you?"

Atieno: "What! Are you tripping or something?"

Dave: "Whatever, this is bull——!"

Authority

Interactive Content

Members typically begin the authority stage by holding the leader responsible for their anxiety. Some members are angry because they see themselves as being abandoned by the leader. Other members interpret their anxiety as the result of the leader's incompetence. Some members continue to believe that the leader can make the group anxiety free, whereas others directly and indirectly express their anger toward the leader. Eventually, members conflict with each other over how best to remove anxiety from interaction. As a result, members engage in heated conflict with each other. This conflict has many variations, depending on how members have dealt with authority issues and their tolerance for anxiety. This conflict draws out members' concerns about participation.

Stage Transition

The intensity of the anger and anxiety in the group is almost unbearable. As members become increasingly angry and frustrated about their failed attempts to avoid anxiety, they begin to understand how sharing their fears and interpersonal concerns can help them. Leaders need to highlight moments when members take risks and share their fears and concerns in the group. They need to enthusiastically use those moments to encourage interpersonal connections and more sharing by other group members. The more members take risks to share their fear and concerns, the less anxious they feel in the group. This stage concludes as members experience profound relief that their conflict has been "resolved."

Dialogue

About halfway through the sixth meeting, Atieno and Dave voice their anger. Wanda and Tracy express their concern that Terry is holding back a strategy that would make interaction easier. Atieno and Dave argue with Wanda and Tracy about how members should interact. Parminder, George, and Susie watch and eventually join in the conflict.

Atieno: "Terry, I don't think you know what you're doing. We can't trust you to run this group in a way that will work for us!"

Terry: "Atieno, I know you're angry with me and that being in this group is frightening for you. I'm not really sure what's scaring you . . ."

Atieno: (*Interrupting*) "Stop! Stop doing that! You're the one that's scary!"

Dave: "Terry, I hope you never push me like that. It only hurts and doesn't do any good."

Tracy: "Terry, I'm sure that with all your experience, you could make this all go so much more easily. Please tell me what I need to do to make this safe."

Wanda: "I kind of agree with Tracy here. I want to get along with everyone. But you keep talking about us being scared or afraid of something or other, when you could do something."

Terry: "Sounds like some of you think I'm holding back on the magic and others think I have no clue. All this seems to be about who's responsible for all these uncomfortable feelings."

Atieno: "I think we should decide that we're going to get along and decide for ourselves what we should talk about."

After 30 minutes of conflict over how the group should operate, members are becoming increasingly agitated.

Dave: "I think we should share what we see as each other's strengths. That would help us all feel better."

Atieno: "Dave, nobody asked for your opinion. We need to decide on topics that deal with our concerns and assign a person to present on a topic each week, and then we can discuss it."

Dave: "Atieno, who made you the queen of the universe?"

Atieno: "Go to h——, Dave! Your ideas are not helpful. I know what I'm doing."

Tracy: "Wow, you two! Cool off. I'm not comfortable with these negative emotions."

Dave: (*Ignoring Tracy*) "Yeah, right. You can't deal with not being in control of everything."

Atieno: "Don't you dare say that about me! That hurts!"

Dave: "How do you think I feel? I've always been scared about making an a—— of myself."

Wanda: "Tracy, you're right on target. These are the kinds of feelings that scare me. They just hurt, and nothing gets any better."

Parminder: "Do you guys see what's going on?"

George: "Yeah, you're fighting over how to make it safe in here, and it's bringing up what you're afraid of."

Parminder: "Terry, what happened?"

Terry: "Parminder, it looks like when people begin to share what's scary for them, something happens to their fears. Let's talk about what's happening."

Individuation

Interactive Content

In the individuation phase, members enjoy a respite after a period of ongoing conflict. They now regard the group as important and meaningful in their lives. Norms emerge that demand the expression of positive feelings and the avoidance of conflict. Some members eventually tire of the phoniness of these norms and angrily challenge other members who enforce "harmony at all costs." The outcome of this conflict is norms that support members in expressing divergent points of view, addressing conflict, sharing the full range of emotions, and prizing the diversity of the membership. As these new norms take effect, members become more accepting of each other, and self-disclosure becomes increasingly intimate.

Stage Transition

Acceptance builds and members feel freer to disclose more personal reactions and emotions. This stage concludes as members become increasingly anxious about the level of intimacy building in the group.

Dialogue

After the preceding conflict, the group is relieved. All the members, regardless of how upset they have been, seem to be enjoying the fact that the group has survived intense conflict and expressions of anger. Interaction has been led by Wanda and Atieno, who seem to enjoy sharing positive feelings and the absence of conflict in the group.

Wanda: "I am so pleased we finally understand that staying positive and not getting into ridiculous arguments is what we need. You know, I wish my family would understand this. Stay positive and your troubles go away."

Atieno: "I never would have guessed that this group could have become so helpful. I'm glad we all agree with what Wanda has been saying. There's no reason to get so upset when staying positive is so productive."

Parminder: "You know, I kind of agree with you two. I like that we're being so positive and not at each other's throats. But I'm not so sure this is real. I don't know if I can agree with the idea of always staying positive."

Susie: "Parminder! Don't go spoiling what we have worked so hard to achieve. I think this is one of those times you need to go along with things. This is so wonderful!"

Atieno: "That's right, Parminder, things are going so well. I know what a positive person you are at heart. You can fit in here, can't you?"

Parminder: "Oh, come on! I'm just saying what's on my . . ."

Wanda: (*Interrupting*) "There! That's it. You know, Parminder, I have some feedback for you. When you say what's on your mind, I get the impression that you're trying to turn our discussions into some kind of whining contest. I feel really positive about you, anyway."

Terry: "Some folks are shifting around in their seats after your feedback, Wanda. Parminder, would you share what you heard Wanda say and your reactions to her feedback?"

Parminder: "Wanda, I'm stunned. No, no I'm not stunned. I'm really ticked off! You said that when I talk about what's on my mind, you think I'm whining but that you like me anyway?"

Wanda: "Yeah, Parminder, that's pretty much it. You shouldn't be ticked off because I can see you becoming such a positive person."

Parminder: "Yeah, whatever. This is feeling a little weird to me. I'm wondering if anyone else agrees with Wanda's feedback?"

Dave: "Parminder, you're right, this is getting really weird. I'm not believing what you said, Wanda. Parminder, it seems to me that you're just trying to be honest. Wanda, what you said to Parminder really annoys me, too!"

Atieno: "Wait a minute, Dave! We don't need to start with this kind of talk. The group is great the way it is!"

George: "I'm not so sure, Atieno. What do you want us to do—pretend everything smells like roses when there's a skunk in the room?"

Over a period of 30 minutes, the interaction becomes intense, with one faction of members arguing to "stay positive" and another arguing for the need for honesty, whether "positive" or "negative."

Tracy: "I've been reluctant to say anything until now, but I'd like to know that I can be honest with you all, even though it's really scary for me. I sure don't want to pretend and go along with what you're saying when I don't. That's always been my problem, and it's got me nowhere."

Dave: "I couldn't say it better! You know, Tracy, I feel like I'm beginning to get to know you. I'm like you, I get into trouble when I pretend. You know, 'Go along to get along.' It works for a while, then it starts to stink!"

Parminder: "Wanda, Atieno, and you, Susie, I know how scary anger is for you three. I don't want to hurt you or frighten you. I just want you to understand that we don't all have to be alike to get along."

Atieno: "Parminder, I hate to admit it, but I am scared of what happens when people get angry. I'm beginning to see that I'm not having much success controlling how you feel about me. That scares me, too."

Parminder: "I had no idea. Atieno, I just thought you hated me!"

Atieno: "No, Parminder, I've wanted you to care about me from the start, but I don't know how to get close to someone who's as honest as you. Funny, that goes for most of you. But now I'm wondering if I really know anyone. Wanda, Susie, I'm thinking I don't really know who you are. I was just comfortable with you."

Intimacy

Interactive Content

In this phase, conflict between members emerges over the acceptable level of intimacy. Interaction addresses fears related to rejection, acceptability, vulnerability, and exposure. These intense interactions include the open expression and experiencing of emotions and the development of insight into members' relationship concerns. Members directly confront issues that contribute to loneliness and isolation and make intense connections with each other. During this stage, leaders try to stay out of the way to allow conflict and resolution to emerge organically within the group. Leaders are attentive to the emergence of any ethical, legal, or safety concerns as well as scapegoating and any behavior patterns that target a member on the basis of their identity rather than their expressed interpersonal fears and concerns. As members take risks to be vulnerable with each other, and as their interactions become more authentic, their connections foster emotionally and psychologically open relationships. It is in this context that termination of the group enters members' awareness.

Stage Transition

As this stage concludes, members may have experienced the most meaningful and open relationships in their lives. Termination means the loss of these relationships. Members' sadness is associated with the impending emptiness of losing meaningful relationships, and their anxiety is associated with fears that they may once again be lonely.

Dialogue

Interaction is emotionally intense as members explore their relationship concerns in the group and understand how these issues influence their family and social relationships. As the group concludes, members become aware of termination.

Susie: (*Looking at Atieno*) "I've been thinking every day about what you said to me a few weeks ago, that you don't really know who I am and that you're just comfortable around me. I was home the other day and was not liking how my kids and husband were not really paying attention to me, and I realized that no one does. Oh, I get along with everybody, but I don't have a real relationship with anybody." (*Starting to cry*) "I'm so lonely and scared."

Wanda: (*Tears in her eyes*) "Susie, I've been having the same reaction. I'm like this 'let's everybody be happy' nice person. But who I am is anybody's guess. I hold back because I'm scared. I don't even know who Wanda is anymore."

A few minutes of silence ensue.

Terry: "As I look at your faces, I see what looks like some intense reactions to what's going on between Wanda and Susie. Some of you are having reactions, but you aren't saying anything."

Tracy: "Yeah, I'm having two reactions. One is, I can't believe how real Wanda and Susie are. I'm amazed and so happy for them! The second reaction is to the feelings I'm having. It's like you two have the exact same hole inside that I have."

Atieno: "I want to know what you two think and how you feel about me. I want to be real with you, and I want you to be real with me."

Terry: "Dave, tears are running down your face."

Dave: "I'm feeling so lonely. I feel like I have a chance right now to do something about it, but I'm really scared."

Terry: "Do it anyway."

Dave: (*Voice shaking*) "Atieno, I feel such a deep connection with you. I share your fears, and I want you to know that I really care about you. I wish I could take your pain away. I really hope you can let me know what's going on inside you."

Atieno: (*Face flushing*) "Dave, I'm so scared of men. I've been hurt so many times, by my father, by my ex-husband, and by any man I've tried to get close to. I feel like 'damaged goods'! I don't want any more pain like that. More so, I have never imagined that I would be able to make a connection with a White man."

Dave: "Atieno, I don't want to hurt you. I care about you. I understand your concerns regarding racism and White men, but that is not who I am. What do I need to do for you to believe me? What have I done to scare you?"

Dave and Atieno continue their exchange for several minutes.

Terry: "Atieno, you seem very open with Dave. Yet I'm not seeing you reacting like you're getting hurt. Instead, you seem to be getting more vulnerable with Dave."

Atieno: "I'm beginning to feel like I can trust Dave. I don't think he'll just use me and leave me. I appreciate the conversations that we have had about race and racism in this group and his perspectives. I can tell by the way he listens and the expression on his face. He's not like the other men, or even the White men, that I have been scared of."

Terry: "Let's talk about what's happening here. How are the rest of you experiencing what's happening here?"

For the next 45 minutes, members process their experiences and apply these experiences to their lives.

Terry: "We have about 15 minutes to wrap up. Who wants to comment?"

Parminder: "This has been so powerful for me tonight. I feel so grateful to have been here. I have never been part of such a dynamic and interracial group. I am really scared, though. I remember what Terry said a few weeks ago about the group ending. We only have three more weeks. I don't know what I'll do when this group ends."

The others nod quietly.

Loss and Loneliness

Interactive Content

The loss and loneliness stage begins as members experience the prospect of losing the meaningful relationships they have in group. The leader reminds members that they have learned how to develop meaningful relationships. If they have not already done so, members discuss how to apply what they have learned in the group to their outside relationships. Eventually, the group concludes.

Stage Transition

The group concludes as members experience loss. At the same time, members experience the excitement of awareness, understand how to confront their needs and fears effectively, and have the relationship skills and understanding necessary to develop fulfilling relationships. Members have learned how to connect and meet their emotional needs in their relationships because they have done so in the group. They have encountered their fears and survived.

Dialogue

At the start of the last meeting, before a structured closing experience, Terry asks members to describe their experiences during the group and how they are applying what they have learned there in their lives. Members are often tearful in describing their experiences, and some suggest ways that members can stay in contact after the group ends. Some members share their reluctance to end the group, whereas others seem ready to do so.

Parminder: "I'll start. I wasn't sure at first if I was going to learn anything in here. Then, boom, it all hit me. I had to deal with how my expectations of other people get in the way of my relationships. I grew up in a traditional Indian family with very high expectations. I realize now that I have never had a chance to be vulnerable and to struggle. I have always just had to get on with it. I have always wanted to be real, and I have never cut any slack for anyone who wasn't. I'm not so Type A about that anymore. I feel like I'm more patient and I want to get to know people more than I did before, you know, before I make some kind of stupid snap judgment. I like me and other people much more than I did before. I'm excited about getting on with my life!"

Wanda: "Parminder, you scared the living s—— out of me at first. I finally figured out why. It was because you were doing what I was so afraid of doing, being real. I have to say, I know this will blow your mind, that I've come to admire you and am trying to be more open myself. I've figured out why I stay hidden, and I've decided that I can't afford to let it get in the way of being close to others. I got that out of this group. I want a real relationship more than I want to be safe. I have shared this insight with my partner, and we're starting family therapy in 2 weeks!"

Tracy: "I have lived my life being afraid of being hurt by other people. Looking back on what it was like for me as a kid helped me make sense of that. But what didn't make sense is that I acted like that was how everyone everywhere would treat me, even though I'm not 'little Tracy' anymore, wanting to please so I wouldn't get screamed at. After a while in here, I realized I had a choice, I could choose to not do that anymore. I could actually act differently. It has been really hard being more honest, really scary at first. Now, after really working hard to be that way in here, it's working. I see some real benefits at work and with my friends. I don't know how to thank you guys."

Susie: "My family does not take me for granted anymore. I won't let them. I found that not holding back gets me what I thought holding back would get me. I feel much closer to my husband, even though I really blew him away at first. I don't know if he had ever really heard any of my opinions before. I think now that he does not have to guess what I think, he likes and loves me even more."

George: "You all have come to mean so much to me. I have made lots of progress, but I don't want to just say good-bye and leave. Does anyone besides me want to stay in touch after group ends?"

The remaining two members make similar disclosures until Terry introduces the closing experience.

Section 2: Conclusion

Interactive group development theory (Kline, 2003) describes core interpersonal issues that members encounter during their group experiences. These issues emerge as members open their interpersonal boundaries. The emergence of these issues is not necessarily linear. Groups will return repeatedly to issues confronted earlier in the group to deal with the anxiety generated by increased intimacy. Increased intimacy can almost always be equated with increased vulnerability. This means that members encounter increasingly intense fears of rejection and alienation as group interaction progresses.

Use group development theories to describe how boundary issues originate and emerge during group interaction and how groups' interactions are influenced by membership composition and the social-cultural context of the group. Being conversant with group development theories helps leaders achieve their potential as effective group counselors and therapists.

Part II

Group Leadership THEORIES and FOUNDATIONS

Chapter 4

Focal Conflict Theory

Outcomes

Level 1 Outcomes

After reading this chapter, entry-level students and practitioners should be able to:

1. Describe focal conflict theory's conceptualization of group process.
2. Explain how focal conflict theory conceptualizes group members' therapeutic experiences.
3. Explain how focal conflict theory conceptualizes the work of the group counselor or therapist.
4. Identify several diversity and inclusion considerations for focal conflict theory.

Level 2 Outcomes

After reading this chapter, advanced-level students and practitioners should also be able to:

1. Apply focal conflict theory's group process concepts to a group or group case.
2. Use focal conflict theory concepts to generate useful group interventions.
3. Outline focal conflict theory's implications for practice.
4. Synthesize focal conflict theory with culturally responsive counseling principles.

Focal conflict theory (Whitaker & Lieberman, 1964) focuses on leaders' understanding of the interpersonal concerns of group members and how these concerns surface in here-and-now group interaction. Unlike several other group leadership theories, it originated from the specific study of groups and was grounded in its authors' experiences as group leaders, in systematic observations of a broad range of group members and group formats, and in research.

Whitaker and Lieberman (1964) presented focal conflict theory as a series of propositions about group therapeutic processes organized into three categories: group process, members' therapeutic experiences, and therapist contributions. The group process propositions include the basic focal conflict model, how the forces of equilibrium and change operate in groups, how themes emerge in members' interaction, how group culture develops, and how group interaction addresses and readdresses vital group issues. The propositions that describe group members' therapeutic experiences include descriptions of members' perceptions and behaviors as well as how members change or maintain habitual interactive patterns. Therapist contributions center around noticing focal conflicts, encouraging beneficial interactions, discouraging unhelpful interactions, and remaining vigilant about not participating in ineffective interaction patterns themselves. The role of leaders is discussed in more depth in Part III.

Although focal conflict theory is useful to most group situations and group member characteristics, its tenets were developed within a White, Western cultural setting. Group leaders who use focal conflict theory should evaluate its application considering their own and group members' intersectional identities and the impact of these identities—and the power or powerlessness that comes with them—on whole group functioning.

At its core, focal conflict theory emphasizes group interaction as a function of group negotiations that are affected by the differential power of group leaders and members in the group. Application of focal conflict concepts relies upon group leaders' perceptions of members' communication styles, needs within the group and outside the group, and fears of social consequences. Group leaders using focal conflict theory must be able not only to think about its neutral application to group interaction but also to see group members' behavioral and emotional responses as functions of their life experience, social identity, culture, and positionality. Only when they are able to do both will leaders be able to create an inclusive group environment and protect marginalized group members from harm.

Group Process

Focal conflict theory's set of propositions related to group process include assumptions and concepts that form *the group focal conflict* as well as assumptions and concepts that describe solutions to the group focal conflict and the process around solutions (Whitaker & Lieberman, 1964). The group process propositions also depict the role of equilibrium and change as focal conflicts play out. Also critical to the group process of focal conflict theory are the emergence of themes in member interactions, the development of group culture, and the recursive nature of member concerns that emerge during interaction.

Group Focal Conflict

Focal conflict theory (Whitaker & Lieberman, 1964) proposes that themes, or regular patterns of interaction, in group members' verbal and nonverbal behaviors reflect their shared concerns. The shared covert wishes of members are termed *disturbing motives*. Disturbing motives are what members wish they could do in the group and are often associated with a need or attempt to meet a need. For example, a disturbing motive may be a group member's wish to make their feelings known to others so they can obtain support. However, the desire to disclose feelings means that members must confront their shared fears about the consequences. In this case, the associated shared fear may be the fear of rejection. These fears are called *reactive motives*. Disturbing motives and reactive motives, in opposition, form the group focal conflict. The group focal conflict invariably causes members to experience *anxiety*. Anxiety occurs when someone feels worried because they are afraid of what might happen during an interaction or experience. This feeling is often caused by past experiences and fears about the future. Anxiety can be about oneself or someone else, but it always involves fear and uncertainty.

Group members' life experience, culture, social identity, and social positionality in the group will influence what they wish to do in the group and their fear of the potential repercussions. For example, at some level most people wish to have their feelings known to others. However, group members whose families of origin or cultures severely limit emotional expression may have increased fear of the social repercussions of making their feelings known. Similarly, members who have marginalized or stigmatized identities may have more fears of expressing their emotions in group because of the potential for further marginalization or erasure. Unfortunately, this has a high likelihood of happening if leaders are not aware of their own biases and the potential to recreate societal dynamics in group.

Solutions

Members' interactions commonly have the goal of responding to a group focal conflict (see Figure 4.1). When members agree, usually tacitly, on a response to a focal conflict, they have developed a solution. For example, in a group where the focal conflict involves a disturbing motive of expressing emotions and a reactive motive of fearing rejection, the group might use a solution such as "talking about safe topics." To be successful, however, the solution requires the agreement of the entire group. The group must also either lower the intensity of the members' anxiety or satisfy the disturbing motive by allowing its expression. Talking about safe topics will succeed as a solution only if all the members agree to talk about safe topics and are no longer uncomfortably anxious.

Group focal conflicts have two types of solutions: restrictive and enabling. *Restrictive solutions* help the group manage its anxiety by avoiding a direct discussion or experiencing disturbing and reactive motives. By avoiding these wishes and fears, group members temporarily reduce their anxiety (see Figure 4.2). Conversely, *enabling*

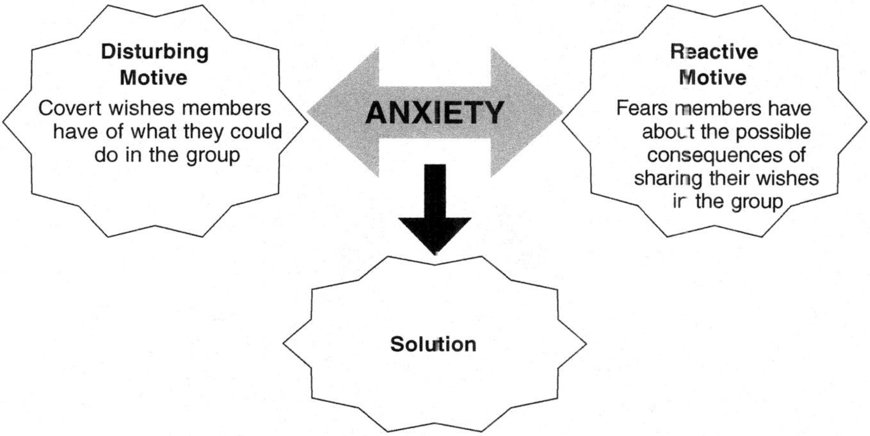

FIGURE 4.1
Group Focal Conflict

Note. Group focal conflict is defined as conflicts that result from opposing disturbing and reactive motives. The conflict causes group members to experience anxiety and negotiate a solution to the conflict.

solutions satisfy disturbing motives and confront the fears associated with reactive motives. Because they confront fears, enabling solutions temporarily increase members' anxiety. If an enabling solution is successful, anxiety eventually decreases because members confront a shared fear and satisfy the disturbing motive.

For example, members who disclose emotions and share fears of rejection may feel intense anxiety at first; but ultimately, they reduce their fear of rejection by talking about it. Once the fear of rejection diminishes and members continue to disclose feelings, the group will demonstrate a sense of accomplishment, become more cohesive, and move on to the next focal conflict. When applying the concept of restrictive and enabling solutions, group leaders should remain mindful that group members' perceptions of the behaviors will be interpreted, at least initially, through their personal lenses, which may include social, cultural, and familial lenses, among others. Table 4.1 provides some examples of focal conflict motives and solutions.

Solutional Conflict

Although group members may agree about solutions to focal conflicts, they may also disagree about them. When members demonstrate opposing solutions, they become involved in a *solutional conflict*. Using the previous example, some members may strongly

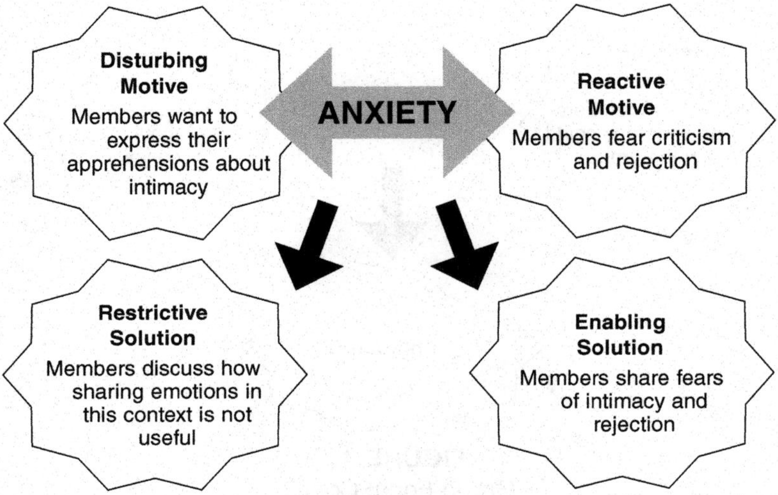

FIGURE 4.2
Group Focal Conflict Enabling and Restrictive Solutions

Note. Solutions to group focal conflict may be either restrictive or enabling, depending on members' anxiety about being intimate and possibly criticized and rejected.

advocate continuing to talk about safe topics to avoid anxiety. At the same time, others may believe a better solution is available. For example, they may advocate for questioning the group leader's competence. In this type of solutional conflict, there are two separate restrictive solutions to avoiding anxiety.

Another type of solutional conflict occurs when members experience varying degrees of anxiety. Members who are not anxious about the focal conflict might advocate an enabling solution, such as "Let's talk about our feelings." Others who are more anxious about the focal conflict might insist on the restrictive solution: "We need to talk about safe topics" (see Figure 4.3).

Members' attempts to deal with the anxiety created by a focal conflict continue until the group has successfully used an enabling solution. Restrictive solutions temporarily reduce anxiety but do not fruitfully attend to the fears behind the reactive motive or to the needs behind the disturbing motive. Consequently, focal conflicts associated with disturbing and reactive motive pairs constantly reemerge throughout the group.

Equilibrium

Focal conflicts are products of group interaction. As members interact, they are exposed to a range of disturbing and reactive motives.

TABLE 4.1
Examples of Focal Conflict Motives and Their Solutions

Disturbing Motive	Reactive Motive	Restrictive Solution	Enabling Solution
Members want to share their emotions.	Fear of rejection and criticism.	Talk about cognitive topics.	Talk about feelings and the fears associated with sharing them.
Members want to openly share what aggravates them about other members.	Fear of being criticized for their "shortcomings."	Ignore "aggravating members" and focus on deciding what it takes to get along in group.	Share reactions and fears of what it would be like to be criticized in the group.
Members want to discuss issues of interpersonal attraction.	Fear of rejection and looking foolish.	Attempt to avoid the issue by talking about relationships outside the group.	Discuss fears about vulnerability and what attracts members to each other.
Members want to resolve conflict.	Fear of others' anger and looking incompetent.	Pretend there is no conflict.	Discuss reservations about being seen as incompetent and areas of conflict.
Members want to disagree.	Fear of being criticized and looking foolish.	Change topics whenever disagreements surface.	Talk about fears of being criticized and desire to disagree.

When focal conflicts emerge, anxieties surface, and solutions are developed and negotiated. Once members develop a successful enabling or restrictive solution, a new focal conflict emerges. For example, a group that has successfully dealt with a focal conflict that consists of a "share your fears" disturbing motive and a "you'll be rejected" reactive motive by using an enabling solution of "discuss your fears" will experience a new focal conflict. The new focal conflict emerges because another disturbing motive, such as "share your perceptions of others" will follow. When this happens, the group begins negotiation around another solution.

The process of finding solutions to focal conflicts is ongoing. The goal of members' interactions is to maintain an acceptable level of anxiety in the group as a whole by establishing equilibrium. *Equilibrium* occurs when a balance between the disturbing and the reactive motives is established with a solution. Groups that reduce anxiety to acceptable levels by avoiding key disturbing and reactive motives can maintain equilibrium. When equilibrium is maintained,

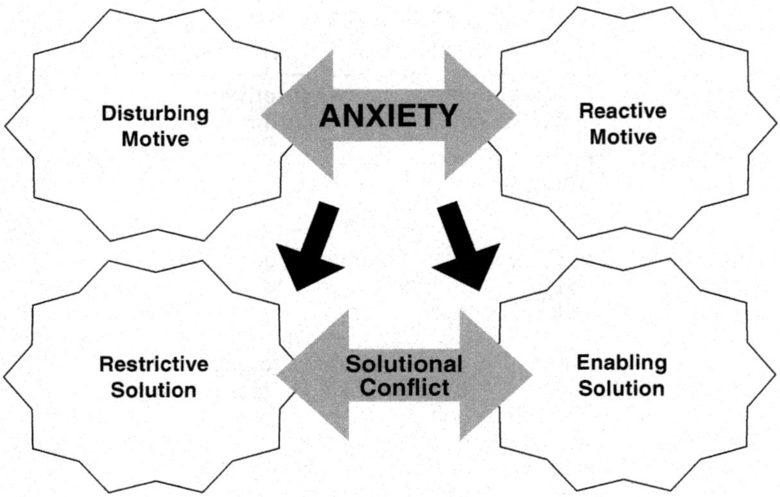

FIGURE 4.3
Group Solutional Conflict

Note. Differences in group members' approaches to resolving interpersonal fears and concerns in the group lead to solutional conflicts.

groups stall, and interactive issues continuously recycle and are repetitively avoided. Consequently, members learn little.

Group Composition and Solutions

How groups navigate solutions to focal conflicts determines how the group progresses. The individual characteristics of group members, or the *group composition*, greatly influence navigation of those solutions. The success of solutions depends on the extent to which members share emotional reactions to emerging disturbing motives. Solutions form readily when members have similar reactions to disturbing motives. An enabling solution that propels the group forward is more likely to occur if members can tolerate the anxiety generated by a disturbing motive. Conversely, a restrictive solution develops quickly if members cannot tolerate the anxiety created by a disturbing motive. Quickly developed restrictive solutions lead to the persistent recurrence of focal conflicts and an overall reduction in the group's effectiveness. When members differ in their reactions to focal conflicts, solutions form slowly, because negotiating a successful solution requires more extensive interaction. Thus, leaders should be aware of group members' ability to tolerate anxiety related to core issues, making decisions first about group composition and later about intervention intensity based on this awareness.

Themes in Group Interaction

Disturbing motives that persistently emerge and reemerge in groups greatly influence group functioning. Reemerging disturbing motives, or "a series of focal conflicts in which the disturbing motives are closely related" (Whitaker & Lieberman, 1964, p. 63), constitute a *group theme*. Group themes surface when members share a desire to avoid the anxiety associated with a particular disturbing motive. A group theme can be identified when members use a variety of restrictive solutions to respond to a reemerging issue. These restrictive solutions, however, do not fully address the focal conflict and only contribute to the reemergence of the disturbing motive at the core of the theme.

For example, over the last five sessions, members of a newly formed group have discussed how to meet their counseling goals. Whenever members begin to discuss being honest about their reactions, one member diverts the conversation for most of the session by introducing a low-intensity conversation. These conversations have included "Let's get to know each other first," "The most important thing we can do is focus on strengths," "Criticism is hurtful," and "Our concerns outside the group are why we're here, so let's focus on those." These are examples of restrictive solutions designed to avoid the disturbing motive of being honest. Because being honest has repeatedly reemerged, it has become this group's theme.

When members are skillful at developing restrictive solutions, the number of group themes multiplies. This is because important disturbing motives and their associated focal conflicts are not successfully resolved with an enabling solution. To counteract this process, leaders should identify and frustrate these restrictive solutions by directing the group to discuss their disturbing motives and reactive fears. Although members respond to these interventions with increased anxiety, interaction eventually becomes more productive.

Groups that develop successful enabling solutions also develop themes. In contrast to groups that develop largely restrictive solutions, these groups demonstrate increasing intensity and intimacy. In other words, these groups develop and remain in the relationship-building phase. Progress in these groups will slow when interaction becomes too intense and an acceptable level of anxiety is not maintained (i.e., equilibrium). At this point, members confront focal conflicts regarding the depth of intimacy, and the relationship issues of the group and its members are progressively resolved.

Group Culture

A group's culture is similar to its normative structure. A group's *normative culture* refers to its established norms, boundaries, and interactive patterns (Cialdini et al., 1991). *Group culture* defines how members can interact, results from negotiations during group interaction, and has a lasting influence on members' interactive behaviors (Whitaker & Lieberman, 1964). Group culture is a composite of all the group's solutions to its various focal conflicts. These solutions become prescriptions for group behavior similar to and overlapping with norms. The solutions that determine a group's culture define how change will take place; shape the relationships between members and leaders; and determine boundaries related to emotions, content, and accepted interaction (Whitaker & Lieberman, 1964). For example, a group that persists in using restrictive solutions such as "don't share your feelings" and "only compliments are acceptable" has developed a culture that severely limits how much members can learn from each other.

Group culture typically resists change because members are most comfortable with solutions that have proven to reduce anxiety. Group culture does change, however, when established solutions no longer eliminate anxiety. This shift occurs when leaders or group members focus the group's attention on its reactive motives and fears. As a result, group members' anxiety escalates, and the group's solution no longer offers protection. At this point, the group begins negotiations to develop new solutions. For example, a leader has frustrated the group's restrictive solution of not sharing feelings by consistently asking members about their fears related to the consequences of sharing feelings. This increases their anxiety to an uncomfortable level again, and they begin to negotiate a new restrictive solution. This negotiation is marked by discussions, such as "How should we solve problems?" "How can we best support each other?" "Logic is the best approach to change," and "Being forced to share feelings is manipulative."

When group members interact to create new solutions, leaders can influence the group to develop enabling solutions. This is accomplished by directly addressing the focal conflict. Ideally, a group's culture will be governed by a majority of enabling solutions.

Group Members' Therapeutic Experience

Group leaders who use focal conflict theory should understand both how it can be used to conceptualize members within the group and how the group environment is connected to the members' learning and growth. The main focal conflict concepts connected to the group members' therapeutic experience are (a) habitual personal solutions, (b) resonance and viability, (c) negotiation of compromise solutions, and (d) deviant members and their relationship to the focal conflict. Social identity, culture, and personal experiences are particularly salient when group leaders consider group members' therapeutic experiences.

Habitual Personal Solutions

Group members enter groups with habitual personal solutions. *Habitual personal solutions* are ways individuals choose to respond to challenging interactions with other people. They develop these solutions in their families of origin and cultural context to manage anxiety attached to their interpersonal concerns (Whitaker & Lieberman, 1964). Often, people join counseling groups because their habitual solutions no longer support healthy relationships or protect them from anxiety as they face developmental crises. For example, Gordon (a fictional person who uses the pronoun "they") joined a group with the habitual solution of "never share your feelings." Gordon came to the group struggling with unsatisfying, disengaged relationships and was unaware of how their life and relationships were being affected by their own habitual solutions.

When group members, such as Gordon, begin to attend a group, they are reluctant to abandon habitual solutions, because these solutions have worked to lower their anxiety in the past. As the group continues, the consequences of members' persistent attempts to use their habitual solutions become more obvious. Members become aware of their habitual solutions and how these solutions function in social interactions. If they become aware that these solutions are problematic in their relationships, members face the anxious prospect of abandoning a solution that has provided them safety in the past for a solution that may or may not work.

Resonance and Viability

In addition to becoming aware that many of their habitual solutions no longer work, members inevitably encounter focal conflicts that are consistent with their habitual solutions. This consistency is referred to as *resonance* (Whitaker, 1989). When members' habitual solutions resonate with the focal conflict, their anxiety escalates dramatically, and they attempt to defend themselves to make the group viable (Whitaker & Lieberman, 1964). For example, Gordon had a difficult time sharing any emotional or personal information that would let others know that Gordon cared about them and wanted to be their friend. Typically, when they wanted to develop a relationship, Gordon would wait for others to share their feelings about their friendship but would never share what they felt. As Gordon's group progressed, members confronted a focal conflict that concerned expressing emotions. During this discussion, Gordon became very anxious. They argued that members should not have to share what they felt and that actions speak louder than words. Whenever another member suggested that sharing emotions was important, Gordon had a strong reaction, making sometimes angry statements that appeared to be designed to shut down the conversation. In this example, Gordon's habitual solution of never sharing their feelings was challenged, and their anxiety escalated. As the group considered enabling solutions to the focal conflict, Gordon did all they could to make the group viable by advocating their habitual restrictive solution.

Viability occurs when a member can avoid a threatening interaction with habitual personal solutions. To maintain the group as a viable environment for their habitual solution, members attempt to influence others to use it. These attempts, however, are usually unsuccessful or short-lived, because group solutions to focal conflicts are constantly evolving and require ongoing negotiation.

In Gordon's case, the success was short-lived, and the viability of their solution was not maintained. The other members decided to share their own feelings. This made being a member very difficult for Gordon, who became extremely anxious. Still, Gordon argued for not sharing emotions. Members who attempt to influence other members to use personally viable solutions and are not successful often settle for *compromise solutions*. Although the group environment continues to be threatening, such solutions are desirable because they make interaction less overwhelming. Gordon, recognizing that the group would not go along with their solution of not talking about feelings, argued that members should participate in whatever way was comfortable for them. The other members could not be convinced to change their "sharing feelings is essential" solution, but this solution would allow Gordon to continue their embargo on sharing feelings.

If an acceptable compromise solution is not established, group members will often withdraw from interaction to protect themselves. Ultimately, all members encounter situations for which they have no personal solutions, their solutions will not work, or the group solution does not reduce their anxiety. Gordon was unable to convince others to back off their "sharing emotion" solution. As a result, Gordon became progressively more anxious and closed off to interaction. Other members' attempts to involve Gordon on a feeling level were unsuccessful.

The motivation to make the group viable increases whenever the group's solutions do not reduce a particular member's anxiety. Anxiety escalates whenever the group's solution prescribes interpersonal behaviors that are especially threatening for members. Members feel vulnerable when they become aware that the group solution makes it impossible to avoid anxiety. Whitaker and Lieberman (1964) pointed out that a group member's perception of threat is directly related to a personal solution that is no longer working. When a member's personal habitual solutions do not protect them from anxiety, they become increasingly vulnerable. As the perception of vulnerability increases, this member experiences increasingly uncomfortable anxiety. The energy members invest toward influencing group solutions is proportional to the magnitude of their threat perception.

Group leaders should be cognizant that for group members who are marginalized in society, the perception of threat within the group may be heightened. If the leader is unaware of marginalizing societal dynamics that are operating in the group, the threat may be very real. Although this does not change the negative impact of restrictive personal solutions on the group or the group members' relationships in and out of the group, group leaders should refrain from demonizing behaviors that may have been or are protective. Rather, they should emphasize the result of the behavior within interaction, evaluate the result based on the member's needs and wants, and promote personal choice with regard to decisions about change.

Compromise Solutions and Members' Influence on Solution Negotiation

Solutions to focal conflicts are negotiated and involve compromise. These negotiations are usually conflictual, in that members have different personal habitual solutions and may attempt to influence other members, overtly or covertly, to use theirs. Because this process demands considerable energy, the group experiences relief when a compromise solution is developed and committed to. At this point, an individual member has little chance to influence the group to change its solution.

However, when the group experiences a situation or event that threatens its equilibrium, attempts to influence the group may be more successful. Influencing the group successfully is not related to a member's personality. Successful change in solutions depends on how much anxiety is generated by the current group situation and the timing of the member's contribution. When a group is experiencing heightened anxiety and has not identified workable solutions, members can more easily influence the group to adopt their habitual solutions—if those solutions offer relief from anxiety. For example, Gordon could have convinced the others to use Gordon's solution if the others were very anxious about sharing emotions and were unable to come up with a solution that immediately lowered their anxiety. In Gordon's case, however, these conditions did not exist, and they were unsuccessful.

The anxiety experienced by an individual member depends on the member's perceptions of group events, the extent to which their interpersonal fears resonate with the current disturbing motive and reactive fears, and how inconsistent their habitual solutions are with the group's solutions. In Gordon's group, other members were not as uncomfortable or anxious about sharing emotions. Gordon, on the other hand, feared what would happen if they shared their feelings. The group's solution was inconsistent with Gordon's habitual solution, and Gordon's interpersonal fears were highly resonant with the group's reactive motive. Gordon began to perceive the group as a hostile environment and other members as having the power to harm them. Consequently, Gordon became even more anxious.

Deviant Members

The perceptions each member has of other group members shift. These shifting perceptions are influenced by other members' contributions to making the group viable during interaction. Members perceive others more favorably when the others support solutions they support and less favorably when they do not. When a member is perceived as blocking the success of a group's solution, that member tends to be perceived negatively by the other members. This member is known as the *deviant member*.

Over the course of their interactions about the "expressing emotions" disturbing motive and various solutions, Gordon's perception of other group members changed, and the other group members' perceptions of Gordon changed too. Early in the group, when conversations were superficial, all members shared positive impressions of each other. As the other members committed to their solution of sharing feelings, believing it to best serve their needs, they began to see Gordon as an obstacle to their progress.

The term *deviant* describes members who do not behave according to group-developed solutions (Stock et al., 1958). Members become deviants when they enact and endorse an enabling solution when the group as a whole has endorsed a restrictive solution. They also become deviants when they endorse a restrictive solution in the context of an enabling group solution. Gordon became a deviant member because they enacted a restrictive, habitual, personal solution in the context of the group's enabling solution (see Figure 4.4).

Deviants' interactions call attention to the focal conflict—that is, deviant members' energetic advocacy for their habitual personal solutions within a group that has otherwise found a successful solution to their anxiety stirs up the disturbing motives and reactive fears that cause the anxiety. Thus, hard-earned group solutions become unsuccessful, and the group as a whole becomes uncom-

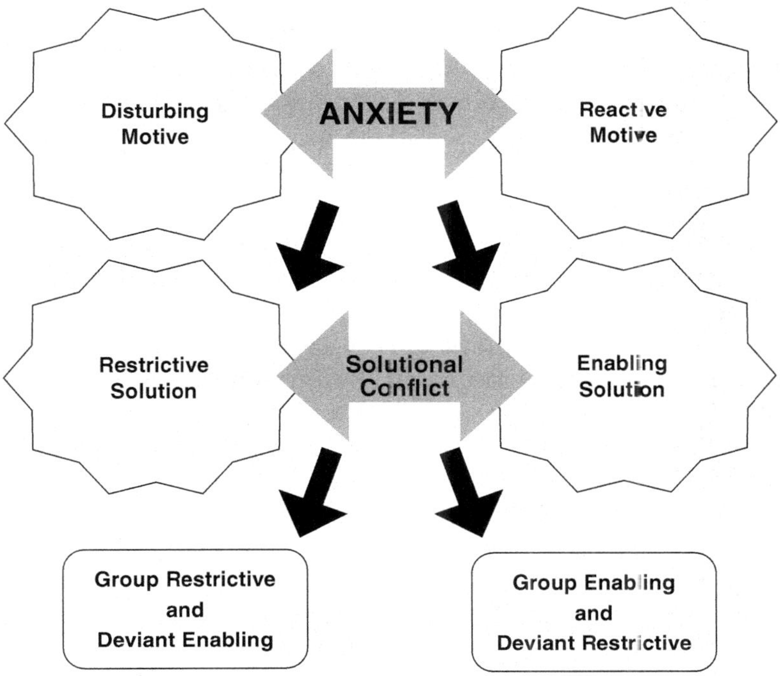

FIGURE 4.4
Group Solutional Conflict and Deviant Members

Note. Deviant group members can frustrate the group's restrictive or enabling solution to the focal conflict by adopting an opposing solution.

fortable again. When this happens, the group reacts emotionally and attempts to persuade the deviant member to agree with the group solution (e.g., "Gordon, you really need to start sharing your feelings. We have a real problem with you withdrawing and not sharing your feelings!"). The group may also, in response to a deviant member's continued anxiety-raising noncompliance, reframe the deviant member's behavior so that it does not threaten the solution (e.g., "Gordon really doesn't understand what they are feeling, so it's OK that they withdraw.") or modify their solution to accommodate the deviant member's disagreement (e.g., "When Gordon withdraws, we can ignore them.").

The quality of deviant group members' experiences is threatened when they frustrate the group solution by not conforming to it. This frustration leads others to actively pressure them to agree with their solution. Typically, groups are intolerant of members who do not conform to agreed-on solutions and will criticize the deviant member for the anxiety experienced in the group. As members continued sharing their feelings, they became progressively uncomfortable with Gordon's withdrawal from interaction. Members made statements such as "Gordon, if it weren't for you, we could actually accomplish something in this group. Maybe you shouldn't be here."

Scapegoats

The crucial issue affecting deviant members is their potential for becoming a group scapegoat. When a member is condemned for group difficulties, that member becomes a *scapegoat*. This is a problematic role that serves a purpose for the group and is a group function rather than an individual failing. The leader must protect the deviant member from becoming a scapegoat by supporting solutions that deal with the deviant in a manner that has therapeutic benefit for the deviant and the group. This is particularly salient when the deviant solution is linked to culture of origin or has a protective function in a group that is differentially threatening to the deviant member—potentially for good reason.

Gordon's group leader intervened when she recognized that Gordon was becoming a scapegoat. She first directed members to address what it would be like for them to be pressured to do something that scared them. She focused on what it was like for them to believe that others did not honor their fears and apprehensions. Then, she initiated a conversation with Gordon that focused on relating their fears with what the group had just discussed—what it was like to have others not respect their fears. Ultimately, by continuously connecting Gordon with others who shared similar reactions, the leader encouraged Gordon to be open about their fear of sharing feelings with others.

Therapeutic Process

The focal conflict approach has the objective of helping members develop effective interpersonal solutions and self-perceptions that are more complementary. These objectives also assume that members entering groups use restrictive habitual personal solutions that limit their interpersonal effectiveness outside the group. For individuals to benefit from their experiences as group members, they must be involved in interactions that elicit change.

To elicit change, leaders intervene whenever needed to establish a level of anxiety that energizes members' interactions. Sometimes, this means elevating the anxiety of a group by directing members to discuss reactive fears and disturbing motives rather than allowing them to avoid these issues. Conversely, when anxiety threatens to shut down group interaction, leaders may introduce or allow the group to use a restrictive solution. Change is also initiated when leaders identify and frustrate restrictive solutions that block the expression of disturbing motives and reactive fears in group interaction. Most importantly, leaders establish a group environment that provides sufficient safety for members to take risks and to self-disclose. These objectives can be realized using a variety of interventions described in later chapters.

Necessary Conditions for Change

Group members must experience several essential conditions to change. First, group members must encounter group focal conflicts that resonate with their own concerns. Second, to learn effective interpersonal solutions, members must participate in group interactions that do not allow their habitual restrictive solutions to lower anxiety and meet interpersonal needs. Finally, members must have opportunities during group interaction to learn about and use effective alternative solutions—that is, enabling solutions. Group members are successful when they develop effective interpersonal solutions, greater tolerance for anxiety, and flexibility in their interactions with others.

Therapeutic Environment

Members are likely to develop effective interpersonal solutions when their group's culture is dominated by enabling solutions and they feel safe. Safety in the context of enabling solutions allows members to abandon habitual personal solutions without being overcome by fear. When this happens, they develop a greater tolerance for anxiety. When a group feels safe, members also experiment with interpersonal solutions, abandon limiting habitual solutions, and develop greater flexibility and resilience in their relationships with others. When group culture is dominated by restrictive solutions, members may not share sufficient personal information or experience enough anxiety to motivate them to abandon their habitual solutions.

In a group culture dominated by enabling solutions, members obtain information that leads to increased self-understanding and more effective personal solutions. This information emerges from members' presentations of solutions to satisfy the group's focal conflict. For example, in a group in which members are developing a solution for a focal conflict related to interpersonal boundaries, members might hear alternatives to their habitual solutions. These alternatives might include, among others, sharing emotional reactions, asking for what they want, disagreeing, and stating preferences. This learning process is especially productive when the group's focal conflict resonates with a member's concerns and the member has an opportunity to experiment with alternative solutions. In addition, as members receive feedback, become aware of their reactions to focal conflicts, and observe the reactions of others, they obtain information that can increase their self-understanding.

Groups that are dominated by restrictive solutions limit the usefulness of the information and experiences members can gain through group interaction. These restrictive solutions are established through group negotiation that involves conversations about how to escape anxiety. These conversations suppress enabling solutions that can lead to more effective relationships. Because solutions developed in a group dominated by restrictive solutions are focused on avoidance, the information members obtain about alternative solutions is suspect.

Unsuccessful Group Experiences

Focal conflict theory (Whitaker & Lieberman, 1964) conceptualizes several reasons why members will be unsuccessful. First, group experiences are unsuccessful when members can continue using ineffective habitual personal solutions. This allows members to avoid the levels of anxiety needed to motivate abandoning ineffective solutions and to experiment with more effective solutions. Second, members who successfully protect themselves from anxiety by withdrawing from interaction will also be unsuccessful. Withdrawal allows group members to avoid helpful interaction that renders their solutions ineffective. Finally, members who can avoid anxiety by replacing their ineffective habitual solutions with new equally restrictive solutions will not be successful. This type of substitution is unfortunately common in groups dominated by restrictive solutions.

Consistently withdrawn or silent members are the members least likely to benefit from group interaction. By simply observing the emotions, personal concerns, and enabling solutions that emerge in the group, silent members achieve limited awareness and insight. Because silent members do not interact, they do not receive direct feedback, are unlikely to overcome fears, and cannot experiment with different solutions. Group leaders must carefully assess their group and the group environment to determine if they are adequately encouraging enabling solutions and identifying and thwarting restrictive solutions.

Group Activity Exercise

Watch the assigned group interaction video. Following the focal conflict theory group observation guidelines for supervisors and peer observers, reflect on your observations of the group. Consider the following questions:

1. What events increased anxiety during the group? How did these events affect members, leaders, and the group as a whole?
2. What might have been the disturbing motives of the members, leaders, and group as a whole? (What do you believe they wanted to talk about?)
3. What might have been the reactive motives of the members, leaders, and group as a whole? (What fear prevented them from talking about the disturbing motive?)
4. What was the most persistent focal conflict? What were some other focal conflicts?
5. What were the restrictive solutions developed by the group? How did those solutions allow the group to avoid the disturbing and reactive motives?

6. Were there any enabling solutions? How did solutions that allowed the group to discuss the disturbing and reactive motives affect the interaction?

Conclusion

Focal conflict theory (Whitaker & Lieberman, 1964) is a powerful tool for group leaders. It provides leaders with a conceptual framework for understanding the outcomes of group interaction and, thus, helps them comprehend group dynamics and formulate interventions. In addition, this theory provides a clear description of how to use group interaction to benefit members. Finally, focal conflict theory can help leaders develop an effective group environment and intervene when a group's culture limits what members can gain. How leaders use focal conflict theory to conceptualize interventions is discussed specifically in Chapter 11.

Chapter 5

General Systems Theory

Outcomes

Level 1 Outcomes

After reading this chapter, entry-level students and practitioners should be able to:

1. Discuss general systems theory concepts relevant to interactive groups.
2. Describe how general systems theory can be used as a framework for understanding group interaction.
3. Explain how leaders use their understanding of boundary functioning to understand and modify group interaction.
4. Describe the role of a leader who uses general systems theory.
5. Describe how general systems theory can be used to help leaders understand the dynamics of social-cultural contexts of groups and their impact on group functioning.

Level 2 Outcomes

After reading this chapter, advanced-level students and practitioners should also be able to:

1. Describe the assumptions and therapeutic processes that derive from general systems theory.
2. Discuss the implications for practice presented by general systems theory.
3. Describe how general systems theory can be used to help leaders understand the dynamics of social-cultural contexts of groups and their impact on group functioning.
4. Describe how general systems theory can be used by group leaders to enhance their understanding of the dynamics of social-cultural issues in groups and how to use this understanding to influence group outcomes.

In 1971, the American Group Psychotherapy Association (AGPA) charged a committee led by Helen Durkin to investigate the applications of general systems theory for group therapy (H. E. Durkin, 1981). This committee developed models for group therapy that departed from the prevailing theories and conceptualizations of the leader's role. This chapter describes applications of general systems theory for group counseling and therapy along with some of the ideas presented by Durkin and her associates. In addition, the work of family therapy theorists provides a more in-depth discussion of a number of concepts.

Essential Concepts: Systems, Subsystems, and Suprasystems

General systems theory describes how the constituent parts of a group interact. The *group system* is a collection of individuals who stand in dynamic relationship with each other. These dynamic relationships involve members interacting with and having a mutual influence on each other. The interaction of members develops a pattern and, thus, becomes a system. "Systems are the product of the interaction of their parts" (H. E. Durkin, 1981, p. 8). Within the group system, each member's interaction performs a function that maintains the group as a system. For example, an anxious member's expression of fears and concern for their performance in the group serves as an outlet and expression for other members who share similar concerns.

Systems are not isolated; rather, they are parts of larger systems, or *suprasystems*, and are composed of smaller systems, or *subsystems* (see Figure 5.1). Subsystems are subgroups of two or more members who share common characteristics. Individual members also constitute individual subsystems. The individual subsystem "defines information about the individual that is known to others. It represents the individual's sense of self" (MacKenzie, 1990, p. 37). Counseling and therapy groups also exist within the context of larger systems. These larger suprasystems include the setting in which the group is convened (e.g., agency, hospital, school) and even larger systems (e.g., immediate community, city, county, state).

Isomorphy

Although systems differ, they all share common characteristics, or *isomorphies*. In a group setting, understanding the concerns of a member sheds light on the related concerns of all other members.

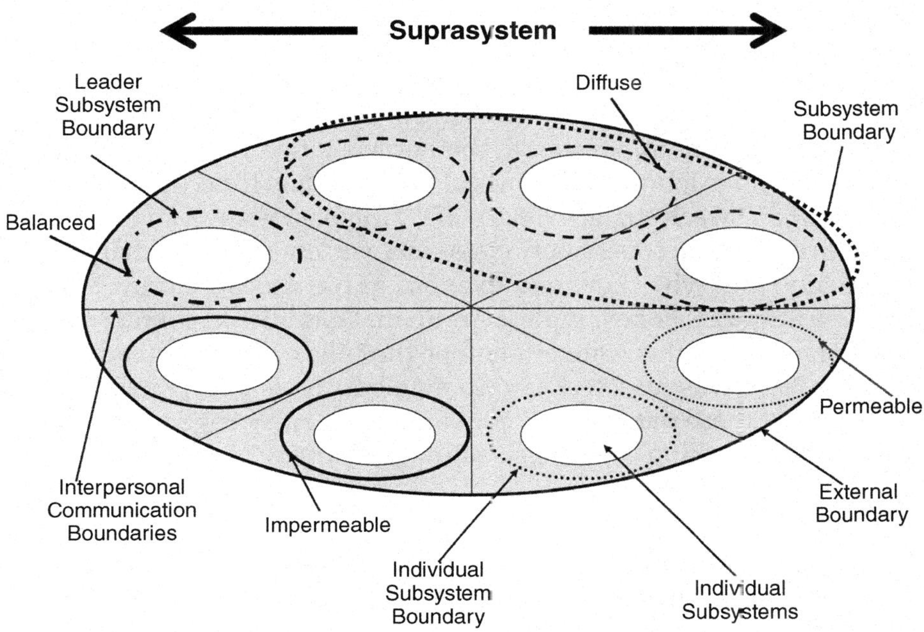

FIGURE 5.1
Group Systems and Subsystems

Conversely, conceptualizing the concerns that characterize group interaction allows leaders to understand the concerns of each member. Thus, a member who describes difficulty with intimacy somewhat describes the intimacy concerns of other members. From the perspective of the group as a system, a group that avoids intimacy has members who have intimacy concerns. Another example is a member who expresses fear of discussing their identity within the group, reflecting fears that others in the group may have about sharing their identities and being their authentic selves within the group.

More broadly, isomorphy implies that counseling and therapy groups reflect the social and cultural conditions of their suprasystems. Thus, all groups demonstrate the issues prevalent in their social and cultural contexts. This isomorphy has an important implication for group leadership in that leaders must confront social-cultural issues, such as racism, sexism, ageism, and other cultural factors that invariably emerge in group interaction.

Homeostasis

All groups attempt to maintain *homeostasis* through interaction that regulates behavior. For example, members' interactions often involve establishing norms that prevent excessive anxiety. The resulting norms include negative feedback loops that limit behaviors that produce anxiety and positive feedback loops that encourage behaviors that manage anxiety. Whenever group norms have changed, as in the process of group development, the group will attempt to regain homeostasis. The homeostatic process involves "times of change followed by times of consolidation to accommodate the change" (MacKenzie, 1990, p. 37). Homeostasis explains why groups avoid issues after periods of intense, emotionally charged interaction and why they tend to avoid implementing norms that increase intimacy. For example, a group that has intense conflict one week may avoid the issue altogether the following week and act as if the issue was resolved. Group members have a responsibility to point out these patterns of behavior and to encourage members to continue working on the issues that previously caused conflict.

Boundaries

In attempting to understand how groups function, group therapists and counselors, like family therapists, have utilized the concept of *boundaries*. Boundary concepts define the functioning of counseling and therapy groups. All subsystems and individual subsystems within groups have boundaries that differentiate them from other subsystems. Groups as systems have external boundaries that separate them from other systems. External boundaries define behaviors that are acceptable in a group, define the group's purpose, and differentiate the group from other groups.

Boundaries "define the amount and kind of contact allowable between members" (D. S. Becvar & Becvar, 1996, p. 191). Because boundaries define how much contact members can have, they also define the information members can share. These interpersonal communication boundaries thus regulate interaction. Groups that have ill-defined boundaries are not likely to have committed members. The lack of commitment occurs in these groups because members are uncertain about their relationships and what they should share. Groups that have rigidly defined boundaries are likely to become stale and boring, because members are not likely to share or receive beneficial information about their relationships.

Subsystems or subgroups have boundaries that separate their members from others (Stapley, 2006). Subgroup members usually share a common perspective, have a common function in the group, or have some common characteristic that defines subgroup membership. Occasionally, subgroups form in response to a particular group issue because of a shared point of view and disband once the issue is no longer relevant. As long as subgroups exist, they have a divisive effect on the group because subgroup boundaries exclude other members. For this reason, subgroups require energetic leader intervention.

In effective counseling or therapy groups, members have psychological boundaries that differentiate them from each other (Stapley, 2006). In effective groups, boundaries allow members to interact meaningfully. When members reciprocally express opinions, emotions, and perceptions, they learn from, influence, and connect with each other and establish their uniqueness.

Boundary Functioning

The development of members depends on how effectively they open and close their boundaries to define themselves and receive and share information. The process of members opening and closing their boundaries is called *boundarying* (J. E. Durkin, 1981). Boundarying implies that individual members have the necessary resources to open their boundaries to receive information and close them to consolidate their learning or protect themselves. Boundary functioning depends on the choices members make to open or close their boundaries.

Ineffective boundarying poses problems for members, subgroups, and the group as a system. These problems are related to boundary permeability, or "how easily [boundaries] permit information to flow to and from the environment" (Goldenberg & Goldenberg, 1991, p. 46). Permeability problems occur when boundaries either do not allow information input or output or do not limit information to be input or output.

Impermeable Boundaries

When members do not consider the input of others or do not share personal information, they have impermeable boundaries. Members with such boundaries become disengaged from the social contexts in which they live and appear unaffected by others' concerns (Barker, 1992). Because these members are disengaged, they are autonomous. This autonomy, however, comes at the cost of not having the capacity to ask for or receive support or to establish emotional connections with others (Minuchin, 1974; Simon, 2015). Consequently, these individuals do not appear sensitive to others' needs for support (D. S. Becvar & Becvar, 1996). Because of their reluctance to share emotion or be psychologically intimate, these members are not likely to develop meaningful relationships with other members. Disengaged members do not benefit from feedback and have the tendency to perseverate over particular issues.

For example, Jim is unemotional in his interactions with others and does not share enough personal information to allow others to know him. Occasionally, other members have a strong reaction to Jim and offer him feedback. Jim, however, ignores this feedback or states that he is not interested in hearing it. Whenever Jim struggles, he does not verbalize his concerns and clearly does not know how to ask for help. During a session, Jim repeatedly complained about not having many friends. He was then offered the following feedback: "Jim, when I ask you how you feel about me, you don't share your feelings and don't even say what you think about me. When you do that, I feel shut out and sad, and I assume you don't want to have a relationship with me." After this feedback, Jim stated, "I heard what you said, but I don't know why I don't have many friends."

Diffuse Boundaries

Members who are overly dependent on others have highly permeable or diffuse boundaries (Simon, 2015). Members with diffuse boundaries develop enmeshed relationships with other members. These relationships are displayed by members who respond immediately to the emotional reactions of others (Minuchin, 1974) as if they cannot tell whether the expressed emotions belong to them or to other members (D. S. Becvar & Becvar, 1996). Members with diffuse boundaries are reluctant to state their opinions and avoid confrontation. They are vulnerable, are overly concerned about the feelings of others, and tend to be very compliant. In effect, they do not seem able to close their boundaries to define themselves or to protect themselves from criticism or unhealthy influence.

Members with diffuse boundaries are depicted by Bowen's concept of fusion (Kerr, 1981). Members who are emotionally fused with others are extremely susceptible to being influenced by the emotions of other members and behave as if their well-being is dependent on others experiencing "positive" emotions. Emotionally fused members tirelessly pursue others' approval. In addition, fused members believe and act as if people cause others' emotions, are reluctant to take responsibility for their own emotions, and blame others for the emotions they experience.

For example, over the last several weeks it had become apparent that Karen was investing most of her energy in trying to keep others happy. She seemed vulnerable and overly reactive to others' emotions and often came to tears over trivial comments. Other members often commented that she was "taking it too seriously." When confronted by another member for being "wishy-washy," Karen responded, "I'm sorry. Please tell me I haven't offended you. I know I shouldn't do that; tell me what you want me to do."

Effective Boundarying

Effective boundarying occurs when members intentionally open and close their boundaries when beneficial. Minuchin (1974) would characterize these members as having clear boundaries. These members are capable of balancing nurturing with receiving nurturing, giving support with receiving support, and belonging with autonomy (D. S. Becvar & Becvar, 1996; Simon, 2015). They open their boundaries to receive feedback, self-disclose, and experiment with new behaviors. They also open their boundaries to connect with others without becoming enmeshed. When it is time to reflect on what they have experienced and consolidate their learning, these members close their boundaries. Members who use their boundaries effectively can close them to protect themselves when necessary or open them to engage with others.

For example, Julie received feedback from four other group members over a 25-minute period. She responded by verifying that she understood the feedback accurately and "checked out" the feedback with other members. Julie took some of the feedback to heart, tried on new behaviors, and openly shared emotions and perceptions related to the feedback. When she believed that she needed to reflect on the feedback she had received and had experienced enough intense emotion, she stated, "I need to stop now and reflect on what just happened."

Just as the permeability of individual boundaries affects interpersonal functioning, the permeability of system and subsystem boundaries affects group functioning. Groups operating with clear boundaries demonstrate fluid communication. These groups effectively negotiate and renegotiate boundaries so that members can learn and change. Change is less threatening when a group has effective boundarying. Members feel free to experiment with new behaviors and express opinions, emotions, and perceptions.

Groups with impermeable boundaries often have a disengaged membership. Members avoid contact with each other by withholding their emotions, opinions, and perceptions. The overall tone in these groups is cognitive and somewhat disinterested. Members in these groups are unlikely to profit from interaction, test out new behaviors, or develop satisfactory relationships with other group members. These groups can be highly cohesive, but this comes at the cost of being disengaged from the environment and potentially productive input.

Members of groups with highly diffuse boundaries, on the other hand, are extremely sensitive to others' reactions. These members are intensely involved with each other and provide a smothering blanket of support. Maintaining comfort and the status quo are highly valued. These members also are overly concerned about others' "negative" emotional reactions and attempt to stifle the expression of these emotions. Members of these groups depend on leaders for direction and often seek leaders' approval. They have little success developing relationships with each other because they are unlikely to risk revealing themselves to others. The learning potential in groups with diffuse boundaries is minimal because members are unlikely to share honest reactions or risk experimentation with new behaviors. These groups are also so open to external input that they often become unproductive, focusing on external concerns as opposed to their own development.

Autonomy

An important goal for group members is autonomy. *Autonomy* means that members have the capacity to act intentionally in their boundarying. Leaders thus have an objective of helping members make choices to open and close their interpersonal boundaries in a way that is self- and relationship enhancing.

Boundarying, as an autonomous system, opens up the possibility for personal development and allows members the freedom to change within the limitations of larger systems (J. E. Durkin, 1981). Individuals, however, have the freedom to be autonomous in terms of their personal boundaries, what they share, and what they choose to experience. The function of autonomy is *wholing*. "Wholing means achieving function through self-organization. Functioning in living structure involves maintaining and developing oneself in the face of environmental forces which work passively or actively against such adaptation" (J. E. Durkin, 1981, p. 37).

Autonomous members decide independently when to participate or not participate and how deeply involved they will be in any interaction. These members can self-disclose to develop intimate relationships and set appropriate limits on how intimate they become with others. The boundaries of autonomous members allow them to become involved but not enmeshed.

However, autonomy can lead to isolation if individuals close their boundaries excessively (Simon, 2015). Although members should strive for autonomous functioning, they need to learn to keep their boundaries open enough to form relationships. Autonomy should be coupled with sufficient permeability to allow members to be open to feedback and be sensitive to others' experiences. Openness to others' experiences, knowing how and when to offer support or share emotions, is essential for members' growth and relationship development.

Hierarchy

Systems exist within suprasystems, and subsystems exist within systems. The activities of a system are organized by the system in which they exist (MacKenzie, 1990), and so the group organizes the behavior of group members. Furthermore, the hierarchical structure of systems affects the roles, behaviors, and impact of individuals within their respective systems. Therefore, to understand the behaviors of a member, the leader should consider how the member's behavior fits how the group is functioning. For example, a person receiving feedback and experimenting with making requests for support may not make sense unless this person's behaviors are viewed in the context of a counseling or therapy group.

Therapeutic Process

Basic Assumptions

Foundational to the therapeutic process is the assumption, as articulated by Helen Durkin (1981), that groups and their members are *living systems*. Effective living systems can open their boundaries to acquire energy and information and use this energy to change. By changing, these systems have the capacity to adapt to environmental circumstances to allow growth and development. In closing their boundaries, these systems can maintain a desired inner state and filter out environmental events that threaten this inner state. Closing boundaries also allows systems to preserve their identity and not become fused with other systems. In this context, relationships involve the reciprocal opening and closing of boundaries—opening for input and connection and closing for identity and integrity.

Living systems open and close their boundaries most effectively when they operate autonomously. "The goal of therapy, to help the group members restore or enhance their own autonomy, is concretized into the more practical goal of helping group members more effectively open and close their own boundaries" (H. E. Durkin, 1981, p. 6). By focusing on boundaries, leaders can simplify their work. "Focusing on system boundaries gives the therapist a single uniform approach to all levels which permit him, at times, to cut through the diversity of content to the underlying structure" (H. E. Durkin, 1981, pp. 11–12). In essence, the desired outcome for group counseling and therapy is members who can open their boundaries to receive and utilize necessary input and close their boundaries when needed to maintain identity and integrity.

Seeing the group, its members, and its leaders as living systems simplifies the understanding of interaction and development of interventions. Because groups operate as hierarchies, interaction observed at one level shows how a system functions at the next lower level. This also means that interventions directed at one level of the group system affect the subsystems of that level. Thus, when leaders intervene to improve group communication, leaders can assume that group subsystems and individual subsystems will be affected.

Isomorphism is a highly significant concept in general systems theory for group counseling and therapy. Because all levels of the group system share characteristics, leaders can learn about the issues of each member by identifying the issues encountered by the group as a system. The assumption of isomorphy also allows leaders to identify group issues by understanding the concerns of individual members.

Implications for Group Counseling and Therapy

The use of general systems theory in group counseling and therapy is all about boundarying. Leaders have the essential tasks of assessing boundary functioning and intervening to help members alter boundaries that limit their capacity for adaptation and growth. The concept of autonomy serves as the criterion for assessing members' boundaries and as the objective for leaders' interventions. Once boundaries are assessed, interventions attempt to modify excessively closed or open boundaries at all levels of the group system. Additional concepts, such as isomorphism and hierarchy, are useful aids for leaders to use to comprehend group boundary functioning, understand the issues present at all group system levels, and develop and implement interventions.

Change involves modifying the inner structure of members' internal systems. For this to occur, the boundaries of the members must be flexible enough to permit penetration (Gray, 1981). Thus, the essential objective of group counseling and therapy is to help members develop the ability "to restructure themselves by regulating the permeability of their intra- and interpersonal boundaries" (H. E. Durkin, 1981, p. 19).

Dynamics of Process

The application of general systems theory to group counseling and psychotherapy involves a therapeutic process that focuses on the boundarying occurring at multiple levels of the group system. The primary role of leaders is to identify ineffective boundary structures and to intervene to alter them (H. E. Durkin, 1981; MacKenzie, 1990). More specifically, leaders have the objective of optimizing the group's external boundaries, interpersonal communication boundaries, subsystem boundaries, and individual boundaries. Autonomy is the goal.

To assess boundary functioning, leaders select one level of the system to observe—be it individuals, subsystems, or the group as a system. When interaction indicates diffuse or impermeable boundaries, leaders can intervene. These interventions have the goal of helping members develop autonomous boundary functioning.

When boundary functioning indicates diffuse boundaries, interventions focus on helping to "firm up" boundaries. Leaders should help members with diffuse boundaries become more independent in their actions and thinking. These members can benefit from numerous interventions, including experimenting with sharing independent opinions, stating what they want as opposed to asking, and experimenting with anger and disagreement. For example, a leader can assist a member with diffuse boundaries with the process of autonomy by reminding them of their group goals. A leader might draw their attention to contradictions in the various positions they take in the group to align themselves with various members or to specific feedback that they are willing to commit to that might be dramatically opposed to their group goals.

When a group diffuses external boundaries, it spends excessive time conversing about outside events and effort in smothering communication that could increase anxiety. Diffuse external boundaries are commonly seen in groups where members have "safety first" or less permeable interpersonal boundaries. These boundaries often occur in groups that incorporate new members on too regular a basis. Leaders of these groups are clearly challenged in their work to develop sufficiently closed boundaries and trust. Their only resort is to emphasize interventions that keep interaction focused on the here and now, to develop norms that contrast with outside systems (e.g., open sharing of emotions, discussing interactions that are occurring within the group, giving feedback based on behavior observed within the group), and to use language that stresses the group as separate from external systems.

When boundary functioning indicates impermeable boundaries, interventions focus on opening boundaries. Impermeable boundaries require opening to allow the exchange of necessary information. One way leaders can help individuals open their boundaries is by encouraging them to share emotions (MacKenzie, 1990). Procedures such as feedback exchange that encourage effective communication and experimentation with new behaviors can also be effective.

Groups that have impermeable external boundaries can have the advantages of cohesiveness, trust, and intense here-and-now interaction. However, a group with impermeable boundaries that remains intact for prolonged periods can become stale without occasional new members and suffer from being detached from the environment. Leaders can use the boundary-opening intervention of asking members to connect their in-group experiences with similar experiences outside the group. This intervention must be timed well and used carefully so as not to create norms that open the group's external boundary excessively (e.g., talk about outside material).

Groups are effective when boundaries allow communication to flow freely. In these groups, members exchange feedback and experiment with new behaviors that lead to change. Ineffective groups suffer from external boundaries that are too diffuse and internal communication boundaries that are impermeable. Such groups demonstrate an atmosphere of defensiveness that involves constant introduction of topics that have little impact on members to maintain safety and homeostasis. Ineffective groups rarely have meaningful feedback exchange or members who experiment with interpersonal behaviors.

Conclusion

General systems theory is a useful framework for understanding group interaction. The theory's principles define the characteristics of a productive group environment and help leaders conceptualize interventions. The concepts of isomorphy and hierarchy are especially helpful for understanding the shared aspects of members' concerns, the potential effects of interventions, and the impact of larger social-cultural contexts on group concerns. Leaders who stress a systems approach have the primary role of boundary regulator. Leaders who focus on boundarying and who have autonomy as their primary goal can be very effective.

General systems theory greatly simplifies group interaction, so it is a useful framework for understanding the complexities of members' interactions. The theory also helps leaders anticipate and understand the impact of group social-cultural contexts on the emerging concerns of members. By itself, however, general systems theory lacks sufficient depth to explain the dynamics of group interactions or to provide a detailed description of the leader's role. Authors who have utilized general systems theory, such as Donigian and Malnati (1997), Agazarian (1997), and Kline (2003), have added their own conceptualizations of the leader's role and borrowed from other theoretical perspectives to deepen the understanding of members' interactive dynamics. Systems theory concepts will be incorporated into the discussion of leader interventions in Parts III and IV. See Chapter 13 for a discussion of evidence-based research on principles and practices of group systems theory.

Chapter 6

The Interpersonal Approach and Group Theory Summary

Outcomes

Level 1 Outcomes

After reading this chapter, entry-level students and practitioners should be able to:

1. Discuss the theoretical foundations of the interpersonal approach.
2. Explain the essential concepts of the interpersonal approach.
3. Discuss the interpersonal perspective on the group therapeutic process.
4. Describe the role of a leader who emphasizes the interpersonal approach.

Level 2 Outcomes

After reading this chapter, advanced-level students and practitioners should also be able to:

1. Describe how the interpersonal approach can be used to help leaders understand the dynamics of social-cultural contexts of groups, their impact on group functioning, and leaders' role in using that understanding to influence group outcomes.
2. Describe the assumptions and therapeutic process that derive from the interpersonal approach.
3. Outline the seven themes that group counseling and therapy theories share and describe how these themes can be used in group practice.

The *interpersonal approach* to group counseling and therapy emphasizes members learning from each other in a setting that accentuates here-and-now interaction, feedback exchange, the correction of interpersonal perceptual distortions, immediate emotional experiencing, the utilization of essential therapeutic factors, and cognitive processing. It views members' interaction in the group as the basis for interpersonal learning, the objectives of which are awareness, insight, and change in relationships both in and out of the group setting (I. D. Yalom & Leszcz, 2020). The interpersonal approach to group therapy was made prominent by the work of Irvin D. Yalom (1970).

Focal conflict theory, general systems theory, and the interpersonal approach are similar in that they claim that members' interactions inside group mirror their interactions outside group. The interpersonal approach differs from focal conflict theory and general systems theory in that it does not emphasize the group as a social system. Thus, it does not stress group-as-a-whole interventions (Ettin et al., 1997) as an imperative aspect of the leader's role. In addition, the interpersonal approach stresses an interpersonal learning process, which the leader must facilitate. Finally, the interpersonal approach has been heavily influenced by the work of Sullivan (1953), which was originally focused on exploring a developmental approach to psychopathology, rather than being intended as a group approach to therapy. For this reason, group workers who use this approach need to combine it with another theory, such as group systems theory, which provides options for group-level conceptualization and intervention.

Theoretical Foundations of the Interpersonal Approach

In the interpersonal approach to group therapy, group interaction is viewed as the mechanism for change (Leszcz, 1992). This perspective is the product of I. D. Yalom's (1975, 1995) conceptualization of interpersonal learning as a therapeutic process. His ideas were based most extensively on the work of Harry Stack Sullivan. Sullivan (1955) maintained that self-esteem depends on individuals' perceptions of how their significant others evaluate their behaviors. During childhood, "the developing personality embraces those parts of the self that are valued by his or her significant others" (Leszcz, 1992, p. 38). By behaving in a way that has the approval of significant others, individuals can maintain their interpersonal attachments and build their self-esteem. Conversely, behaviors that do not gain the approval of significant others cause interpersonal anxiety, because individuals perceive that such behaviors threaten their attachments with significant others. Because significant others disapprove, individuals' perceptions of their self-worth diminish. The behaviors that create interpersonal anxiety, or are threatened with disapproval, are "disavow[ed] through the process of selective inattention" (Leszcz, 1992, p. 38).

Additionally, the disapproval of significant others can cause individuals to disown personal experiences and avoid using interpersonal behaviors that communicate these experiences. Conversely, individuals learn to value interpersonal behaviors and their accompanying internal experiences when they gain the approval of significant others. People construct their unique personalities through the development of interpersonal schemas and the adaptation of their behaviors according to their perception of feedback from significant individuals in their lives. This intricate process involves the maintenance or eradication of certain behaviors (see Figure 6.1). The resulting composite, although formed at an early age, persists and influences relationships throughout an individual's life (I. D. Yalom & Leszcz, 2020).

For example, when Steve was 5 years old, his parents scolded him for feeling and acting sad and angry. When Steve experienced these scoldings, he perceived he was doing something inappropriate and that being sad and angry was unacceptable. Eventually, so

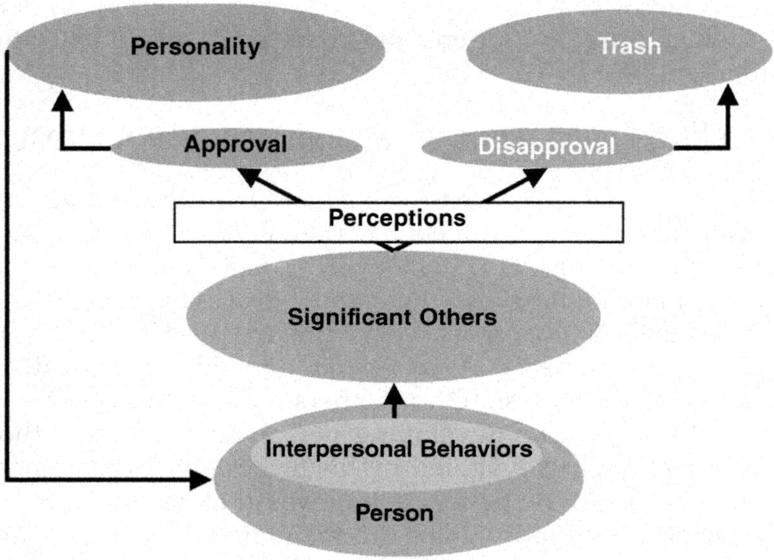

FIGURE 6.1
Developing Interpersonal Schemas

Note. Individuals create their personality by maintaining or eliminating interpersonal behaviors on the basis of how they perceive the evaluations of significant others.

Steve could maintain his parents' approval and his own self-worth, he stopped attending to these unacceptable feelings. Consequently, Steve came to believe that he had to conceal his feelings to maintain attachment with his parents and be worthy. Later, when Steve joined a group at age 28, he described several failed relationships. He discussed feeling unable to meet his needs for emotional support. He also stated that his partners complained they never knew when he was upset and felt shut out by him. When other members encouraged him to talk about his sadness, Steve denied feeling sad.

I. D. Yalom and Leszcz (2020) emphasized Sullivan's (1953) idea that individuals are disposed toward perceiving others in a way that distorts what occurs in their relationship. These distortions are associated with individuals' perceptions and possible misinterpretations of significant others' approval and disapproval. Sullivan (1953) coined the term *parataxic distortion* to describe this perceptual process. As I. D. Yalom and Leszcz (2020) explained, "a parataxic distortion occurs in an interpersonal situation when one person relates to another not on the basis of the realistic attributes of the other" (p. 219). Rather, the individual reacts to the other unrealistically because of their own perceptions and internal reactions. These distortions define acceptable and unacceptable interpersonal behaviors and lead to impaired relationships.

Leaders commonly observe a variety of parataxic distortions emerging in group interaction. The following example occurred during the early meetings of an adolescent group:

> *Renee*: "Brian, you just can't act that way. I won't like you if you do."
> *Leader*: "Renee, I'd like you to try a different way to . . ."
> *Renee*: "Shut up! You are so critical of me and everything I do. You think I can't do anything right! You go to h——!"

In this example, Renee's reaction was due to a parataxic distortion, which is indicated when a member's emotional reaction is far more intense than a situation warrants. Here, Renee's angry reaction was inconsistent with the content of either previous or current interaction. Although this example involved the leader, parataxic distortions occur between members as well.

Parataxic distortions are correctable through the process of consensual validation (Sullivan, 1953; I. D. Yalom & Leszcz, 2020). Consensual validation is a process in which individuals learn how to value themselves, their internal experiences, and their behaviors differently, depending on others' responses and perceived evaluations. In this way, group members who encounter others' reactions that are contrary to their own perceptions can correct their interpersonal distortions. For example, if a member who is ashamed of having shared their feelings of feeling marginalized as a gender minority in society and within the group hears that other members deeply appreciate this sharing, it can change their belief that others will reject them because they are worthless when they share feelings. This corrected interpersonal distortion helps this member value their emotions and become more emotionally open in their relationships.

I. D. Yalom and Leszcz (2020) expressed their view of interpersonal relationships as a critically important human need, stating that "people need people—for initial and continued survival, for socialization, for the pursuit of satisfaction. No one—not the dying, not the outcast, not the mighty—transcends the need for human contact" (p. 21). They, along with Sullivan (1955), viewed mental health in terms of healthy relationships. Therefore, the goal of group counseling and therapy is to help group members learn how to achieve healthy and satisfying relationships.

Essential Concepts

The interpersonal approach focuses on members' interactions "as the nucleus of change, growth, and improvement" (Leszcz, 1992, p. 37). This focus is grounded in the assumption that developing and sustaining relationships is a highly significant human need and that individuals' definitions of self-worth are a function of their relationships.

Therapeutic Factors

I. D. Yalom and Leszcz (2020) described 11 factors that contribute to the process of change in a therapy group (see Table 6.1). I. D. Yalom and Leszcz (2020) compiled a list of therapeutic factors that were influenced by the research of Corsini and Rosenberg (1955) as well as Bloch and Crouch (1985). These researchers studied therapeutic factors and consistently defined them as the process that simplifies the complex interactions that occur in therapy group sessions. They are valued for their utility as leadership objectives and for their precision in identifying tactics and strategies that leaders can use within the group to bring about change.

Unlike the approaches used by previous researchers, two out of the 11 factors identified by I. D. Yalom and Leszcz (2020), interpersonal learning and group cohesiveness, were treated separately to emphasize their importance. Furthermore, the authors subdivided

TABLE 6.1
Group Therapeutic Factors

1955 (Corsini & Rosenberg)	1985 (Bloch & Crouch)	1970 (I. D. Yalom) and 2020 (I. D. Yalom & Leszcz)
• Acceptance • Altruism • Universalization • Intellectualization • Reality testing • Transference • Interaction • Spectator therapy • Ventilation	• Insight • LIA • Acceptance and cohesiveness • Self-disclosure • Catharsis • Guidance • Universality • Altruism • Vicarious learning • Instillation of hope	• Instillation of hope • Universality • Imparting of information (didactic instruction and direct advice) • Altruism • Corrective recapitulation of the primary family group • Development of socializing techniques • Imitative behavior • Interpersonal learning (input and output) • Group cohesiveness • Catharsis • Existential factors

Note. LIA = learning through interpersonal action.

the imparting of information into two parts, didactic instruction and direct advice, to illustrate the multidimensional nature of communicating information to clients. Six other factors—instillation of hope, universality, altruism, corrective recapitulation of the primary family group, development of socializing techniques, and imitative behavior—are also important contributors to change. I. D. Yalom and Leszcz (2020) viewed the final two factors, catharsis and existential factors, as best understood in the context of the other factors. Chapter 7 addresses therapeutic factors in greater detail.

Interpersonal Learning

Interpersonal learning is a comprehensive term that encompasses the processes of consensual validation, corrective emotional experience, the group as a social microcosm, transference, and insight. Although other therapeutic factors contribute to change, interpersonal learning is the most essential mechanism of change (I. D. Yalom & Leszcz, 2020). An interpersonal group approach uses interpersonal learning to alter interpersonal distortions, provide insight, and help members master the interpersonal behaviors necessary to experience more satisfying relationships (Kline, 2003; I. D. Yalom & Leszcz, 2020).

Interpersonal learning involves members gaining an understanding of how others perceive and react to their interpersonal behaviors. When members share their perceptions and reactions, others receive information that can correct interpersonal distortions. In addition, this information provides members with input about alternative interpersonal behaviors that can improve their relationships. As members become more adept at self-observation and effective interpersonal behaviors, they transfer their learning to relationships outside the group.

Consensual Validation

The most significant factor in interpersonal learning is the process of *consensual validation*, the most essential component of which is interpersonal feedback (see Figure 6.2). Leaders encourage consensual validation on the premise that group members can alter their interpersonal distortions when they compare their self-evaluations to others' evaluations (I. D. Yalom & Leszcz, 2020). Thus, when members find that others see certain interpersonal behaviors positively, they can begin to regard those behaviors positively even though they previously have viewed them as unacceptable. Consensual validation also influences behaviors that others view as unacceptable and that the member has viewed as acceptable.

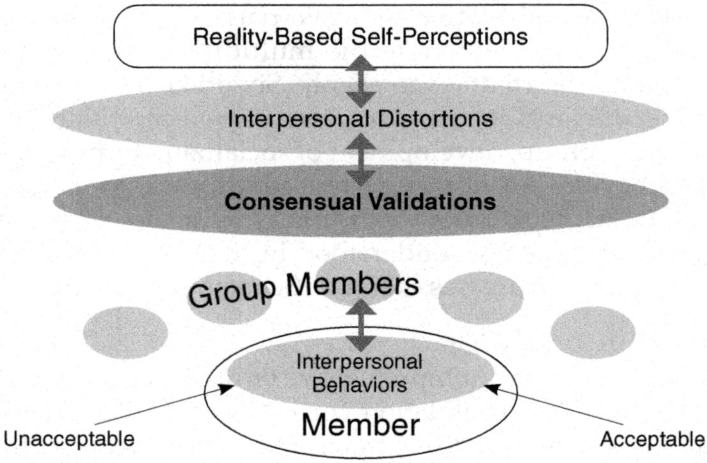

FIGURE 6.2
Interpersonal Theory–Consensual Validation Process

For example, Nguyen believed that sharing emotions was a sign of weakness and thus unacceptable. After an intense interaction with another group member, Nguyen heard that others believed he was being evasive and dishonest because he had not shared the emotions he was obviously experiencing. Nguyen received feedback that challenged his interpersonal distortion that sharing emotions was unacceptable. Nguyen also learned that others experienced his acting as if he had no emotions negatively. Thus, Nguyen received information that challenged his assumptions about acceptable and unacceptable interpersonal behaviors. This input offered Nguyen consensual validation that changed his interpersonal distortion that sharing emotions was unacceptable.

Consensual validation is achieved through feedback exchange. Feedback allows members to learn how others perceive their interpersonal behaviors. Effectively shared and processed feedback offers members information that increases their understanding of how their behaviors contribute to the emotional and cognitive reactions of others and challenges interpersonal distortions (Okech, 2015). This information enables members to self-evaluate based on what happens in their relationships rather than on their distorted perceptions of others' evaluations. Chapter 9 will explore feedback exchange in general and the ORAL model of feedback exchange in particular (Lindbloom et al., 2005) as an example of an effective feedback process that enhances the consensual validation process.

Corrective Emotional Experience

A *corrective emotional experience* is an experience of intense emotion, reality testing, and cognitive processing that corrects interpersonal distortions. For corrective emotional experiences to occur in groups, two important conditions—safety and honest feedback exchange—are necessary (I. D. Yalom & Leszcz, 2020). In this context, safety emanates from a caring, supportive, and nonjudgmental environment that allows the member to take risks with new behavior.

Corrective emotional experiencing includes consensual validation and emphasizes emotion or intense self-disclosure. Corrective emotional experiencing also involves the expression of intense emotion (positive or negative) or the sharing of a revealing and involving self-disclosure, sustained interaction that allows full expression of the emotion or disclosure. The process of consensual validation corrects interpersonal distortions, and this improves members' ability to interact intimately with other members (I. D. Yalom & Leszcz, 2020). Often, it involves a member anticipating a disastrous reaction from others to their disclosure or display of emotion and experiencing a response that is contrary to this anticipation.

For example, Kim believed that expressing her anger when she felt ignored would result in rejection and never gaining the acceptance of others. During the latter part of a session, she felt that others had been ignoring and trivializing her input. Before she could stop herself, she exploded with intense anger. The other members attended to her and did not attempt to shut down her anger. Kim, with the encouragement of the leader and other members, was able to share not only her anger but also her fear of disapproval and rejection. She found that others appreciated her expressions rather than rejecting or criticizing her for them. Others let her know that it was important for them to know whenever she felt ignored or angry. In this experience, Kim confronted her fears of abandonment and rejection and learned to share her anger more openly.

Social Microcosm

Over time, members' relationships in counseling and therapy groups increasingly resemble their relationships with people outside their groups (I. D. Yalom & Leszcz, 2020). This is why groups are often seen as *social microcosms*. This refers to the social and cultural settings in which members interact, as well as the personal relationships and dynamics within those settings. I. D. Yalom and Leszcz (2020) pointed out that the interpersonal concerns that lead members to join a group eventually are demonstrated in the context of the group's interaction. In other words, members' relationship difficulties and interpersonal distortions become evident as members interact. Members' group experiences also take on the characteristics of their families of origin, as members use the same interpersonal behaviors they developed in their families.

The interpersonal issues that bring members to groups become apparent in the members' here-and-now interactions. These interactions are thus relevant to understanding and improving members' relationships. By observing members' interactions, leaders obtain information about members' interpersonal dynamics and their functioning in their interpersonal contexts outside the group (I. D. Yalom & Leszcz, 2020). This information shapes interventions that address relationship difficulties in the group and improve relationships outside the group.

Cohesiveness

Cohesion in group therapy is analogous to the therapeutic relationship in individual counseling and therapy (I. D. Yalom & Leszcz, 2020). I. D. Yalom and Leszcz (2020) defined *cohesiveness* as the commitment and investment that members have in each other and in their individual and collective outcome. A cohesive group has more consistent attendance, higher levels of member participation, more intense self-disclosure, more authentic engagement, more satisfying relationships between members, increased tolerance for hostility, and more effective outcomes overall than less cohesive groups (Kline, 2003). Members of cohesive groups are accepting and supportive of each other and open to being influenced by other members (I. D. Yalom & Leszcz, 2020).

Cohesiveness must exist for the other therapeutic factors to operate (I. D. Yalom & Leszcz, 2020). When a group is cohesive, members accept each other and value each other's opinions and, thus, disclose more and take more risks. Consequently, cohesiveness leads to positive outcomes. The development of a cohesive group environment depends on how effectively leaders have developed a safe therapeutic group culture. For a safe therapeutic group culture to evolve, the social and cultural context of the group and its impact on the dynamics of group members' relationships and interpersonal interactions must take center stage in group members' discussions early in the life span of the group. Additionally, a well-defined and managed feedback exchange process plays a significant role in consensual validation, a key component of group cohesion.

The Here and Now

An extremely important task for leaders is developing a group culture that emphasizes the here and now. When a group is engaged in the here and now, interaction focuses on what is occurring in the present between members in the group, not on past or outside events. This emphasis is critical for two reasons. First, interactions occurring in the group at any particular moment contain the interpersonal distortions that have brought members to the group. Second, interactions in the here and now are more likely to be immediate and laden with affect. Such interactions have a greater impact and are more challenging to interpersonal distortions (I. D. Yalom & Leszcz, 2020). I. D. Yalom and Leszcz (2020) put the importance of the here-and-now experience into perspective, stating that "to the degree that the therapy group focuses on the here and now, it increases in power and effectiveness" (p. 27).

Two conditions must be present if the here and now is to have a therapeutic impact. First, members must be in spontaneous, open, and authentic contact with each other. Second, members must reflect back on their experiencing of one another to make their experiencing therapeutically useful. This is a self-reflective loop that involves cognitive processing of experience and offers members opportunities to develop insight. I. D. Yalom and Leszcz (2020) strongly cautioned leaders against viewing emotional experiencing in the here and now alone as adequate for therapeutic progress: "There [is] clear evidence that a cognitive component [is] essential; some type of cognitive map [is] needed . . . that [frames] the experience and [makes] sense of the emotions evok[ed] in the group" (p. 29).

It is, however, critical for leaders to consider what must happen in a group to create a safe place for members to engage authentically and to take risks in addressing interpersonal concerns. Social-cultural context plays an important role in this consideration. The perspectives held by racial minority groups and other underrepresented groups can easily be perceived as interpersonal distortions by leaders who do not recognize the significant social and psychological impacts of oppression, marginalization, and injustice. A culturally responsive group leader should be able to distinguish between interpersonal distortions and valid intercultural concerns that are grounded in prolonged exposure to systemic oppression and marginalization.

Therapeutic Process

The interpersonal approach uses necessary therapeutic conditions and a therapeutic process that stresses interpersonal learning. The goal is to optimize members' interpersonal functioning. To meet this goal, members' concerns are conceptualized as interpersonal difficulties stemming from interpersonal distortions. Next, by focusing on here-and-now interactions, leaders help members identify and correct the interpersonal distortions that hinder their interpersonal functioning while validating interpersonal concerns that are grounded on legitimate direct experiences of oppression, marginalization, and injustice.

Necessary Conditions

I. D. Yalom and Leszcz (2020) stressed the primacy of cohesiveness and interpersonal learning for the success of group members. These two therapeutic factors allow other therapeutic factors to emerge and operate. Whether cohesiveness and interpersonal learning are present depends on how effectively leaders have developed a facilitative group culture. For a group culture to develop and use necessary therapeutic factors, two conditions must exist: "(1) the members must experience the group as sufficiently safe and supportive so that . . . tensions may be openly expressed[, and] (2) there must be sufficient engagement and honest feedback to permit effective reality testing" (I. D. Yalom & Leszcz, 2020, p. 25).

Process of Therapy

The therapeutic process is a process of interpersonal learning that includes consensual validation, corrective emotional experience, the group as a social microcosm, the activation of the here and now, and processing that uses the self-reflective loop. Members who are involved in this process learn to function more effectively in their relationships in group. This learning then transfers to relationships outside the group.

In brief, this process flows in the following way:

1. Members interact openly and honestly in the here and now.
2. Members' interpersonal distortions emerge in their here-and-now interactions.
3. Members become aware of these distortions because of interpersonal feedback and self-observation.
4. Interpersonal distortions are corrected through consensual validation and corrective emotional experiencing.

5. Members gain insight into how others perceive them, their motivations, and the causes or origins of their interpersonal distortions and behaviors.
6. Members take responsibility for using and changing ineffective interpersonal behaviors.
7. Members learn about and use behaviors that are consistent with more effective interpersonal functioning.
8. The behaviors that are consistent with more effective interpersonal functioning are then used in interpersonal situations outside the group.

I. D. Yalom (1995) stressed that the success of group members depends on both emotional experiencing and developing a cognitive structure to define, gain insight, and change interpersonal distortions. Socially and culturally embedded concerns must be addressed in the process of group creation and construction in order for the conditions outlined above to emerge and to thrive within the group. Leaders must be sufficiently knowledgeable and responsive to the larger social-cultural contexts of the group to be appropriately responsive to cultural concerns within the group and to differentiate them from interpersonal distortions. Such a group can provide room for generalizations of interpersonal and social concerns (e.g., cisgender vs. sexual gender minority, majority White vs. racial minority groups, gender-based conflict) to be addressed in the group while being culturally responsive and creating room for deliberations on social-cultural concerns that interfere with the development of effective interpersonal relationships in communities.

Role of the Leader

The basic objective for leaders using the interpersonal approach is to mobilize the interpersonal learning process. Once in operation, interpersonal learning builds group cohesion and activates other therapeutic factors. To accomplish this, objective leaders perform roles that establish a safe and facilitative group culture and perform essential functions.

Creating a Facilitative Culture

"Leaders of interpersonal groups must initially work to create a safe, supportive, and therapeutic environment" (V. J. Yalom & Vinogradov, 1993, p. 190). To accomplish this objective, leaders must first carefully compose their groups with members who meet five criteria: being able to examine their own interpersonal behaviors, being motivated to change, being open to giving and receiving feedback, being willing to experiment with new interpersonal behaviors, and being committed to regular attendance (V. J. Yalom & Vinogradov, 1993).

Then, leaders must establish the group as a therapeutic social system that supports members' growth and change. This system should be developed with the guiding principle that the most effective and desirable outcome is members helping members—that is, "the group is the agent of change" (I. D. Yalom & Leszcz, 2020, p. 109). Accomplishing this objective involves developing a normative structure much like the facilitative group environment discussed in Chapter 2.

The norms recommended by I. D. Yalom and Leszcz (2020) include self-monitoring, self-disclosure, procedural, importance, agents of help, and support norms. *Self-monitoring norms* help group members become responsible for group functioning. These norms include members making comments about interaction, pointing out conflict, encouraging each other to stay in the here and now, and monitoring each other's feedback. *Self-disclosure norms* facilitate members' disclosing of here-and-now reactions and other information relevant to interaction. Examples are norms that do not force disclosures, that allow members to make choices about what to disclose, and that do not criticize self-disclosure. *Procedural norms* promote free-flowing and spontaneous interaction. I. D. Yalom and Leszcz (2020) warned that overly structured procedural norms would prevent spontaneous interaction and make groups boring. *Importance norms* concern the importance of the group to its members and are articulated in how members utilize the group for help. When such norms are in place, members participate with the belief that interaction is helpful. Norms that communicate that members are the *agents of help* are in place when members turn to each other for input and feedback as opposed to looking to leaders for help. Examples are norms in which members are allowed to ask each other for help, encourage each other to take risks, and give feedback when others need it. *Support norms* establish safety and security in the group. Norms that communicate support include accepting each other's feelings nonjudgmentally, never criticizing the person but sharing reactions to behaviors, staying with a member as long as work is productive, guarding against feedback overload, and encouraging members to take risks.

Activating the Here and Now

I. D. Yalom and Leszcz (2020) stressed that one of the leader's primary responsibilities is teaching members about *here-and-now* interactions. During the early stages of a group, leaders must continually instruct members to share their immediate emotions, discuss what is happening in the present, share their immediate reactions to each other's behaviors, and give immediate feedback. Donigian and Hulse-Killacky (1999) stated that in order to activate the here and now, leaders must help members focus on their interactions and reflect on group events. Attention to process is an important part of activating the here and now (Donigian & Hulse-Killacky, 1999).

Process and the Self-Reflective Loop

The concept of process is a hallmark of the interpersonal approach. *Process* describes "the nature of the relationship between interacting individuals" (I. D. Yalom & Leszcz, 2020, p. 130). Process characterizes how interaction occurs (e.g., volume or rate of speech, nonverbal behaviors) and the purpose of the interaction. I. D. Yalom and Leszcz (2020) considered process to be the how and why of interaction. Thus, leaders who pay attention to process observe interaction, wonder about the motivations or purposes behind interaction, and consider what the interaction says about the relationships of the interacting members. We maintain that leaders who pay attention to process are also knowledgeable about the cultural contexts in which their group exists, understand how the dynamics of social-cultural interactions and histories will emerge in the group, and are prepared to help members navigate such issues when they inevitably emerge within the group.

Process describes not only a discrete interaction but also a series or sequence of interactions. These interactions may involve several members or the entire group. Examples of process include interactions designed to reduce anxiety, negotiate norms, or make decisions. In terms of dyadic interaction, process could involve developing a relationship, criticizing, supporting, and challenging. The interpersonal approach stresses the importance of leaders making statements that identify process. I. D. Yalom and Leszcz (2005) argued that process "is indispensable and a common denominator to all effective interactive groups" (p. 137). Becoming aware of process allows members to learn from their interactions and to develop a different understanding of themselves (I. D. Yalom & Leszcz, 2020). Process observations that help members reflect on their interactions are instrumental to this learning.

Leaders using the interpersonal approach perform several tasks to utilize process for interpersonal learning. The first task is activating a here-and-now focus. This is achieved by directing members to interact about what is transpiring in the group at the moment and directing members away from discussing events that occur outside the group (I. D. Yalom & Leszcz, 2020). Once here-and-now interaction takes place, the next task is process illumination (I. D. Yalom & Leszcz, 2020). *Process illumination* occurs when leaders make statements that describe the how and why of interaction. Examples of such statements include "The group seems to want to avoid talking about Mary's issue," "John, it looks like you're trying to convince Shelley to like you," and "Some of you want to confront the issue of how much emotion to share in here, while others would rather not talk about it." Leaders must be cautious that in directing members away from events that are occurring outside the group, they do not minimize the impact of such events in the dynamics of the group, the assumptions group members make about each other, or the choices members make about what to disclose within the group.

I. D. Yalom and Leszcz (2020) characterized the sequence of here-and-now experiencing and then reflecting on that experience as the *self-reflective loop*. Interacting in the here and now openly and with emotional honesty—and then reflecting back on this experiencing—is an essential aspect of interpersonal learning. The self-reflective loop allows members to conceptualize their experience and gain insight. Insight leads to understanding about relationships and interpersonal behaviors.

Conceptualization of Members' Concerns

The effectiveness of the interpersonal approach relies on leaders being able to conceptualize members' concerns as interpersonal difficulties (I. D. Yalom, 1995). Thus, the issue that caused a member to join a group is not as significant as how that member relates to others. Members' concerns and treatment goals are expressed in terms of altering interpersonal distortions, improving members' ability to relate effectively, and achieving healthy relationships. For example, members who enter group because of "depression" could be seen as individuals who have restricted relationships. Possible goals of these members could include increased involvement with others, improved relationship skills, and spontaneity. The perspective that the life satisfaction and difficulties of individuals manifest themselves in interpersonal relationships is the foundation of the interpersonal approach.

To summarize, the major strength of the interpersonal approach is its conceptualization of interpersonal learning. Interpersonal learning and its related concepts are rooted in a model of interpersonal relationships. This model accounts for how members develop and can change ineffective interpersonal functioning. Additional strengths of the interpersonal approach include its conceptualization of therapeutic factors that lead to the therapeutic progress of group members.

The interpersonal approach acknowledges that groups operate as therapeutic social systems and describes procedures for developing an effective therapeutic culture. Although I. D. Yalom and Leszcz (2020) recognized that groups operate as therapeutic social systems, they did not emphasize conceptualizing the group as a social system or interventions that would address the group as a system. This limitation compromises the interpersonal approach's conceptualization of groups within their social-cultural systems and the pervasive impacts of the social-cultural dynamics of such systems on group dynamics, patterns of members' initial interactions, content of group discussions and vital contextual knowledge, and skills required of leaders in such contexts.

Essential Themes in Group Counseling and Therapy Theory

The theories presented in this part—focal conflict theory, general systems theory, and the interpersonal approach—are important to the practice of group counseling and therapy. They reduce the complexity of group interaction, present models of effective interaction, and suggest interventions necessary to help members meet counseling and therapy goals. Leaders who use these group-focused theories are likely to increase their confidence and ability to conceptualize and implement interventions. Clearly, these theories are more appropriate for group work than those designed to understand clients in individual counseling and therapy settings (Kline, 2003). They aid group leaders in conceptualizing individual functioning with groups, interpersonal functioning within groups, group-as-a-whole dynamics, and the importance and appropriateness of leader intervention at each of the three levels of group functioning (Rubel & Okech, 2006). These theories share common themes that illuminate essential objectives, processes, and operational assumptions of group counseling and therapy.

Origin and Significance of Interpersonal Difficulties

Focal conflict theory, general systems theory, and the interpersonal approach share common assumptions about the origin and significance of interpersonal difficulties. First, each recognizes family-of-origin experiences as the most common source of interpersonal difficulties. These perspectives agree that interpersonal behaviors and perceptions of self and others result from interaction with significant others in the family of origin. The intent of these interpersonal behaviors and perceptions is to obtain acceptance, develop and maintain positive self-perceptions, moderate anxiety, and maintain essential relationships. Early in life, these behaviors and perceptions become part of the individual's personality, form their approach to interacting with others, and persist into adult life. Often, the behaviors and perceptions developed in the family of origin interfere with the individual's ability to develop and maintain satisfactory relationships.

Interpersonal difficulties form as individuals attempt to get their own needs met as children. Whitaker (1985) described essentially the same process presented by I. D. Yalom (1995), although their respective ideas originated from different theoretical perspectives. H. E. Durkin (1981) discussed how family-of-origin systems influence the interpersonal boundaries of individuals—that is, interaction with others, most commonly in the family of origin, shapes how individuals interact and estimate their self-worth. When family-of-origin experiences do not meet their needs, individuals protect themselves from emotional damage by developing dysfunctional interpersonal behaviors to meet their needs.

I. D. Yalom (1995), Whitaker (1985), and H. E. Durkin (1981) also agreed that the patterns of relating formed at an early age persist into adult life. These patterns (interpersonal distortions, habitual restrictive personal solutions, and diffuse or impermeable boundaries) have a distinct influence on relationships and life satisfaction. Individuals, as Whitaker (1985) put it, use solutions that usually originate in the family of origin "and remain important in adult life" (p. 204). There was also agreement that people function as if they are in their family of origin throughout life, even though circumstances obviously differ and their interpersonal behaviors are no longer useful.

From the perspectives of focal conflict theory, general systems theory, and the interpersonal approach, the significance of difficulties in interpersonal relationships is that individuals can function only as effectively as they relate to others—that is, effective interpersonal functioning is the basis of mental health, and mental health concerns are viewed as interpersonal difficulties. Thus, therapeutic goals—whether they involve correcting interpersonal perceptual distortions, developing autonomous boundary functioning, or implementing enabling solutions—are all grounded in interpersonal relationships. One drawback of the three theories' view on challenges in interpersonal relationships is that they do not consider how social and cultural contexts, as well as histories of oppression and marginalization, can affect individuals' interactions in groups. These factors can have a significant impact on people's interpersonal behavior, particularly in groups where there is a mix of majority and marginalized members, such as those related to gender identity and sexual orientation (Okech et al., 2023; Rubel & Okech, 2010). It is critical for group leaders to view these theories and their value within the context in which they were created and the limited perspectives at the time in the field of counseling regarding addressing issues of diversity; multiculturalism; identity development; the impact of privilege, marginalization, and oppression on how individuals function in groups; and the importance of leaders using this knowledge to conceptualize groups, their functioning, and effective interventions.

Relatedness of Members' Concerns

Each of the perspectives presented in this chapter indicates the relationship of members' concerns in three different contexts. First, to some extent, all members share common concerns. Second, the interpersonal issues that members demonstrate in their interactions in group are identical to the relationship problems members have outside the group. A third context considers the impact of social-cultural factors in communities, histories of marginalization and oppression of certain members of communities, and the impact the dynamics of privilege, marginalization, and oppression have on interpersonal patterns and group dynamics (Okech & Rubel, 2007).

Members become involved in groups because of interpersonal difficulties. These difficulties are manifested as dysfunctional interpersonal behaviors intended to meet relationship needs, moderate interpersonal anxiety, and maintain self-esteem. Thus, to some extent, all group members share each other's concerns. Shared disturbing and reactive motives, the isomorphic qualities of members' concerns, and common anxiety-laden issues (I. D. Yalom & Leszcz, 2020) are seen as fundamental realities of the group social system.

Because all members' concerns are related, interventions or interactions that have an impact on one member are likely to affect other members. This premise should cause leaders to encourage all members to share their reactions to significant group events, such as noteworthy interventions, feedback exchanges, or corrective emotional experiences.

These perspectives also view the interpersonal issues, attitudes, perceptions, and behaviors that members demonstrate in group as consistent with those that members experience outside group. The concepts of isomorphism, habitual personal solutions, interpersonal perceptual distortions, and the group as a social microcosm share the contention that the interpersonal perceptions, apprehensions, and interactions of members both in and out of group are essentially identical. These premises mean that group interactions are significant and that helping members deal with the interpersonal issues they experience in group is highly relevant to meeting counseling or therapeutic goals.

Here-and-Now Interaction

Focusing on here-and-now interaction is indispensable. The solutions that members negotiate to deal with shared disturbing and reactive motives, the restrictive habitual personal solutions used by each member, the isomorphic qualities of members' concerns, as well as interpersonal perceptual distortions all unfold in the context of here-and-now interaction. This assertion emphatically challenges the usefulness of dealing with members' reports of interpersonal concerns outside group. Activating the here and now is even more effective when a group leader recognizes social-cultural factors that permeate the society in which the group is situated and how they might play out in the group. For example, rather than asking members about the impact of racism in their lives in the community, leaders can focus on exploring and discussing how racism could be playing out in the group and how group members' experiences of privilege and oppression within the group can impact members working on interracial relationships and intercultural conflict. Interventions focusing on here-and-now interaction have a considerably more powerful effect on members than interventions aimed at helping members deal with problems they are not currently experiencing. Most important, here-and-now interventions are more likely to stimulate emotional expression and influence members' interpersonal perceptions and behaviors. In addition, because members enact their interpersonal difficulties in the here and now, interventions that improve how members interact in group ultimately help them become more effective in their relationships outside the group.

Intervention Focus

In addition to focusing interventions on here-and-now interaction, leaders should focus interventions on different levels of the group as a system: the individual, interpersonal, and group-as-a-system levels. Perhaps the greatest consistency in these approaches is the primacy of interpersonal interventions. Whether the intervention process involves identifying and correcting interpersonal perceptual distortions, opening or closing interpersonal boundaries, or identifying restrictive solutions and developing enabling solutions, the objectives are basically the same. Although focal conflict theory, general systems theory, and the interpersonal approach agree on the usefulness of individual interventions, they differ in their intent. General systems theory and focal conflict theory view individual interventions as a vehicle to intervene in the shared concerns of members and the group as a system. On the other hand, the interpersonal approach is not as concerned with the group as a system and is directed more toward dealing with an individual member's perceptual distortion.

Focal conflict theory, general systems theory, and the interpersonal approach agree that interventions focused on the group as a system are useful. I. D. Yalom and Leszcz (2020) viewed group-as-a-system intervention (i.e., mass group commentary) as a means to optimize the effectiveness of the group environment but were the least enthusiastic about group-level interventions and warned against their overuse. The interpersonal approach does not articulate how interventions at the group-as-a-system level influence individual and interpersonal levels. General systems theory and focal conflict theory more clearly and completely describe the usefulness of group-as-a-system intervention and its connection with other levels of the group system. These two approaches see group-as-a-system intervention as a way to effect communication, influence individual members and subgroups, reveal and address shared concerns, define boundaries, and so on.

Members benefit significantly when leaders are able to facilitate interpersonal learning. This conviction is predicated on theoretical assumptions and research that indicate that members learning from each other is far more powerful and memorable than learning from interactions with leaders (I. D. Yalom & Leszcz, 2020). Leaders' interventions, therefore, should emphasize interpersonal and group-as-a-system intervention. This perspective also suggests that interventions focusing on individuals should include efforts to involve other members. Although individually directed interventions are potentially useful, an overemphasis on them ignores the potent forces of interpersonal learning.

The Therapeutic Group Environment

The three theoretical perspectives discussed in this chapter all describe a group environment that is most conducive to the therapeutic progress of members. Each approach requires leaders to establish a safe environment. Whitaker and Lieberman (1964) stated this clearly as a "shared sense of safety is an essential condition for therapeutic progress" (p. 217). In general, there is agreement that leaders and members should communicate acceptance and caring. Desirable outcomes are also connected with members sharing the perception that participation is in their best interest. The establishment of a shared perception of safety in the group is one of the leader's more important responsibilities (Kline, 2003).

Interpersonal Objectives

The three theories all view interpersonal relationships as the origin of interpersonal difficulties and as the means to resolve these difficulties. Leaders who successfully enable members to improve their relationships in group will succeed in helping members make important changes in their lives. Leaders' objectives are to establish a group environment that supports interpersonal learning and to involve members in interpersonal learning processes. It is this process that distinguishes group from other therapeutic treatment modalities.

Phases of Therapeutic Process

The perspectives presented in this chapter share some common ideas about the essential phases of group counseling and therapy. All seek to improve relationships in an interpersonal environment and include similar processes. In general, these perspectives agree that the group therapeutic process includes the following 11 phases:

1. Individuals join counseling or therapy groups because of difficulties in their interpersonal relationships. These difficulties involve ineffective interpersonal behaviors, interpersonal communication problems, limiting interpersonal perceptions, and diminished perceptions of self-worth.

2. When members begin group, they interact using customary interpersonal behaviors. Over time, members' here-and-now interactions progressively reveal the ineffective behaviors, communication problems, limiting perceptions, and diminished perceptions of self-worth that have brought them to group.
3. Here-and-now interaction brings progressively into members' awareness their ineffective behaviors, communication problems, limiting perceptions, and diminished perceptions of self-worth. Awareness is the product of interaction, observation of self and others, reflection, and feedback.
4. Members find that the dysfunctional behaviors and perceptions that have become increasingly ineffective in meeting their needs before coming to group are very ineffective in group, and they experience a range of emotional reactions.
5. Members and leaders find that groups are not immune from the influences of the social-cultural contexts in which they are situated. Dynamics of privilege, marginalization, and oppression will inevitably emerge in groups situated in contexts in which such dynamics exist. Leaders have a responsibility to highlight these social-cultural dynamics to group members and to confront and help members focus on addressing barriers to effective interpersonal relationships as they emerge within the group.
6. Members are led to decide to change by a combination of increasingly uncomfortable emotions associated with not meeting interpersonal needs, building frustration with ineffective interpersonal behaviors, corrective emotional experiencing, consensual validation, and increasing confidence in the group's caring and support. At this point, members clearly understand that what they are doing is not working and that they need to do something differently.
7. When members decide to change, they become open to input, ask for input, and more openly share their emotions and experiences in the group. The input of others educates members about alternative interpersonal behaviors that could meet their needs more effectively.
8. Members experiment with alternative interpersonal behaviors and receive feedback that helps them evaluate how well these behaviors meet their needs and how they affect other members.
9. As members continue to use and become adept with effective interpersonal behaviors, they experience satisfying relationships in the group.

10. As relationships with other members become more satisfying, members strengthen their perceptions of self-worth and alter their limiting interpersonal perceptions.
11. As members become more proficient with interpersonal behaviors and satisfied with their relationships in group, they experience more satisfying relationships outside group. At the same time, perceptions of self-worth grow, and distorted interpersonal perceptions are corrected.

Group Activity Exercise

Watch any group interaction video. Following the interpersonal approach, reflect on your observations of the group. Consider the following questions:

1. What therapeutic factors did you observe operating as the group interacted?
2. What interventions did the leaders use to activate the mechanisms of interpersonal learning (e.g., here-and-now interaction, feedback, process/self-reflective loop)?
3. What norms were operating to support interpersonal learning? Were there any norms that could have been developed to more effectively support interpersonal learning?
4. Describe any interpersonal interactions that may have involved perceptual or parataxic distortions.
5. What issues in members' interpersonal relationships were most dominant in the group's interactions?
6. What were some of the leaders' interventions? How effective were these interventions in initiating interpersonal learning?
7. What are some alternative interventions that you might use?

Conclusion

Leaders who use theories designed for group counseling and therapy have distinct advantages over leaders who use theories designed for individual counseling or therapy. These advantages include having a means to simplify observation of group interaction, to conceptualize an effective group environment, and to understand the processes and advantages of members learning from each other, and also having a structure that provides a framework for conceptualizing interventions and intervention objectives. Each of these advantages shows why individual theories are deficient in the group setting.

Leaders who use these theoretical approaches in their practice are working from a solid foundation. The themes described in this chapter represent a theoretical consensus about group dynamics and how individual members can change in the group setting. Leaders who base their practice on these themes can lead with the knowledge that they are using perspectives that were developed in group counseling and therapy research and that were drawn from the experiences of theorists who practice group counseling and therapy.

Chapter 7

Interactive Group Leadership

Outcomes

Level 1 Outcomes

After reading this chapter, entry-level students and practitioners should be able to:

1. Describe and identify the core therapeutic factors.
2. Define and identify the essential leadership functions.
3. Describe the various leadership styles and their advantages and disadvantages.
4. Discuss the essential attitudes that facilitate effective leadership.
5. Articulate the culturally responsive leadership objectives that contribute to inclusion, effective group environments, and interpersonal learning.

Level 2 Outcomes

After reading this chapter, advanced-level students and practitioners should also be able to:

1. Analyze the development of therapeutic factors from an inclusive perspective.
2. Analyze group situations and prioritize the application of leadership functions.
3. Develop a personal leadership style that is appropriate for inclusive and effective group work.
4. Analyze the interaction of groups with diverse membership and conceptualize appropriate leadership objectives.

Interactive group leadership focuses on group members benefiting from interaction with each other. The powerful influence that counseling and therapy groups have on group members is the consequence of immediate, congruent, and honest member-to-member interaction within the group. These often intense interactions most commonly occur in group environments where members experience sufficient trust, safety, and support to risk disclosing their emotions, perceptions, and reactions. Many factors affect the development of group environments that promote members' growth and learning. These factors include group composition, the group setting, leaders' personal qualities, and the interactive norms established in the group. For growth and learning, group members must have sufficient interactive skills to communicate clearly, offer effective feedback, share emotions and perceptions, and present interpersonal challenges. All of these factors depend on the efforts of group leaders. This chapter introduces the primary concepts of trust and group boundaries and developing effective interactive skills before describing factors that affect the leadership role. The relationship of therapeutic factors, leadership functions, and leadership style to interactive group leadership is then examined in depth. Finally, the interactive group leader role is defined and summarized.

Trust and Group Boundaries

Interactive group leadership focuses on building trust through influencing group boundaries. Trust among group members is central to a productive group environment. A critical first step in building trust within the group is developing interpersonal and external group boundaries that promote members' learning. *Interpersonal boundaries* describe how openly members share emotions and perceptions with each other, whereas *external boundaries* describe the extent to which members' interactions focus on relationships within the group as opposed to events occurring outside the immediate group environment.

In successful counseling and therapy groups, leaders encourage members to develop interpersonal boundaries that allow them to share how they experience one another and to learn from feedback given by other members. *Functional interpersonal boundaries* are open enough to allow members to disclose emotions and perceptions and to provide honest interpersonal feedback. Leaders must ensure that these boundaries are sufficiently open to allow members to accurately hear, thoughtfully consider, and productively respond to the disclosures and feedback of others. The establishment of these boundaries depends on the amount of trust members have in one another.

Trust within the group is established when sufficient flow of immediate and authentic communication occurs between members. From the interactive perspective, *trust* is defined by how confidently members believe they can predict that others will respond usefully to their self-disclosures (Kline, 1986). Useful responses include both affirming, supportive, and sympathetic responses and also challenging, confronting, clarifying, or encouraging responses. Members base their predictions of usefulness on observations of others' responses to prior self-disclosures during group interaction. Members' personal experiences of self-disclosure are a significant basis for anticipating responses to self-disclosures in group. Members who have a history of receiving negative responses to their self-disclosures, often within their family of origin and at an early age, will be hesitant to disclose. They may need to develop a positive self-disclosure history in group before risking the disclosures necessary for growth and learning in group interaction. This occurs when these members can observe other members benefiting from self-disclosures and feedback exchanges. Their participation often starts when they are encouraged to take "safe" self-disclosure risks. This task may be more difficult for group members who have experienced marginalization or discrimination in and outside the group.

The level of trust that develops in a group influences the depth and content of members' self-disclosures. Trust is high in groups where members have routinely experienced helpful and positive responses to self-disclosure during group interaction. In such groups, members feel safer and tend to share more intimate personal information. As this sharing becomes common, members experience an increasing level of trust in each other, and the group develops communication norms that encourage immediate and intimate disclosures. These norms depend largely on the development of permeable interpersonal communication boundaries. Additionally, trust within a group may be negatively affected by societal norms that have made intimate disclosures about race, culture, and identity risky and emotionally charged.

Early and ongoing resistance to here-and-now communication is a sign of mistrust. Such resistance may appear as ongoing conversations about people and events outside the group and the group's objectives. These conversations indicate overly permeable external group boundaries. As leaders attempt to open boundaries within the group, they must also ensure that external boundaries are sufficiently closed. External boundaries are necessary to develop cohesion and a productive group culture. When external boundaries are sufficiently closed, interaction about events not useful to the group or group members is infrequent. The longer groups discuss external content, the less members can benefit from crucial here-and-now contact. The longer members avoid here-and-now contact, the more difficult it becomes to establish sufficiently closed external boundaries and permeable interpersonal boundaries.

Developing Effective Interactive Skills

Helping group members establish and maintain effective interactive skills is an essential ongoing activity for group leaders. Leaders should instruct and remind members to use interactive skills during all phases of the group's life. The objective of group is that members learn to use effective interactive skills both in and out of group. Ideally, using these skills will become a group norm, and members will remind each other to use them.

It is not reasonable to expect new members to possess effective interactive skills at the beginning of group. Thus, one of the leader's early tasks is to teach members to communicate in the here and now and to use responsible language. Leaders also have the crucial task of teaching members skills for effectively giving and receiving feedback.

The level of trust and the communication boundaries that develop in group depend heavily on how effectively members use necessary interactive skills. When members continue to use effective interactive skills, leaders will observe that trust increases. This is because productive outcomes for member disclosures and feedback exchanges are more frequent and predictable when members use effective interactive skills. Based on this increased trust, interpersonal boundaries become more permeable, and disclosure norms evolve in a way that supports increasing levels of intimacy.

Factors Influencing the Leadership Role

Numerous factors influence how leaders perform the leadership role, including members' expectations for leaders, leaders' beliefs about how the leadership role should be performed, leaders' socialization and interpersonal needs, and the way leaders interact with members. Leaders should be aware that group members' expectations define what they believe their leader should do, which can strongly influence what the leader does. Thus, the leadership role is influenced by the familial, sociocultural, and professional socialization of leaders and members, as well as by the power dynamics within the group.

Typically, during the initial stages of most groups, members will expect leaders to lower their apprehension about group membership. These expectations usually include "Tell us exactly what we should do" or "Make our group less frightening." Whether or not these expectations are made clear, leaders will feel pressure to comply. When leaders submit to this pressure, they will find themselves choosing not to be critical and refraining from using potentially challenging interventions. As groups progress, leaders should be aware that their group members' expectations will continue to influence what they do. Most leaders will become aware of expectations such as "The members want me to ignore emotionally charged issues." If leaders comply with these expectations, their effectiveness will be compromised.

Leadership actions are also influenced by leaders' beliefs about what they should do to be effective in their role. Most leaders support common beliefs about effective leadership, such as "I should be honest, direct, and clear in my communications with the group." When leaders act according to beliefs consistent with effective leadership, they are more likely to be effective leaders. However, problems occur when leaders' beliefs are inconsistent with effective leadership. When leaders act on beliefs such as "I must be involved in every interaction to ensure that learning takes place," they are choosing to be ineffective leaders. Acting on beliefs that are unconscious is especially problematic if these beliefs are inconsistent with effective leadership. Leaders who are not aware that they are acting on detrimental beliefs will not understand that they are sabotaging the effectiveness of their groups.

Leaders' interpersonal needs may also have a negative impact on their effectiveness as leaders. Leaders whose interpersonal needs include such conscious or unconscious ideas as "Everyone must like me" or "I must protect group members from intense feelings" are likely to use members to meet these needs. This results in groups that do not benefit and may harm members. All group leaders should be highly committed to understanding their own unmet interpersonal needs. Leaders must maintain awareness of these unmet needs so that they can guard against interacting with members in a detrimental manner. The most appropriate settings for leaders to work on getting their own interpersonal needs met are in supervision, in their own therapy, and in their own personal relationships.

The way leaders interact with members as they attempt to meet objectives during the early phases of group is particularly important. Early on, members focus on their initial and intense anxieties as they join the group. Group members often want leaders to fill such roles as caretaker, rescuer, teacher, or parent. Often leaders will experience a sense of conflict between the professional role of assisting members to become collaborative mutual helpers and the urge to meet members' expectations that leaders should take care of them. Members often blame leaders for the presence of anxiety and expect leaders to eliminate the anxiety associated with self-disclosure and feedback.

Initially, leaders should aim to modify members' erroneous expectations of the group leaders and establish expectations that are consistent with interactive group work. The process of clarifying member expectations is important for interactive group work, because it defines how members will establish communication norms and develop interpersonal boundaries. This process establishes members' responsibilities and normalizes challenging leader objectives and interventions meant to promote inclusive and effective group interaction.

How leaders interact with members has important implications for members' expectations of leaders. For example, leaders who frequently interact with individual group members to solve interpersonal issues establish that leaders, rather than members, are responsible for addressing these issues. Members will interpret this pattern as meaning that only leaders can address members' personal concerns or interactive conflicts. Another example is leaders who often "take care" of group anxiety by encouraging interaction that reduces group tension. These leaders prolong the group's anxiety by confirming members' fears about being unable to deal with difficult situations and solidify members' erroneous beliefs that leaders are in charge.

Conversely, leaders who direct group members to interact with other members to practice new ways to resolve interpersonal difficulties help members believe they can solve their own problems. Groups with this belief are energetic, have permeable interpersonal communication boundaries, frequently exchange feedback, and gain interpersonal learning. When members perceive that they can tolerate their own emotions and respond productively to others' emotions, they become increasingly autonomous and effective in interpersonal relationships, consistent with the interactive approach.

Establishing Therapeutic Factors

Creating group environments that demonstrate essential therapeutic factors is a key aim of the leadership role. Therapeutic factors are the critical elements of the group change process (I. D. Yalom & Leszcz, 2020). Corsini and Rosenberg (1955) conceptualized these factors when they reviewed research describing therapeutic processes in group therapy. They collected, categorized, and labeled statements about the therapeutic elements of therapy groups, which resulted in nine therapeutic factors: acceptance, altruism, universalization, intellectualization, reality testing, transference, interaction, spectator therapy, and ventilation. Later, I. D. Yalom (1970) presented 11 factors that were the products of his research, clinical experience, and theoretical approach. These factors were instillation of hope, universality, imparting of information, altruism, the corrective recapitulation of the primary family group, development of socializing techniques, imitative behavior, interpersonal learning, group cohesiveness, catharsis, and existential factors. Both Corsini and Rosenberg's and I. D. Yalom's (1970) lists reflected the theoretical perspectives of their authors (i.e., transference and existential factors, respectively).

Bloch and Crouch (1985) used a research process similar to Corsini and Rosenberg's (1955) process. They reviewed the group therapy literature, noted the themes and consistencies appearing in the research, and developed a classification of therapeutic factors. Bloch and Crouch's goal, however, was to uncover therapeutic factors independent of theory. Their research resulted in a more specific definition of the term *therapeutic factors*, a list of six discrete factors, and a cluster of additional factors. This chapter uses the factors presented by Bloch and Crouch because they depict themes across the group literature and because they are the least theoretically biased. However, leaders should note that the concept of therapeutic factors is culturally influenced, that all groups will tend to display predominant sociocultural dynamics, and that individuals will respond to group conditions based, in part, on their social positionality and culture. Leaders should understand that, depending on the context, one member's therapeutic factor may be another member's marginalization. For example, instances of altruism, one of I. D. Yalom and Leszcz's (2020) therapeutic factors, may be experienced by a group member who has been marginalized within society as patronizing without sufficient prior trust and communication.

Bloch and Crouch (1985) indicated that therapeutic factors are elements of group therapy that support group members' growth and change and are dependent on the actions of the group therapist and group members. They also indicated that therapeutic factors are different from the conditions of the group and techniques used by the group leader, which they viewed as prerequisites for change. Bloch and Crouch presented the following factors and definitions:

- *Insight* (self-understanding): The essence of insight is that the group members each learn something important about themselves. This may include learning how they affect others in group and learning about the nature and origin of interpersonal difficulties.
- *Learning from interpersonal action*: The core of interpersonal learning is a group member's attempt to respond to and connect with others in the group adaptively based on their needs and feedback from others. Members learn from interpersonal action when they try out new and potentially better ways of interacting with other group members, either as a response to other group members or on their own initiative.
- *Acceptance and cohesiveness*: These two therapeutic factors are conceptually similar and closely related. Acceptance is an individual's perception of belonging and being valued within the group, whereas cohesiveness indicates a perception of the group's attractiveness shared by group members. Bloch and Crouch regarded cohesiveness as a precondition for other therapeutic factors. More specifically, they indicated that acceptance is unlikely without group cohesiveness.

Bloch and Crouch's (1985) research also identified the factors of self-disclosure, catharsis, and guidance. They defined *self-disclosure* as the "act of revealing personal information to the group" (p. 128), *catharsis* as "an emotional release . . . which brings some measure of relief" (p. 162), and *guidance* as "the imparting of information and the giving of direct advice" (p. 171). Additionally, Bloch and Crouch clustered the factors of universality (seeing similarities in self and others), altruism (helping others), vicarious learning (learning through observation), and instillation of hope (perceiving that change is possible) because their study revealed insufficient depth in the research to support these factors as distinct. Despite the lack of research, the identification of these factors made an important contribution to helping people change in groups.

Ultimately, any conceptualization of these therapeutic factors is an oversimplification of the complicated and intertwined forces of change that occur in groups (I. D. Yalom & Leszcz, 2020). Therapeutic factors are metaphors for beneficial elements of the group environment and are not independently existing entities. Rather, they are complexly related and mutually influential (I. D. Yalom & Leszcz, 2020).

Interactive Therapeutic Factors

Therapeutic factors are systemically related. It is impossible to examine one factor without considering its reciprocal relationships with other factors. For example, learning from interpersonal action cannot occur unless members self-disclose. Self-disclosure generally will not occur in sufficient depth if members are not experiencing the group as cohesive and not feeling accepted. Accordingly, if self-disclosure, acceptance, cohesiveness, and learning from interpersonal action are not present, insight is unlikely. The reciprocal relationship of these factors extends to universality, vicarious learning, instillation of hope, and altruism. All the therapeutic factors depend on one another.

The interactive perspective regards the therapeutic factors as conceptually labeled "chunks" of a continuous interactive process. This perspective allows leaders to focus on establishing several of these factors, knowing that the other factors will be set into motion as a result. For example, if learning from interpersonal action occurs, members will become more hopeful about their own learning (instillation of hope) and will be able to identify similarities between themselves and other members involved in the group's learning processes (universality). In addition, learning from interpersonal action probably cannot occur without members' self-disclosure (e.g., offering feedback, sharing personal reactions, disclosing emotions), and that disclosure depends on that member experiencing some level of acceptance in the group.

Consequently, the process of engaging members with each other is perhaps the most crucial objective of the interactive leadership role because then therapeutic factors will emerge. Because the interactive perspective focuses on managing interpersonal boundaries and facilitating members learning from each other, the most essential interactive therapeutic factors are learning through interpersonal action, acceptance, self-disclosure, and insight. Leaders whose interventions work toward developing these factors set the interactive process into motion. The development and implementation of therapeutic factors result from leaders performing essential leadership functions.

Leadership Functions

Leadership functions are the responsibilities and tasks necessary to accomplish specific leadership objectives. In general, leadership functions should establish an environment in which learning can occur. This environment is one in which members can learn from each other; develop flexible interpersonal roles and behaviors; learn about interpersonal relationships; experiment with interpersonal behaviors; and develop awareness, self-understanding, and insight. Additionally, this environment should be inclusive and provide all group members equal access to learning and change processes.

Lieberman et al. (1973) defined four primary leadership functions that encompass many of the responsibilities and tasks in which leaders engage. These functions are emotional stimulation, caring, meaning-attribution, and executive function. The leadership function of *emotional stimulation* was described by Lieberman et al. as leader interactions that elicit emotional reactions, including anxiety. These actions may include empathizing, challenging, connecting members, confronting, processing personal values, examining attitudes and beliefs, and self-disclosing. *Caring* as a leadership function was depicted as a function and a style and described as leaders' expressions of protection, kindness, love, affection, support, praise, and encouragement. The leadership function of *meaning-attribution* was defined as a process of conceptualizing group interaction and how group members can change. When leaders interpret group events, offer information that helps members understand interactions, or encourage members to observe and make sense of interaction, they are enacting the meaning-attribution function. *Executive function* is a leadership function focused on administrative tasks that are the group leader's responsibility. Lieberman et al. indicated that this function includes setting limits, suggesting rules, offering norms, setting goals or group directions, managing time, pacing, stopping the group, blocking harmful interaction, and facilitating decisions.

From the interactive perspective, theory influences how group interaction is conceptualized. Then conceptualization forms leadership objectives, and these objectives determine leadership functions. Leadership functions define how leaders use skills, interventions, and strategies to achieve the objective of each function. Thus, interactive group leadership functions are those functions that are essential or helpful to creating a group environment where group members learn primarily from each other. The interactive leadership functions are norm setting, boundary management, structuring, instruction, regard, languaging, and administration.

Norm Setting

Norm setting is an essential early and ongoing responsibility of leaders. The norm-setting leadership function requires leaders to structure the interactive group environment by helping members establish norms for interaction and participation. Examples of norms that leaders can introduce and support early in the group include using personally responsible language, being on time for group, not talking while others are interacting, and giving direct feedback. Later, leaders can implement norms such as completing work before moving on (e.g., complete feedback exchanges), honoring members' requests for ending feedback, or checking feedback for consensus.

Leaders who are enacting the norm-setting function should be aware that members may agree on how they should interact but not act accordingly. For example, members may agree that they should not interrupt other members but regularly interrupt. Thus, the norm is "interrupt work," not "finish work." Leaders who are norm setting must monitor group interaction to discern whether suggested and agreed-upon norms have come to fruition or norms that hinder group effectiveness are present. Strategies and interventions that leaders can use to identify and stop norms that block effective interaction are discussed in Chapter 11.

The norm-setting function involves a continuum of actions that can range in style from authoritarian to democratic—for example, the continuum might range from presenting useful norms to the group and energetically enforcing them to involving the group in discussing the norms they want and then supporting them. When enforcing a norm, leader actions also may range in style from identifying norm-breaking behaviors and then directing members to conform to asking the group to identify existing norms and then discussing how they contribute to group interaction.

Leaders should begin groups having carefully considered a few norms that are crucial for effective group functioning and should commit to establishing these norms. Leaders who attempt to initially establish too many norms will find enforcing them difficult and will find themselves distracted from other necessary functions, diminishing their effectiveness. The optimal number of norms depends on leaders' careful consideration of group purpose, composition, structure, and the necessity of an interactive environment. Leaders should commit to implementing the norms they present to the group, because presenting norms and not enforcing them erodes the leader's credibility. A benefit of enforcing only a few important norms is that leaders then can intentionally support inclusive norms and discourage marginalizing norms.

Leaders should think of norm setting as an additive process in which several important norms are developed early. When members use these norms without prompting, leaders can work to develop additional norms as needs become apparent. As groups interact, they will develop additional effective norms (i.e., those that promote effective interaction) after some early norm-setting work by leaders. They will also develop counterproductive norms (i.e., those that block effective interaction) that will require ongoing intervention. Leaders' use of the norm-setting leadership function affects members' expectations of the leader, members' expectations about their interactions with each other, the group environment, the issues that surface in group, and the group's eventual effectiveness.

Boundary Management

Through the boundary management function, leaders note and shape group boundaries to promote effective group interaction and group member change. This requires leaders to attend to communication content and process, directly facilitating open communication between members. Such action helps members develop interpersonal boundaries that permit the sharing of emotions, perceptions, attitudes, beliefs, and assumptions about others' motivations. It also helps members make informed relationship choices. Boundary management often involves directing members to disclose their emotions to each other and to share their perceptions of other members, such as in the following example with Gordon, the group member introduced in Chapter 4:

Leader: "River, tell Emma the emotions you are feeling toward her now."
Leader: "Chandra, tell Gordon what you think their silence is about."

Boundary management also involves leaders establishing external group boundaries. Effective external boundaries promote effective interpersonal relationships within the group and define how much communication about events external to the group occurs within the group. Effective external boundaries aid in developing group cultures with different communication boundaries from social systems outside the group. The boundaries leaders establish in a group create that group's unique culture. Effective group cultures feature here-and-now interaction that includes emotional content. Inclusive group culture features communication that allows disparate experiences to be voiced and heard, power dynamics to be openly discussed, and harmful interaction (e.g., microaggressions) to be identified and processed. This communication is also open, honest, immediate, direct, and related to the goals of the group.

To establish effective external group boundaries, leaders help members develop awareness of how interaction within the group differs from experiences outside the group and how this difference makes the group experience valuable. Leaders help meet this objective by describing helpful group processes, such as sharing emotions, and by directing members to describe how group interaction differs from interactions outside the group. Leaders who hear members share the following have evidence of effective external group boundaries:

Member: "I couldn't wait to get here this week. I just had to find some people who would tell me, honestly, how they feel about me. And would listen to what I had to say."
Member: "I can say stuff in here that I can't say anywhere else."

Member: "It's refreshing to talk about racism and have people ask if it's happening here in the group."
Member: "When we get into a conflict in here and actually resolve it, that blows me away!"

Examples of other approaches that can contribute to effective boundaries include directing members who have shared emotions with each other to describe to the group what that experience was like or asking members who have observed the honest sharing of emotions to describe what they observed and the feelings they experienced. Leaders will find it helpful to bring the effects and benefits of productive emotional exchanges to the attention of the group. By highlighting how group interaction works, leaders build effective group boundaries.

Sometimes leaders will find that boundary development is elusive. As a group develops, leaders will often observe members experimenting with intimacy by being emotionally open and then retreating by closing their boundaries. Leaders should understand that members are especially vulnerable after intense, emotionally charged experiences and will often close their boundaries and reflect on their work before considering change. Members who remain persistently vulnerable are less able to give meaning to their interactions and make useful choices about changing. This is because they are not as able to think clearly. In such cases, leaders can ask the member to temporarily withdraw from group interactions to reflect on these experiences. Alternatively, leaders can direct other group members to not interact with a member to allow that member an opportunity for reflection.

Structuring

Leaders performing the structuring function instruct, direct, and shape how group interactions occur to facilitate interpersonal learning. Examples of interaction supporting include directing feedback exchanges, coaching interaction to teach communication skills, and establishing interactive procedures for conflict management. This function also includes leaders giving instructions for structured procedures, such as icebreakers and opening or closing rounds.

Structuring is a directive function that can be used when it is useful for members to interact in a structured or specific manner. Circumstances that require clear communication between members are one such instance. For example, leaders may decide to use the structuring function when members are in an emotional interaction where clear communication is difficult. Other examples of times when structuring is useful are initial feedback exchanges when members are less skilled and feedback norms are being formed, when members' interactions evidence persistent communication problems, or when a member is being harmed by unclear communication.

The structuring function is also useful when managing time is critical. For example, structuring in the form of closing rounds or each member briefly sharing in order is a way to ensure all members have a chance to share at the end of group. Leaders can instruct members to share a type of information (e.g., emotions, lessons learned, thoughts) and amount of information (e.g., no more than a sentence) about what they experienced during a group session. Part of structuring in this case is limiting interaction so all members have a chance to contribute during a limited time.

Instruction

Instruction is an active and directive leadership function with the objective of teaching members skills or concepts that contribute to their ability to learn. An example is when leaders teach members effective interactive skills, such as giving and receiving feedback, making direct requests, and paraphrasing to ensure effective communication. Instruction also includes teaching group members how to transfer new behaviors learned in group to outside relationships and environments. Teaching members about transferring their learning to real-life situations is important because members may not fully understand the effects that new interpersonal behaviors can have on their relationships.

The instruction leadership function may be useful at any point during the group. However, leaders should not overuse this function in groups whose aim is for group members to learn from each other. The most essential objective of the instruction function is to help members develop interactive skills for the purpose of interacting with each other. These skills are necessary for members to learn how to become effectively engaged with each other as active, not passive, learners. Leaders who overuse instruction by engaging in philosophizing or academic discussions will observe progressively disengaged groups. This is the product of norms that develop largely because of leaders' conceptual rather than emotionally stimulating conversations.

Leaders observing a disengaged group should reflect on the extent to which their interventions may have had a cognitive focus. Leaders who overuse the instruction function become characteristically cognitive in their interactions with group members and contribute to members closing their boundaries.

Regard

The interactive leadership function of regard involves leaders demonstrating attitudes and actions consistent with a caring relationship in their interactions with members. The following attitudes and actions demonstrate regard as a leadership function:

- *Genuineness*: Leaders demonstrate genuineness when they behave as if authenticity and congruence are important in relationships. For example, a leader demonstrates genuineness when they appear sad as they give feedback that a member's self-destructive behavior saddens them.
- *Acceptance*: Leaders demonstrate acceptance when they behave as if they believe in the inherent worth of others and the value of unconditionally accepting them. For example, a leader demonstrates acceptance when they express interest in and engage the group process to help a member who is being scapegoated by others for norm challenging and distancing behaviors.
- *Empathy*: Leaders demonstrate empathy when they value and express a cognitive and emotional understanding of the internal experience of others. An example is a leader intervening at the individual level to connect with an angry group member to say, "Auna, I can see that you are really angry, but you're also hurt by the feedback David gave you and uncertain what to do."

Empathy, genuineness, and acceptance were considered by Rogers (1961) to be necessary and sufficient conditions for change. From an interactive perspective, however, they are necessary but not sufficient. Furthermore, although unconditional positive regard (Rogers, 1961) is an important leadership function from the interactive perspective, leaders must also perform functions necessary for members to interact effectively and learn from one another. Leaders must effectively demonstrate regard or risk their groups not developing the trusting climate conducive to learning. Leaders who do not consistently communicate empathy, genuineness, and acceptance will observe that members fear criticism, develop facades, and do not express emotions.

Unconditional positive regard is consistent with Lieberman et al.'s (1973) caring function. They stated that it is important that "leaders express considerable warmth, acceptance, genuineness, and a real concern for other human beings in the group" (p. 238). The goal of group leaders in performing this leadership function is to demonstrate a real human concern for the welfare and the learning of group members. However, this does not mean that leaders should avoid confronting ineffective interpersonal behaviors. Rather, group leaders should communicate honestly and show sincere concern while challenging members to confront their fears, develop awareness, and initiate change. These behaviors, like most other leader behaviors, exist on a continuum with many ways to express each element.

Languaging

The languaging interactive leadership function is similar to the instructional function in that it involves presenting concepts to the group. The difference is that the languaging function describes specific group interaction events, focuses members on their perceptions and experiences of those events, and is not a skill-building process. The languaging function expands Lieberman et al.'s (1973) function of meaning-attribution from a process of conceptualizing group events to helping group members understand and change to a process of co-constructing language about effective learning processes with group members. The basis for the languaging function is the social constructionist principle that languaging about solutions helps solve problems, whereas languaging about problems maintains them (R. J. Becvar et al., 1997).

The languaging function includes a continuum of activities that vary with respect to the extent of leaders' and members' involvement. At one end of the continuum is leader input that does not involve group discussion. Examples of this include process commentary, educational input regarding a group event, and educational input about interaction. At the other end of the languaging function continuum is member languaging. Examples of this include member-centered discussion about how the group solves problems, about the positive impact of a facilitative norm, or about effective member interactions that resulted in learning. To facilitate member-centered languaging, leaders involve members in discussions to describe and label interactive processes that have facilitated connection and the growth of the group and its members. Leaders initiate member languaging until the group begins to do it on its own.

The member-centered languaging process can be used once interactions that work have occurred. Then, leaders initiate a conversation directing members to describe what worked. This conversation can include members presenting observations, describing interactions, discussing outcomes, sharing emotional and cognitive reactions, and labeling what worked. The following are examples of leaders' statements designed to engage the languaging function.

Leader: (*Gesturing to the entire group*) "What did you observe that worked just now?"

Leader: "What did you all see happen as a result of Bernie sharing their emotions?"

Leader: "How are you all reacting to what just happened?"

Leader: "What does the group want to call what happened in River and Chandra's interchange?"

Leader: "It seems that it would be useful to name what happened so that we can do it again when we need to."

Languaging involving such statements causes members to increase their awareness of what they did that worked and accept responsibility for it. When members understand what they did that worked, they can function more effectively, because they know what to do and have ownership of it. Member languaging about what works also magnifies the members' confidence in the helpfulness of the group. These conversations build group cohesion because group members increasingly believe in the group's ability to affect members positively. Effective member languaging increases trust and involvement in the group.

Leader languaging occurs when leaders explain group events that work. Languaging at this end of the languaging continuum is more consistent with the meaning-attribution function described by Lieberman et al. (1973). This form of intervention helps members conceptualize group events and develop a framework for change. Typically, leader languaging has less impact than member languaging because members value languaging processes that involve them. In addition, leader languaging reinforces the perception that the leaders are the experts. This perception places the responsibility for learning on the shoulders of leaders and limits the potential of group interaction.

Leader languaging, however, is time efficient and can heighten member awareness. When leaders use languaging to describe what works, members focus their attention on interactions that work. In addition, leaders can use languaging to bring an interaction or pattern of interactions to the attention of the group. Such is the case when leaders point out norms (e.g., "The group seems to have agreed that everyone should be listened to."). However, leaders will not see the immediate change in group interactions as a result of this intervention because heightened awareness alone rarely results in groups learning to operate more effectively. Whenever possible, leaders should use terms developed during member languaging processes because such terms may be more significant, meaningful, and memorable to members. Terms that leaders introduce in their languaging interventions are less likely to be significant, understandable, or memorable to members.

Administration

Leaders perform the interactive administrative leadership function when they engage in and lead activities that contribute to the practical and logistic aspects of group management, particularly those activities that support effective group interaction. Examples of this function include scheduling sessions, selecting a location, and setting the length of sessions. This leadership function also includes two procedures that are vital to a group's ultimate effectiveness: pregroup screening and orientation.

Pregroup screening is an essential part of the administrative leadership function because ineffectively composed groups seldom become usefully therapeutic (I. D. Yalom & Leszcz, 2020). Usually, screening involves the group leader interviewing each prospective group member (Gladding, 2019) and assessing a potential group member's readiness to benefit from the group. Piper et al. (1998) listed several characteristics that group leaders should assess for during the screening interview. These include a baseline level of interpersonal skill, motivation to participate in group, positive expectations about the group, current psychological discomfort, an identified problem suitable for interpersonal work, openness to relationship behavior changes, susceptibility to group influence (moderate approval dependency), and a willingness to help others.

Pregroup orientation is also an important contributor to group effectiveness and part of the administrative leadership function (I. D. Yalom & Leszcz, 2020). Leaders can orient members during the initial group meeting after members have been screened or during the screening interviews. Pregroup orientation should include information about the processes, techniques, and interactions that will likely occur during the group. It should also describe the potential risks related to emotional or psychological stress. Orientation information should present leaders' theoretical perspectives, areas of expertise, credentials, and experience as group leaders.

Leader Beliefs and Member Attitudes

When leaders perform the interactive leadership functions, they are making choices about the content and purposes of their interactions. Leaders' choices are simplified when their chief priority is engaging members in interaction with each other. This objective is grounded in the leader's belief that group members, with sufficient trust and interactive skills, learn best from each other. Engaging members with each other enables them to develop attitudes that positively influence participation and learning. When members are engaged with each other, they learn from each other and develop the attitude that they are responsible for the amount and depth of their participation and, consequently, what they learn. As members experience productive outcomes from group interactions, they become increasingly confident that they can trust each other to act in the group's interest. The attitudes of being personally responsible for learning and trusting the intentions of other members help members to become increasingly honest and immediate in their interactions.

Leadership Style

When developing their leadership roles, leaders must be clear about the group environment they want to establish. As leaders develop this environment, they should consider that the way they interact with members establishes how members perceive the leader and the leadership role. A leader's approach to developing the environment that supports members' learning is a significant contributor to the group's effectiveness. Leaders whose styles are ineffective will limit their group's effectiveness even if their intent is to develop an effective group environment. This discussion focuses on leadership style, the ways leaders interact to achieve objectives, and potential reactions of group members to leadership styles.

Lewin's (1944) classic research depicted leadership style on a continuum of authority that ranged from authoritarian to laissez-faire. Hansen et al. (1980) described leadership styles as varying along several continua. These variations include from leader centered to group centered, from autocratic to anarchistic, and from directive to nondirective. From the interactive perspective, leadership styles exist and vary along authority, activity, and personal involvement continua. The *authority* continuum is the range of persistent leader choices related to who has the power to make and implement decisions that impact the group. The *activity* continuum is the range of persistent leader choices related to how frequently and how intensely leaders interact in the group. Finally, the *personal involvement* continuum is the set of persistent choices that leaders make related to how transparently and personally they become involved in group interactions (see Figure 7.1).

Leaders' customary manner of interacting with groups informs members about what they, as group members, should do. For example, leaders who persistently do not disclose emotions, continuously conceptualize interactions, and frequently enforce group norms communicate to group members that they should interact cognitively and wait for leaders' directions. Leaders' styles define how members perceive leaders, the behaviors members expect from each other and leaders, and ultimately the atmosphere and interpersonal issues that surface in the group.

The Authority Continuum: Authoritarian, Democratic, and Laissez-Faire Leadership

The authority continuum ranges from authoritarian to democratic at the midpoint to laissez-faire. It depicts the range of leaders' beliefs about who is competent and responsible for making and implementing decisions: leaders only, leaders and members in

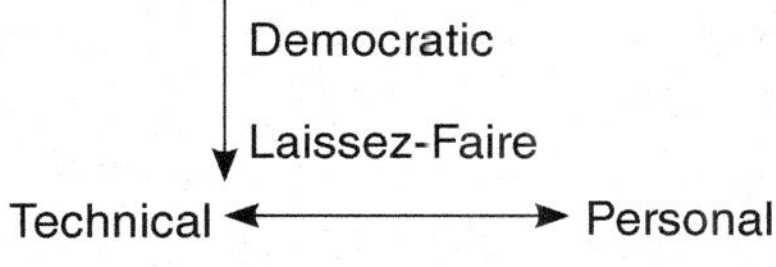

FIGURE 7.1
Leadership Style Dimensions

collaboration, members only, or no one. Regardless of leaders' style, authority issues will emerge in groups. Leaders' authority styles shape how authority issues present in group interaction—that is, a leader's own stance toward authority as part of their group leader role emerges and is played out in the group in diverse ways, depending on the stance.

Authoritarian Leaders

Authoritarian leaders demonstrate the belief that group members are incapable of engaging in effective behavior and developing the insights necessary to support group and member changes (Hansen et al., 1980). These leaders believe that members do not understand their problems adequately, do not gain insight without explanation, and cannot function in the group without ongoing direction. Therefore, persistently authoritarian leaders are not likely to develop a group in which members can learn effectively from interaction with each other.

Nevertheless, authoritarian leadership behaviors are essential in a wide variety of common group situations. For example, groups' early implementation of norms and boundaries such as owned language, complete feedback exchanges, finishing work before moving on, here-and-now communication, and sharing feelings requires consistent prompting on the part of the group leader. In addition, leaders need to be authoritarian in situations that require decisive action, such as enforcing norms that involve the safety and well-being of members.

Members have characteristic responses to leaders who are persistently authoritarian. Dependent members (Bennis & Shepard, 1956), who are predisposed to rely on others to direct them, will initially enjoy authoritative leadership. The behaviors of authoritarian leaders minimize responsibility for group member problem-solving and change, thereby lowering risk and group anxiety. Counterdependent members (Bennis & Shepard, 1956), who have a pattern of challenging authority, will rebel against leaders who continuously attempt to direct their behavior. Independent members (Bennis & Shepard, 1956), who base their opinions about authority on its effect, will not have an immediate reaction to an authoritarian leader. Instead, they will wait to experience how well their needs are met in the group before deciding how to react. Once dissatisfied, they are likely to challenge the authoritarian leader.

Leaders who rely on an authoritarian leadership style should carefully examine their interpersonal needs. In the group environment, the interpersonal needs of authoritarian leaders are often marked by a desire to avoid the rejection of group members and accompanying fears of intimacy. By controlling interaction, these leaders do not have to fear the possible rejection that goes with being authentic and encouraging authenticity in the group. Their fear of rejection and fear of intimacy will likely mirror the members' experiences as they struggle to engage one another openly. When leaders also have these concerns and use an authoritarian leadership style to defend themselves, their groups are likely to stall. This is because members' fears and leaders' fears will permit only a superficial level of intimacy.

Democratic Leaders

In contrast to authoritarian leaders, democratic leaders use collaborative actions that engage members in decision-making and carrying out group responsibilities. Democratic group leaders use a variety of skills, such as clarification, synthesis, feedback, and evaluation of process, as their main group leadership tools. Their aim is to involve members so that each participant contributes to the welfare of other individuals in the group. The democratic group leader works with the group members to determine group goals and how to achieve them. Democratic leaders believe that members can learn from each other and grow. These leaders know that group members, given the proper conditions, are capable of learning from each other and developing self-understanding and insight.

Democratic group leaders have attitudes and behave in ways consistent with interactive group leadership principles. However, issues surface when leaders do not feel free to use authoritarian interventions. Authoritarian interventions are occasionally necessary when members of a democratic group make decisions that can slow or stall the development of a facilitative group environment. For instance, when members agree to not share "negative" emotions in group, leaders must intervene authoritatively. If a leader is purely democratic, they will allow members to make the decision to not share negative emotions. Then, the purely democratic leader will have to wait until members experience the negative consequences of this decision. Then the democratic leader can initiate a renegotiation of the "sharing negative emotions" rule. This lengthy process is a waste of time in groups intended to be therapeutic and can easily be avoided through brief authoritarian interventions.

Purely democratic leaders develop operating procedures in collaboration with group members. As soon as members agree to procedures, they are responsible for implementing and cooperating with the procedures. Democratic leaders are then responsible for observing members' compliance with the agreed-upon procedures and facilitating the renegotiation of these rules when members agree that the rules are not helpful. However, purely democratic groups use time that could be devoted to members' personal work to reach agreements about how the group should operate. Group objectives that include efficiently forming a facilitative environment and promoting member change require the situational use of authoritative interactions to perform the necessary leadership functions. While members of groups led by leaders with a democratic style tend to have ownership of the process and outcomes of their groups, this is not an adequate reason for adhering to a purely democratic approach.

The nature of the interaction between purely democratic leaders and group members is also important to consider. Leaders who use an extensively democratic style should clarify that their choice of style is not based on a strong personal need for acceptance. Leaders who are consciously or unconsciously concerned about acceptance may use a democratic style to avoid conflict with group members and reduce the risk of rejection. Even if a personal need for acceptance is not interfering, leaders must still be clear about the congruence of the democratic approach with group objectives. A focus on promoting interpersonal learning based on naturally occurring group interaction is more consistent with members' growth and change than a focus on participation in democratic group processes.

Although democratic leaders may appear to avoid authority issues, this is not the case. Dependent members (Bennis & Shepard, 1956), who tend to look for protection and direction from leaders, often perceive democratic leaders as neglecting their responsibility to direct the group. Counterdependent members (Bennis & Shepard, 1956) assign responsibility to leaders and challenge leaders' competence, regardless of leaders' attempts to encourage group member responsibility. Of the group member types, independent members (Bennis & Shepard, 1956) respond most favorably to the democratic leadership style. They initially see the sharing of responsibility as an opportunity to learn but may become frustrated when interaction becomes unproductive.

Laissez-Faire Leaders

In contrast to authoritarian and democratic group leaders, laissez-faire leaders minimally participate in the development of group procedures, norms, or boundaries. The laissez-faire style is difficult to describe as a leadership style because leaders using this style assume no responsibility for the direction, content, or processes of their groups. These leaders do not actively participate in directing group interactions, and their involvement resembles that of group members (Hansen et al., 1980).

The laissez-faire leadership style is generally inconsistent with the interactive approach because laissez-faire leaders are not actively involved in developing a facilitative interactive environment. This group leadership style is occasionally appropriate. For example, simply observing and reflecting on the group can be useful when leaders are not certain about what is occurring or when they want members to wrestle with an issue to elevate group anxiety. Observation and reflection are also useful when an intervention fails. In this case, leaders can profit from observing and reflecting to clarify what is going on in the group. A pause such as this allows leaders to gain emotional distance from a failed intervention before reengaging with group members. However, leaders should avoid using a passive observational style for any extended time.

Members of all personality styles who experience leaders as persistently employing a laissez-faire style have authority issues with the leader. These reactions stem from leaders' nonperformance of necessary leadership functions. Truly laissez-faire leaders are never there when someone needs them. Hansen et al. (1980) pointed out that laissez-faire leaders often have a strong need to be liked. By acting more as members than as leaders, laissez-faire leaders try to gain the approval and acceptance of the group members. To gain the approval of group members, the leaders choose not to interact in a way that best serves their needs.

Interactive Authority Style

Although interactive group leaders use behaviors found in all three leadership styles, the behaviors and attitudes that are characteristic of the democratic leadership style are essential. Especially important is the attitude that members have the resources that allow them to learn from each other and to learn to function autonomously within the group. However, leaders must also actively direct group interaction or observe and reflect to maintain an effective group environment, encourage interpersonal learning, and protect group members. The interactive approach is not consistent with the attitudes held by authoritarian and laissez-faire leaders or with the persistent use of authoritarian or laissez-faire styles.

Depending on circumstances, interactive group leaders use behaviors consistent with the different leadership styles to meet group needs. For example, early in the group, members need to learn and practice interactive skills, and the group needs to develop and use facilitative interactive norms. To accomplish these objectives, leaders are often active and directive. Later, when facilitative norms and members' interactive skills have developed, group leaders increasingly use observational and democratic procedures. Just as group members grow to more flexibly use interpersonal roles, group leaders must be flexible in how and when they enact the various authority roles and must have a wide repertoire of interpersonal behaviors to meet the dynamic needs of their groups.

Active Versus Passive

To perform interactive leadership functions effectively, group leaders actively participate early in the group. This early emphasis on leader activity establishes effective interaction norms, develops effective interpersonal skills, and manages interpersonal and external group boundaries as the group forms. Later, as members demonstrate increasing self-sufficiency, interactive group leaders become progressively less active. Despite this general trend, leaders' involvement depends on what is transpiring in the group. For example, leaders may become highly active when they observe that a feedback exchange is incomplete, when a member is at risk of being scapegoated for instigating conflict in an otherwise peaceful session, or when a microaggression occurs against a group member with a minoritized identity.

Active participation can be described, in general, as leaders frequently engaging in group interactions. In some cases, highly active and authoritarian leaders frequently share their knowledge because they believe their expertise is necessary for effective group work. This type of persistently active leader establishes a communication pattern in which they become the center of group interaction. This form of active leader participation eventually creates more intense authority and dependency issues. In other cases, persistently active leaders participate to establish group norms and ground rules, develop permeable interaction boundaries, structure group interaction, and direct members to interact with each other. Despite their admirable intentions, these persistently active leaders also create authority and dependency issues. Their group members experience a demand for open interaction. However, in this case, these issues are necessary steps toward group autonomy.

Persistently active leaders and their supervisors should consider two potential interpersonal issues: overengagement and group dominance. These issues often affect leaders who are persistently active in conceptualizing group events or lecturing. Frequently, these leaders are apprehensive about emotional intimacy and rejection. In this case, the persistently active leaders' overengagement blocks intimacy in the emerging group relationships. The leaders' ongoing and dominant conceptual activity encourages members to engage with each other at a conceptual level but no further. Members' interactions will eventually mirror their leaders' interpersonal fears.

Passive leaders usually believe that minimal group leader interaction with group members is essential for group effectiveness. Although occasionally observing and reflecting on group interaction is useful, it is doubtful a persistent passive, observational approach is useful. In some cases, passive leaders may believe that minimal participation offers members an opportunity to explore their projections and transference relations with leaders. More commonly, persistently passive group leadership indicates leaders' interpersonal concerns and results in distrust in leaders.

Leaders who persistently use a passive approach to group leadership should be cognizant of several potential interpersonal issues. These interpersonal issues include fear of being rejected and fear of being perceived as incompetent. When these fears are present, leaders tend to believe that by remaining passive in the group, they can maintain personal safety—that is, they can maintain safety by remaining hidden from group members and abdicating their leadership roles and responsibilities. Paradoxically, members often criticize persistently passive leaders for being distant and judgmental.

Interactive Activity Style

Interactive group leaders' activity level depends on what is going on in their groups. Active participation or passive, observational, and reflective leader involvement can be appropriate for what is occurring in the group. Interactive group leaders should self-monitor their activity level on an ongoing basis. Persistently passive participation is not responsive to the needs of the group, because all groups require active leader participation at some point in time. At the same time, persistently active participation by the group leader deprives group members of learning opportunities. Members should never develop the impression that leaders do "all the talking." To lead groups effectively, leaders' activity level must be responsive to the needs of the group. Monitoring activity level is especially important in situations where coleaders are struggling to have equal "airtime" or are competing for the attention of the group members.

Figure 7.2 presents a facilitation sequence that shows how leaders can help group members build relationships and interact better. The leader's actions are focused on redirecting the group's attention, asking open questions to encourage participation, giving direction when necessary, and making observations about group dynamics. The sequence also demonstrates clarifying skills, such as paraphrasing and reflecting on group statements, using open questions and directions to stay engaged, and teaching these skills to group members (see Table 7.1). Finally, Figure 7.2 shows the role of connecting skills, which are crucial for effective interpersonal interventions in the group. These skills include bridging members who may not see commonalities, opening up interactions between members and the leader of the group, directing members to talk directly to each other, sharing observations and feelings, and commenting on group interactions while inviting members to reflect on their interpersonal connections.

Personal Involvement and Technical Skills

Interactive group leaders must balance their leadership between demonstrating their competence and confidence in using skills,

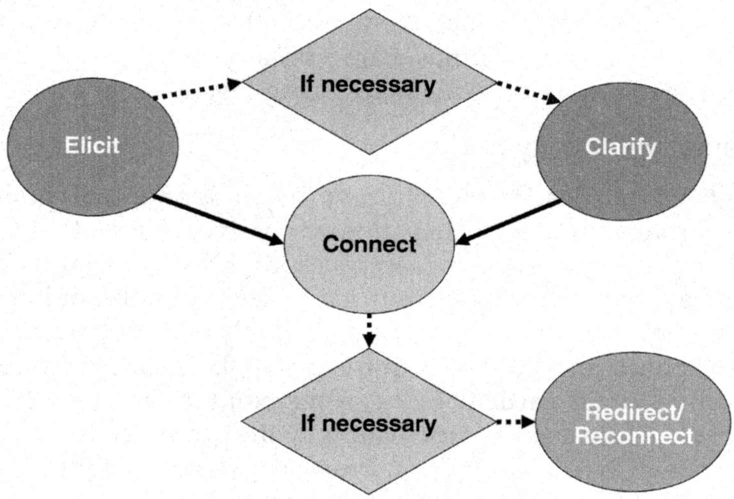

FIGURE 7.2
Basic Facilitation Sequence

TABLE 7.1
Basic Group Intervention Skills

Eliciting Skill	Clarifying Skill	Connecting Skill
• Open questions • Directions • Observations	• Paraphrasing and reflection • Open questions • Directions and invitations	• Bridging • Open • Directed • About interactions

interventions, and strategies and demonstrating their genuine, trustworthy, and caring personal reactions and emotions. Leaders limit their effectiveness by overemphasizing either one of these polarities, because the extensive use of either approach creates member expectations that limit productive group outcomes. Leaders should be adept at using interventions and comfortable sharing personal reactions. Most importantly, leaders must be mindful of the implications of participating exclusively in either mode.

Group members learn to trust each other when they exchange increasingly intimate self-disclosures over time. As members become increasingly intimate and learn that other members accept them, they develop a sense of trust and safety. When leaders rely heavily on technical expertise and avoid sharing personal reactions, they block this process. Often, leaders who rely heavily on technical expertise are anxious about how others perceive them. These leaders find that using a leadership style that emphasizes their technical competence decreases this anxiety. However, this style has its problems.

Leaders who rely heavily on technical expertise will observe members behave as if interacting in group is a very scary experience. Often, these reactions involve members attributing their fears of interacting with each other to leaders whom they perceive as distant, manipulative, and judgmental. Often, these members do not trust these leaders because they do not have information about the personal reactions of leaders. Group members may assign critical or judgmental characteristics to group leaders who rely heavily on technical expertise.

In contrast, leaders who rely heavily and persistently on personal engagement experience a different, but also problematic, array of group reactions. Initially, these reactions include being liked and admired by members. This reaction feeds leaders who are apprehensive about their relationships with group members and helps the leader become more comfortable. However, as groups proceed, this overly personal behavior becomes confusing to members.

Members' confusion about the roles of persistently overpersonal leaders is the outcome of the ambiguous messages sent by these leaders. Ambiguity emerges because the personal involvement of these leaders blurs the necessary line between membership and leadership roles. Members become confused about what behaviors to expect from leaders and begin to expect leaders to behave more like members. These expectations are especially problematic when leaders inevitably need to address critical group needs using authority. For instance, after interacting like other group members, persistently overpersonal leaders may become intensely directive to establish necessary boundaries or to protect a member from harm. This change in leader behavior confuses members. Leaders who rely heavily on overpersonal engagement to avoid challenges and gain acceptance ultimately face heated leadership challenges in situations where it is necessary to direct the group.

Group leaders who use excessive or inappropriate personal disclosure to develop close bonds with members will find themselves conflicted when they must perform necessary and authoritative leadership functions. Once leaders' participation begins to resemble that of members, members' expectations begin to conflict with leaders' necessary use of expertise or authority. Leaders who use persistent overpersonal engagement experience leadership dilemmas similar to the dilemma of enmeshed parents when they attempt to maintain family rules with their children.

Interactive Involvement Style

Using a leadership style that balances technical expertise and personal involvement is essential. Leaders must demonstrate regard for the experiences of members and be transparent enough to allow group members to know them and trust them. At the same time, leaders should use interventions that are sufficiently correct, active, and direct to establish effective interpersonal boundaries and confront group issues.

To balance these leadership dimensions, leaders must judge the group's needs based on what is occurring in the group at the time. For example, group leaders' emotional disclosure is usually not useful in a feedback exchange that requires use of the structuring function. Conversely, using techniques to address members' fears may not be as useful as an emotional disclosure that demonstrates understanding of members' fears.

Interactive Leadership Role

The interactive leadership role is based on theoretical assumptions that leaders demonstrate through seven objectives:

1. Interact and intervene with the goal of developing therapeutic factors that support interpersonal learning.
2. Enable and support group member interpersonal communication boundaries that allow sharing of emotions and perceptions.
3. Establish external group boundaries that sustain group environments that promote interpersonal learning and cohesion.
4. Facilitate and support a normative structure that encourages interaction, self-disclosure, feedback exchange, and experimentation with new interpersonal behaviors.
5. Provide sufficient structure to ensure group member learning and members' languaging of solutions.
6. Teach members communication and feedback skills that facilitate learning.
7. Actively counter oppressive dynamics that become a part of group interaction.

This perspective suggests the actions leaders perform to meet their group objectives. To achieve group objectives, leaders perform core roles that are influenced by their leadership style. These roles are demonstrated through the leader's skills, interventions, and strategies. Leadership style has significant implications for the group environment, group members' expectations of leaders, and how members perceive their responsibilities for learning.

As group leaders gain experience, they should reexamine their beliefs about how group interaction helps group members. As their beliefs evolve, leaders can experiment with small changes in their leadership approach to see what works best for them. By using this experimentation process, leaders can develop their most congruent and helpful leadership approach. Leaders who participate in this process are much more likely to sustain their enthusiasm and ongoing development as group leaders. Leaders will find that they are most effective when their leadership is consistent with their experiences and beliefs.

Conclusion

Essential attitudes and objectives can reduce the complexity of the group leadership task. Leaders should direct members to interact with each other. This means that the leadership role focuses on enabling and facilitating interaction. Leaders must establish and reinforce the members' personal responsibility for learning and interacting congruently as well as help members develop interpersonal boundaries that allow communication of feelings and the disclosure of perceptions. Interactive group leaders challenge the group to develop here-and-now norms and sufficiently closed external group boundaries. In terms of style, interactive leaders strike a balance between technical expertise and presence as a person. Leaders cannot develop an effective learning environment without establishing their presence as open, authentic, and direct people. They engage members in identifying interactive concerns that are being avoided and work diligently to involve the group in confronting and resolving these concerns, while continuously demonstrating the attitude that members, not leaders, are the primary sources of therapeutic change. Most of all, interactive group leaders act with confidence in the belief that members are capable of dealing with difficult, emotionally charged, interpersonal issues effectively.

Part III

Interactive GROUP LEADERSHIP in ACTION

Chapter 8

Basic Group Leadership Skills and Interventions

Outcomes

Level 1 Outcomes

After reading this chapter, entry-level students and practitioners should be able to:

1. Describe and identify affective, behavioral, and cognitive objectives for basic group leadership skills and interventions.
2. Define and identify intervention levels and describe their importance.
3. Discuss the timing, balance, and intensity of interventions and their implications for skill and intervention use.
4. Describe and identify culturally responsive basic group leadership skills and interventions.
5. Apply the basic facilitation sequence.

Level 2 Outcomes

After reading this chapter, advanced-level students and practitioners should also be able to:

1. Apply culturally responsive basic group leadership skills and interventions to meet affective, behavioral, and cognitive objectives.
2. Apply culturally responsive basic group leadership skills and interventions appropriately for all three intervention levels.
3. Evaluate group scenarios for appropriate timing, balance, and intensity of skills and interventions.
4. Explain why basic skills and interventions occasionally do not work and what to do when this happens.

Group leadership skills and interventions are most effective when they are culturally responsive, are used to establish inclusive and safe group environments, and mobilize the powerful forces of group interaction for the benefit of all members. This premise is grounded in the conviction that group members learn most effectively from each other. It follows that the leader's role is to facilitate culturally responsive and increasingly intimate here-and-now interaction, self-disclosures, honest feedback exchanges, appropriate risk-taking, confrontation, experimentation with alternative interpersonal behaviors, and members' efforts to change. Group leader responsibilities also include protecting members from harm and providing cognitive structures to make sense of group interaction. Group leaders should also model effective interpersonal behaviors, help members process group events, and offer only necessary educational input.

Basic skills are group leaders' most fundamental response to group interaction. These skills are simple actions and statements designed to focus members on specific aspects of the group and to facilitate effective interaction. Basic interventions are a sequence of basic skills. Generally, these interventions use first one basic skill to illuminate a potentially fruitful issue within group interaction and then additional skills to facilitate interaction around this issue. Basic skills and interventions are the tools leaders use to perform their various functions (see Chapters 7 and 10).

All skills and interventions may address one or more levels of the group system. These levels are the group as a system, subgroups or interpersonal exchanges, and the individual group members. Effectively used skills and interventions help leaders meet several important global group objectives, such as orienting group members to the culture of group work and developing a shared within-group culture; encouraging affective experiencing and expression; providing a cognitive structure; and changing, encouraging, and directing group members' within-group behaviors. Leaders should be aware of the timing, balance, and intensity of the skills and interventions they use.

Affective, Cognitive, and Behavioral Objectives

Learning in groups is most effective when group members have consistent opportunities for emotional experiencing, cognitive understanding, and experimentation with new behaviors. Thus, effective group leaders are adept at engaging with their groups to meet affective, cognitive, and behavioral objectives. They are also aware of and can adapt to the variety of ways that social and cultural identity, power, and safety can affect how group members relate to these important objectives. The process and ultimate goals of interactive group work are to assist group members to more fully and effectively experience and express emotions, to develop cognitive frameworks that lead to insight and intentionality, and to learn more personally effective relationship behaviors.

Affective Objectives

Affective objectives are those associated with the expression of feelings and emotions. To learn and grow, group members must experience and express emotions. Members who do so are more likely to encounter their most limiting personal concerns within here-and-now interaction and to receive meaningful feedback from the group. Developing comfort with expressing and experiencing emotions also liberates members to become more self-accepting, honest, and spontaneous in their relationships.

Group members who experience and effectively share their emotions also experience changes in their interpersonal communication boundaries (MacKenzie, 1990). Once members' boundaries are open enough to experience and share emotions, they become more intensely involved in interaction. When members are emotionally involved, they are more likely to experience interactions that lead to change (I. D. Yalom & Leszcz, 2020). Emotionally involved members are more committed to and intensely engaged with one another. This allows them to be more open to sharing and receiving feedback, to appropriately confront and be confronted, and to experience the emotional interactions that lead to meaningful change.

Members have met affective objectives when their interactions include open, spontaneous, and honest expression of emotions. At this point, leaders have an indication that the group is cohesive and that members perceive the group as a safe environment.

Group members must have consistent opportunities to experience and express emotions, and group leaders must work at each level of the group system to meet affective objectives. At the group-as-a-system level, leaders strive to develop group norms and cultures that support and include the expectancy of expressing emotions. At the subgroup or interpersonal level, leaders promote the effective expression of emotions in relationships between group members. At the individual member level, leaders help each member learn to identify, openly share, and value their emotional experiences, while remaining responsive to each member's cultural orientation and readiness to examine and share their emotions.

Although affective objectives are critical to group and group member learning and growth, individual group members may assign different meanings to their and other group members' emotions and expressions of emotion, depending on their experiences in society, social identity, and culture. For example, experiencing, exploring, and appropriately sharing anger is a common and important occurrence in groups, particularly during the storming stage of group development. However, some group members may view their own and others' anger expressed in a way deemed appropriate by the group leaders as rude, offensive, dangerous, inauthentic, impossible, liberating, or good communication on the basis of their own experiences in society, social identity, and culture. Thus, the leader must be aware of this very real potential and be prepared to protect, guide, and support members as they make sense of and act on their differences in lived experience, power, and worldview.

Cognitive Objectives

Although affective objectives are critical to group member learning and growth, they are not sufficient for change (I. D. Yalom & Leszcz, 2020). Equally critical are *cognitive objectives*, which take the form of language or information members require to make sense of their interactions and relationships and to develop solutions that lead to change.

Experiencing emotion opens the door to change, but members must develop cognitive structures to understand their emotional experiences. These cognitive structures help them name, define, and evaluate their experiences as well as understand and plan desired changes. These cognitive structures take shape when members receive feedback, learn language about productive group events, and process here-and-now interactions. The value of these cognitive objectives is especially evident during effective feedback exchanges, when group members come to understand and name the impact of their ineffective relationship behaviors and identify more effective ones.

Like affective objectives, cognitive objectives should be promoted at all group levels. At the group-as-a-system level, leaders meet cognitive objectives by ensuring group members have the information needed to optimize their learning. This information includes how to exchange feedback, how to communicate more effectively, and what to do to develop more effective interactive norms. Group leaders also meet group-level cognitive objectives by languaging about group events that are particularly meaningful or have productive or destructive outcomes. Leaders move toward interpersonal cognitive objectives by providing information that helps members understand and work through relationship issues they experience with each other. Leaders meet cognitive objectives at the individual level by helping members understand their relationship problems, here-and-now experiences, and what they must learn to make desired changes.

Despite the necessity of promoting cognitive objectives, leaders must be cautious and intentional about how they accomplish them. A common issue is excessive cognitive input, which encourages group members to disengage and may inadvertently communicate an unproductively authoritative leadership style. Additionally, an overemphasis on cognitive objectives may promote group norms prioritizing content and reflection over emotion and relationship. Group leaders may effectively promote cognitive objectives through the judicious use of interventions that fall into three broad categories: educational input, languaging, and processing.

Educational Input

Educational input to promote cognitive objectives is appropriate to meet several categories of group needs. For example, educational input is appropriate when the information is necessary to facilitate interaction and promote change. Information that enables members to interact effectively, such as information about basic listening skills and effective ways to give and receive feedback, is useful if it is correctly timed, presented clearly, and supported throughout interaction. Similarity, information that helps group members understand challenging interventions and interactions in group may also be useful if well timed. Examples of this type of information include information about cross-cultural communication and the role of healthy conflict in groups. Information that helps orient group members early in the group is also useful. This may include information about goals and objectives, boundaries, and group culture.

Another category of appropriate educational input is information that is required to uphold professional ethics, protect the rights of group members, and promote group members' safety and well-being. Leaders are obligated to provide information necessary for the well-being of the group members (e.g., discussing safe sex when members talk about being sexually active). Leaders also have the ethical responsibility at the beginning of the group to reiterate informed consent information. Regardless of purpose, educational input must be closely connected to current or recent interaction to be meaningful to members. For example, coaching group members on effective feedback exchanges during or immediately after a shared experience with ineffective feedback will have more impact than a lecture that is not connected to a shared experience.

Languaging

Languaging is the process of describing and naming solutions to members' problems that have emerged during group interaction (see Chapters 7 and 10). Languaging has several goals, including increasing members' confidence in the group's helpfulness, cocreating shared language for effective learning processes, and identifying and illuminating interactions that lead to effective learning. Because languaging is a discussion of group processes that lead to effective outcomes, it encourages members to become more focused on solutions. This focus disrupts members' tendency to overemphasize problems. Overemphasizing problems or maintaining a problem focus sustains problems and decreases the probability of change. Languaging is both a cognitive process and an objective whereby the leader and group members conceptualize helpful interactions so that they can be repeated.

Processing

Processing, along with languaging, is an essential ongoing leader task and a vital tool for meeting cognitive objectives. Leaders *process* group events to help members reflect on and learn from here-and-now interaction. This self-reflective loop (I. D. Yalom & Leszcz, 2020) allows members to discuss what has immediately occurred or is occurring to make sense of it and, potentially, develop insight. Processing is discussed in detail as an aspect of leaders' ongoing responsibilities in Chapter 10.

Behavioral Objectives

Group members' opportunities for affective experiencing and cognitive understanding must be coupled with opportunities to identify and try out effective relationship behaviors. Members learn most effectively when they (a) receive feedback about interpersonal behaviors, (b) discover effective alternative behaviors, (c) experiment with alternative behaviors, and (d) incorporate into their relationships the alternative behaviors that work best for them. These outcomes are most likely to be achieved when behavioral objectives are met at the group-as-a-system, interpersonal, and individual levels.

At the group-as-a-system level, behavioral objectives involve establishing norms that develop a facilitative interactive group environment (see Chapter 2). These norms support feedback exchange and experimentation with alternative behaviors. Interpersonal-level objectives focus on identifying and learning more effective relationship behaviors. For example, two members might learn and practice listening skills to better navigate a conflict that has been further fueled by interrupting each other. Objectives for the individual level are met when members conceptualize their personal goals in terms of relationship behaviors. For example, a member who learns that they come across to other members as critical might find that experimentation with listening and paraphrasing skills deepens their understanding and receives improved reactions from others.

Change is possible when group members identify and understand the relational impact of their ineffective behaviors. This understanding happens when they receive input from others about potentially more effective relationship behaviors. Behavioral objectives are met when members feel empowered to choose behaviors that meet their own needs, experiment with alternative relationship behaviors, and find behaviors that both enhance their relationships and meet interpersonal needs. Focusing on relationship behaviors also helps members refine their perceptions of self and others. By focusing on relationship behaviors, members learn to think in terms of behaviors that do not work, rather than attributing what goes wrong in relationships to their own worth and the worth of others. Ongoing feedback about the effectiveness of relationship behavior experiments is an important step in members experiencing change. Feedback provides information that allows members to learn behaviors that can improve the quality of their relationships. When a member receives feedback that experimental behaviors work for others and determines that those behaviors achieve what they want and are personally viable, the member can then make choices about maintaining those behaviors in their relationships. For example, River experimented with several ways to express disagreement. After several experiments, River received feedback that others understood their point of view and believed that River invited the others to engage in a discussion about their differences. This is what River wanted, and River felt comfortable using these behaviors. River then decided to make these behaviors a habit in all relationships.

Intervention Levels

Group leaders who understand and work with the systemic levels inherent in groups are essential for forming effective group environments and promoting effective group interaction. Groups are social systems composed of individual, subgroup (or interpersonal), and group-as-a-system levels. All interventions and skills that leaders use address one or more of these levels and have an impact on all levels. Regardless of the level addressed, all interventions and skills should be used to actively engage members with one another or set the stage for such interactions. Less important are the target of the intervention or skill or the way the intervention or skill is implemented.

Individual-Level Skills and Interventions

The most overused and least effective skills and interventions are those directed toward individual members, although these skills and interventions have their place. Leaders who overuse individual-level skills and interventions often fail to engage members sufficiently with one another. When they do this, they fail to utilize the most powerful source of learning and change—members' interactions with one another. Leaders overemphasize individual-level communications for many reasons. This may be a habit formed during individual counseling and therapy training or a result of inadequate group leadership training. It may also result from the interpersonal fears and needs of leaders.

Interventions and skills directed toward individual members are, however, occasionally necessary. They are appropriate to use occasionally to involve and support a member's participation, particularly before sufficient cohesion has developed for group members to support and challenge each other. At the same time, these skills and interventions should be used with an awareness of the associated dangers. The most obvious danger is overuse. Overuse of individually focused skills and interventions comes with the risk of establishing norms that place leaders as experts in charge of each member's change. This encourages passive membership. Passive members are much less likely to help each other or to develop meaningful relationships in the group.

Subgroup or Interpersonal Skills and Interventions

Group leaders should prioritize subgroup or interpersonal skills and interventions. Skills and interventions aimed at members' relationships are important because helping members develop healthy and satisfying relationships is the essential purpose of group counseling and therapy. Interpersonal skills and interventions should be aimed at (a) promoting interaction, (b) initiating feedback exchanges, (c) opening interpersonal boundaries, (d) challenging habitual restrictive solutions to focal conflict, (e) confronting interpersonal perceptual distortions, (f) initiating and completing interpersonal learning processes, and (g) initiating changes in members' relationships. The bulk of the most meaningful work that group members do will occur at the interpersonal level.

Group-as-a-System Skills and Interventions

Skills and interventions that focus on the entire group membership are intended to address issues experienced by all members. One critical goal of group-as-a-system-level skills and interventions is to establish norms that make the group an effective learning environment. These norms, discussed in depth in Chapter 2, promote safety, cohesion, acceptance, and risk-taking.

Group-level interventions are also used to confront issues that block the group's progress. These interventions identify and direct all group members to deal with shared concerns, group-as-a-whole boundary issues, and focal conflicts. By identifying shared concerns, group-level boundary issues, and focal conflicts, group-level interventions can noticeably elevate the anxiety and stimulation present in the group.

Although group leaders and members generally perceive group-level skills and interventions as less risky and challenging than subgroup or interpersonal skills and interventions, overuse presents a danger. Leaders who overuse group-level interventions may be perceived as distant or impersonal (I. D. Yalom, 1975), and members may respond to the overuse of group-level skills by disengaging from the process. However, the careful use of group-level skills and interventions is indispensable because it can greatly enhance members' learning and group effectiveness.

Intervening: Timing, Balance, and Intensity

The goal of getting members to interact therapeutically is the basis for making decisions about when, how often, and how powerfully to intervene as a leader. In the absence of concrete guidelines, the following discussion offers some ideas that can be useful when making intervention decisions. With experience, leaders will gain a sense of the timing, balance, and intensity of interventions.

Timing

The timing of skills and groups of skills that form interventions is crucial. When considering an intervention, leaders should remember that members' interactions are often intended to manage anxiety. These attempts consist of solutions that include avoidance and denial, maintaining open external group boundaries, clinging to closed interpersonal boundaries, or disconnected cognitive discussion. Although these solutions normally require the group leader to robustly intervene, interventions are not always advisable. Generally, the timing of interventions depends on group development, the level of membership skills, the level of anxiety, members' ability to cope with anxiety, and group member safety.

Early in group development, leaders should be mindful of the lower levels of trust members have in each other and the leader, as well as their uncertainties about group rules. Group members' early uncertainties may call for more frequent interventions than would be called for later in the group. However, both early group conditions also raise members' anxieties. Group leaders should be careful during this time, as interventions that confront members' anxieties directly and attempt to develop enabling solutions may make anxiety overwhelming and produce defensiveness. Later in the life of the group, however, these interventions can be highly productive. Consequently, knowing when raising members' anxiety will be productive is important when considering when to intervene. Generally, leaders are encouraged to increase anxiety but never to the extent that it destroys members' perception of safety. Group members' sense of safety tends to become more resilient as the group develops over time.

When members are interacting productively, leaders should feel free to develop enabling solutions and frustrate restrictive solutions to focal conflicts. At this point, members have developed a sense that the group is a safe environment and that they can face uncomfortable anxiety. They will also have developed sufficient group membership skills to feel empowered to communicate through anxiety and conflicts. Interventions that significantly escalate anxiety should not be used before members have developed the skills and attitudes necessary to manage intense emotion. Once group members have developed a critical mass of these skills, leaders can more directly address focal conflicts and increasingly risky boundary issues.

Regardless of a group's stage of development and the group members' skill development, leaders should be able to identify when group member anxiety has become overwhelming and their sense of productive safety has been threatened. When anxiety is high and it appears that interaction may shut down, leaders should consider using temporary "escape hatch" restrictive solutions. Such solutions allow members to regain or maintain their sense of safety in the group. Leaders can manage the group's anxiety by either ignoring or introducing restrictive solutions. The following examples show how a leader can lower a group's anxiety by introducing an escape hatch restrictive solution:

Leader: "Well, we've been dealing with some nerve-wracking stuff tonight. I'm wondering how everyone is going to destress after group."

Leader: "Wow! I think it's time we all take a deep breath. It seems like we can all be proud of how we faced some difficult issues today."

Knowing when to intervene is particularly difficult for beginning group leaders, but it can be helpful to know a handful of situations that can be categorized as low, intermediate, or high in the sensitivity required. The timing of some interventions is not particularly sensitive, but the interventions are very important to group functioning. These interventions include bridging members who are not interacting, initiating feedback exchanges, and establishing a facilitative group environment. Important interventions that require more sensitivity to timing are modifying ineffective communication behaviors, identifying and modifying interpersonal perceptual distortions, helping members and the group develop effective external boundaries, and encouraging the development of autonomy. Interventions that are critical to group effectiveness and require an even greater sensitivity to timing include challenging restrictive solutions and identifying focal conflicts, developing enabling solutions, and confronting. These lists do not include all possible interventions leaders can make. The essential point is that interventions that produce increasingly greater anxiety require increasingly greater sensitivity to timing, and leaders should become familiar with common interventions in each category.

One circumstance requires no consideration for timing: Leaders must intervene whenever a member has the potential of being harmed. Harmful interactions include but are not limited to interactions that diminish or attack a member's personhood, take away their autonomy, or introduce or reinforce destructive roles. Harmful interactions do not include interactions that raise anxiety and may cause fruitful discomfort, such as giving feedback, expressing disagreement, and expressing anger or other emotions appropriately. Interactions intended to do harm are always unacceptable. Whenever it becomes clear that a member may be harmed, leaders must intervene immediately and decisively. These interventions should establish clear boundaries that prevent damaging interactions. Leaders should also intervene when they understand that unintentional patterns of interaction may cause harm. Common unintentionally harmful interactions include the marginalization of underrepresented or culturally different group members and scapegoating. Accordingly, leaders must carefully monitor interactions for these dynamics.

As indicated earlier, intense interactions are not necessarily harmful interactions. Leaders should carefully consider when to intervene in intense group interactions. Ordinarily, leaders should not intervene when members are engaged in an intense interaction and the interaction promises to have a productive outcome. It is especially important not to intervene to preempt members' attempts to deal with emotionally intense issues on their own if these attempts show promise of progress.

Emotionally intense interactions should conclude with the interacting members having shared openly, communicated effectively, clarified their concerns, and understood how to address their relationship concerns. As emotionally intense interactions progress, leaders should intervene only when necessary to help conceptualize the meaning of the emotional expression and the events associated with the expression. Emotionally intense interactions in which members are clearly having communication skill problems are another opportunity for leader intervention.

Leaders should monitor their interventions to avoid the habit of intervening whenever interaction becomes intense. This pattern of intervention communicates to members that they are incapable of handling such interactions themselves and will not allow self-sufficiency to develop further. Leaders who find they have this tendency should look carefully at their own tolerance for emotional expression. Anxiety associated with members' emotional expression should be addressed with leaders' supervisors, in consultations with other professionals, in debriefing with coleaders, or in their own counseling or therapy.

In general, while intervention may become less frequent as groups continue to develop, the timing of interventions becomes more critical. Attempts to intervene whenever needed early in the life of a group for the purpose of developing a facilitative group environment usually pay off. The payoff of a facilitative environment is the group becoming progressively more self-sufficient. However, leaders who continue to intervene whenever it seems necessary and do not allow group members to take increasing responsibility for interactions will limit the effectiveness of their groups. These groups will lack creativity and spontaneity, be dependent on leaders for ongoing direction, and be much less likely to develop autonomous boundaries. Members must have opportunities to become self-sufficient. Allowing members to struggle with group and interpersonal issues is the first step in members discovering that they have the necessary resources to confront their issues.

Balance

Balance describes how leaders distribute their interventions in terms of form, objective, level, frequency, and amount. *Form* describes the types of skills or interventions used. *Objective* includes the affective, cognitive, and behavioral goals of each intervention. *Level* describes the part of the group system an intervention addresses—individual, interpersonal, or the group as a system.

Frequency refers to how often leaders intervene, and *amount* refers to how long they speak when they intervene. Balanced use of skills and interventions involves group leaders using various forms and objectives directed at various parts of the group system. Balance also means that leaders aim to talk much less than group members.

When considering intervention balance, leaders must keep in mind the goal of creating a largely self-sustaining group. Members respond to frequent leader interventions by withdrawing and waiting for the leader to tell them what they need to do. These members become disempowered, quickly lose their energy, and do not feel capable of taking charge of their own learning. Optimal frequency of leader intervention is demonstrated when groups become increasingly self-sufficient. This usually means that at the beginning of the group, leaders intervene frequently enough to facilitate the development of effective interactive norms. They have focused on teaching members interactive skills, and members have become personally responsible for learning. Members of these groups do not depend entirely on their leaders, because they have learned how to learn effectively from each other.

Leaders should also consider the duration of their interventions. Lengthy interventions are detrimental because they direct members' attention away from interaction with each other and toward listening to the leader—shifting from active participation to passive listening. Leaders should attempt to balance interventions to maintain or energize interaction. In general, leaders should strive to make their interventions as short as possible. Direct, concise interventions have greater impact and maintain members' contact with each other.

Intensity

Intervention intensity refers to the extent to which an intervention raises members' anxiety. More intense interventions directly respond to disturbing motives and reactive motives by naming them. These highly intense interventions may direct members to act on disturbing motives, thus directly confronting their reactive fears. The least intense interventions direct the group away from disturbing motives and reactive fears, serving as restrictive solutions that dramatically reduce members' anxiety. By appraising the group's tolerance for anxiety, leaders can develop a sense for how intense their interventions should be.

It is not useful for the group environment to have either an insufficient or a consistently uncomfortable amount of anxiety. If anxiety is too low or too high, the group will be ineffective. When anxiety is excessive, members will persistently attempt to implement restrictive solutions or disengage. If anxiety is too low, restrictive solutions are operating. Leaders should allow restrictive solutions only when anxiety is suddenly intolerable or chronically excessive (Whitaker & Lieberman, 1964). When anxiety has been overwhelming, these escape hatch restrictive solutions can reestablish a sense of safety within the group. Leaders must decide which restrictive solutions avoid issues and should be confronted and which are responses to overwhelming anxiety and should be ignored.

Basic Skills and Interventions

With an understanding of intervention objectives, levels, timing, balance, and intensity, group leaders can begin to use basic group leadership skills and interventions effectively. The following discussion describes three types of basic skills (listening skills, directives, and observations) and nine of the most useful foundational interventions.

Listening Skills

Listening skills are fundamental to individual counseling and therapy (Ivey, 1994; Young, 1992) and serve as a building block for effective group leadership through limited use at the individual level. The most *basic listening skills* are simple restatements that are used to encourage interaction and promote effective communication between leaders and members. By accurately restating the affective or cognitive content shared by members, leaders can validate their understanding, communicate attention to members, and stimulate introspection. Basic skills also include open-ended questions that begin with "how" or "what" (Ivey, 1994). Open-ended questions encourage members to share or expand upon their thoughts and emotions. Closed questions, another basic skill, begin with "do," "are," or "have" (Ivey, 1994). These questions confirm understanding and close down interaction.

More *advanced listening skills* used at the individual level confront discrepancies in members' actions, emotions, or verbalizations; increase immediacy in the relationship; and probe more deeply into members' emotions and thinking (Ivey, 1994). These more advanced skills help members gain a better understanding of their thoughts, emotions, and behaviors. These skills also promote more intimate relationships, can initiate change, and help support the formation of norms around self-disclosure and here-and-now interaction.

All listening skills use statements or questions. In the group context, leaders should use listening skills to involve individual members with one another rather than to initiate extended interaction with a particular member. Examples of useful application of listening skills include using a question to draw out a member, restating what a member has said to ensure that others understand, making a statement that identifies the emotions a member is experiencing, and drawing out a member's reaction to another member or to a group event.

In group, leaders should limit their focus on the individual level. Consequently, the two most important uses of listening skills are aimed at supporting shifts from the individual to the interpersonal level. Listening skills can be used (a) to connect group members to one another through the basic facilitation sequence (or other interventions that connect members to one another) or (b) as a skill set to be taught to all group members. When members learn these skills, the effectiveness of their communication with each other increases dramatically.

Directives

Directives are leader statements that instruct members to participate in the group in a specific way. Directives are the most efficient way to connect or redirect interaction and initiate members' experimentation with alternative behaviors. This skill can halt a prolonged verbalization by a member that blocks productive interaction by the group. Finally, directives can instruct a member to offer feedback or share information, reactions, or emotions with the group, a particular subgroup, or a particular member. Examples of directives include:

Leader: "Gordon, you've been talking for a while, and I can see others have something to share. Please hold that thought."
Leader: "John, say 'I' instead of 'you.'"
Leader: "This concerns Shay. Say that directly to Shay."
Leader: "Isabelle, before we move on to your topic, we need to let Jet finish. Jet, please continue."
Leader: "Jenn, you've received lots of feedback and look flustered. Please tell the group to stop when you've had enough."
Leader: "Let Harley finish before you jump in."
Leader: "Stay with the feelings you're having now."

Developing directive skills can be helpful for members who are working on clarifying their interpersonal boundaries. Leaders can direct members to use directives, such as in the following examples:

Leader: "Tell them what you want."
Leader: "You can tell others when you've had enough feedback."
Leader: "You're in charge of defining your own boundaries here. Tell the others what you want them to know."

Directives that target the entire group are a very effective management tool. Group directives are simply statements to the entire group that instruct about and ask all members to engage in desirable behaviors. These directives can be used to manage communication, promote the establishment of facilitative norms, or manage the group's boundaries. Some examples follow:

Leader: "Be here on time. The group starts at 8:00 sharp."
Leader: "When members say they want to stop receiving feedback, stop giving it."
Leader: "When you have a strong reaction to another member's behaviors, it's a good time to give that member feedback."

Using directives can be an effective way for group leaders to catalyze and shape group interaction. However, leaders should also be aware that directives focus their considerable power in a way other skills do not. The use of directives usually raises anxiety in the group; thus, leaders should consider optimum intensity levels for the group at the moment. Also, on account of the power-laden nature of directives, group leaders should carefully consider the sociocultural appropriateness of what they are requesting. Often, if the group leader determines, or a group member's response indicates, that a particular directive may not be culturally appropriate, the directive may still be introduced or supported with information about its therapeutic intent and framing to support group member autonomy.

Observation

Observation as a basic skill involves watching and listening to interaction and making a statement about what has been seen and heard. Observation may include statements about members' nonverbal expressions, what members say or do during specific interactions, or patterns in a member's interactions. A more sophisticated form of observing involves looking for process. Observing process involves reflecting on the possible and likely purposes of members' interactions. For example, does a particular member appear to be intimidating, controlling, manipulative, caretaking, or acting out a victim's role while attempting to get what they want?

Sharing observations is an effective way to increase members' awareness of their interpersonal behaviors. This is important because most individuals interact in their social environments with a limited awareness of the larger personal and interpersonal impact of their behavior. Thus, most people have no understanding of what specifically they are doing that preempts them from meeting interpersonal needs. When members hear observations of their behaviors, they become aware of these behaviors. With awareness, members can choose to use a behavior and observe for themselves how others react. If the reaction is undesirable, they can choose to experiment with different behaviors.

Leaders can share observations when a member is being silent about a noticeable reaction they are having and when a member appears to be disengaged. Observations should be simple statements that avoid overinterpreting a members' behaviors. The observation "Ben, you're wrinkling your brow and setting your jaw. It looks like you're having a reaction to what Darby just said" avoids overinterpretation of a member's behaviors. Conversely, the observation "Ben, you're wrinkling your brow and setting your jaw. It looks like you're really taking offense with what Darby just said" is an overinterpretation. Although overinterpretation should be avoided, leaders should include empathically generated statements about the feelings a member appears to be experiencing in observations, such as "Pam, you're wrinkling your brow and setting your jaw. You look angry."

Leaders sharing observations of members' interactions helps members develop more effective interpersonal behaviors. By sharing an interaction observation, leaders identify potential relationship issues and can initiate experimentation with alternative relationship behaviors. Interpersonal observations should contain an objective description of what leaders have seen or heard. This snapshot of interaction includes the identification of specific verbal and nonverbal behaviors. The following are examples of some interpersonal observations:

Leader: "Jamel, when you respond to the suggestions everyone is giving you, you start with, 'Yes, but.'" (*Observation of verbal behavior*)

Leader: "Auna, when you waved your finger in Bernie's face, they jumped back." (*Observation of behavior and consequence*)

Leader: "David, after you said, 'I don't care what you say,' several group members sat back in their chairs." (*Observation of verbal behavior and consequence*)

Leaders should also promote observation as a membership skill. When members share observations of each other's behaviors, all members increase their potential for learning. In addition, observation is an essential aspect of feedback exchange. Effective feedback, like effective group leader use of observation, includes a description of specific behaviors or words and consequences so that feedback receivers can understand what they are doing that leads to others' reactions. Thus, leaders should look for opportunities to involve members in sharing their observations:

Leader: "I'm going to ask everyone to hold on for a second. Group, what exactly do you see going on in River and Auna's discussion?"

As members share observations, leaders should help or coach members to offer specific and objective observations. Members should understand that observations are not interpretations of the meaning or intention of a member's verbal or nonverbal behaviors. Interpretations presented as observations commonly produce defensive reactions. The following examples compare an objective observation and an interpretation offered as an observation:

Emma: "You're trying to scare other members." (*Interpretation*)
Emma: "You're shaking your fist and talking very loudly." (*Observation of verbal and nonverbal behavior*)

Observations of the group as a system are an important foundation for several types of interventions. The simplest form of group observation increases the group's awareness of how it interacts. Observations can also identify counterproductive or productive group norms. Finally, observations of group interactions can initiate languaging. Following are some examples:

Leader: "Whenever the topic of expressing emotions comes up, every member leans back in their chair and looks at the floor." (*Observation to increase awareness of interactions*)
Leader: "It seems like whenever conversation becomes intense, someone changes the subject, and the rest of the group goes with them." (*Observation of a limiting group norm*)
Leader: "The group seems to be learning something very important right now. What do each of you think it is?" (*Observation and invitation to language*)

The Basic Facilitation Sequence

The *basic facilitation sequence* is the most basic intervention or series of skills. It is designed to draw group members out to engage with each other and shift interaction from the individual to the interpersonal level. This sequence follows a simple and easy-to-remember progression.

1. *Elicit*: The leader uses a listening skill to elicit a member's sharing about a current or recent group interaction.
2. *Clarify*: If needed, the leader uses a question or a statement to clarify the cognitive and emotional content of what the member said.
3. *Connect*: The leader then uses a question or statement to generate member-to-member interaction if other members do not respond on their own.

The basic facilitation sequence invites interaction. However, members frequently will feel less anxiety addressing the leader instead of each other. In these cases, leaders must add a fourth step to the facilitation sequence, a directive. The directive redirects interaction so that members speak with each other.

Examples of the basic facilitation sequence follow. The first example shows an elicit and connect sequence, and the second shows an elicit, clarify, connect, and redirect sequence.

Example 1
Leader: "Chandra, you look very angry. What's going on?" (*Elicit*)
Chandra: "I'm really annoyed with Gordon."
Leader: "Tell Gordon what you're annoyed about." (*Connect*)

Example 2
Leader: "River, I can see you're having a reaction you're not sharing." (*Elicit*)
River: "Something just happened that really bothers me."
Leader: (*Gesturing to the whole group*) "Tell us what you're reacting to." (*Clarify and connect*)
River: (*Speaking to the leader*) "Chandra just gave Gordon some feedback that I don't buy."
Leader: "River, you need to be saying this to Chandra. Tell Chandra." (*Redirect*)

These examples show how individually directed interventions are transformed into interpersonal exchanges using the basic facilitation sequence. Member-to-member interaction should be the goal for all individually focused interventions and skills.

Bridging

Bridging (Ormont, 1990) is an interpersonal intervention that leaders use to establish and develop emotional connections between members. In much the same way as the basic facilitation sequence, bridging should be used whenever members do not spontaneously connect with one another. Although bridging is useful throughout the life of a group, it is especially important during the initial stages of group development. During the early stages of group, bridging has the goal of establishing member-to-member interaction and connecting as norms.

Leaders use bridging at its most basic level to involve and connect members who share issues, thoughts, emotional reactions, defenses, or perspectives on interaction. A more sophisticated use of bridging involves identifying an underlying theme of group interaction and drawing all group members into a discussion of how they are impacted by the theme. Creating a bridge between members requires initiating a conversation between them about what they share in the here and now. Ideally, bridging eventually involves all group members with each other (Ormont, 1990). Ormont (1990) described three basic forms of bridging: (a) open bridge, (b) directed bridge, and (c) bridging about an interaction.

Open Bridge

An *open bridge* is an open-ended request for a member's reaction to a group event. This is the lowest intensity type of bridge. This type of bridge does not pursue a specific topic; instead, it opens interaction to new topics. For example:

Leader: "River, what do you think is going on with David?"

This question creates a bridge between River and David and raises other members' awareness of both River's and David's reactions. Ormont (1990) pointed out that the member responding to this bridge is revealing their own feelings as well as the feelings of the person to whom they are reacting.

Directed Bridge

Unlike an open bridge, which does not pursue a specific topic, a *directed bridge* specifies the topic of the bridge. Directed bridges are somewhat more intense than open bridges because they use more power and aim to purposefully move interaction toward issues that are significant to members. For example:

Leader: "Jamel, do you see that Auna is angry about what you just said to her?"

This bridging question is presented to Jamel for several reasons. These include bringing Auna's feelings into the group's awareness, helping Jamel to create a bridge with Auna, and involving Jamel in an interaction that can increase their sensitivity to the effects of their communication.

Bridging About an Interaction

Bridging about an interaction involves drawing out a group member's observations and perceptions to help other members become more aware of their interactions. This can be a lower or higher intensity intervention, depending on the centrality of the issue and the directness of the bridge. Following are examples of lower and higher intensity bridges with Gordon, the group member introduced in Chapter 4:

Leader: "Gordon, what do you see going on between River and Jamel?"

Leader: "Gordon, how are River and Jamel struggling to work through conflict affecting you? What do you feel and believe about this?"

In these examples, Gordon was asked these bridging questions because their earlier interactions had demonstrated similar issues. By including a member who has had similar experiences, the leader increases the impact and depth of the bridge. In these examples, Gordon can share experiences and how they perceived the issue being experienced by River and Jamel. Any member who observes an interaction can be involved in this type of bridge, with an intention to open interaction to a broad range of reactions. This form of bridging is also useful in identifying and resolving relationship issues.

It may be necessary to employ the basic facilitation sequence (i.e., elicit, clarify, and connect) when using bridging questions.

This sequence is useful when clarification of a member's response to a bridging question is needed or when it is necessary to redirect a member's response. The following examples depict how bridging can be used in conjunction with the basic facilitation sequence:

Chandra: "I am really scared to talk about my feelings in here. I'm just not used to sharing my feelings with anybody."
Leader: "Bernie, I noticed that while Chandra was talking, you were nodding as if you were agreeing with her about how hard it is to share feelings." (*Observation and directed bridge*)
Bernie: (*Speaking to the leader*) "I know exactly what she . . ."
Leader: (*Interrupting*) "Bernie, can you speak directly to Chandra?" (*Redirect*)
Bernie: "OK. Chandra, I know exactly what you mean. I'm not used to sharing my feelings, either. It scares the sh— out of me."

At this point, the leader has several options: (a) wait to see what develops between Chandra and Bernie, (b) direct Chandra and Bernie to talk more about their shared fear, or (c) bridge to other members. If the leader sees others reacting nonverbally, the leader can follow up if Chandra and Bernie become bogged down. Following is an example:

Leader: "I'm seeing other members reacting to what Chandra and Bernie are saying about being afraid to share their feelings. Who would like to share the feelings you experience when you think about sharing feelings in here?" (*Observation and directed bridge*)

Another common application of bridging involves connecting members who have shared consistent reactions or similar concerns during the life of the group. This is a powerful way to connect members who can use each other's support:

David: "I am really uncomfortable with having to share my feelings when I give feedback. It really shouldn't be that important."
Leader: "Gordon, you shared this same concern last week. Tell David where you are with that now." (*Directed bridge and connect*)

If the leader is interested in expanding on David's concern and hearing the reactions of other group members to what David has said, the leader can bridge to another member. This intervention can be repeated to generate the participation of additional members whenever desired:

> *Leader*: "Auna, what are your reactions to what David has said?" (*Open bridge*)

Leaders can also bridge to the entire group by not selecting a particular member. When bridging to the group, the leader gives members the choice to share or not share. This approach is useful when the leader believes that identifying a specific member for the bridge will create too much anxiety. The risk in presenting this type of group-level bridge is that no one will respond:

> *Leader*: "I'm wondering who would like to talk about how uncomfortable it is to talk about being sexually attracted to another member." (*Directed bridge to group*)

If group members do not respond to a directed bridge or if the leader believes that sharing is unlikely, a direction to share can be used to involve members who seem to be having the strongest reactions to the interaction:

> *Leader*: "Gordon, you look like you're having a very strong reaction to Chandra and Bernie's conversation. Share with them what's going on with you." (*Open bridge and connect*)

Despite their valuable nature, bridges can also be misused. Ormont (1990) discussed uses of bridging that impede interaction. First, bridging is an inappropriate way for leaders to avoid being challenged. Second, leaders should avoid bridging to a member who is not likely to share useful emotions or reactions. Finally, when several members are interacting meaningfully and including other members in the interaction, additional bridging would be distracting.

Confrontation

Confrontation as an intervention is a variation of observing. It can be used as an individual, interpersonal, or group-as-a-system intervention. *Confrontation* involves observing discrepancies in members' behaviors. Young (1992) described five areas of incongruence that can serve as the foundation of appropriate confrontation. These are as follows:

- When incongruities exist between verbal and nonverbal behaviors (e.g., member talks about being sad with a smile)
- When a member's self-perception differs from the perceptions of others (e.g., a member's self-description of being an unacceptable person when others admire and like the member)
- When what a member says they will do is inconsistent with what they do (e.g., a member says they will participate more frequently but remains withdrawn)
- When what a member wants is incompatible with the reality of their concern and their history (e.g., a member wants to have an intimate committed relationship when they are closed to others' input and have a history of failed relationships)
- When one of a member's verbal messages contradicts another (e.g., a member says they want feedback, then says they are not interested in others' perceptions)

Because of their intensity, confrontations can be powerful tools that initiate change, or they can elicit defensive reactions. Carroll et al. (1997) and Donigian and Malnati (1997) agreed that group leaders' intentions and attitudes while confronting members largely determine the impact of the confrontation. A confrontation offered with respect, care, and sensitivity is more likely to be effective than a confrontation made in anger with the intention of demeaning. The latter is likely to elicit a defensive and potentially harmful reaction.

Confrontations have the goal of increasing awareness and initiating change. Change resulting from confrontation involves a member becoming aware of their inconsistencies and learning to develop more consistent words and actions. This change helps a member become more congruent and communicate more honestly in relationships. Members who change successfully in response to confrontation will often hear that others perceive them as becoming more honest and trustworthy as a result. This change in perception is related to members losing the trust of other group members because of their inconsistencies.

As with most interventions, leaders should make confrontations with the eventual goal of member-to-member interaction. Usually, this means that confronting a member should lead to feedback exchange. After a confrontation, the reactions of the member receiving the confrontation should be elicited and clarified. Then other members should be invited to offer feedback. The following dialogue illustrates this sequence:

Leader: "Emma, you say you are bored, and you aren't happy with what you're getting out of group. It worries me that that's your experience. At the same time, I notice that you haven't participated very much and, when asked, say you prefer sitting back and watching." (*Confrontation of inconsistency of words and actions*)

Emma: "But, I am bored."

Leader: "You're bored, but you prefer sitting back and watching?" (*Reiteration of earlier confrontation*)

Emma: "I see what you mean. I'm kind of boring myself."

Leader: "As a way to start being 'unbored,' would you like to get some feedback about how other members are reacting to you?" (*Confirm openness to initiation of feedback exchange*)

Emma: "Umm . . . I'd rather—wait, OK. I'll give getting feedback a try."

Leader: "I saw several of you reacting to the conversation Emma and I were having. Emma wants to experiment with getting some feedback. Can someone share their reactions with her?" (*Observation and question to initiate feedback exchange*)

Interpersonal confrontation also involves the observation of the destructive interaction patterns that choreograph many relationships. Relationship issues involve all parties concerned, not just the members who may appear to be the victim or the cause of the problem. For example, a member who manipulates another member first needs to find another member who is willing to be manipulated. If this is a pattern for either group member, bringing this dynamic to their attention may spur productive change for both.

For example, Grace tells Evan, "Evan, I really vibe with you here in group. I really connected deeply when you shared about how you feel powerless when others are really sad in here. I'd really like to hear more." Evan responds by sharing more about his current feelings and how they connect to his painful childhood being raised by an aunt who struggled with alcoholism. Grace then criticizes Evan for being "sexist and ableist." Later, Grace repeats her request; Evan complies and is hurt again. In this example, Grace could easily be described as the "bad guy" and Evan as the victim. However, it is important to note that Evan willingly complies, although he will be hurt again. This pattern, much like other interpersonal patterns, recycles. Even leaders who are experienced and knowledgeable about destructive relationship patterns may not identify these patterns until they have been repeated several times. Confrontation of both members is indicated when a sadomascchistic setup is identified. These confrontations initiate ongoing feedback and experimentation with alternative behaviors. Either of the following confrontations might be used:

> *Leader*: "Evan, you complain that Grace is hurting you, and at the same time, you continue to volunteer yourself to get hurt. She asks you to open up, you do, and you get criticized."
>
> *Leader*: "Grace, you tell Evan you want to be close to him and ask him to be more open to you. When he does, your words label and reject him. You ask for vulnerability, then find a way to reject what he shares."

Interpersonal confrontations should use the same skills and conditions that lead to effective individual confrontations. As is the case with individually directed confrontation, interpersonal confrontation uses observations that identify contradictions and discrepancies in actions and words. Leaders should remember that a goal of confrontation is to initiate behavior change. Confrontations that result in defensive behaviors are not useful, whereas those offered with respect and sensitivity are most likely to succeed.

Leaders should also encourage group members to use confrontations when appropriate. Encouraging this opens more pathways for members to interact and participate in each other's growth. As members begin to use confrontations, however, leaders should strongly monitor their use. Confrontations that attack or are not sensitive to the reactions of the member receiving the confrontation should be preempted. Helping members learn how to make caring and sensitive confrontations is an important goal for group interaction and ultimately an effective relationship skill.

Challenges

Whereas confrontations draw attention to current ineffective behaviors or relationships, challenges are forward-looking and meant to motivate. Challenges focus on encouraging members to use new interpersonal behaviors, such as engaging in boundary-opening self-disclosures designed to increase the intimacy in relationships. Challenges, although related to directives, differ because they offer members a choice about taking risks and trying new behaviors. Challenges vary in intensity, from low-intensity comments that merely suggest experimental behaviors to high-intensity direct comments that strongly recommend experimental behaviors. Leaders vary the intensity of their challenges based on the amount of anxiety they want a challenge to create and how much anxiety the member or group can manage.

Because challenges direct members to interact, they usually do not require a follow-up connecting or eliciting intervention. These are needed only when members do not respond to a challenge. Before challenging a member, leaders should clarify that members are in charge of choosing how they interact. A challenge should always be presented as a choice, and members should not be pressured or coerced into performing challenges. However, leaders should follow up with questions or directions that explore members' choices.

Challenges that promote experimentation with new behaviors can be implemented by leaders following feedback exchanges or confrontations, or they can be generated by leaders in the absence of feedback exchanges and confrontations as an invitation to experiment with new behaviors. Following are examples of both situations:

Leader: "Emma, you just got some feedback that suggested how you can look angry when you feel angry. You seem to be really annoyed with Grace. If you feel ready, you can try that out now." (*Challenge as feedback follow-up*)

Leader: "Evan, if you're interested, I'd like you to try an experiment. Here it is. Whenever you hear another member indicate they expect you to agree with them without question, try saying something like, 'I think for myself. You need to give me a good reason why I should agree with you.'" (*Leader-generated challenge*)

Challenges that encourage risk-taking can also follow a confrontation or feedback exchange or be initiated as a leader-generated experiment. The goal of risk-taking challenges is to increase members' involvement in their relationships. This is an intentional way to influence members to open their interpersonal boundaries and abandon habitual solutions that keep members isolated. Following are a few examples of risk-taking challenges:

Leader: "River, you might find this experiment useful. If you want, you can try it a couple of times tonight and let us know how it works. Here it is. When you hear someone say something and you feel even a little sad, say to that member, 'I felt sad when I heard you say that.'"

Leader: "Jamel, when you have a strong reaction to what another member says, I'd like you to try something different from being silent. If you're up for it, I'd like you to say, 'I'm really reacting strongly to what you're saying, but I don't understand how I feel. I'd like you to give me some feedback that might help me understand better.'"

Leader: "Bernie, you and River haven't connected much with each other yet. The two of you have not really interacted at all. Here's an experiment I'd like you to try, if you're willing. During the next three sessions, observe each other from time to time. When you have any kind of reaction, share it. Or, better yet, share some feedback. I'd like each of you to do this at least twice a session." (*Leader challenge to try a boundary-opening experiment*)

Challenges directed at the group as a system are the same in form and content and are directed at the entire group. These challenges occur for the same reasons as those directed at individual members or relationships. Group-directed challenges encourage the group to experiment with different norms or different communication boundaries. See the more complicated intervention strategies in Chapter 11.

Leaders should experiment with challenges to find an approach that works best for them. Some leaders believe they need to offer a rationale for their challenges. Other leaders prefer not to share a rationale. Instead, they might tell the member who is being challenged to try the experiment a few times and then to share what they have discovered in the process. Leaders should also consider that challenges can create anxiety, and group members should experience these experiments as a choice. Group interactions are meant to expand group members' array of responses and actions. However, members will vary individually—as influenced by experiences, personality, culture, and positionality—in what works and is growth producing for them. Particularly in the case of challenges, group leaders should be cognizant that culture, social identity, and power distribution in the group may leave some group members less empowered to choose.

Communication Clarification

Another intervention useful to many groups is communication clarification. Leaders use communication clarification when members' interactions demonstrate communication problems. As described in Chapter 9, communication problems include bypassing, inference making, polarizing, and signal reactions (Tubbs, 1992). The objectives for communication clarification are to clarify members' intended messages and to ensure understanding. Improving communication has important implications for the effectiveness of member interaction. Most critically, communication clarification supports the usefulness and potency of feedback exchange.

Communication clarification interventions can include observations, listening skills, directives, and feedback exchanges. Communication clarification is a process that begins by stopping interaction that evidences a communication problem and continues by describing the observed communication problem. This intervention then concludes with the leader directing and supporting members to use more effective communication skills.

Leaders can involve members in this process by stopping an interaction that demonstrates a communication problem and asking members to share their observations of the interaction. This approach supports previous interventions designed to develop communication skills and involves members in monitoring each other's communication skills. A variation of this intervention involves interrupting an interaction that has communication problems and directing members to give the interacting members feedback about how they have been communicating. Ultimately, leaders should closely monitor members who are involved in the process and support them until communication is clarified and new communication behaviors are identified and used.

Leaders should ensure that members receiving feedback about communication problems learn more effective communication behaviors to use in their interactions. Once the interacting members have defined more effective communication behaviors, these behaviors should be used immediately. This process involves three steps. First, the leader directs the interacting members to repeat their interactions, this time using effective communication behaviors. Second, the leader asks the interacting members to discuss their experience using the communication behaviors. Last, the leader directs the group to offer feedback on the communication behaviors, as shown in this example:

Leader: "Gordon, you and Jamel have been having some problems communicating with each other. The two of you were given feedback that you might try something new, repeating what you heard the other one say before you respond. As I recall, your disagreement started while sharing the feelings you were having about other members in here. Why not start over? This time try to use the feedback you got." (*Summary and direction to experiment with alternative behaviors*)

After Gordon and Jamel experiment with the alternative behaviors, the leader makes a suggestion.

Leader: "Jamel and Gordon, how did repeating what the other said work for you?" (*Question to elicit reactions*)

Jamel and Gordon share reactions, after which the leader directs them to interact with each other briefly about their experience with each other when trying out the new behaviors. Then, the leader turns to the group.

Leader: "Group, what feedback do you have for Jamel and Gordon?" (*Question to initiate feedback exchange and bridge*)

Another application of communication clarification involves improving a member's ability to communicate effectively. Although this is an individually focused intervention, its intent is to improve interpersonal relationships. When members demonstrate a pattern of communication problems, leaders can offer feedback or direct the group to offer feedback that identifies the problematic communication behaviors and supports developing effective communication skills. Similarly, communication clarification interventions directed at the group as a system have the goals of improving the communication skills of the entire group and developing groupwide facilitative communication norms, as shown in the following example:

Leader: "You know, I've noticed that as we've gotten into some more intense and emotional interactions, communication kind of falls apart. What have you all observed?"

Several members identify examples of poor listening skills.

Leader: "How can you all help each other when this happens again?"

Contracting

Contracting as an interpersonal intervention is an agreement, usually between two members, that specifies an experimental behavior, an interaction to promote that behavior, and the circumstances in which it is to be applied. Contracting can involve more than two members, or even the entire group. It can be used to follow up a feedback exchange, confrontation, challenge, communication clarification, or any other intervention that addresses the relationship behaviors of the contracting members. Contracting involves members in helping each other change. Contracting distributes responsibility for monitoring how members progress toward their goals and helps build norms that establish a shared responsibility for change. This, in turn, increases members' involvement in interpersonal learning. Contracting engages members and helps to establish how members can assist each other and open interpersonal boundaries.

Contracting provides several useful support functions. It helps members follow through when attempting to develop new interactive skills. Contracting can involve members who effectively manage their boundaries in helping members who have difficulty managing their boundaries. Thus, members can learn more effective boundary management skills from each other. In addition, contracting can assist in the ongoing monitoring of members' behaviors.

Contracting is very useful when several members are working on developing the same behaviors. When they contract with members to encourage each other to use a behavior, leaders do not have to monitor these members as closely. At the same time, the contracted members get to experience offering and receiving support. In addition, when members monitor each other's behaviors and continuing experimentation, they become more personally responsible for their changes and less reactive than they would if monitoring were left only to the leader.

Leaders initiate contracts by identifying or acknowledging a member's goals. Once goals are described, the leader asks the members involved whether they would like help in achieving their goals. As several members assent to helping each other meet the goals, a group agreement is developed. Leaders can promote this process by suggesting that mutual support might increase members' chances of reaching their goals. Contracts should be clear and uncomplicated. Leaders should avoid developing contracts that involve multiple behaviors or complicated sets of circumstances in which to perform the contract.

Contracts are agreements between members to provide support for ongoing experimentation, to remind each other to use experimental behaviors, or to encourage risk-taking. These ongoing agreements can involve members who are skilled in using a particular behavior helping other members become proficient with that behavior. Contracts can also challenge members to use experimental behaviors when it is uncomfortable to do so.

The following example illustrates how a leader can initiate a contract after feedback exchange:

Leader: "Bernie, it seems as if you've decided that, sometimes, it might be useful for you to close your boundaries when Auna struggles with her feelings. Did I get that right?" (*Summary and question to ensure understanding*)

Bernie: "Yeah, I think I need to sit back and let her have her feelings and not try to 'fix' how she feels. I feel so guilty when she's hurting. I just imagine that guilt eating me up."

Leader: "Would you like some help with that?" (*A question that invites the initiation of a contract*)

Bernie: "I could use all the help I can get."

Leader: "Who do you think can help you best? This would be a person who can reliably let you know when it's time to sit back. Now ask." (*Direction, contract initiation, and connect*)

Bernie: "Jamel, can you help me out? You seem like you can let people have their feelings. And you're great at observing what's going on."

Jamel: "Sure, Bernie, what can I do?"

Leader: "Tell Jamel exactly how you want him to help you out." (*Direction to ensure understanding*)

Bernie: "Jamel, just tell me to 'chill' when Auna is talking about her feelings. Look my way and tell me to chill if I look like I'm ready to get in her business."

Contracting involves the leader more intensely when the leader directs another person to offer help and specifies the help to offer. This strategic move is used to involve two members who are closed to each other or to ensure that a member who will follow through with a contract is involved. A variation here would be to ask Bernie to develop a contract with the entire group. There are many ways to develop and initiate contracts. The essential components of contracts and their initiation are specific behaviors and clear agreements between members about when and how they will support each other's changes. Leaders, as they experiment with using contracts, will find many strategic uses and diverse ways to initiate and shape interpersonal and group-as-a-system contracts.

Steps for developing interpersonal contracts are as follows:

1. The leader initiates the contracting process by asking the member or members (in the case of a relationship-focused intervention) whether they are willing to continue the use of new interpersonal behaviors.

2. If the member or members agree to continue, the leader asks whether they would like some assistance in continuing the use of the behaviors. Often, it is useful to frame this step as an inquiry about whether a member or members would like to receive support from other members in continuing to develop new ways of interacting in the group.
3. If the member or members are willing to receive support or help to continue the use of the new interpersonal behaviors, the leader initiates the contract.
4. To initiate the contract, the leader secures an agreement with other group members or a particular member to participate in the contract. This agreement involves making a commitment to remind and encourage the member or members developing the new behavior to use the new behavior whenever it is useful. One way of doing this is to ask the member or members using the new behaviors to identify a member they would like to ask to serve as their support person.

Boundary Setting

Boundary setting is a specific set of interventions that helps leaders perform their boundary management function (see Chapter 7). These interventions involve helping members define their communication and relationship boundaries and move toward more autonomous functioning and choices that help them engage in more fulfilling relationships. Autonomous functioning can be viewed as making informed and empowered relationship choices. Boundary-setting interventions are designed to help members make better choices about when and how much to open or close their boundaries.

Boundary-Opening Interventions

Boundary-opening interventions are those intended to help group members who are in some way closed off become more receptive, open, and emotionally available. They are helpful for members who have boundaries that are not permeable enough to develop and support healthy relationships. Impermeable boundaries can also limit how these members benefit from interpersonal learning. Boundary-opening interventions encourage behaviors such as expressing emotion, self-disclosing appropriate personal information, asking for and using feedback, giving effective feedback, sharing reactions, expressing concern for other members, and offering and asking for interpersonal support. Boundary-opening interventions require the leader to use observations and confrontations to increase member awareness, exploratory listening skills to engage closed members with others, and directives and challenges to initiate behavior change. An example of a boundary-opening intervention follows:

Leader: "Gordon, you haven't shared much and haven't asked for any feedback." (*Observation*)
Gordon: "Your point is?"
Leader: "I get that you'd like me to leave you alone. At the same time, you appear vulnerable and sound angry." (*Confrontation and attempt to invite disclosure*)
Gordon: "What of it?"
Leader: "Gordon, I'm not going anywhere, even though you want me to back off. I'd really like to know what's scaring you so much." (*Listening skill to explore reaction and invite interaction*)
Gordon: "Leave me alone. This is making me really uncomfortable."
Leader: (*Speaking to the group*) "I wonder what the rest of you are noticing here?"

The leader invites group interaction to keep others engaged and possibly to bridge with Gordon.

Jamel: "I know what it's like to be scared to share what's going on with me. Gordon, the only way to make it easier is doing it and finding out you can survive."
Gordon: "I am getting really mad now . . ."
Leader: (*Interrupting*) "Gordon, you look scared and sad, not mad." (*Confrontation*)
Gordon: "This is stupid. What if what I feel is wrong? And everyone gets mad? Now that I say that, it sounds f'd up. Maybe I do need some help with it."
Leader: "Gordon, I've got an experiment that could help. The experiment is to notice when you have an emotional reaction to anyone in the group and to make a feeling statement to the member right then. Just try it once. Anybody want to help Gordon with their experiment?" (*Challenge to use a boundary-opening behavior and invitation for a support contract*)

This example shows how a leader could challenge a member with closed boundaries to be more open. The use of a challenge and the invitation for a support contract reflect the leader's sense of the member's fearfulness about trying on a very uncomfortable behavior. In many cases, members with rigidly closed boundaries are very resistant to boundary-opening interventions. These members require patience and will become engaged in interaction only after they have built significant trust in the group and become less fearful about being vulnerable. These members' issues can amplify trust issues in the entire group, and they have great potential for becoming scapegoats.

Boundary-Closing Interventions

Boundary-closing interventions are intended to help members who demonstrate excessively open boundaries develop behaviors that support personal autonomy and make informed and empowered choices about their relationship behaviors. Members with diffuse boundaries may seem overly concerned about others' feelings, struggle with taking responsibility for their own emotions, seem overly compliant, and may persistently try to gain approval. Some boundary-closing behaviors members can experiment with include allowing others to experience intense emotions, stating opinions that are different from others' opinions, expressing anger, and saying "no" to requests. Boundary-closing interventions utilize listening skills, observations, confrontations, challenges, and directives. Exploratory listening skills engage members with diffuse boundaries in dialogue about their behavior. The following is an example of a boundary-closing intervention:

Leader: "Chandra, whenever another member starts to share their feelings, you jump right in. You change the subject or tell the person not to get upset." (*Observation*)

Chandra: (*Speaking to the leader*) "That's so overwhelming. It's like you're mad at me. . . . What did I do to make you mad? Tell me so I can stop it."

Leader: "You think I'm upset with you now, and you want to make me happy so you won't have to be scared." (*Immediacy*)

Chandra: "Yes, yes, I am. You're so present. I wish I could be more like you."

Leader: "I want you to do an experiment. I know you will because you want to be a good group member. Here it is. Disagree with me now and disagree three more times with other group members during this session." (*Direction*)

In this example, the leader uses the member's need to please as leverage to involve a member with diffuse boundaries in a boundary-closing experiment. Disagreeing is boundary-closing because it defines a member's opinion and differentiates that member from others.

Requesting Input

Requesting input is an intervention that assists the leader by generating and substantiating information about the group, empowers group members by valuing their perspectives, and shifts some responsibility for the group to group members. Leaders request input by asking questions, seeking suggestions for alternative behaviors and problem-solving ideas, and encouraging sharing of personal experiences that relate to the current situation. This information can facilitate progress and collaboration within the team. Other examples include asking or directing members to share group culture or norms with a new member, to describe their experiences with experimental behaviors outside the group, or to describe their experience with a shared concern.

When asking members for informational input, leaders should be cautious. Asking for information directs the group into cognitive conversation and may lead the group away from meaningful, emotionally engaged interaction. Thus, leaders should request information only when it can contribute to group empowerment and autonomy. In addition, after requesting input, leaders should be prepared to quickly direct members back to the here and now. The following are examples of leader statements that elicit information:

Leader: "Emma, I'd like you all to share with Garret what's expected from members in this group—the expectations you have for each other and how we go about learning in here."

Leader: "Gordon, you were going to try on some different relationship behaviors after our last session. Could you share how they worked for you?"

Leader: "Chandra, you have been working on making some changes that are very similar to those Bernie has just started to face. Would you share with them what it has been like for you?"

Requesting input can generate possible approaches to conflict management or potential solutions for problem-solving. In terms of managing conflict, this intervention is appropriate when members are involved in nonproductive conflict, which occurs when there is an impasse in interaction that consists of a repeated argument that covers the same issues. When leaders observe that conflicts between members are becoming unproductive, they can intervene with a request for input. This intervention involves the use of an observation and a directive or question, such as in the following example:

Leader: (*Interrupting and looking at the group*) "Auna and River seem to be covering the same issues repeatedly. They seem frustrated, as do the rest of you. I'm wondering if any of you have ideas about different ways that they can approach their disagreement." (*Observation and request for input*)

The most useful application for requesting input follows feedback exchange. When a member has received feedback but has not identified an experimental behavior, the leader can follow the feedback exchange with a request for input. This follow-up involves asking or directing specific members or the entire group to generate ideas for experimental behaviors, as in this example:

Leader: "What ideas for new behaviors do you all have for Gordon to try?" (*Question requesting input*)

Structuring

Structuring interventions are the specific actions leaders use to perform the structuring function (see Chapter 7). Structuring shapes the interaction of group members and uses observations and directives. Observations about interaction and directives to reshape interaction are the basic structuring sequence. Structuring is used to teach feedback and communication skills as well as to manage interpersonal or group interaction. Managing group interaction can influence interactive norms or control chaotic interaction. Structuring interpersonal interaction is a management tool intended to ensure understanding, maximize learning and change, and minimize chances for harm. The following examples illustrate how leaders can initiate structuring interventions:

Leader: "Wow! You folks are really engaged and feeling some intense emotions. I'm having a hard time understanding what's going on, though, because we have a lot of talking over each other. I'd like you to speak one at a time so each of you can be heard." (*Observation and direction*)

Leader: "River, your feedback didn't include exactly what Emma was doing that you reacted so strongly to. Restate your feedback and include exactly what Emma was doing." (*Observation and direction*)

Once members have finished participating in structured interactions, leaders should direct the interacting members to discuss or process their experiences. This reaction-sharing phase can highlight what worked in the structured interaction. This phrase starts with a directive. A directive to share reactions often leads to languaging about what has worked in the interaction, as in this example:

Leader: "Emma, River included some specific behaviors in their feedback to you. Tell us about how those worked for you." (*Observation and direction*)

Emma: "When they told me the specific things that I was doing, I didn't feel attacked. I felt a little ashamed, but at least I knew what I did that got them upset."

Leader: (*Speaking to the group*) "What happened here that was helpful for Emma?" (*Question to initiate languaging*)

When Basic Skills and Interventions Do Not Work

Leaders should question the effectiveness of skills and interventions that are not successful. Besides poor timing, there are several reasons why interventions may be ineffective. A common reason is inaccurate diagnosis of interactive problems in the group. Interventions can also be ineffective because they fail to address or appreciate members' fears. Leaders who have not accurately identified focal conflicts or boundary issues or defined members' shared fears may continue to intervene using ineffective interventions with the same negative results. When these persistent interventions are based on an inaccurate assessment of group issues, leaders often become increasingly baffled about why the group is not cooperating.

When leaders are uncertain about why their interventions are ineffective, they need to examine and reassess the goals of their interventions. Occasionally, leaders can experiment with not intervening as a method to understand more accurately what is occurring in the group. Not intervening when intervention is apparently called for is an excellent diagnostic tool, especially for beginning leaders, who are often overwhelmed by the complexity of their role.

Not intervening allows leaders to observe interaction and more clearly define existing norms and their impact on interaction. By not intervening, leaders can also gain a better idea of what members' motivations are for not responding to an intervention. Withholding interventions allows leaders an opportunity to diagnose focal conflicts or to determine whether the group has become overly dependent. Not intervening encourages members to assume more responsibility for group interaction and norm development and maintenance. Leaders who choose not to intervene to diagnose interaction should be careful. This diagnostic process does not release leaders from their responsibilities.

Ultimately, persistent misdiagnosis of interactive problems or misperceptions of group members' fears may stem from two causes. The first is lack of knowledge about group interaction or issues faced by group members that may affect group interaction. For example, leaders may not understand a group theory, such as focal conflict theory or systems theory, well enough for it to be of use them, or they may not have sufficient multicultural counseling knowledge or skills to work meaningfully with diverse group members. The second is leaders' own interpersonal patterns and distorted perceptions disabling effective diagnosis of group interactive problems and addressing of members' fears. For example, group leaders may habitually avoid emotion or underestimate their power and privilege in group. These issues may be addressed through training and supervision but may require the leader to do personal work via therapy or group counseling in the case of leaders' interpersonal patterns.

Conclusion

The skills and interventions presented in this chapter are fundamental for facilitating interactive groups. Whenever leaders use these skills and interventions, they must maintain awareness that their goal is for members to interact and learn from one another. Group leaders' most fundamental responses to group interaction are basic skills or simple actions designed to focus members and to facilitate effective interaction. They may also engage in a series of skills in sequence or basic intervention to highlight a useful issue within and process that issue. Leaders should enact basic skills and interventions with consideration given to intervention objective, intervention level, timing, balance, and intensity. These fundamental skills and interventions are needed for leaders to perform their ongoing tasks and responsibilities. The ongoing tasks of leaders and strategies for dealing with problems in group interaction are discussed in the remaining chapters of this part.

Chapter 9

Developing Effective Group Membership Skills

Outcomes

Level 1 Outcomes

After reading this chapter, entry-level students and practitioners should be able to:

1. Outline the membership skills necessary for effective group functioning and interpersonal learning.
2. Outline how to teach members to be interculturally aware and self-sufficient.
3. Explain how to identify effective and ineffective group membership behavior.
4. Describe effective and ineffective forms of self-disclosure and their impact on the group membership experience.
5. Outline the necessary components of effective feedback exchange and experimentation.
6. Explain how to teach and structure feedback exchange.
7. Discuss how to initiate and monitor experimentation with new membership behavior.

Level 2 Outcomes

After reading this chapter, advanced-level students and practitioners should also be able to:

1. Describe how leader understanding of effective membership and communication skills can help guide interventions that are culturally responsive and encourage the success of all group members, irrespective of their identities or social and cultural backgrounds.
2. Describe and model through specific examples how leaders can teach effective communication skills within the group.
3. Describe and model through specific examples how members can engage in effective feedback exchange, self-disclosure, and experimentation through specific skill acquisition and demonstration processes.
4. Describe the assumptions and interventions that derive from monolingual cultures and how to modify them in order to be effective with multilingual group members.

Learning how to interact effectively is critical for members of groups that emphasize interpersonal learning. The effectiveness of members' interactions depends on the development of several essential membership skills. As members develop these membership skills, leaders will observe that the frequency and quality of members' learning increases. These skills include effective interpersonal communication skills, self-disclosure, feedback exchange, and experimentation.

Because members need to have certain skills to benefit from interpersonal learning processes, leaders have the goal of helping members become skilled interpersonal learners. As members become skilled, they become increasingly interculturally aware and self-sufficient and can learn with increasingly less active leader intervention. Being interculturally aware involves members demonstrating understanding of their own cultural values, beliefs, and behavior as well as understanding those of fellow group members. Intercultural awareness in a group is demonstrated through patience, understanding, and respect for fellow group members who communicate differently (e.g., choice of language, words, expressions) and have different values and boundaries around personal self-disclosure. Being self-sufficient, on the other hand, involves demonstrating autonomy in initiating interactions and responding appropriately to fellow group members. As members become interculturally aware and self-sufficient, leaders can attend more fully to observing interaction dynamics, shared concerns, and impediments to group development. These observations are the basis of accurate leader interventions that eventually have the greatest impact on group interaction and members' learning.

The most crucial component of interpersonal learning is members having the skills necessary to give and receive feedback. Giving and receiving feedback works best when members have the communication skills needed to clearly present and understand the feedback they are given. Leaders must be aware of the impact of differences in English language proficiency in multilingual groups and try to ensure clear, thoughtful, and effective communication. Communication and feedback exchange skills, however, do not necessarily lead to change. To change, members must define new behaviors to experiment with and develop in group, then incorporate the new behaviors that have worked in group into their relationships outside group.

Training members to use communication skills increases the quality of feedback exchange. When members paraphrase and question to ensure understanding and reflect feelings to communicate awareness of others' emotional experiences, they have the skills necessary to participate meaningfully in interpersonal learning, even in intercultural contexts. In addition, as members self-disclose to share their immediate experiences and establish emotional connections, the group progresses as a highly effective learning environment. Leaders play a significant role in communicating the value and impact of self-disclosure as members of varied cultural backgrounds negotiate appropriate and necessary self-disclosure within their group.

Members' use of effective communication skills creates an environment that increases opportunities for interpersonal learning. In addition, effective communication, along with meaningful self-disclosure, is the foundation for the development of trust. When members trust each other, their fears of rejection diminish. Consequently, an atmosphere of safety develops, and members become less concerned about cultural differences and interpersonal risks.

Effective Interpersonal Communication

Interpersonal communication is the "process of creating meanings in the minds of others. These meanings may or may not correspond to the meanings we intend to create" (Tubbs, 1992, p. 212). When attempting to facilitate effective communication in groups, leaders should be mindful that cultural differences do exist (Geroski et al., 2021; Ivey et al., 2011; Okech et al., 2015). Several cultural factors influence how we create meanings and how others receive them. For example, members' racial and/or gender identity may influence how they communicate and how they interpret communications from others resulting from cultural and socialization norms and values. Language proficiency may also impact communication skills and meanings attributed to messages communicated from the leaders and fellow group members. Finally, members' chronological age and cognitive status may also have considerable influence on group member interpersonal communications. It is critical for group leaders to be aware of the characteristics of their group members and to be intentional about facilitating effective communication with and between group members. Group members make progress as they learn how to communicate their experiences and perceptions effectively and understand the meanings of others' communications; therefore, it is essential that members learn how to understand each other, and encouraging members to use effective communication skills is the way to ensure that this happens. In essence, effective communication allows members to exchange information that helps them learn from the group experience.

Guidelines for Effective Communication

Effective communication is the shared responsibility of members who both send and receive messages. D. W. Johnson and Johnson (2000) indicated that because communication is interpersonal, it involves both a member effectively sending a message and another member effectively receiving the message. The guidelines D. W. Johnson and Johnson described are relevant for group environments that focus on interpersonal learning. Leaders may use these guidelines as they guide group interaction, as content for discussion during pregroup orientation meetings, or as ideas they can infuse into the interventions they use to address communication problems.

Sending

Effectively sent messages have eight characteristics (D. W. Johnson & Johnson, 2000). These characteristics increase the chances that others will understand and respond nondefensively to the messages they receive:

1. Members should "own" their statements by using the pronouns "I" or "my." Using these pronouns demands that members assume responsibility for their statements. Those who receive an owned statement are more likely to believe it. Consider the following statements: "You get sad when you get ignored" and "I feel sad when you ignore me." Although these statements can express the same meaning, the member who offers the latter statement expresses themself more clearly. Making owned statements of emotion also connects speakers more meaningfully with their own experience (Champe et al., 2013).
2. Members should include necessary information and make statements specific. Partial or vague statements increase the chances of miscommunication. By omitting information, speakers increase their chances of being misunderstood. The member who states, "When you do that, it upsets me and I feel differently about you," offers the receiver insufficient information. If the receiver of this message does not ask what "that" and "feel differently" mean, he or she can only assume what the sender means. The consequence of these assumptions is that the receiver will draw erroneous conclusions about their behavior and relationship with the sender.
3. Members should send congruent messages to be believable. Members perceive others whose verbal and nonverbal behaviors do not agree as insincere. A common example of incongruent messages is members who state that they are angry while they smile or laugh while they cry. Members who receive incongruent messages will be confused, not understanding which part of the message to respond to: the words or the smile, the tears or the laughter. Believable and accurately heard messages are most likely when members match their verbal and nonverbal behaviors.
4. Members should repeat parts of their messages to increase the chances of being heard and understood. When members communicate effectively by restating a point clearly and succinctly, others will also understand that the point is important to the speaker.
5. Members should ask for verification from the receivers of their messages in order to clarify their communication and improve their interactive behaviors. When receivers respond to verification statements like "Tell me what you heard me say,"

senders can determine whether they have been heard accurately. When members are frequently misheard, it is useful for them to explore what happened to cause the miscommunication. Questions like "What did I do to make it difficult for you to hear what I said?" can be used to initiate this exploration. Responses can help members develop greater awareness of how their style of verbal and nonverbal communication affects their relationships with others.

6. Members should use terms that are understandable to the receiver. Members who use terms that are convoluted, jargonistic, metaphoric, or abstract are often misunderstood. When members communicate in this manner, receivers are less likely to hear a message specifically related to the sender's intentions. Receivers may also experience the embarrassment of having to admit they do not understand what the sender is trying to say. In multilingual and multicultural groups especially, language that is simple, clear, and easily understood is more effective than complex vocabulary or contextual slang that may distract from the message being communicated. Leaders should encourage all members to use words that others will understand and should ask members to translate easily misconstrued language into clear and specific terms. This process often has a powerful effect on both the speaker and the receiver, leaving little room for misunderstanding.
7. Whenever possible, members should include words that describe the emotions they are experiencing. The messages that offer the clearest indication of the sender's intentions include statements of emotion. Receivers who hear "I'm really hurt by what you've said" will have a clear understanding of the sender's message. On the other hand, receivers who hear "I can't believe you said that" are left to wonder whether the sender is angry, joking, sad, or hurt. In this case, if others do not guess the sender's feelings accurately, miscommunication occurs (Champe et al., 2013).
8. When members react to the behaviors of other members, they should specifically identify those behaviors and not attach evaluative terms. Members should also avoid interpreting the meaning or motivation behind these behaviors. A nonevaluative message that does not interpret the motivations of others is less likely to elicit defensive reactions. For example, the statement "You did that stupid grin again—you're just trying to confuse me" will probably elicit a defensive reaction.

Conversely, the statement "When you finished talking, you smiled. I'm not sure how to respond to you" allows receivers to develop awareness of the impact of their behaviors and provides an opening to talk about their intentions.

Receiving

Effectively receiving others' communications requires effort (Okech, 2015). This often means that leaders will need to monitor interaction to ensure that members hear each other's messages accurately. D. W. Johnson and Johnson (2000) offered three guidelines for effectively hearing the messages of others:

1. To ensure that they hear a message accurately, members should restate both the information and the emotions shared by the sender. These restatements should be made in the receiver's own words and should not include an evaluation of the message, attach or remove information, or draw conclusions about the motivations behind the statement.
2. The effectiveness of responses to a sender's statements increases when receivers state their perception of the sender's emotions. These statements should be tentative and owned as the receiver's perceptions.
3. After receivers have paraphrased and shared their perceptions of a sender's emotions, a negotiation process begins that has the objective of reaching agreement about the meaning of the message. Receivers initiate this process by making statements like "I think you're saying that . . . " or "I believe you mean . . . "

Teaching Communication Skills

Group leaders can teach members specific communication skills that will help them learn from each other and communicate more effectively in their daily lives. These include reflecting feelings, paraphrasing, and questioning.

Reflecting Feelings

Ivey (1994) described elementary reflection of feelings as noticing another's emotional expression, then stating the observed emotional expression to the person. Reflection of feelings can note overtly expressed feelings or be a statement of a member's perception of another's feelings. Reflections use emotion words, such as *angry, happy, hurt, scared, sad, empty*, and *lonely*:

Steve: "Well, I had to say something to her because who else was going to say anything?"
Bill: "You look angry." (*Reflection of observed feelings*)

or

Bill: "No one saying anything is really scary for you." (*Reflection using an imagined feeling*)

Leaders should encourage members to use reflections when

- members are having emotional experiences and are not recognizing these experiences,
- a member attempts to understand another member and does not include an effort to understand the other's emotional experience (Champe et al., 2013), or
- two members are having emotional reactions to each other but are not stating their feelings.

Teaching members to reflect each other's feelings helps members put words to the emotional connections they are experiencing. "Putting words" on emotional connections brings these connections clearly into awareness and increases group cohesion. Directing members to use reflections is one of the most fundamental ways to help members open their communication boundaries:

Leader: "Dave, it seems that you and Jill are experiencing some emotions here and you're not sharing them. Try this. Tell Jill what you understand her saying and add how you think she is feeling to your statement."
Dave: "Jill, you're telling me to stop being late, and you're angry."

Paraphrasing

Ivey (1994) described *paraphrasing* as a person stating in their own words what they have heard another person say. This restatement should include key words the other has said and should attempt to be a shorter statement than the one made. By shortening the restatement, the paraphrasing member can focus on what he or she perceives to be the most important aspects of the other member's communication. Paraphrases ensure that members accurately hear each other's words. After hearing a paraphrase, members can indicate how well the paraphrasing members have stated what they have said:

Steve: "Well, I had to say something to her because who else was going to say anything?"
Bill: "You say things when you don't know who else will."
Steve: "Yeah, somebody had to."

Paraphrasing is an important first step in helping members understand and act on feedback. Leaders should teach members to paraphrase to clarify their understanding of any important communication and as an initial response to receiving feedback. After members paraphrase, if they still do not understand the feedback they have been given, they can ask questions to gain further clarification (Okech, 2015). Directing a member to paraphrase is also useful when members' emotional responses to each other do not seem consistent with the words they are using.

When a member's reaction to what another member has said seems inconsistent with the statement made, it is often because of a misunderstanding. Members involved in emotionally charged interactions can occasionally benefit from accurately paraphrasing what others have said before sharing their own reactions. The following example shows how leaders can teach members to use a paraphrase to clarify interaction:

Cindy: "I don't know where I stand with you, Art. You seem to be trying to keep me away."
Art: "Cindy, you don't seem to care about me."
Leader: "Art, I'm not sure you understood what Cindy was saying. Say to Cindy in your own words what you heard her say."
Art: "You basically said I'm a real jerk and you don't care for me."
Cindy: "No, Art, that's not what I said."
Leader: "Cindy, say what you want to say to Art. Art, before you respond, say what you heard her say in your own words to see if you heard her accurately."

Questioning

Leaders should teach members to use questions to confirm understanding, ask for clarification, and request information from others. There are two basic types of questions: open and closed. Closed questions can be answered in only a few words (Ivey, 1994) and usually start with the words *are* and *do*. Closed questions are especially useful for verifying understanding:

Steve:"Well, I had to say something to her because who else was going to say anything?"
Bill: "Are you saying you're in charge of saying things when no one else will?"
Steve:"Well, someone has to say something."

Open questions (Ivey, 1994) encourage others to describe their thoughts and feelings more fully. Open questions usually start with the words *what*, *how*, and *could*:

Steve:"Well, I had to say something to them because who else was going to say anything?"
Bill: "What do you think will happen when no one says anything?"

or

Bill: "What are you thinking when no one says anything?"

If members appear to be making assumptions or to not understand each other's communications, leaders need to teach questioning skills. Be cautious when encouraging the use of questions because members often will substitute questions for feedback or for more honest and direct statements. When this happens, leaders should direct them to offer feedback or make a direct statement:

Jane: "Ken, what are you trying to do when you argue with me?"
Leader: "Jane, it seems that you have some feedback for Ken. Restate your question as feedback."
Jane: "Ken, when you argue with me by giving me fact after fact, I assume you're trying to control me, and that really ticks me off!"

Leaders teach members to use communication skills so that they can communicate effectively. The objective is to help members communicate their awareness of others' emotional experiences, establish emotional connections, and ensure and deepen understanding. By paraphrasing and questioning, members develop their understanding of information others share and how others share that information. When members use reflection of feelings, they experience what it is like to be more intimate in their relationships and understand others at the deepest and most meaningful level.

Timing and Teaching of Communication Skills

Ironically, there are drawbacks to teaching group members the skills and processes necessary to ensure effective communication. First, learning and using effective communication skills requires considerable effort. Second, in multilingual groups, learning may be slowed by language proficiency issues. Third, using communication skills, especially before members use them fluidly, can reduce the spontaneity of group interaction. Fourth, when these skills are first used, interactions can feel artificial. Finally, the time needed to develop these skills could otherwise be devoted to the issues that concern the group's members. Because of these drawbacks, leaders should consider carefully when to direct members to use effective communication skills.

Leaders should teach members to use communication skills whenever they are involved in an interaction that has communication problems. This does not mean that leaders should stop their groups and teach all members communication skills. Doing so would not demonstrate respect for the members involved. Rather, leaders should stop the members who are having trouble communicating, instruct the members involved, and immediately direct the involved members to apply the skill in their interaction as other members observe. Leaders should help members differentiate between difficulties based on language proficiencies and those based on differences in perspectives of a situation and choice of language or words used in dialogue. Leaders should make every effort to make this instructional intervention as brief as possible.

From a timing perspective, teaching members to use communication skills has more impact when members are encountering communication difficulties. The motivation for learning communication skills is far greater when the skills are associated with an immediate need. In addition, teaching particular members to use communication skills when they need the skills is a learning experience observed by the entire group. When members demonstrate how effectively the skills work in their interactions, the entire group observes and learns vicariously how to use the skills and what the skills accomplish.

Communication Problems

When members communicate ineffectively, experiences can be destructive and harmful. Ineffective communication creates a group climate of distrust and competition (Gibb, 1961; D. W. Johnson & Johnson, 2000). Members perpetuate these outcomes by not using the skills needed to interact effectively. Evidence of ineffective communication in a group includes the following:

- Members make but do not verify their interpretations of the meaning of others' statements.
- Interaction includes assumptions about the motivations of others.
- Frequent conflicts appear more semantic than substantive.
- Members have emotional reactions to others that seem inconsistent with the content of their interaction.
- Conflicts escalate with increasingly intense member statements and emotional expression regardless of the importance of the issue.
- Misunderstandings about expectations lead to emotional reactions.
- Members use language that causes others to have immediate and intense negative reactions.
- Members agree on an issue when they clearly do not understand what the others mean.
- Disagreements emerge over issues that members agree on but do not know they agree on because they are using different words to say the same thing.

As leaders help members learn to communicate more effectively, they must be aware of some basic problems in communication and be ready to intervene. Members understand communication when they accurately hear the meaning of the messages they receive. Often members do not understand messages they receive in the way the sender intended, and at times the words used cause strong reactions. Frequently, misunderstandings and emotional reactions are the result of basic communication problems. Tubbs (1992) described four common problems in interpersonal communication: bypassing, inference making, polarizing, and signal reactions.

Bypassing

A common cause of misunderstanding in interpersonal communication, *bypassing* occurs when the sender and the receiver assign different meanings to a word or phrase that they use in their interaction. Tubbs (1992) and Tubbs and Carter (2020) identified two instances of bypassing. One occurs when people have different meanings for a word or phrase, and the other occurs when people use different words to express the same thought.

A consequence of bypassing is that group members may not know when they are agreeing on a point. This results in a conflict connected not to the point being made but rather to the words being used. Intense disagreements can occur when members actually agree. Leaders need to help members state the meanings of the words and phrases that are key to their contentions. Members are often surprised to discover they are using different words to say the same thing and are actually agreeing.

Bypassing also happens when members use a word or phrase to agree with each other when they really disagree. This occurs when members attach a different meaning to the words they use. Leaders will commonly see members agreeing on how they will interact and later react emotionally because others have not lived up to their agreement. Leaders should frequently check with members who agree to clarify what each believes they are agreeing to.

Inference Making

Inference making occurs when members make assumptions about the motivations behind others' communication. These usually erroneous conclusions shape the interpretations a member makes about the meaning of others' interactions. Leaders will commonly observe inference making when members have a reaction to each other that does not seem to fit with the content of their interaction. These "out of proportion" reactions are often related to the assumptions made about others' intentions. When leaders observe a receiver of a communication having a disproportionate reaction, it is useful to explore the receiver's assumptions about the intentions of the sender. Asking the sender to state their intentions should follow this.

Polarizing

Polarizing occurs when members have intense disagreements and exaggerate their perspectives. As one member overstates their point of view, the other, to make their point as powerfully as the first, does so as well. The effect of these reciprocal exaggerations is that the people involved get farther away from possible agreements.

When leaders observe polarizing interactions, they can ask the disagreeing people to restate what the other has said before stating their own point of view. This procedure reduces the emotional intensity of the interaction and results in clearer communication

(Tubbs, 1992). By lowering the intensity and increasing the clarity of communication, the resolution of disagreements is far more likely.

Signal Reactions

Tubbs (1992) stated, "All of us learn to react to certain verbal and nonverbal stimuli in some strong and predictable ways" (p. 238). Occasionally, group members use certain phrases or words that have a dramatic effect on interaction. *Signal reactions* are the strong emotional reactions that commonly follow the expression of these words and phrases. Words and phrases that produce signal reactions include profanity and terms that denote strong cultural, gender, racial, or religious biases. Other instances of signal reactions include phrases like "I've tried that, and it doesn't work," "You don't get it, do you?" or "What do you know about my problems?" When signal reactions occur, leaders should direct members to discuss how these words or phrases affect them and initiate feedback exchange. When members use terms that indicate insensitivity to differences, leaders must intervene to address the damaging effects of the words and confront the associated prejudices.

By addressing communication problems and strategically teaching communication skills, leaders increase group effectiveness. First, by helping members communicate more effectively, opportunities for learning increase, and these opportunities are more productive. Second, effective communication increases the level of trust members experience in the group. Finally, the group environment becomes safer because communication problems are resolved. Each of these outcomes contributes to group development and to the establishment of an effective learning environment.

Self-Disclosure

Self-disclosure refers to the process of sharing personal information with another person (Kline, 1986; Vinogradov & Yalom, 1990). It is often done to establish intimacy, but in some cases, clients may feel pressure to share in group settings (Vinogradov & Yalom, 1990). Personal disclosure in groups involves sharing information that others would not know unless disclosed by the member. This can help build trust and connections within the group. In groups, personal disclosure includes information others are not likely to have unless the disclosing member shares it. Self-disclosure implies that members perceive the content of their disclosure as sufficiently intimate that they would not openly disclose to it everyone (Kline, 2003; Minds Tools Content Team, n.d.; I. D. Yalom & Leszcz, 2020).

Counseling and therapy groups cannot function as productive learning environments without self-disclosure. Learning depends on members sharing their emotional reactions and perceptions of others' behaviors. In addition, self-disclosure is indispensable for a group environment that features mutual trust and acceptance. Porter and Mohr (1982) described the role of self-disclosure: "Until individuals have had (and used) opportunities to reveal how they see and do things: they are not likely to receive information that will help them decide whether they want to make behavioral changes" (p. 10). In addition, meaningful self-disclosure allows group members to check out their perceptions, engage in feedback exchange, develop relationships with others, and accept themselves more fully (I. D. Yalom & Leszcz, 2020).

Members who avoid self-disclosing often fear rejection. Contrary to this is the corrective emotional experience of members disclosing what they perceive as the unacceptable aspects of who they are, only to find that others do not reject them. As members offer progressively intimate disclosures, they learn that acceptance based on the facades they use to gain approval is hollow. A significant part of the healing process in groups is members experiencing others' acceptance in spite of their own imperfections. This cannot occur without self-disclosure.

There are many important reasons for self-disclosure in groups that focus on interpersonal learning. These include:

- Experiencing acceptance
- Making emotional connections with others
- Learning how to develop increasingly intimate relationships
- Sharing personal experience related to the immediate content of group interaction to connect with others and make information available so others can learn
- Offering reactions and emotions in order to obtain support, feedback, and cognitive input
- Reality-testing cognitive reactions and experience
- Learning how to take interpersonal risks and tolerate the anxiety associated with these risks
- Learning how to be congruent in interpersonal relationships

Effective Self-Disclosure

Effective self-disclosure initiates and sustains interaction (I. D. Yalom & Leszcz, 2020). When members express their immediate emotional and cognitive reactions, they learn from each other and become increasingly intimate. Self-disclosure of "my experience of you right now, as we look at each other" is one of the most personal forms of interpersonal expression. As members approach this level of intimacy, they discover the powerful impact of interpersonal learning.

Effective self-disclosures are the product of a member choosing to disclose. Because of this, leaders need to be especially aware of how groups pressure individual members to disclose. Ideally, group participation helps members develop awareness of their thinking and feeling. It also helps them to understand the potential risks involved in disclosing thoughts and emotions and how to make a conscious choice to disclose. This is especially important in multicultural groups, where beliefs and values about self-disclosure may differ, and where members may have different perceptions of self-disclosure based on the dynamics of social-cultural identity groups represented in the group. Preliminary conversations about identities and fears about intercultural relationships may lay a sound foundation for appropriate self-disclosure in the group. This process has important implications for the relationships that members have outside the group.

When members coerce others to disclose, the process of members choosing to disclose is short-circuited. Leaders must decide whether members encouraging a member to disclose are coercive or supportive of that member's learning. When a member resists encouragement to self-disclose, leaders should explore the reluctance rather than push for a disclosure. Premature self-disclosure due to group coercion can be damaging to a member and impact their healing process as well as their trust and investment in the group.

Effective self-disclosure develops trust and increasingly intimate interaction. As members share progressively intimate information, they develop confidence that they can predict how others will respond to their disclosures. Trust builds as members have productive experiences with their disclosures. As trust builds, the group becomes a safer place to disclose increasingly intimate information. This trust-building process occurs most readily when disclosures include immediate emotional and cognitive reactions within the group.

Finally, effectively communicated self-disclosure is most potent. Self-disclosures that include "owned statements," feelings, specific information, congruent statements, understandable language, and nonevaluative terms are most effective.

The following example demonstrates how a leader might encourage the use of self-disclosure and the impact of effective self-disclosure:

Moses: "You don't understand me. I just want you to give me some attention."

Okoth: "Stay away from me, leave me alone. I don't want you to hurt me."

Leader: "Moses and Okoth, the two of you are not communicating what your fears and emotions are. Try sharing what you're feeling and what you're fearing the other will do."

After a long pause, Moses speaks.

Moses: "I'm really feeling scared, like I'm doing something wrong or unacceptable. All I want to do is be your friend, but I'm afraid that you'll just ignore me."

Okoth: "Moses, I'm afraid you'll hurt me somehow. I'm scared that if I allow you to get close to me that I will experience the racism and hurt that I have encountered with other White men."

Defensive Self-Disclosure

Defensive self-disclosures isolate the discloser from others in the group. Members who fear making themselves known to others commonly make these disclosures, which include content that keeps others at a distance. Some commonly observed types of defensive self-disclosure include distancing, shocking, expressing painful vulnerability, and monopolizing.

Distancing self-disclosures persistently focus on differences to establish interpersonal boundaries that exclude others. Members making these disclosures imply that others cannot possibly understand or appreciate their experiences. For example, a member might say, "I feel so lonely in here because no one can possibly understand me and what I've been through. You can't even begin to know how to help me!"

When a member persists with distancing disclosures, other members have angry reactions and withdraw their attention. When leaders observe a member using a pattern of distancing disclosures, they should state their observations. Most important, leaders should urge other members to share their reactions to the distancing disclosures and help distancing members recognize the impact of their behavior and help them address their interpersonal fears.

Shocking self-disclosure uses intensity as a means of keeping others away. Members who use shocking self-disclosure may offer stories of horrible trauma, be extremely intimate, or express extremely intense emotions when these disclosures are inconsistent with group interaction norms. Shocking commonly occurs in the initial stages of a group when members disclose overly personal information before other members have developed a sense of safety or trust. Later, shocking self-disclosures more commonly present as intense emotional expressions or disclosures that exceed the group's norms for intimacy. Leaders should confront members who use shocking as a defense, and this intervention should incorporate feedback from members who are having profound reactions to the shocking disclosures.

Expressing painful vulnerability involves overstating emotional fragility. Members who use this defense present themselves as extremely fragile. These disclosures suggest that virtually any interaction would devastate them. For example, such members may cry quietly as other members receive constructive feedback or ask for a break from a feedback process after receiving one benign feedback. The message communicated by this defense is "Stay away from me, unless you want to destroy me." Other members will commonly withhold their reactions and feedback from and attempt to reassure or protect the fragile member. Leaders identifying a member's use of this defense should offer observations about this member's behavior and the reactions of other group members. For example, "Lucy, it seems that the more you tell others how fragile you are, the more you keep them away" or "Telling Steve how frightened you are seemed to push him away. Seems that you're more afraid of being close than you are of being hurt." The intervention goal is to involve the "fragile" member. Even if this member is experiencing painful emotions, it is crucial for them to engage with others and learn how to obtain and respond to interpersonal support.

Monopolizing Controls Other Members

As long as a member controls conversation, that member controls the group. Monopolizing occurs when individuals present a prolonged and usually personal narrative. This narrative is difficult for other members to interrupt because it contains sensitive material, and the monopolizing member will not stop talking. Monopolizing members usually use prolonged storytelling to avoid intimacy and the intensity of interpersonal contact. This can be challenging if a member comes from a culture of storytelling. However, even in communities that use storytelling as a central tool for teaching, participants manage the time allotted for such activities and steer away from individuals monopolizing social events.

Although self-disclosure is essential, it can be counterproductive. Leaders, as they listen to self-disclosures, need to remain aware of process—that is, the objectives of members' self-disclosure. Leaders should consider intervening when a member's self-disclosure causes others to retreat. This involves initiating a feedback exchange process in which others share the impact of the member's self-disclosures.

Encouraging Effective Self-Disclosure

Encouraging self-disclosure is important throughout the life of most groups. When disclosure is risky, leaders may need to direct members to disclose how they are currently experiencing each other. Self-disclosures in the context of here-and-now interaction commonly involve members sharing the emotions they experience in response to other members' verbal and nonverbal behaviors.

Leaders can follow the direction to self-disclose with an invitation to exchange feedback. Following up with an invitation to exchange feedback is most useful when the interacting members have not shared enough to have learned from the interaction. When members exchange disclosures that allow them to learn and make emotional connections, leaders should allow interaction to continue without intervention:

Leader: "Dave, you seem to be having an emotional reaction to what George is saying. Share that emotion with him."
Dave: "George, I'm really angry with you."
George: "Oh, really?"
Leader: "Dave, give George some feedback about what he is doing that angers you."

To summarize, self-disclosures that communicate immediate emotional experiences are very powerful. These disclosures increase intimacy and enhance members' perceptions of connection. When members share a full range of immediate emotional reactions, it is an indication that their group is developing as an effective interpersonal learning environment.

Feedback

Feedback is a form of self-disclosure in which members offer their emotional and cognitive reactions to others regarding their behaviors, which may include either words or actions. Feedback exchange is one of the most important learning processes in interactive groups (Kline, 2003; Okech, 2015; I. D. Yalom & Leszcz, 2020).

Unfortunately, many people describe feedback as positive or negative, which places a value on the content of the feedback. Negative, or corrective, feedback indicates that the sender reacted negatively (e.g., disliking, disapproving) to the receiver's behavior, whereas positive feedback indicates that the sender reacted positively (e.g., liking, approving, admiring) to the receiver's behavior. When leaders or members describe feedback as positive or negative, members who receive negative feedback get the message that they are doing something wrong. This perspective impedes feedback exchange, because most members are reluctant to evaluate others and potentially damage their relationships. In addition, the feedback format "When you _____, I feel_____" attaches a value to the receiver's behavior. For example, "When you talk loudly, I feel scared" assigns responsibility to the loudly speaking person for another member's emotions and implies that the person talking loudly should change their behavior if they want the sender to feel differently—a form of emotional coercion.

From the interactive perspective, effective feedback is simply data; it is neither positive nor negative. Feedback is not an evaluative process intended to correct or compliment; rather, it is members sharing their reactions to others' behaviors. Members who receive feedback have the freedom to make choices about changing or continuing their interpersonal behaviors in light of the feedback.

To be complete, feedback must describe how the member giving the feedback interprets the behavior of the member receiving the feedback. Such interpretations are closely associated with the sender's emotional reactions to the receiver's behavior. For example, when a member interprets another's behavior as intimidating, that member will be afraid. This perspective emphasizes the interpretations and assumptions of the person giving the feedback and the intentions of the person receiving the feedback.

When feedback statements include the sender's interpretation of the receiver's behavior, feedback has a different tone. A person hearing "When you talk loudly, I feel scared because I assume you are trying to hurt me" is less likely to feel evaluated and more inclined to discuss their intentions. This is because the sender's "owned" interpretation removes the implication that the receiver's behavior should change. Instead, the conversation moves to examining how members interpret other members' behaviors. When this occurs, the leader can initiate a discussion with the person receiving the feedback about their intentions.

Feedback exchanged in this manner also becomes a process in which members who give feedback can learn how their assumptions about others' behaviors affect their relationships. This occurs when the interpretations of others in the group are different from the interpretations of the member giving the feedback and do not match the intentions of the receiver. At this point, the sender of the feedback has a chance to examine how their interpretations of others' behaviors affect their relationships in and outside of the group. This examination occasionally leads to members gaining insight into the origin of their interpretations. For example, a terrified member who interprets another member's loud voice as dangerous could learn how family-of-origin experiences explain their fear of others' anger. Members' choices after receiving feedback reflect their interpersonal and intrapersonal goals and objectives in and outside the group. Leaders have an obligation to help members make choices that support their interpersonal growth and learning.

Feedback is either effective or ineffective, depending on what information is communicated from the sender to the receiver and how it is communicated (see Table 9.1).

Effective Feedback

Effective feedback includes the following:

- Presentation of immediate observations and reactions to a pattern rather than an isolated occurrence of a behavior
- Specific descriptions of behaviors and/or words used by the feedback recipient
- An owned statement of the assumptions and interpretations being made about the motivations and purposes of the receiver's words and/or behaviors
- Disclosure of the feelings experienced by the feedback giver

TABLE 9.1
Effective Versus Ineffective Feedback Approaches

Effective Feedback	Ineffective Feedback
Is checked for understanding and clarity	Meaning is assumed and communication is incomplete
Considers the readiness of the receiver	Receiver is not ready or able to hear feedback
Receiver is asked about willingness to receive feedback	Feedback is offered without the consent of the receiver
Does not imply a requirement for change	Suggests behavior must be changed
Involves the sender as much as the receiver	Centers on the sender in one-way communication

An effective feedback statement is "You changed the subject and looked away from me. When you did that, I assumed you were afraid and trying to avoid me. Right now, I feel sad about that."

Effective feedback exchange is complete only when the member receiving feedback has defined alternative behaviors for experimentation. This occurs when other members agree about the impact of the receiver's behaviors, the receiver recognizes that their behaviors are not getting the desired result, and the receiver chooses to experiment with different behaviors. The following example demonstrates this:

Leader: "Maria, it seems like many group members are having a similar reaction to your teasing. They seem annoyed by it and want to avoid conversations with you. I'm guessing that that's not what you want to happen."

Maria: "I'm only teasing to make friends. I want all of you to like me."

Leader: "So, what you're doing to make friends isn't working in here."

Maria: "No, it's not! This really sucks. Now I understand why I felt like nobody in here liked me."

Leader: "Maybe you could get some ideas from the group about some different ways to start relationships with them."

Maria: "OK, you folks have some ideas for me?"

Rhonda: "Wow, Maria, I didn't know you were trying to be friends with me. For me, making friends starts with showing interest in me and sharing what's going on with you."

This interaction continues until the group has offered Maria some ideas about different behaviors, and Maria agrees to experiment with some of them. Maria's experiments until she achieves the results she wants, and other members perceive her behavior as she intends.

For an illustration of the cycle of interpersonal learning, see Figure 9.1.

Ineffective Feedback

Feedback that reflects a delayed reaction to another member's behavior is often ineffective. Other examples of ineffective feedback include (a) feedback that expresses conclusions about the intentions of the person receiving the feedback, (b) feedback that characterizes and evaluates the person receiving the feedback, and (c) feedback

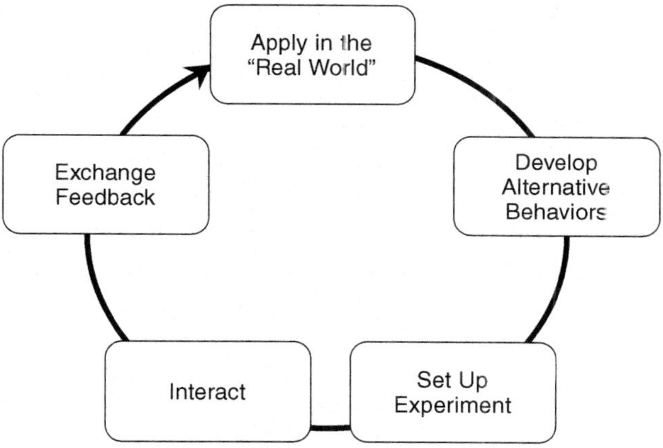

FIGURE 9.1
The Cycle of Complete Interpersonal Learning

that implies an understanding of the motivations of the person receiving the feedback (Kline, 2003; Lindbloom et al., 2005; Mead, 1977; Okech, 2015).

"Last week, you were nasty! You obviously wanted to hurt Steve" is a clear example of ineffective feedback. Ineffective feedback is likely to create misunderstanding, be based on untested assumptions, be evaluative, be used to punish, initiate angry exchanges, and use value-laden terms that elicit emotional reactions. If ineffective feedback continues, the group environment will deteriorate. Members will learn to distrust each other and regard feedback exchange as a damaging process. Whenever leaders recognize ineffective feedback, they must intervene.

Feedback and the Interactive Group Environment

Members learn the most when effective feedback exchange flows freely. When members exchange feedback, they learn about the impact their interpersonal behaviors have on others. Members also learn how their interpretations of others' behaviors affect their relationships in and outside the group. As members examine their interpretations, they acquire insight into the origin of their interpersonal behaviors and relationship problems.

Teaching Feedback Exchange

In order to teach effective feedback exchange, members should be encouraged to interact, share their perceptions, and offer their immediate emotional reactions (Kline, 2003; Lindbloom et al., 2005; Okech, 2015). This process can be modeled using the ORAL (Observation, Report, Assumptions, and Level) model of feedback exchange, which consists of four steps of member engagement (Lindbloom et al., 2005). The first step, Observation, is when members pay attention to what is being said and to the behavior of other members. Next, members Report by describing what they saw and heard in the group. The Assumptions step involves sharing interpretations of what was heard or seen, allowing for correction or agreement from other members. Finally, the Level step allows members to share their feelings and emotional reactions. It is most effective to teach feedback skills when members have strong emotional reactions but struggle to share and respond to them. The ORAL model (see Figure 9.2) helps members engage in feedback exchange even when they are feeling vulnerable and emotional but still want to remain connected to other group members.

Leaders can begin the process of teaching feedback exchange by teaching feedback skills to a member who is involved in sharing reac-

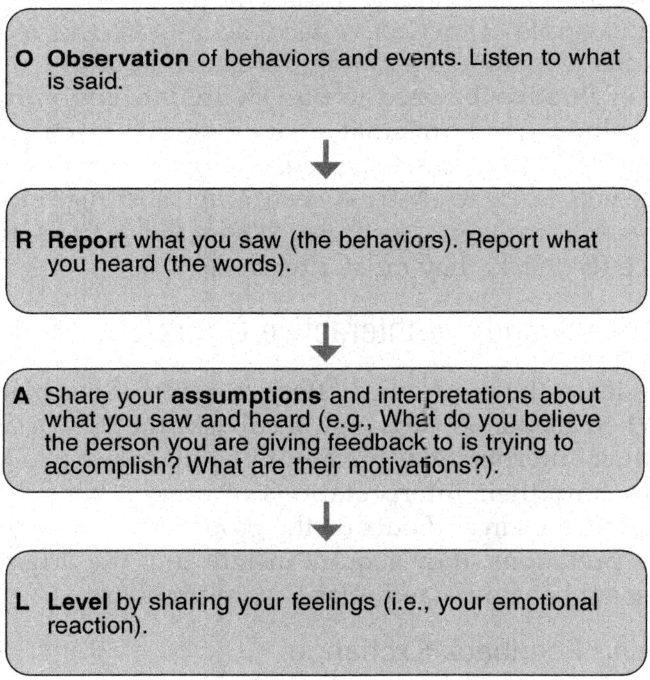

FIGURE 9.2
The ORAL Model of Feedback Exchange

tions with another member. This individualized approach to teaching skills helps the member learn how to interact more effectively with another member while other members observe. The intention is not to involve a single member in a prolonged leader intervention but rather to initiate skill development for the entire group.

As groups progress, members will continue to need coaching with feedback exchange. Leaders must consistently ask all members to follow the principles and steps of the feedback exchange. This is necessary both for learning to occur and for members to commit to using the feedback skills. Continued coaching, whenever needed, reinforces members' learning. Thus, more formal skill instruction is seldom necessary. When effective feedback exchange behaviors become group norms, members will take over the coaching process by prompting each other to use feedback skills. When members assume the coaching role for each other, leaders can be less heavily involved in monitoring feedback exchange.

Teaching Members to Send Feedback

When leaders identify a member who has a need to give feedback, leaders ask the member about their reactions to another member. If these reactions are persistent, and not a one-time reaction to an unusual behavior, leaders should proceed. Once leaders confirm that the member reacting to another's behaviors is willing to learn a different way to share their reactions, leaders begin the teaching process.

Leaders begin the process of teaching feedback exchange by directing the member involved to state the specific words and/or behaviors that initiated that member's reactions. Next, leaders ask the member to state their assumptions about the intentions of the words and/or behaviors that the other member used. Next, leaders direct the member to share the emotions experienced when the other member used those words and/or behaviors. Finally, leaders direct the member to put all these components together in a statement made directly to the member who is to receive the feedback. Figure 9.3 provides a visual representation of the process for sending feedback.

Initially, the process of teaching feedback exchange skills requires the sequential teaching of very specific skills. This process can be frustrating for members who would rather use their usual pattern of offering feedback even if it is ineffective. Leaders must be patient and persistent in encouraging members to stay the course and trust in the feedback exchange process and in the effectiveness of the new skills they are learning. The ultimate goal is for feedback

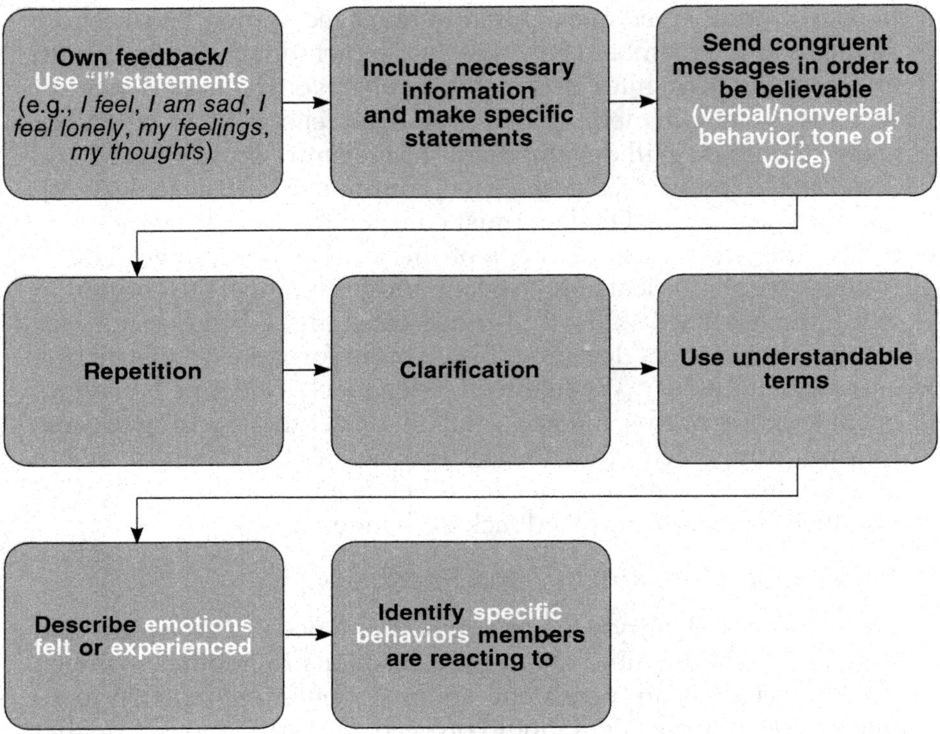

FIGURE 9.3
Process for Sending Feedback

exchange skills to become norms monitored by group members. The following example shows how a leader would initially teach feedback exchange skills:

Julie: "Robert, you just don't understand. You can't control me that way."
Leader: (*Interrupting*) "Julie, you seem to be having some definite reactions to Robert."
Julie: "I am!"
Leader: "I'm wondering if these reactions have been going on for some time?"
Julie: "Yes, I just got to the point where I had to say something."
Leader: "Would you like to give Robert some feedback that could help both of you?" (*Confirm willingness to give feedback*)
Julie: "I guess so, but I kinda thought that's what I was doing."

Leader: "Feedback needs to have three parts for it to work. First, tell us exactly what Robert is doing that you're reacting to." (*Teach and direct*)

Julie: "Well, lots of stuff. He's trying to convince me to do things his way."

Leader: "What exactly is he doing to convince you?" (*Question to specify behaviors*)

Julie: "He keeps giving me all these reasons to do something I don't want to do. He keeps going and going and going and doesn't seem to listen to me."

Leader: "What do you mean when you say he doesn't listen to you?" (*Question to further specify behaviors*)

Julie: "He won't stop when I ask him to."

Leader: "OK, let's see if I've got this right. Robert keeps on giving you reasons to do something you don't want to do even though you ask him to stop." (*Paraphrase to confirm understanding*)

Julie: "Yes!"

Leader: "The second part of feedback has to do with what you believe Robert is trying to do—that is, your assumptions about the intentions of his words and behaviors. So, when he gives you these reasons and won't stop, what do you assume he's trying to do?" (*Teach and direct*)

Julie: "It feels like he's trying to control me, to act the way he wants me to act. Like my way isn't right."

Leader: "OK, so he keeps on giving you reasons to do something even though you ask him to stop, and you assume he's trying to control you." (*Paraphrase to confirm understanding*)

Julie: "Yeah."

Leader: "Julie, you seem to be having an emotional reaction to Robert. Your emotions are the third part of feedback. Tell us what your emotions are when you assume Robert's trying to control you." (*Teach and direct*)

Julie: "He annoys the h—— out of me!"

Leader: "Now, Julie, say this to Robert. Tell him what he's doing, what you think he's trying to do, and how you feel when this happens." (*Direct and connect*)

Julie: "Robert, when you keep on giving me reasons to do something even though I tell you to stop, I feel like you're trying to control me and that I'm unacceptable the way I am."

Leader: "And your emotional reaction . . ." (*Prompt*)

Julie: "Yeah, when you do that, you really tick me off!"

At the next opportunity for feedback exchange, the leader abbreviates this process by asking members to share feedback and using prompts to ensure that the components of effective feedback are included. After several exchanges, members will begin to initiate the process of feedback exchange and coach each other. Members' participation in initiating and monitoring feedback exchange increases as leaders take a progressively less active role in feedback exchange. Leaders should feel free to encourage members to take charge of feedback exchanges by directing members to assume responsibility for this role.

Teaching Members to Receive Feedback

Effective feedback exchange requires the member receiving the feedback to use some necessary skills and demonstrate several important attitudes. These skills and attitudes include effective communication skills, knowing how to use the perceptions of other group members to validate the feedback, openness to hearing and understanding feedback, and willingness to give and receive feedback. In addition, the feedback exchange loop is complete only when the receiver has defined alternative behaviors for experimentation. Teaching members to effectively exchange feedback, define experimental behaviors, and experiment with these behaviors are crucial ongoing leadership tasks. The process for receiving feedback is shown in Figure 9.4.

When members learn how to receive feedback effectively, they usually become less defensive and more open to hearing it. Teaching members to receive feedback is the second step in teaching feedback exchange skills. When leaders teach a member to give feedback and the feedback has been given, leaders then must teach the member who has been given the feedback how to receive it. Occasionally, while teaching a member to give feedback, it may be necessary for the leader to direct the feedback receiver to listen and not interrupt the feedback sender.

Mead (1977) described an effective feedback exchange as follows:

1. Effectively receiving feedback means that receivers should listen intently to the words of feedback givers. Feedback receivers who stop listening to the feedback to prepare a response will not hear the feedback accurately.
2. Once sent, feedback receivers should paraphrase the feedback to ensure that they accurately heard and understand the feedback. By ensuring that they accurately heard and understand

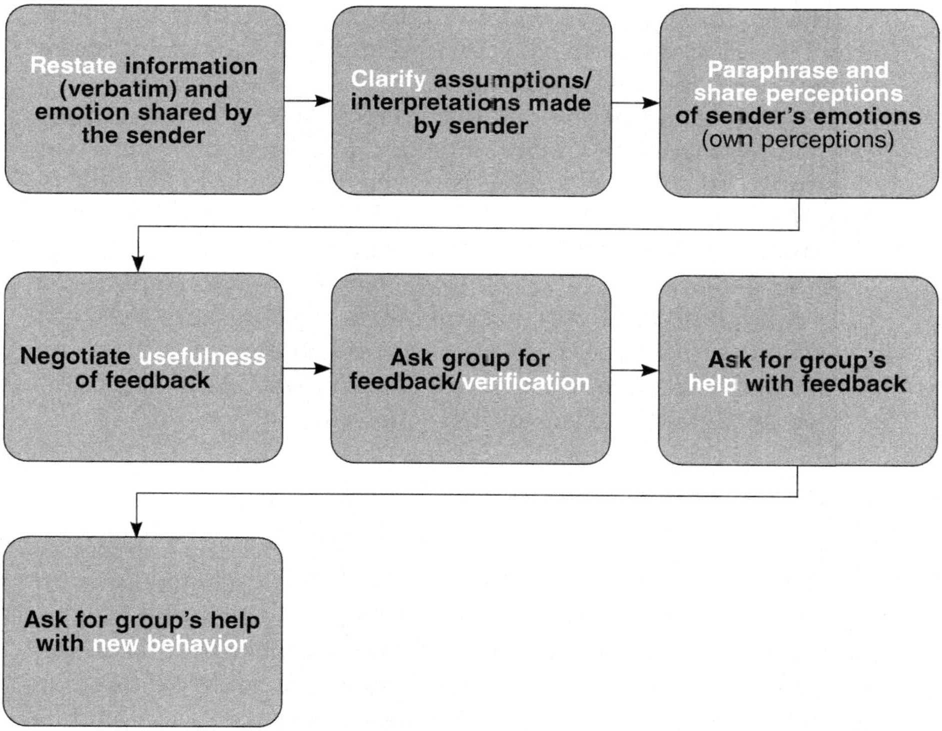

FIGURE 9.4
Process for Receiving Feedback

feedback, receivers reduce the possibility that they are making assumptions about the meaning of the feedback. Receivers listen more intensely when they understand they are responsible for accurately paraphrasing feedback. Leaders should coach members who are unclear about the meaning of the feedback to ask clarifying questions.

3. Once feedback receivers have accurately paraphrased the feedback, they should check for consensus with other members. Checking for consensus determines whether other members share the feedback giver's perceptions. If other members do not have similar perceptions, leaders can explore the perceptions of the member who has given the feedback. Occasionally, when feedback is not validated by group consensus, members who have given the feedback should either receive feedback or begin to look at their own possible perceptual distortions. Also, the fact that other members do not share the same perception does not necessarily mean the feedback is inaccurate.

The leader should pay attention to group dynamics at points when accurate feedback is offered and the other group members are reluctant to endorse it.

4. It is important that members who receive feedback retain autonomy. Members are not obligated to change their behavior simply because they have received feedback. Nonetheless, feedback that has been validated by group consensus often implies, in the minds of group members, that behavior change should follow. Leaders need to be cognizant of this implication because it means that group members may pressure feedback receivers to change. Leaders must protect members' freedom to make choices about change and to understand the interpersonal consequences of their choices.

If a member does not change in response to ongoing feedback, leaders need to explore both the group's needs to change the member's behaviors and the member's reluctance to change. Occasionally, the group's need to change a member's behavior is an indication that a feedback receiver is frustrating the group's solution to a focal conflict or evidence that the member is breaking an important norm or role expectation. The same could be the case when group members are unwilling to validate feedback that has been offered to one of them.

Teaching feedback-receiving skills thus involves coaching members to listen, paraphrase, check for consensus, and retain autonomy. When members decide to change behaviors, leaders instruct them to ask for alternative behaviors and help them set up experiments with selected behaviors:

Robert: "Julie, I'm really hurt that you don't think I care about you."

Leader: "Robert, before you respond more to Julie, I'd like you to say to Julie what you heard her saying to you. This is the first thing you should do when you get feedback." (*Direct, connect, and instruct*)

Robert: "Julie, you said that I don't care about you and that all I want you to do is to act the way I want."

Julie: "That's not it. I don't think you heard what I said."

Leader: "Julie, give Robert your feedback again. Robert, I want you to listen carefully. When Julie is done, I want you to say back to Julie what you heard her say." (*Direct and connect*)

Julie repeats her feedback and Robert accurately paraphrases it.

Involving the Group in Feedback Exchange

It is not only the members involved in a feedback exchange who should be taught to give and receive feedback. Feedback exchange is a group event that affects and involves all members. In addition to learning feedback skills through observation, other group members can learn about the effects of certain behaviors, how to validate feedback, and how to offer input about alternative behaviors.

The group's active participation in a feedback exchange begins after a member has received feedback and has accurately paraphrased it. At this point, leaders direct the member who has received the feedback to ask other members to validate the feedback. Once feedback is validated and the receiving member decides to change behaviors, the group again participates by helping the feedback receiver develop alternative experimental behaviors. Once the receiver selects an experimental behavior, the group continues to participate by offering ongoing feedback on the experimental behavior. Thus, the entire group actively participates to support both the feedback exchange and the experimentation processes.

The role of members in validating feedback is to develop consensus about the accuracy of the feedback. *Consensus*, in this case, means that members who have not been directly involved in the feedback exchange share a common perception of the feedback receiver's behavior. To validate feedback, leaders direct the member who has received feedback to ask the other members whether their perceptions align with those shared by the member giving the feedback:

Leader: "Robert, it's important to check out feedback with other group members to see if they have similar perceptions as Julie. Ask the others how they see it." (*Instruct, direct [consensus], connect*)

Robert: "Does anybody else have the same reactions that Julie does?"

Leslie: "Robert, I couldn't put my finger on my reactions to you until now. What Julie said totally fits with my reactions. I feel like I have to do things your way, or you'll badger me."

Ted: "When you try to convince me to see things your way, I just tune out. I can't handle the intensity of your arguments. I just say to myself, 'There he goes again.'"

Leader: "It seems like most of the other members agree with Julie's feedback. We'll stop now. Robert, what are you learning from this?"

Seeing members agreeing with Leslie and Ted, the leader cuts off conversation that could be damaging to Robert.

During the feedback validation process, leaders should allow members to add reactions that may provide more information to the feedback receiver:

> *Janice*: "Robert, I agree with the feedback. Something that's a part of what you do is the tone of voice you use when you offer your reasons. From the way you sound, I assume you believe you know what others need to know. It's part of what's annoying to me."

Leaders also need to guard against receivers becoming overloaded by feedback. Feedback overload occurs when receivers become overwhelmed by the amount of information they are hearing and/or become overwhelmed by the emotions they experience as a result of the feedback. To benefit from feedback, receivers need to develop a clear idea about their behaviors and the effects of these behaviors. This task becomes overwhelming if the diverging points of view of other members, which are necessary to clarify feedback, include more information than the receiver can manage. Thus, the receiver becomes confused, and the impact of the feedback is lost. In addition, when members become extremely emotional, they stop hearing feedback. As feedback is validated, leaders must monitor receivers for overload and remember that the validation process is not an opportunity for members to dump their frustrations on another member. Rather, it is intended for the benefit of the feedback receiver:

> *Leader*: "Robert, you've been hearing a lot from other members about their perceptions of you. You think you could say what their main reactions are?" (*Boundary setting and question to monitor understanding*)
>
> *Robert*: "I could at first, but it's getting confusing. I've heard so much that I'm not able to keep it all straight."
>
> *Leader*: "OK, let's stop now and see if we can pinpoint exactly what others are reacting to." (*Direction*)

Another problem that occurs during the validation process is when members begin to give new feedback that addresses behaviors not included in the original feedback. Leaders should prevent the introduction of new feedback during the feedback validation process. Such feedback confuses receivers and reduces the impact of the original feedback. Leaders should limit feedback validation to the words and/or behaviors included in the original feedback:

Al: "Robert, I agree with the feedback you got. There's also this other thing you do that . . ."
Leader: "Stop there, Al. This is something you can take up with Robert later. Right now, we're dealing with Julie's feedback. Robert, tell the group what you're hearing so far." (*Boundary set and direct*)
Robert: "I've heard a lot from almost everyone in the group. It's beginning to get confusing."
Leader: "Robert, it seems that others agree with Julie's feedback. This may mean that your behavior is not working the way you want. It's up to you now to decide if you want to change your behaviors." (*Summarize and direct*)
Robert: "I don't want people to see me as controlling and judgmental. I guess I need to do something different."

Members' involvement is also important at the conclusion of feedback exchange and validation. When feedback receivers indicate that they want to experiment with new behaviors, the collective creativity and knowledge of members is used to help receivers define alternative behaviors. To generate alternative behaviors, leaders direct feedback receivers to ask the entire group or selected members for possible alternative behaviors.

Experimentation

Experimentation with new behaviors is the primary objective of feedback exchange in interactive groups. Members who experiment with new behaviors take advantage of the opportunity to receive ongoing feedback that helps refine new interpersonal behaviors in a supportive environment. Feedback exchange makes information available, but it does not necessarily lead to changes in behaviors, attitudes, or emotions. Experimentation is the key.

Members experiment with new behaviors when they decide that their behaviors do not achieve the interpersonal results they want. Figure 9.5 shows the disclosure-feedback-experimentation cycle in detail. The process begins with self-disclosure. As members interact, they react to one another.

Members use feedback exchange to share their reactions. At this point, members discover how well their interpersonal behaviors get

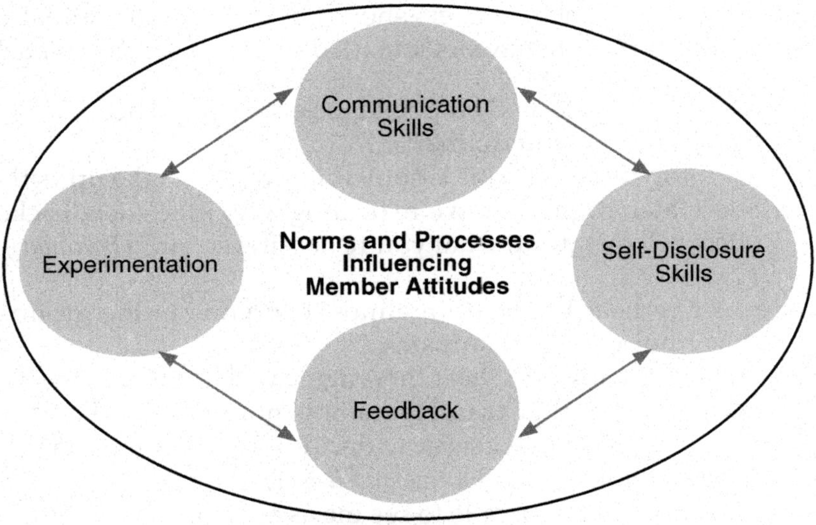

FIGURE 9.5
Disclosure-Feedback-Experimentation Cycle

the results they want. For example, members who want to develop relationships with other members may get feedback that confirms or disconfirms that their behaviors invite closer relationships. If members then want to develop behaviors that are more likely to get the interpersonal results they want, they ask for input about alternative experimental behaviors. Once members get some ideas about different behaviors, they can experiment with the behaviors they select.

Feedback and experimentation continue so that members can refine new behaviors until they get the interpersonal results they want. At any time during the experimentation process, members can decide whether their experimental behaviors are congruent with how they want to view themselves and how they want to be perceived by others. If they are not, the group helps generate different experimental behaviors. Then experimentation resumes until members get the results they want.

Finally, members, in consultation with the leader and the group, make choices about using the behaviors developed in group outside group. Leaders should periodically help members explore how they experience the impact of their experimental behaviors. Frequently, this exploration is a process that leads to additional insight and refining of the experimental behaviors. This is one of the few times in a counseling or therapy group when spending a significant portion of the group's time describing experiences outside the group is actually welcome and beneficial to the group's interactions and the goals of the group.

The disclosure-feedback-experimentation model focuses on members' interpersonal behaviors, but it is not behavioral to the extent that it ignores a complete range of experience. Experimentation leads to behavioral, attitudinal, and emotional change. Leaders need to involve members in conversations with each other as they experiment and eventually incorporate new behaviors. In particular, it is essential to initiate conversations with members that focus on the emotional aspects of their experience. As members share their experiences with each other, they commonly describe how faulty assumptions have constricted their relationships (e.g., "I never thought I could just ask" or "I could disagree and others could get mad, and I felt like I didn't have to please them!"). The process of experimentation uses an initial behavior focus that attempts to initiate change in all facets of members' experience.

To begin the process of developing alternative behaviors, members need first to clarify their intentions and develop experimental behaviors others see as more consistent with those intentions. Leaders can begin this process by asking feedback receivers what they were attempting to accomplish by using the behaviors identified during the feedback exchange. In cases where a member's intentions are inappropriate, leaders need to help that member explore those intentions with other members. In general, inappropriate intentions are associated with behaviors that violate boundaries, manipulate, or harm others in any way.

The process of generating alternative behaviors influences the entire group membership. The behaviors produced during this process offer all members ideas about more effective interpersonal behaviors. Ideally, following several repetitions of this process, norms develop that support the generation of alternative behaviors after feedback validation. Eventually, leaders will only need to prompt members to generate these behaviors.

The following example demonstrates how a leader clarifies a member's intentions and helps generate experimental behaviors:

Leader: "Robert, what did you want to communicate to Julie?" (*Question to clarify intentions*)

Robert: "I don't want Julie to get hurt. I thought I could give her reasons that would convince her to be more cautious about what she shares. I wanted her to know that I care about her and want her to be happy. This is something I've been struggling with for a long time."

Leader: "Robert, to learn other ways to communicate what you intend to communicate, you'll need to make a specific request for input. What exactly is it that you're not getting across that you want to get across?" (*Instruction and question to explore intentions*)

Robert: "I want people who I care about to understand that I care about them."

Leader: "Ask the rest of the group for some ideas about what you could do differently to help others understand that you care about them." (*Direct and connect*)

Robert: "Can anyone give me some ideas about what I can do to help you understand that I care about you?"

As members offer suggestions for different behaviors, leaders monitor interaction for excessive input that could overload the receiver and listen for consensus in the suggestions. When members inundate receivers with suggestions or begin to offer irrelevant suggestions, leaders should conclude the process of generating alternatives. When there are several viable suggestions, leaders direct receivers to choose a behavior that makes the most sense to them for experimentation. Remember that when members generate alternative behaviors, all members are hearing suggestions about potentially useful interpersonal behaviors:

Leader: "Robert, you've heard a number of good suggestions. Which one do you think might work for you?" (*Boundary setting to conclude generation of alternative behaviors and direction to select a behavior for experimentation*)

Robert: "Well, Gurpreet's idea to say that I care and that I'm available for support and not say what the other person should do seems like it would work. It would be hard to do, but I think I could do it."

Leader: "OK, you want to experiment with saying that you care and are available for support instead of supplying lots of reasons." (*Paraphrase to confirm understanding and to initiate experimentation*)

Robert: "That's right."

Once behaviors for experimentation have been identified, leaders can structure an initial experiment to help the member "try on" the behavior. First the leader coaches the member to use the experimental behavior in an interaction that initiated a feedback exchange. If the behavior produces the results the member wants and other members react positively to the behavior, the member trying on the behavior then uses it in ongoing experimentation during group interaction.

A leader-developed feedback contract with selected members or the entire group facilitates ongoing experimentation. The purpose of using a feedback contract is to involve the group in monitoring experimental behaviors and giving feedback about the effectiveness of the experimental behaviors. The processes of receiving feedback (i.e., listen, paraphrase, validate, and autonomy), generation and selection of alternative behaviors, and the initial "try on" experiment are completed once ongoing experimentation begins. As experimentation continues, ongoing feedback is used to refine experimental behaviors, so they become increasingly congruent and effective. When experimental behaviors are ineffective, alternative experimental behaviors are generated, selected, and employed. Occasionally, the experimentation process reveals concerns of the experimenting member that were not initially confronted. For example, it may become clear that Robert's "caring" for Julie disguised Robert's rigid expectations for others' behaviors or the projection of his own fears onto Julie:

Leader: "Robert, you want to say that you care and are available to give support instead of attempting to get others to do what you want." (*Paraphrase to ensure understanding*)

Robert: "Yeah, that's what I want to try."

Leader: "Before you do this on your own, let's try an experiment to be sure you're on the right track. Try doing this with Julie to see how it works." (*Set up "try on" experiment and direct*)

Robert: "Julie, I didn't know that I could just say . . ."

Leader: (*Interrupting*) "Just say it." (*Direct and connect*)

Robert: "Julie, I want you to know that I care about you. I'm scared you might get hurt. If you want my support, I'm here to give you whatever kind you want."

Leader: "Julie, give Robert some feedback about how what he said worked for you." (*Direct and connect*)

Julie offers feedback, and other members describe their reactions to Robert's experimental behaviors.

Leader: "OK, Robert, do you like how you came across enough to keep experimenting on your own in group?" (*Question to explore and confirm ongoing experimentation*)

Robert: "You know, that was really scary, but I like that Julie and the others understood what I wanted to communicate."

Leader: "Robert, it's useful when you're learning a different behavior to get some ongoing feedback about how well the behavior is working. Sometimes you can change it to work better and feel more natural for you. To do this, you need to make a feedback contract with other group members." (*Instruction and direction to set up ongoing experimentation and feedback contract*)

Robert, with the leader's prompting, develops a feedback contract with the entire group.

Conclusion

When members communicate effectively, self-disclose, exchange feedback, and experiment with new behaviors, they become highly skilled group members. Research shows that this level of interpersonal activity and learning leads to positive group outcomes for engaged members (see Chapter 13). Essentially, group members who learn from its process and have developed enhanced interpersonal skills achieve the greatest benefits from group participation. These benefits include corrective emotional experiences, interpersonal insight, improved interpersonal boundaries, improved intrapersonal processes, intercultural competence, and changes in the habitual personal solutions that limit their satisfaction in relationships. To achieve these benefits, group members must be open to learning new interpersonal skills, examining their intrapersonal processes, and examining their worldview and its impact on their intercultural interactions. They also need to be willing to take risks to try out new behavior, which requires willingness to be vulnerable and to make mistakes. Members who invest in learning the skills described in this chapter will achieve the results they seek in groups and also positively influence the experiences of others in and outside their groups.

Chapter 10

Ongoing Leadership Tasks

Outcomes

Level 1 Outcomes

After reading this chapter, entry-level students and practitioners should be able to:

1. Identify leadership tasks that leaders must perform throughout the lives of groups.
2. Describe essential processing skills.
3. Explain how to maintain a group environment that promotes diverse members' learning.
4. Discuss how to protect members from harm.
5. Explain how to promote diverse individuals' chances of success as group members.
6. Describe how to monitor group interaction for focal conflicts.

Level 2 Outcomes

After reading this chapter, advanced-level students and practitioners should also be able to:

1. Analyze group interaction and select essential leadership tasks.
2. Apply essential processing skills to group interaction.
3. Evaluate a group environment for its likelihood to promote members' learning.
4. Outline a frame of reference and the strategies that lead to members sharing a perception of safety in the group.
5. Demonstrate how to protect diverse group members from harm.
6. Illustrate how to promote diverse individuals' chances of success as group members.
7. Analyze group interaction to identify focal conflicts.

Ongoing leadership tasks support the primary objective of interactive group leadership—that is, to help group members benefit from their interactions with each other. This chapter describes how previously discussed concepts, such as group development theory, basic leadership and membership skills, and interactive leadership, are integrated in a leader's thoughts, actions, and tasks to be performed throughout the life of the group. See also Table 10.1.

The two main ongoing leadership tasks are developing a facilitative group environment and supporting interpersonal learning. Early in group, leaders intervene to develop a facilitative environ-

TABLE 10.1
Fundamental Leadership Skills: Objectives

Individual	Subgroup (or Interpersonal)	Group as a System (Whole)
• Engage a member in therapeutic factors	• Engage selected members in therapeutic factors	• Engage the entire group in therapeutic factors
• Affective	• Affective	• Affective
• Cognitive	• Cognitive	• Cognitive
• Behavioral	• Behavioral	• Behavioral

ment. The same types of interventions may be used as the group progresses through its life to maintain the quality of the group environment. In the same way, leaders use a flexible but consistent set of interventions to facilitate interpersonal learning throughout the group's life. Leaders intervene to facilitate interpersonal learning from the first session and continue until the group's final meeting.

Leaders should be aware of the systemic nature of the ongoing tasks involved in developing a facilitative group environment and facilitating interpersonal learning. These tasks are systemic in the sense that the interventions used to develop a facilitative group environment also influence the quality of interpersonal learning, and the interventions used to enhance interpersonal learning affect the quality of the group environment.

Because the group environment and interpersonal learning are systemically connected, leaders could focus on either developing the group environment or facilitating interpersonal learning and likely be successful. However, by balancing the two interventions, leaders can deal more directly and responsively with members' needs and emerging group issues.

To elaborate, when leaders observe that the group environment is not facilitative, they can focus on directly encouraging effective interpersonal learning. If they do this, leaders will find that the group environment becomes more facilitative as members observe and experience productive interpersonal learning. Conversely, when leaders recognize that interpersonal learning is not productive, they can look to the group environment to determine what shared concerns, restrictive solutions, boundary issues, or blocking norms are inhibiting interpersonal learning. When leaders accurately diagnose group environment issues and effectively intervene, interpersonal learning becomes more frequent and productive.

Often, members' ineffective use of interpersonal learning and group membership skills has little to do with how successfully leaders have taught these skills or how well members have learned. Rather, the ineffective use of interpersonal learning and group membership skills is often the consequence of *obstacles* in the group environment. These obstacles may include norms that preclude the expression of emotions, restrictive solutions that allow members to avoid sharing impressions, oppressive power dynamics, and shared fears of evaluation and judgment.

To maintain a facilitative group environment and facilitate interpersonal learning, leaders must continue to perform a range of essential ongoing tasks that include processing, optimizing the facilitative qualities of the group, establishing a shared perception of safety, protecting members from harm, and increasing individual members' chances of success.

Processing

Within the context of ongoing leadership tasks, processing is a set of tasks that direct members to share, reflect on, and more fully understand their here-and-now experiences, thereby encouraging and capitalizing on interpersonal learning. Processing involves having a discussion among the members about their experiences and thoughts related to group interaction or a series of interactions in the group over time. Although processing can take a number of forms, it should spur identification of interaction processes and increase members' understanding of how they are interacting and the consequences of their interactions.

Processing and languaging are closely related. Languaging is a form of processing and specifically directs members to define and make sense of interactions in the group that have led to learning. However, the function of processing is more general. Processing includes discussing and making sense of not only successful learning interactions but also any interactions that have had an impact on group members, such as emotionally charged interaction and frustrating or nonproductive interactions. Leaders begin processing by doing the following:

- Initiating discussion designed to describe, define, and understand any effective group interaction (languaging)
- Sharing observations about issues occurring at the group-as-a-system level and encouraging discussion
- Starting a discussion of group members' reactions to group interactions they have either experienced or observed
- Directing members to discuss experiences as a part of structured activities for the purpose of conceptualizing and generalizing learning

The common element unifying the tasks that are a part of processing is the goal of helping members make sense of what has occurred during group interaction, immediately or in the recent past. Processing is similar to the learning processes described by I. D. Yalom and Leszcz (2020), who referred to the process of helping members reflect on their experiences and develop a cognitive framework to understand these experiences as the "self-reflective loop." The self-reflective loop is a sequence of events that involves members having open, honest, here-and-now interactions with each other and then reflecting on these interactions to understand, conceptualize, and gain insight. In addition, the processing task of sharing observations and beginning discussion of group-as-a-system issues is similar to I. D. Yalom and Leszcz's (2020) leader process commentary (see Chapter 6).

Processing Skills

Processing generally involves stopping the group after a significant interaction or series of interactions and directing members to share and discuss their emotional and cognitive reactions. Once members share their reactions, leaders direct them to reflect on and make sense of these reactions. Successful processing outcomes include members conceptualizing their personal and shared concerns, defining their desired changes, and gaining insight into their interpersonal behaviors. Other successful outcomes include connecting emotionally with each other, developing language to describe what works, and reality-testing their reactions. When members share emotional and cognitive reactions, they also feel more connected and less lonely.

Well-timed processing provides members with learning opportunities. Leaders can start processing at almost any time during a group session to highlight a significant group event. Processing is not appropriate, however, if it diverts members' attention from productive member interactions such as intense emotional interactions, feedback exchanges, or the confrontation of a member's behaviors. When they begin processing, leaders should be mindful that their intention is to deepen members' learning and not avoid their own emotional reactions to group interaction. Another use of processing is to "buy time" when leaders are uncertain about what to do next. Commonly, when leaders are in doubt, so are the group members. The expression "When in doubt, process" is not far from the truth.

Although not an exhaustive list, the array of approaches described here illustrate how processing can be used in various situations. As a rule, processing should immediately follow group interactions that produce reactions that leaders expect members will need to discuss. Leaders who perceive almost all interactions as very meaningful may overuse this intervention. On the other hand, leaders who limit processing to events they perceive as profound will probably underuse this intervention.

Leaders' judgments about the benefits of processing determine when to process. When leaders believe that processing could help members sort out their reactions to a significant group event or produce important learning, they should start processing. At the same time, leaders should begin processing only when productive group interaction is at a point where it can be interrupted. Processing is useful in the following situations:

- Current interaction defines an issue that blocks effective group interaction (e.g., members are focusing on external events or avoiding expressing emotions)
- An intense interaction between several members has an unacknowledged emotional impact on the group (e.g., members are avoiding the expression of emotion that relates to their shared fears or the group focal conflict)
- Members are interacting in a way that poses a threat to a member (e.g., a member is being scapegoated)
- Members are avoiding giving feedback to a member whose behaviors are having an adverse effect on interaction (e.g., a member is monopolizing interaction, and other members are watching passively)

Leaders should not begin processing when doing so would stall meaningful interaction, unless they believe that an interaction is becoming harmful to the group or to the members involved in the interaction.

Helping Members Share Reactions

Processing encourages members to share their reactions to a group event. To accomplish this, group leaders can simply stop interaction and use a directive or a question to initiate discussion of the event and members' reactions to it. Following are some examples of how leaders might initiate processing of a group event:

Leader: "Let's stop here. What did you all just see happen?"
Leader: "I want to hear how each of you is reacting to the interaction that River and Chandra just had."
Leader: "Something just happened, and the entire group got quiet. Who wants to start talking about it?"
Leader: "That was intense! What emotions are you all feeling right now? Jamel, you seem full of emotions."

Leader: "I see a lot of reactions to what just happened, but no one is talking. All of you seem uncomfortable. Something happened that we need to talk about. Who wants to start?"

Helping Members Conceptualize Concerns

When members identify and label their concerns, they can identify what they want to change. Helping members conceptualize their concerns, however, usually requires a shift in most leaders' thinking. Instead of seeing themselves as in charge of defining what is wrong, leaders should think in terms of solutions that are not working for the problems at hand. When leaders see members struggling to interact with each other, they are observing members' failed solutions (Watzlawick et al., 1974), most often to the problem of interpersonal anxiety. For example, the member who withdraws from group interaction does not have the problem of being withdrawn. Instead, this member's solution of withdrawing is not working. The more other group members attempt to involve the withdrawn member, the greater that member's anxiety becomes, and the more the member withdraws. As the group doubles its efforts to involve the member, the member continues to use withdrawal. Withdrawing fails to lower the member's anxiety because the other members will only increase their attempts to "help" the member become involved. Withdrawal fails because it only invites other members to try harder.

During interaction, group members commonly develop norms organized around reducing anxiety. Interaction thus moves from solution to solution to minimize the anxiety created by pressure to interact honestly, openly, and congruently. When members find solutions that lower their anxiety, members perceive interaction as safer. However, these solutions work only temporarily because members are not developing solutions that confront the issues that created their anxiety in the first place (e.g., being rejected, ignored, judged). When members choose the solution of "talking about anxiety" as the means to lower anxiety and decide that solutions aimed at avoiding anxiety do not work, they can effectively interact and address their shared interpersonal concerns.

When leaders help members identify and understand failed solutions for their anxiety about group interaction, the members are then in a better position to develop solutions that work. These solutions involve a range of interpersonal behaviors that will improve the quality of group interaction and will contribute to better relationships for members in their lives outside the group. In a manner consistent with the languaging leadership function, leaders should first direct the group to discuss what is not working. This discussion will help group members develop language to describe the failed solution. The following examples show how leaders can initiate the processing task of helping members conceptualize their concerns:

Leader: "There's something going on right now that's preventing the group from talking about what's happening. What do some of you think is getting in our way now?"

Leader: "It looks like the group has come up with a way to stay stuck. Who can describe what the group is doing?"

Leader: "Every time the group gets close to dealing with the fear of being honest, something happens to shut down the conversation. Let's talk about what it might be."

Leader: "It looks like the group has committed to being totally safe in here at the expense of growth. Let's talk about what we're doing to keep us stuck."

Helping Members Define Change

Processing is also a way to help members define the changes they want to make. This processing intervention is an important follow-up to conceptualizing concerns. The following examples illustrate how leaders can help members define change as an aspect of processing:

Leader: "You all seem to understand that changing the subject when someone gets uncomfortable is not working. What do you all think you can do in here that would work better?"

Leader: "Given your group goal of helping each other more and giving more honest feedback, what are some ways to interact that will help you do these things?"

Leader: "What have you all noticed that helps us learn from each other?"

Helping Members Develop Insight

Although processing occasionally leads to insight, leaders should not conclude that they have the power to offer members insight. Developing group member insight is impossible as an intentional leader activity. Most commonly, member insight is part accident, part culmination of a facilitative environment, and part individual commitment. Insight emerges when members understand how the interactive behaviors they use within the group mirror situations and behaviors that have occurred in their past and in their everyday lives. For example, a member becomes aware that he reacts angrily whenever he is not involved in group discussions. Reflecting on these reactions, he recalls feeling sad and lonely when left out of his older siblings' activities. If he reacted angrily, the siblings would include him.

Processing also can lead to insight when members discuss motivations for the interpersonal behaviors they use during particular interactions. As members discuss their motivations for interpersonal behaviors, they may describe an "aha" moment. When members have this experience, they suddenly become aware of how and why certain interpersonal behaviors developed. They have developed interpersonal insight when they become aware of the motivations for their interpersonal behaviors. Members who make these discoveries might say, "So that's why I do that!"

Leaders who make it a point to direct members to discuss the motivations behind their behaviors may help members develop insight:

Leader: "David, what did you want to happen when you challenged Emma?"

Leader: "I'm wondering, Gordon, what it is you're getting from taking care of the other members."

Although it is quite likely that members will not be aware of the reasons for their behaviors, asking members to reflect on their motivations enhances awareness. Occasionally, enhanced awareness over time can lead to insight. Developing group member insight is not something leaders do. Leaders can make conditions in the group right for the development of insight only by processing group interactions and directing members to discuss reactions and motivations. Insight happens serendipitously; virtually any statement made during the processing of group interactions can lead to members gaining insight.

Optimizing the Group's Facilitative Qualities

Leaders' ongoing leadership tasks have the overall objective of optimizing the environment and facilitative qualities of the group. To reach this objective, leaders focus on supporting enabling solutions, on identifying and frustrating restrictive solutions, and on building a shared perception of safety, among other tasks.

Supporting Enabling Solutions

An essential leadership task is establishing and maintaining a group environment that optimizes each member's chance of having a successful group experience. One way leaders can move toward achieving this objective is by encouraging members to develop and implement enabling solutions. Recalling Chapter 4, enabling solutions are essentially norms that support directly addressing what group members wish to do in the group (disturbing motives) and the fears they have (reactive motives) about pursuing those wishes. If leaders do not encourage enabling solutions, restrictive solutions will dominate the group's interaction. Groups dominated by restrictive solutions deprive members of opportunities for interpersonal learning and significantly lower their chances of success.

Leaders should expect the regular emergence of restrictive solutions. As a leader, it is important to anticipate the frequent emergence of restrictive solutions that may limit the group's progress. When forming a group, it is crucial to clearly communicate the expectation for members to share personal information and expect that they may feel uncertain about the outcomes of their initial interactions. To combat the anxiety generated by this uncertainty, group members devise restrictive solutions.

While group members are developing restrictive solutions to manage their anxiety during initial interactions, most group leaders are trying to lay the groundwork for a productive and safe-enough group environment. To do so, many leaders encourage group members to engage in open here-and-now interaction by establishing ground rules. Ground rules that advocate for open here-and-now interaction are, in essence, prescriptions for enabling solutions (e.g., share your immediate emotions, honestly state your reactions). Unfortunately, the strategy of attempting to establish ground rules that promote enabling solutions has serious limitations. Regardless of what leaders attempt to prescribe, members will devise restrictive solutions. Group members respond first to their fears, not to their group leaders.

Experienced group leaders discover that the most useful strategy is to establish ground rules that satisfy ethical standards and then expect restrictive solutions. By expecting restrictive solutions, rather than attempting to establish ground rules that "eliminate" restrictive solutions, group leaders will be in a better strategic position. For example, by attempting to enforce ground rules such as sharing immediate feelings and staying in the here and now, leaders directly challenge members' initial fears about the consequences of interaction (e.g., offending others and being rejected) and may drum up a paralyzing amount of anxiety or resistance. On the other hand, by diligently asserting the need for confidentiality, anticipating that members will need to work out how open they can be with each other, and remaining vigilant for restrictive solutions, leaders can quickly begin dealing with interpersonal concerns.

Leaders who install only ethically necessary ground rules are more efficient because they do not have to determine why ground rules that prescribe how to interact are ineffective. From a strategic perspective, promoting ground rules that are destined to fail erodes members' confidence in leaders, sets up early leadership challenges, and leads to power struggles over how members should interact. By installing ethically necessary ground rules and expecting restrictive solutions, leaders can be ready to identify restrictive solutions as they emerge and intervene to frustrate their use.

Identifying and Frustrating Restrictive Solutions

To begin establishing enabling solutions, leaders must first identify restrictive solutions. This involves carefully observing group interaction. Although leaders can easily observe some restrictive solutions, many are not as obvious. Restrictive solutions are used by group members whenever interaction creates too much anxiety. The most obvious restrictive solutions are those that have been overtly negotiated and agreed upon. These restrictive solutions are usually products of group discussions that label some aspect of group interaction unnecessary or harmful. For example, members may reach a very quick consensus that interaction should always focus on each other's strengths and not on weaknesses.

The most difficult focal conflicts to identify are those that are created covertly. Chapter 2 described how obstructing norms develop from a process of covert negotiation. The covert processes that develop restrictive solutions and those that develop obstructing norms are identical. In fact, when restrictive solutions become long-term patterns in group interaction, they have become obstructing norms. For the most part, however, restrictive solutions come and go as members continue to negotiate and renegotiate the most effective means to manage anxiety.

Identifying covertly developed restrictive solutions involves observing interaction for patterns. These patterns often take shape as interaction that seemingly approaches an issue, only to detour quickly to safer topics. For instance, members may discuss how interaction is better when it includes members' emotional expressions but then suddenly enter a discussion about how demanding members' jobs have become.

Restrictive solutions are also present when obvious issues exist in group interaction but members do not speak about them. An example of an unspoken issue is when several group members do not participate, and the other group members do not mention their nonparticipation. Another example is when some members are having visibly strong emotional reactions and other group members avoid mentioning the emotional display. In both cases, the observed patterns illustrate what group members do to avoid interactions that will elevate anxiety. Restrictive solutions are the things that group members do to avoid interactions that elevate anxiety.

Leaders should intervene when they identify restrictive solutions. As they confront restrictive solutions, leaders should think and plan in terms of a series of interventions, because members will predictably cling to restrictive solutions that allow them to avoid anxiety. Also, members are adept at generating new restrictive solutions to replace those that have been thwarted by the leader or no longer spare them from anxiety.

The most effective approach to taking power away from a restrictive solution is to verbalize the disturbing motive and the reactive fears. By doing so, leaders frustrate the restrictive solutions and move members toward developing enabling solutions. Verbalizing disturbing motives and reactive fears repeatedly is successful over time because leaders continue to state aloud the issues members want to avoid. Thus, members are unable to avoid them. When leaders elevate anxiety to the point that members must face the disturbing motives and reactive fears, the restrictive solution fails. When a restrictive solution fails, members become much more open to trying an enabling solution. The following are examples of leader statements that initiate the process of frustrating restrictive solutions:

Leader: "The group seems intent on talking about how tired you are, but you might make more progress if you talk about how scary it would be to share how you feel about each other."

Leader: "The longer you focus on how River handles feedback, the longer you avoid talking about how scared you are to be rejected."

Leader: "The group is spending a lot of time talking about the last meeting. I wonder how this helps you all deal with the fear of being hurt if you share how you really feel right now?"

Group leaders can also frustrate group members' attempts to develop restrictive solutions during interaction. When leaders begin to understand that members' current interaction has the goal of developing a restrictive solution, leaders should direct the discussion toward the disturbing motive and reactive fears. When leaders do this, they should also help members see how a restrictive solution will not satisfy their needs:

Leader: "So, you seem to be set on giving only positive feedback to each other. Let's talk for a minute about how this helps you deal with being afraid to be honest with each other."

Leader: "Help me understand. What do you hope to gain by talking in depth about each of your home lives? It seems like under that, everyone is afraid that, if they show who they really are here in group, they will be judged and rejected."

Whitaker and Lieberman (1964) maintained that when leaders choose not to intervene on an identified restrictive solution, they are making a mistake that will inhibit the formation of a facilitative environment. It is also harmful when leaders do not notice restrictive solutions emerging. In both cases, by not intervening, leaders support the continuance of restrictive solutions. Leaders must support the use of enabling solutions—meaning that leaders continuously observe group interaction to identify and discourage restrictive solutions and diligently intervene to develop enabling solutions.

Building a Shared Perception of Safety

A shared perception that participation in group interaction is safe is a necessary condition for meaningful interpersonal learning. When members feel and believe it is safe to take risks and engage in emotionally intense interactions, the group becomes a powerful learning environment. However, taking risks and engaging in emotionally intense interactions is inconsistent with most members' everyday patterns of what they need to do to stay safe.

Most members begin groups with boundaries and habitual solutions that do not support the types of interaction that lead to interpersonal learning. At the beginning, group members often attempt to protect themselves from interpersonal harm by hiding—that is, by not expressing reactions and emotions. This hiding allows them to control the amount of anxiety they experience. Unfortunately, staying hidden is a solution that does not allow members to develop relationships, gain acceptance, overcome loneliness, establish emotional connections, experience congruent interactions, or get feedback. Although staying hidden is a solution that does not work to promote growth, those who use it experience less anxiety even as they may remain miserable. Being hidden, especially if it becomes a group norm, creates interpersonal boundaries that obstruct interpersonal learning and threatens the facilitative potential of the group environment.

When groups first convene, members usually agree that the group is a risky place to share personal information beyond a few facts about or occurrences in their life. To cope with this risky environment, members usually negotiate avoidance as the best way to stay safe. When this is agreed upon, members avoid meaningful interaction, support each other's avoidance, and develop the perception that avoidance leads to safety. This flawed perception of safety is persuasive because staying hidden allows members to manage their anxiety. The outcome is a hidden membership that shares a perception of safety in an environment members perceive as threatening. The price, however, is deeper connection and growth.

A real sense of safety occurs only after members have confronted their fears and engage in conflict. To confront their fears, members must risk interacting with others in a more open and intimate way than they are accustomed to. Members become secure in their perception of safety when they witness and experience productive interpersonal learning and come to believe they have the skills to interact in productive ways. As mentioned earlier, interpersonal learning and the facilitative nature of the group environment are systemically related. As one develops, so does the other. Real safety is built upon trust in self and others to engage in and successfully manage self-disclosure and interpersonal learning.

Fortunately, leaders can take steps to develop a shared perception of safety in their groups. Developing safety begins with leaders' group composition choices (Whitaker & Lieberman, 1964). When groups are composed of members who diverge dramatically in their interpersonal boundaries and tolerance for anxiety, development of safety is nearly impossible. Developing safety is nearly impossible in a poorly composed group because members with extremely permeable boundaries are likely to share personal information that threatens members who are protective of their impermeable boundaries. Differences in boundaries, or *boundary incompatibility*, result in a group divided between members feeling frustrated that sharing is not open and members feeling threatened by what others want to share. In addition, when members have a widely varying tolerance for anxiety, solutions that satisfy the needs of some members are either overly threatening or overly stifling for others.

Groups composed of members with similar enough boundaries and tolerances for anxiety are more likely to develop interactive norms that ultimately lead to a shared perception of safety that allows interactive learning. Boundaries that permit members to share concerns, reactions, and emotions while maintaining adequate autonomy allow members to interact honestly without creating excessive anxiety or excessively threatening the group's perception of safety. This perception is further promoted when group members' anxiety tolerances are reasonably similar.

Safety further develops when enabling solutions allow members to speak openly and deal directly with their interpersonal fears—that is, interpersonal boundaries become progressively more open as members risk disclosing and develop trust. When members' productive learning experiences are witnessed by the group, boundaries open further, the perception of safety increases, and the group environment becomes progressively more facilitative. As the group becomes more facilitative, a shared perception of safety builds.

However, a shared perception of safety is not permanent. As groups continue, leaders and members will differ on how to approach and resolve members' relationship issues. This conflict occurs because leaders have the objective of helping members learn how to manage relationship issues and members have—along with their desire to grow—the objective of avoiding uncomfortable anxiety. Leaders thus face the ongoing balancing act of urging members to confront relationship issues and maintaining a shared perception of safety. Thus, leaders must weigh their goal of confronting relationship issues against the goal of maintaining a shared sense of safety in the context of the group's ability to tolerate anxiety and the potential for successful resolution of the issues. When maintaining this balance, leaders should consider two factors. If leaders believe that members are operating at the edge of their anxiety tolerance and members' avoidance of difficult group issues is an "escape hatch" for intolerable anxiety, they may choose not to confront members' avoidance. This action involves ignoring members' avoidance and supporting members' efforts to redevelop the shared belief that group interaction is safe. Some possible ways leaders can support and initiate escape hatches are as follows:

Leader: "Let's shift topics now. What are some of the interactions that happened tonight that you learned from, and what did you learn?"

Leader: "The tension in here is intense! Jamel, say more about what you've been learning."

If, on the other hand, leaders believe that members are avoiding issues they could successfully resolve, they should challenge members' avoidance. Successfully intervening to challenge members' avoidance depends on leaders identifying what members are avoiding and continuously frustrating members' attempts to shift discussion to safe topics:

Leader: "Gordon and Emma still have not talked about their anger with each other, and the group seems willing to let that slide."

Leader: "River, Chandra, Jamel, and David, I'm very confused about why you're talking about work. The four of you seemed furious a minute ago! You are having some strong reactions, and you're sitting on them."

It is not useful for the group environment to have a constant uncomfortable level of anxiety. Groups with a consistently high level of anxiety will become ineffective because members shift their attention from interpersonal learning to closing their interpersonal boundaries and negotiating how to make the group reasonably safe. To be sensitive to members' perceptions of safety, leaders should assess the level of anxiety present in their groups. They can do this by observing members' nonverbal behaviors and the content of their interaction. When anxiety is excessive, leaders should shift, or allow members to shift, the discussion to less threatening escape hatch topics on a temporary basis. Escape hatches, carefully and sparingly used, can support a shared sense of safety in groups.

Protecting Members From Harm

Closely associated with developing a shared perception of safety is the ongoing leadership task of protecting members from harm.

Safety in the group is also contingent upon other ongoing tasks, but when members understand that they can depend on leaders to protect them from harm, their confidence in the safety of group increases. In her discussion of group leader responsibilities, Whitaker (1985) emphasized the role of leaders in establishing safety:

> Persons in groups are supported in feeling safe enough to take risks if they can hold on to the sense that there is one person in the group who retains sufficient understanding, strength, courage, and disinterest to handle acutely difficult situations and emergencies should they arise. (p. 382)

To establish a perception of safety, leaders should be alert to, and preempt, situations that harm members or identify and remedy them. There are several situations that lead to member harm: members excessively pressuring other members, members in persistent isolation, group boundary problems, and unaddressed harmful societal dynamics within the group that mirror members' trauma. *Members pressuring other members* refers to situations in which group members coerce other members to engage in behaviors that those members do not wish to perform. This includes situations where group members blame a single member for group issues. The issue of *members in isolation* includes occasions when members persistently do not share the emotional reactions they experience in group or make choices about using behaviors observed in group outside the group without first discussing them during group. *Group boundary problems* concern both the group's internal interpersonal boundaries and its external boundaries. *Unaddressed societal dynamics* refers to group situations where the leader and most of the members reenact societal oppression within the group at the expense of minority members.

Members Pressuring Other Members

Members excessively pressuring other members occurs when group members pressure another member to conform to their personal requirements. Interactions that illustrate the pressure to conform occur when one or more group members attempt to convince another member to participate more actively, to take risks, or to receive and act on feedback. Although these attempts can be beneficial for the pressured member, there is a point at which pressure to conform becomes damaging.

Although it is critical for leaders to define when pressuring to conform becomes damaging, it is also difficult because leaders may often find themselves pulled into being on the side of the members who are doing the pressuring. For example, leaders want all members to be actively involved in feedback exchange. When several group members pressure another member to be more actively involved in feedback exchanges, leaders will find themselves supporting the members' efforts to involve the pressured member.

It is not necessarily negative when members urge another member to become involved. In fact, it can be very positive. However, when pressure becomes coercive or abusive in any way, leaders should intervene to support the pressured member's choices about participating in feedback exchanges. The group leader should also address other members' apprehensions about the pressured member's participation—that is, the group leader should encourage the group to examine what fear is behind the requirement they are trying to impose on their fellow member. For example, group members who strongly pressure other members to participate more actively often fear more intimate participation. They are absolved of any pressure to share more intimately if they must "wait" for the pressured member to perform as instructed.

Other unacceptable instances of pressuring a member to conform are more easily identified. Some obvious cases include demanding that a member share personal information, pressuring a group member to agree with a group decision, or exhorting a member to interact in a way that is unacceptable to that member. Leaders should be assertive in supporting the right of all group members to make their own choices, unless these choices involve harm to self or others.

Leaders should be aware that members who do not conform to the expectations of others in the group may experience negative consequences. One consequence they may experience is being blamed for the anxiety other members experience. The process of group members coming to believe a particular group member is the cause of their anxiety is well explained by focal conflict theory.

Focal conflict theory describes circumstances in which individual members are blamed for other members' anxieties. One of these cases occurs when a member enacts a restrictive solution, and the group is attempting to implement an enabling solution (deviant restrictive). Another circumstance occurs when a member enacts an enabling solution, and the group is attempting to implement a restrictive solution (deviant enabling). In each case, the noncomplying member is pressured to conform. If the noncomplying member does not conform, other members may blame that member for the group's problems. This is an indication that a member is at risk of becoming a scapegoat and being potentially harmed.

The following scenario illustrates this dynamic. David insisted that he would not share his emotions during the group. This represents a restrictive solution. Other members, however, had just openly negotiated an enabling solution whereby they decided that sharing feelings was necessary because it promoted connection and safety. As the whole group interacted, the group began to develop an opinion that David was holding the group back. As this opinion took shape, interaction grew in its intensity and members other than David became angry. Finally, Chandra stated, "David, if you were more open, we could actually get something done in here. Instead, we are all stuck in this boring loop."

Members become scapegoats when they do not comply with the other members' solutions to focal conflicts. Noncomplying members are seen as the reason group-developed solutions are not working the way group members had hoped. When members are scapegoated, other group members may become abusive and critical, blaming the scapegoated member for problems in group interaction. Scapegoated members, especially those who are emotionally fragile, may feel rejected and can be hurt by the harsh comments of other members. If leaders are not aware of the scapegoating process and fail to intervene, scapegoated members can be harmed.

Leaders should be alert to problems that involve coercion and scapegoating. Once leaders identify coercion or scapegoating, their interventions should be decisive and clear. These interventions should focus on the group as a whole and not on the members being pressured or scapegoated. In each of the following examples, the leader interrupts conversation that pressures or scapegoats a member:

Leader: "It seems that sharing emotions is important and that trying to talk David into it is not helping you do that. I'd like all of you who want to share your feelings to go ahead and share them. Certainly, David's not trying to stop you."

Leader: "Most of you believe that sharing emotions is important, and so do I. It's time we started doing it. Who wants to start?"

Leader: "It seems that sharing your feelings is scary, and it's even scarier if everyone is not on board. What's so scary about having someone hold back? Jamel, you can start."

Members in Isolation

Members in isolation pose difficult problems for group leaders, especially in two common situations. The first is when members have profoundly disruptive experiences, such as an intense emotional reaction, and do not talk about it. The second is when members use behaviors outside group that they have observed in group without communicating their intent or experience with it. The issue that ties both cases together is that members are not disclosing their intentions or experiences in group. When this happens, leaders may be totally unaware of what is happening. The goal for leaders in dealing with members in isolation is to do all they can to prevent problems.

When members experience an emotionally intense reaction to a group interaction and do not share it, they cannot be helped by the group or the leader to process their experience. Thus, they are much less likely to develop an understanding of their experience or draw on the support of the group or group leader. Dealing with intense feelings in isolation may increase their sense of isolation within the group and exacerbate preexisting issues. A possible implication of this is that the member may leave the group and be at risk of harming themself or others without the awareness of the leader.

Members who decide to use behaviors they have observed or experimented with in group in regular social settings without first processing the implications may risk damaging their relationships. Customary social interactions, including those in primary relationships, usually do not involve the openness or honesty found in the interactions of members in effectively functioning groups. Members who choose to interact with significant others as they have with other group members will shock unprepared significant others. Irreparable harm is possible in relationships that are not based on openness and honesty. For example, a member who confronts an employer as they would another group member may lose their job.

To prevent the problems posed by isolated members, leaders should work toward several objectives related to what members should share in group. Leaders take a step toward preempting potential problems by establishing and maintaining the norms "share reactions, especially strong ones" and "don't try a behavior outside group before discussing it in group." After emotionally intense interactions, leaders should carefully scan group members for nonverbal reactions. Members who are not sharing should be strongly encouraged to enter group interaction to process their reactions. In addition, members who are experimenting with alternative interpersonal behaviors within the group should be cautioned to discuss the implications of using these behaviors outside the group.

Group Boundary Problems

Boundary problems surface at the internal and external boundaries of groups. These problems can negatively impact the interactive environment if not addressed by the leader. Internal boundary problems include, but are not limited to, verbal and physical assault and coerced self-disclosure. External boundary issues include, but are not limited to, breaches of confidentiality and the inclusion of inappropriate members. Unacceptable interpersonal boundaries are exemplified by verbally or physically violent behavior directed at another member. Because the group environment encourages and relies upon safety, such behavior is particularly harmful. When leaders screen new members, present group ground rules, and develop group norms, they must state explicitly that verbally and physically assaultive behaviors are unacceptable in the group and clearly indicate the consequences of these behaviors.

To protect group members, leaders must immediately eliminate from the group individuals who physically assault or seriously threaten another member, either in or outside of group. Group members should never have to consider the possibility that another member may physically attack them. The presence of a member who assaults or threatens physical assault on another member totally undermines leaders' efforts to establish an environment of safety.

The case of verbal assault is not as clear-cut as the case of physical assault or threat of physical assault. Verbal assaults present leaders with room for interpretation. In some cases, members who are learning to express anger appropriately may not immediately have the interpersonal skills necessary to do so in a productive manner. Until they develop the necessary skills, these members may come across as verbally abusive. Clearly, these members can benefit from feedback and experimentation with appropriate communication of anger. Leaders must judge what to do on the basis of whether a member has the ability and the skills to share anger productively, whether they are instead choosing to remain verbally abusive, and whether their inappropriate expression of anger unfairly limits other members' growth or harms other members.

When leaders believe a member will continue to be verbally assaultive or abusive in spite of feedback exchange, they must remove that member from group. In this instance, leaders should speak with the individual involved about their removal from the group, but this discussion could occur outside of the group. During this discussion, leaders should be prepared to provide appropriate referrals. When a group member is removed, the group leader needs to process the member's removal thoroughly in group.

External boundary problems commonly include breaches of confidentiality and the inclusion of members who are inappropriate for group work. During screening interviews and the group's initial meetings, leaders should emphasize the importance of confidentiality, explain their ethical and legal responsibilities in terms of confidentiality, and clearly illustrate ways to maintain confidentiality. When group members breach confidentiality by discussing outside of group information that was disclosed by others in group, leaders have several courses of action.

Some leaders may stipulate during screening and initial meetings that members who breach confidentiality will be immediately dropped from the group. This stipulation presents the clearest boundary for members and contributes to external group boundaries that enhance members' perceptions of safety and trust. Other leaders may devise ways for group members to confront a member who has broken confidentiality and give group members the responsibility of retaining or removing the errant member. This approach raises several important issues. First, by giving members responsibility for this decision, leaders send members an ambiguous message about leadership role responsibilities. If leaders need to plan later about removing or including a new member, the existing members may not understand why they have suddenly lost one of their responsibilities. Second, when members are permitted to remain in the group after breaking confidentiality, members' perceptions of trust and safety may always be insecure. Finally, asking members to make this decision places them in the difficult position of trying to make a reasoned decision about a person they may have grown close to and who has betrayed their trust.

The external boundary problem of an individual who is inappropriate for group work can usually be prevented by careful pregroup screening. During screening, leaders should carefully consider a prospective member's history of treatment and current mental status in addition to the criteria presented in Chapter 7 in the discussion of leaders' administrative function. As leaders screen individuals for inclusion in their groups, inevitably they will decide not to admit some individuals. They should be aware of referral sources that are more appropriate for these individuals. Finally, leaders should understand that they are making choices about group composition during screening interviews. Important considerations for screening interviews are noted during the discussion of developing a shared perception of safety and also in the discussion regarding members' personality styles in Chapter 3.

Unaddressed Societal Dynamics

Clearly, members cannot have a successful group experience without sharing, to some extent, a perception of safety. How to establish a shared sense of safety was previously discussed in this chapter. However, one common situation warrants attention and involves the ongoing task of developing a shared perception of safety as well as the ongoing task of protecting members from harm. This is when a group member who differs in social identity from other group members, in ways that are visible or invisible, struggles to experience a shared perception of safety within the group and becomes isolated, silenced, invalidated, or even scapegoated. This occurs when a group member experiences systemic oppression outside of the group and the environment within the group mimics, as it often does, the outer world. When a group member who has a lived experience of oppression or discrimination reexperiences this within a therapeutic group, safety is impossible, and harm is probable without leader intervention. Prevention and intervention should be used to address this issue as part of preventing the harm of group members.

First, the leader must be aware that this is always possible, even in a group without visible diversity, and they must be open to conceptualizing low participation or nonparticipation by a member as a diversity issue. The leader must be aware of their own potential biases and how these may show up during interaction. During screening and orientation, leaders should ask members if they have identities or life experiences that have caused them to be marginalized, if they have apprehensions about this occurring in the group, and how they would like to handle that information within the group. This early foundation will provide a basis for safety. Early in the life of the group, leaders should encourage the expectation that social identity is potentially important in the group and that reactions related to social identity may be useful to share.

As interpersonal interaction develops, the leader should monitor group member participation and also monitor the content of interaction for bias and microaggressions, particularly if several members share these interactions. How the leader intervenes depends on the likelihood of the potentially marginalized group member being able to voice their concerns with support, the egregiousness of the group's marginalizing behavior, and the leader's own resolve to prevent inequality from dominating the group. If the marginalizing behavior is clear, persistent, and intentional, leaders should be confident and directive:

> *Leader*: Emma, I've noticed that several times you have eased the tension after someone reminds you to listen by mimicking the speech patterns of someone with a hearing impairment. This could be very hurtful, and I'd like you to stop.

If the marginalizing behavior seems unintentional, and the leader believes the individual who is affected can voice their concerns with some support, the leader may work at the individual level to elicit the concern:

> *Leader*: Gordon, you seem pretty quiet, and your face looks frustrated. What's going on?
>
> *Gordon*: I feel invisible and hurt, but I'm scared to talk about why.
>
> *Leader*: I can see that you are pretty scared, but I think you'll keep feeling invisible if you don't talk about it.
>
> *Gordon*: It's just that everyone talks in here like there are just men and women. I told everyone in the first session my pronouns are "they/them," but I've been misgendered several times. That hurts. But I'm super tired of telling people when it happens. And sometimes it doesn't go well, either.

Regardless of how the leader chooses to intervene to prevent harm, they should monitor the rest of the group members for reactions and provide opportunities to process, language, or provide feedback.

Ensuring Individual Members' Chances of Success

Another essential ongoing leadership task is ensuring that every member has the opportunity for a successful group experience. Successful group experiences occur when members have enough opportunities for interpersonal learning to make their group experience useful. These opportunities occur when members experience sufficient safety in the group, self-disclose significant emotions and perceptions, give and receive feedback, and experiment with new behaviors that are relevant to their well-being. On the other hand, when members do not share a perception of safety and they participate superficially or not at all, they are unlikely to have a useful group experience. To ensure that members make the most of their opportunities, leaders must intervene to address the factors that prevent members from participating in meaningful interaction.

Focal conflict theory (Whitaker & Lieberman, 1964) conceptualizes how members use customary interpersonal behaviors or habitual personal solutions to avoid the anxiety associated with group participation. When members' habitual solutions interfere with opportunities for interpersonal learning, leaders should identify the events that lead to the use of these solutions. In other words, when a member uses a defensive interpersonal behavior for an extended period of time, leaders should identify what is occurring in the group that may be causing that member to be uncomfortably anxious.

Once leaders have identified a situation in which a member uses a habitual solution, leaders can use several interventions. One of these involves interfering with what the group is doing to evoke a member's anxiety. A group may be dealing with issues that a member finds especially threatening, or the group may be unreasonably challenging a member to change their behaviors. Whenever leaders recognize that the group is challenging one of its members unreasonably to address its own anxiety, leaders must intervene by blocking the challenge. For example, a leader could make the following intervention when the group is unreasonably challenging one of its members to stop being angry:

> *Leader*: "It seems that the group is having a hard time dealing with Chandra's anger. Bernie, perhaps you can talk about what it's like for you to experience anger in here."

When leaders determine that a member's habitual solution is a response to a reasonable challenge by other group members, leaders use a different intervention. The goal of this intervention is to frustrate the member's habitual solution. For example, when members are challenging another member about not being open to feedback, leaders might say the following to frustrate the member's habitual solution:

> *Leader*: "River, several members have attempted to give you feedback and have tried to talk you into listening to it. You've been really angry with them and have told them you don't

> want to hear it. Your anger doesn't seem to be working because they keep trying to get you to listen to their feedback. Go ahead and ask them for some suggestions on a better way to say 'no.'"

Habitual solutions are most problematic when members use them to avoid interactions that could lead to interpersonal learning. For example, members who use anger to shut down productive interactions or refuse to listen to feedback are using habitual solutions that block opportunities for interpersonal learning. At the same time, other group members lose opportunities for learning because of the time and energy they invest in persuading these members to change. When they overinvest in changing other members' habitual solutions, these members also avoid their own interpersonal learning, risks of self-disclosure, and potentially helpful feedback.

To ensure that members' habitual solutions do not block opportunities for learning, leaders should share their observations about the habitual solutions with the group. If observations, subsequent confrontation, and feedback from others do not help to engage the member who is using habitual solutions to avoid interpersonal learning opportunities, leaders need to examine the group as a system.

When examining the group as a system, leaders should try to determine how a member's continued use of a habitual solution supports the group operation. For example, a member who refuses to be involved sustains a group system organized around avoiding the anxiety associated with participation. This happens when a group focuses much of its energy on trying to include a member who refuses to be included. By using group time to convince a very reluctant member to participate, the group is able to avoid talking about their fear of participation. For as long as the member refuses, the group system of interaction and avoidance continues.

By observing how a member's role operates in the group system, leaders can better understand how other group members are, in reality, supporting the member's continued use of a habitual solution. These observations also provide leaders with important information about the shared fears of all group members. When observing a group to see how a member sustains a group system, leaders may find it useful to consider the following questions: What is the group's pattern of interaction? How does this member's behavior help the group continue this pattern? What *is not* happening while this pattern *is* happening? What shared fears are members attempting to avoid?

Leaders should consider interventions that target both the member using the habitual solution and the entire group. Interventions that address both these targets are the most effective way to deal with a group system that supports a member's continued use of a habitual solution. When using these interventions, leaders should not expect immediate results. Such results are not likely because these interventions attempt to reorganize a group system so that all members can experience learning opportunities. The success of interventions designed to reorganize a group system requires repeated attempts to frustrate how the system operates. In other words, what the system is organized to do (e.g., avoid feelings) does not work because leaders continue to frustrate how it operates (e.g., direct members to talk about feelings). Following are some examples of how leaders might initiate interventions to change members' patterns of using habitual solutions and to address group systems that maintain the use of habitual solutions:

Leader: "It seems that each of you is really invested in helping Emma stay angry. Tell me what would happen if she weren't so angry."

Leader: "It seems that each of you is really invested in helping Emma stay angry. Let's experiment with interacting the way you would if she weren't angry."

Leader: "You've all worked really hard for half the group to involve David. He simply does not want to, so I think it's time to move on. Who wants to begin?"

Leader: "You know, Jamel, if you did something different, the rest of the group would have to take some responsibility for making sure different points of view are shared."

Interventions that challenge a member's habitual solution modify that member's interpersonal boundaries and address their interpersonal perceptual distortions. Once members elect to abandon their habitual solutions without replacing them with other habitual solutions, they will open their boundaries to more meaningful interaction. During this process, members encounter perceptual distortions that have led them to stay closed to others. For example, Gordon kept their feelings to themself (i.e., their habitual solution) because of their experiences with their family of origin, who would criticize them for sharing feelings. When Gordon witnessed other members sharing feelings without criticism, they decided to open their boundaries to allow sharing of feelings in group.

Monitoring Group Interaction for Focal Conflicts and Themes

Removing blocks to interpersonal learning often involves identifying focal conflicts and group themes that interfere with meaningful interaction. Group themes and focal conflicts are impediments to interpersonal learning because they represent what members are attempting to avoid. When leaders identify group focal conflicts and themes, they gain insight into the dynamics of group interaction, can understand the motivations of group members, and then can define intervention objectives.

Stock and Lieberman (1962) described various pieces of data (or clues) that help leaders identify focal conflicts and group themes. These clues include group interaction content, the way members interact, and members' nonverbal behaviors. In focal conflict terms, a group organizes around the avoidance of the anxiety that is created by interpersonal issues. Avoidance of an interpersonal issue influences the content of group interaction and impedes interpersonal learning. Consequently, the avoidance of an issue organizes the content of interaction, and the content of a group's interaction reflects its current focal conflict.

By accurately identifying the theme in group interaction, leaders can identify elements of the focal conflict. For instance, as group members interact around the issue of how they should participate, leaders may hear a theme in members' discussion that indicates the group shares a fear of being criticized. This theme identifies the reactive motive (i.e., fear of criticism), which is a potential target for intervention. The leader in this example could offer one of the following interventions, which are presented in order of increasing intensity:

Leader: "The group seems to be suggesting that you might get criticized in here. Let's talk about what it's like for you to be criticized."

Leader: "Being criticized can really hurt. River, you start. Tell us what it would be like for you to be criticized by another member."

Leader: "Bernie, you and other members seem fearful of being criticized in here. Tell the person in here you think is most likely to criticize you why you think they would do that and how you would feel if that happened."

A leader in this example could intervene to assist members in developing a group norm that facilitates personal responsibility for words and actions in the group:

Leader: "It seems that most group members have developed a pattern of saying 'we' when they are really talking about their own point of view. From now on, I would like to encourage each of you to say 'I' when you present your own perspective."

Leader: "Whenever a member begins to describe how they feel, they are cut off, and the subject is changed. We need to adopt the ground rule that members expressing their feelings should be allowed to complete their expression before anyone else speaks."

Leader: "David, could you repeat what you said? This time remember to use 'I' instead of 'we.'"

Leader: "Judith, stop. Let Randy finish saying how he's feeling."

Any discussion members have about circumstances outside the group is an additional clue regarding the current focal conflict. From the focal conflict perspective, all content included in group interaction is in some way related to the focal conflict the group is experiencing in the here and now of group interaction. For example, a discussion about how the press has wrongfully accused a community member can indicate fears group members have about being misunderstood in group.

Leaders should frustrate the restrictive solution of extensive externally focused conversation because it is commonly used to avoid the anxiety of more intimate and productive interaction. However, before shifting interaction back into the group, leaders should listen for the theme that reveals the core issue of current group interaction. When shifting conversation back into the group, leaders should relate the theme to members' here-and-now experience in the group. To accomplish this, the leader might say the following in reference to the conversation about the wrongly accused community member:

Leader: "Let's switch our focus slightly. It seems like the group may need to talk about what it would be like for other members to get the wrong idea about you."

Leaders can become confident that members are talking about issues related to a focal conflict by observing the way members respond to the content. Clues to look for include nonverbal and affective reactions, the energy and pace of interaction, and the emotional tone of the discussion. For example, when members are uncomfortably shifting about in their chairs, not looking at each other, and talking rapidly and anxiously, the discussion is likely getting very close to the most pertinent focal conflict.

In addition, leaders should consider the context of the group discussion. For example, an abandonment theme in interaction content might be explained by the fact that the group is about to conclude or that the leader is about to go on vacation. The group leader needs to attend to context clues to help them understand group themes, connect these themes to focal conflicts, develop interventions, and then intervene.

Conclusion

Interactive group work focuses on leaders interacting in group to develop a facilitative environment that encourages group member autonomy and member-to-member learning. Leaders use their leadership role and basic leadership skills and interventions to facilitate this environment. Maintaining this environment throughout the life span of the group requires the leaders' attention to a set of ongoing tasks. The ongoing leadership tasks described in this chapter have the singular goal of optimizing members' opportunities for learning. By helping members communicate effectively and exchange feedback in a productive manner, leaders are on their way to reaching this goal. When leaders also successfully confront group environment issues that slow learning, members are likely to have productive learning experiences, and leaders will attain their goals.

Because the group environment and member-to-member or interpersonal learning are mutually influential, leaders can focus on either and have some positive effect. But a balance between the two allows leaders to deal responsively with both. Regardless of emphasis, maintaining a facilitative group environment and facilitating interpersonal learning requires leaders to regularly perform a range of essential ongoing tasks. Leaders must attend to processing the concerns of members and the group. They must monitor and optimize the facilitative qualities of the group. Finally, they must also continuously strive to establish a shared perception of safety, protect members from harm, and increase individual members' chances of success.

Chapter 11

Intervention Strategies

Outcomes

Level 1 Outcomes

After reading this chapter, entry-level students and practitioners should be able to:

1. Discuss how to use intervention strategies for confronting obstructing group norms and implementing facilitative group norms.
2. Describe intervention strategies designed to deal with interpersonal and relationship issues and how to use them.
3. Explain "problematic" member roles from a focal conflict perspective.
4. Outline intervention strategies for addressing problematic member roles and how to use them.
5. Discuss the dynamics of social/diversity issues and how they emerge during group interaction.
6. Describe how to use intervention strategies to address social/diversity issues in counseling and therapy groups.

Level 2 Outcomes

After reading this chapter, advanced-level students and practitioners should also be able to:

1. Describe how leaders' understanding of effective intervention strategies can lead to culturally responsive interventions that encourage the success of all group members, irrespective of their identities or social and cultural backgrounds.
2. Describe and provide examples of how leaders can help problematic group members overcome challenges to interpersonal effectiveness and productive group membership.
3. Describe and provide clear examples of how members can effectively exchange feedback, practice self-disclosure, and experiment by acquiring and demonstrating specific skills.

Intervention strategies are sequences of interventions made over the course of a session or several sessions to improve the facilitative qualities of the group environment and encourage member change. Intervention strategies may involve a number of interventions focused on specific ongoing objectives (e.g., developing a group's normative structure). Other intervention strategies may have objectives that require a session or several sessions to accomplish (e.g., helping members change their group roles and improving certain aspects of their relationships).

Leaders use intervention strategies once they have observed group-as-a-system interaction patterns that impair group productivity or identify the need for changes in some members' patterns of interpersonal relationships. These patterns include obstructing norms, interpersonal and relationship issues, problematic member roles, and sociocultural issues that emerge in group interaction.

Obstructing Norms

Obstructing norms are patterns in interaction that support behaviors that are inconsistent with group objectives. Ordinarily, these interactive patterns hinder effective communication, feedback exchange, experimentation, and the development of a facilitative group environment. Examples of obstructing norms include implicit rules for interaction, such as sharing compliments but not feedback, discussing thoughts but not feelings, focusing on external experiences but not immediate group experiences, and interrupting others when what they are sharing causes anxiety (see Chapter 2).

From the focal conflict perspective, obstructing norms are restrictive solutions members use to avoid confronting the anxiety produced by disturbing and reactive motives. Restrictive solutions become obstructing norms when members use them for extended periods of time and these solutions become a pattern in group interaction.

Leaders need to remember that obstructing norms develop subtly and are initially difficult to recognize. For leaders to recognize obstructing norms, they must identify the pattern of interaction that slows group progress. By reflecting on the reasons behind ineffective group interaction, leaders can then identify the reactive motives that members are attempting to avoid. For example, whenever a member begins to express emotions, other members change the subject. Whenever leaders observe an obstructing norm, they should intervene, especially in the early phases of the group when norms are under development; otherwise, they allow obstructing norms to become a more entrenched interactive pattern that becomes increasingly resistant to change.

Once leaders identify obstructing norms and decide to modify them, they can choose from an array of interventions. These interventions include implementing new ground rules, observing the obstructing norm, directing the group to discuss the obstructing norm, experimenting with a helping norm, or confronting the obstructing norm. Whichever interventions leaders choose to use, they must remember that they are intervening in a social and cultural system. Such intervention means that members must understand the problems associated with an obstructing norm, be clear about the benefits of implementing a helping norm, and commit to following through on working with other members to change "the rules" of group interaction. Successful norms interventions occur only when facilitative norms replace obstructing norms. Norms interventions are energy intensive but can have a profound impact on the quality of group interaction.

Implementing New Ground Rules

Often the simplest norms intervention is to implement new ground rules. Although frequently effective, this intervention requires considerable energy on the part of leaders to monitor and direct implementation, and it may not address the dynamics that caused the development of the obstructing norms. Leaders should use this intervention sparingly and attempt to implement a new ground rule only infrequently. New ground rules will be unsuccessful if leaders do not follow through by monitoring implementation. In addition, members will begin to question the importance of the new ground rule and the earnestness of the leaders' interventions.

Leaders can consider implementing a new ground rule whenever they observe a problem in group interaction that suggests the presence of an obstructing norm. The objective of implementing a new ground rule is to create a norm that will improve group interaction. This intervention differs from the essential ground rules that leaders implement at the onset of the group to protect members and define the external boundaries of the group (e.g., confidentiality, no abusive behaviors). To intervene, leaders simply point out the problem in interaction and direct members to follow a new ground rule:

Leader: "It seems that most group members have developed a pattern of saying 'we' when they are really talking about their own point of view. From now on, each of you need to say 'I' when you present your own perspective."

Leader: "Whenever a member begins to describe how they feel, they are cut off, and the subject is changed. We need to adopt the ground rule that members expressing their feelings should be allowed to complete their expression before anyone else speaks."

The following examples depict how leaders can attempt to legislate new group norms by directing members to use them. These interventions require consistency and ongoing leader monitoring to be successful, which involves redirecting interaction:

Leader: "Fatima, repeat what you said. This time remember to use 'I' instead of 'we.'"

Leader: "Judith, stop. Let Mohamed finish saying how he's feeling."

Observing Obstructing Norms

Obstructive norms develop subtly and often escape leaders' awareness. When leaders notice an obstructing norm, a useful initial intervention is simply to identify the obstructing norm. This intervention is most effective in mature working groups where it is necessary only to raise members' awareness. In mature groups, members will understand the intervention and will often develop more facilitative norms independently.

In less mature groups, where members experience intense anxiety when facing difficult disturbing and reactive motives, this intervention is much less effective. Leaders who share their observations of obstructing norms in less mature groups will often observe members ignoring the intervention. In less mature groups, leaders can be satisfied when this intervention performs an educational function. The trick is ensuring that members actually hear the intervention and, at least, reflect for a moment on the norms that guide their interaction. Following are examples of this intervention:

Leader: "It seems the rule the group is following now is to change the topic whenever the issues get too intense."
Leader: "The norm the group is using to deal with disagreements is to ignore them."
Leader: "Everyone in the group seems to have forgotten that sharing feelings is important."

Sharing an observation of a group's obstructing norm identifies a restrictive solution that members have developed to avoid anxiety. Sharing a group's obstructing norm will raise anxiety if members discuss it. In less mature groups, leaders should repeat this intervention and direct members to discuss the obstructing norm to have maximum impact.

Observing and Directing Members to Discuss Obstructing Norms

As a follow-up to sharing their observations of obstructing norms, leaders can observe and direct members to discuss obstructing norms. This substantially increases the effectiveness of observing obstructing norms in most groups.

In this intervention, leaders ask or direct members to discuss how the obstructing norm blocks the group's effectiveness. Leaders may also direct members to reach a consensus about a norm that would be more effective and to develop an agreement to use the more effective norm.

Although this intervention is effective, it can be quite time consuming. At worst, a protracted discussion of an obstructing norm can serve as an alternative restrictive solution if the discussion becomes excessively cognitive. Thus, leaders should consider the group's purpose, needs, and time limitations when determining whether to use this intervention.

Following are some examples of observation and direction to discuss an obstructing norm:

Leader: "It appears that whenever a member shares their feelings, the group responds by changing the subject. Tell me what you all think about how changing the subject is helping you make progress in this group."

Leader: "I've been observing how group members have been giving feedback, and it looks like there's a rule that whenever a member asks for feedback, others take turns giving compliments. Let's talk for a moment about how well this is helping you all learn in here."

Following are examples of using this intervention with an additional direction to reach consensus on a more effective norm:

Leader: "It appears that whenever a member shares their feelings, the group responds by changing the subject. I want you all to talk about how that's getting in your way and come up with a different way to handle your feelings."

Leader: "I've been observing how group members have been giving feedback, and it looks like there's a rule that whenever a member asks for feedback, others take turns giving compliments. You all need to talk about this for a while and decide on what you believe is a more productive way to exchange feedback."

The direction to reach consensus on a facilitative norm to replace an obstructing norm can also be a separate intervention that follows a group's discussion of the obstructing norm. A covert leader strategy here is to frustrate a group's restrictive solution. The rationale for this sequence of interventions is that the longer a leader involves members in discussing a restrictive solution (obstructing norm) and enabling solutions (facilitative norms), the more likely it is that members will face disturbing and reactive motives.

The combination of sharing observations of obstructing norms, directing members to discuss these norms, and directing members to develop more facilitative norms is powerful because it sustains members' focus on issues that they want to avoid. Avoided issues, when discussed in a progressively open fashion, lead to members facing difficult interpersonal issues and developing more effective interpersonal behaviors.

Experimentation With New Norms

Norms experimentation involves a mixture of leader-directed interventions and member participation to develop norms that are more effective. This intervention is usually very productive in less mature groups, where interventions that more directly involve members in confronting restrictive solutions may excessively threaten homeostasis. This intervention also spreads the responsibility for the development and implementation of facilitative norms to members. Because all group members and the leader share responsibility, less energy is required on the part of the leader and a more democratic group atmosphere develops.

Norms experimentation is, however, a complicated intervention that requires time for implementation and follow-through. Five steps are required:

1. Leaders identify a pattern in group interaction and ask members whether they would like to try an experiment.
2. Leaders suggest a norm to experiment with, carefully describing when to use the norm and the interactive behaviors involved.
3. The leader contracts with the members to use the norm for a specified period of time (e.g., the remaining meeting time, several meetings). This period is the "experimentation period."
4. The contract includes the agreement that members will commit to monitoring each other's interactions to ensure that all members are using the norm. The contract should also include the understanding that the experimental norm can be renegotiated if it is too disruptive.
5. The experiment begins, and members remind each other to use the behaviors included in the norm.

At the end of the experimentation period, leaders initiate a discussion of how well the norm worked. The goal is to decide whether to continue or discontinue the use of the norm.

Following is an example of how a leader might implement a norms experimentation intervention:

Leader: "Something I've noticed is that members who are sharing their feelings are frequently cut off by others who either change the subject or interrupt to reassure the one expressing their feelings that everything is OK. Would you all like to try an experiment?"

Members usually are uncertain what "trying an experiment" means and are curious about what the leader is asking. At this point, the leader moves to the second step:

Leader: "What I'm asking you to do is to consider experimenting with a different way of interacting. I'm suggesting that whenever another group member shares their feelings, each of us allows that member to finish. Then, before changing the subject or reassuring that member, respond to what that member has shared. Are you all willing to try this experiment?"

Group members are usually willing to try the experiment but remain unsure of what the leader is asking:

Leader: "Here's what the experiment will involve. First, let's try the experiment for the rest of this session and during the next time we meet. At the end of our next session, we will talk about how our experiment worked and whether we want to continue to not interrupt or reassure and instead respond to a member's feelings before moving to another topic or issue. I'd like to ask each of you to commit to reminding each other to use these behaviors whenever someone does not use them. We can always talk about these behaviors if they disrupt what we're doing too much. Everyone agree? Any questions?"

Once the leader has clarified what is involved in the norms experiment, members begin using the new behaviors as an experiment. Usually, members require only minimal prompting by the leader to monitor the experimental behaviors. Ideally, monitoring norms experimentation by members involves simply identifying the behaviors another member is using and reminding that member to use the experimental behaviors. It is important that these reminders not have a judgmental tone. Reminding each other to use the experimental norm behavior is also an opportunity for members to practice feedback exchange. On occasion, reminders to use behaviors associated with an experimental norm escalate the anxiety of members who would rather avoid interactions that involve the experimental norm behaviors. This is an opportunity to explore the apprehensions of these members.

At the end of the experimentation period, the leader summarizes what has happened and initiates a discussion of the experimental behaviors:

> *Leader*: "Well, we've completed the experiment. I got the impression that it was scary at first, and then as we got more accustomed to using the experimental behaviors, some good things started to happen. I want to hear how the experiment went for each of you."

After members share their experiences with the experimental behaviors, the leader processes their experiences. If the norms experiment was successful, the leader asks whether members would be willing to continue to use and remind each other to use the experimental behaviors:

> *Leader*: "If you are willing, I think we should make our experimental behaviors a part of how we interact in this group. Would you all be willing to continue using these behaviors and to remind each other to use them?"

At the conclusion of successful norms experiments, members are usually willing to continue using the experimental behaviors. Resistance to using the new behaviors usually expresses itself when members "forget" to remind each other to use the behaviors. Commonly, these behaviors become norms, and the need for reminders decreases.

Confronting Obstructing Norms

Confronting obstructing norms is essentially the same as identifying restrictive solutions that have become "permanent fixtures" in group interaction. This intervention approach involves challenging members to consider their interactive behaviors in the context of their expressed objectives for group participation. When using this approach, leaders should not judge members' interactions by conveying that the interactions are inappropriate or inadequate.

Such conveyance is often an indirect expression of leaders' frustration. Rather, leaders should have a clear understanding of their own reactions to group interaction before using this intervention. When frustrated about group interaction, leaders should consider offering clear and specific feedback to group members. Following are examples of how leaders can confront obstructing norms:

Leader: "Help me understand why you all continue to block the expression of your fears in here when you've all stated that you need to confront your fears to reach your goals."
Leader: "It seems like you all are still trying to avoid exchanging feedback even though you all have agreed several times that it's essential that you do it."
Leader: "When members agreed to supporting the expression of each other's feelings, I thought you were interested in doing that, and not discouraging each other's sharing as you are all doing now."

Confronting obstructing norms forcefully calls attention to problems in group interaction. As discussed previously, identifying obstructing norms may be sufficient to change norms in mature groups. In less mature groups, confronting obstructing norms is an effective way to elevate members' anxiety. Elevating members' anxiety by confronting obstructing norms can be an effective way to minimize the benefits members experience by using a restrictive solution. However, leaders must never use this strategy to elevate members' anxiety without the clear intention to minimize restrictive solutions and to support enabling ones.

Confronting obstructing norms is a more intense intervention than simply observing obstructing norms. A potential pitfall in using this intervention is that members could perceive these confrontations as judgments of their participation. Confronting obstructing norms is most useful when leaders determine that the intensity of their norms interventions is not sufficiently challenging to gain members' attention. A challenge that follows members not acting to change a norm they have committed to change is a powerful reminder and a means to elevate members' anxiety.

Norms Interventions: Final Considerations

Leaders use norms interventions to change group social systems, which requires changes in members' interactions and the expectations they have about each other's participation. Thus, to be successful, norms interventions require members' cooperation. When members choose to avoid experimenting with or following through on new group norms, leaders' only recourse is to be diligent about sustaining a sufficient amount of anxiety to make the enactment of obstructing norms less comfortable. In other words, when members avoid the implementation of new norms, all leaders can do is to call attention to the obstructing norm and to the disturbing and reactive motives it is being used to avoid.

Interpersonal and Relationship Issues

Members come to groups because of problems in their interpersonal relationships. Thus, leaders should expect members to experience inevitable struggles in establishing, developing, and maintaining relationships in group. Leaders should regard the relationship issues that surface in group as important opportunities to address members' most critical concerns as they occur during the process of here-and-now group interaction. However, some relationship problems occurring between group members may be particularly resistant to leaders' interventions and may limit the group's effectiveness—for example, members who persistently engage in protracted arguments or members who repeatedly rescue another member. Relationship problems that are resistant to intervention can pose particularly difficult barriers for group progress, because groups rely on members' relationships as the medium of change.

According to the group counseling and therapy theories discussed earlier in this book, members' relationship issues may emerge as distorted interpersonal perceptions, ineffective boundary functioning, or restrictive habitual personal solutions. These interpersonal problems are observed in members who isolate themselves from others, defend themselves from meaningful involvement, attempt to control the content of interaction, and develop enmeshed or fused relationships.

Interpersonal boundary interventions and interpersonal contracts offer two possible approaches for dealing with these interpersonal problems. However, another issue to consider is whether an interpersonal problem is a role problem. Role problems are particularly resistant to interpersonal interventions because roles are an integral part of the group's social system and require interventions that involve the entire group. It is highly likely that when interpersonal interventions do not work, it is because the group supports the continuation of problematic interpersonal behaviors associated with a member or members' roles. Thus, interpersonal boundary interventions and interpersonal contracts are considered first steps toward changing interpersonal behaviors. In cases where these interventions are not effective, role interventions and possibly group norms interventions can be more effective.

Interpersonal Boundary Interventions

Interpersonal boundary interventions involve the leader directing members with excessively closed boundaries to share information that they have withheld. For example, a leader may ask or direct members to share their emotions or offer feedback. Interpersonal boundary interventions also involve directing members to withhold information that leads to overinvolved or fused relationships with other group members. This may occur when a leader directs a member not to rescue another member from the experience of sharing painful emotions. Members with overly diffuse boundaries may also benefit from sharing information that more clearly defines their boundaries with other members. In this case, interventions may include directing members to experiment with using assertive language, disagreeing with others, or asking for what they want.

As members interact, opportunities arise to use interpersonal boundary interventions. In some cases, these interventions attend to issues emerging in particular relationships. In other cases, these interventions are useful when particular members demonstrate relationship problems in all their relationships with other members. Such interventions are useful in developing the relationship between two members or helping a member in all of their relationships in the group.

Following are some examples of interpersonal boundary interventions. The first few demonstrate boundary interventions with relationships that demonstrate excessively closed boundaries:

Leader: "Otieno, tell Sharon how you feel."

Leader: "Sally, you seem to be reacting to what Beth is saying. Give her feedback about the reactions you're having to what she is doing."

Leader: "Mark, you and Michael really have strong reactions to each other. I'd like each of you to tell the other what you think he is trying to do."

These demonstrate boundary interventions with relationships that have excessively open boundaries:

Leader: "Colleen, you seem to agree with almost everything Jack says. Tell him how you disagree with him."
Leader: "Gina, you really seem to want to get along with me. I want you to know that I only get along with people who can disagree with me and state different points of view."
Leader: "Sanchez, before any of the other members share their reaction to what just happened, I'd like you to say what you think."
Leader: "Gina, tell Yvonne how your point of view differs from her point of view."

Interpersonal Contracts

Interpersonal contracts are a useful follow-up to interpersonal boundary interventions and experimentation with new behaviors and one of the final elements of a feedback exchange process. The objective of interpersonal contracts is to continue a member's use of new interpersonal behaviors. By doing so, a member is in a position to continue receiving feedback and develop the effectiveness of new behaviors.

Interpersonal contracts follow these steps:

1. The leader initiates the contracting process by asking the member or members (in the case of a relationship-focused intervention) whether they are willing to continue the use of new interpersonal behaviors.
2. If the member or members agree to continue, the leader asks whether the member or members would like some assistance in continuing the use of the behaviors. Often, it is useful to frame this step as an inquiry about whether a member or members would like to receive support from other members in continuing to develop new ways of interacting in the group. Also, referencing a member's goals to connect better with others may be persuasive when the member is reluctant to take risks to work on their goals in the group.
3. If the member or members are willing to receive support or help to continue the use of the new interpersonal behaviors, the leader initiates the contract.
4. To initiate the contract, the leader secures an agreement with other group members or a particular member to participate in the contract. This agreement involves making a commitment to remind and encourage the member or members developing the

new behavior to use the new behavior whenever it is useful. One way of doing this is to ask those using the new behaviors to identify a member who they would like to help them and ask that member to act as a support person.

Another option involves the leader strategically selecting a member to participate in the contract. For example, if the contract involves helping a member to use "I language," the leader can ask a person who struggles with using I language to act as the support person. Alternatively, the leader can ask a member who is especially effective at using I language to act in the support role.

A fourth option is to involve the entire group in the support role. By doing so, the leader can also consider this contract as a means of norms intervention. For example, asking the group to remind a member to ask for what they want is a way of reinforcing the idea that all group members should use this interpersonal behavior.

The following is an example of how a leader might use an interpersonal contract with a member developing a new interpersonal behavior:

Leader: "Joan, when you were direct and told Todd to not boss you around, it looked like it worked for you. What was it like to be that direct?"

Joan: "It was really scary at first, and when he backed down, it felt really good, like I had some power."

Leader: "Is being direct by saying how you feel and what you want in your relationships in here something you want to continue?"

Joan: "It's a little scary, but I'd like to."

Leader: "How would you like to get some support from another group member to help you continue working with being direct?"

Joan: "Oh, I'm not too sure, I don't know what . . . "

Leader: (*Interrupting*) "Practice being direct with me. Tell me what you want."

Joan: "That's right, OK. Yes, I want support."

Leader: "Great, Joan! I'd like you to directly ask another member to remind you to be direct when you need to be direct but forget. This person will be your support person."

Joan asks Ruth to be her support person, and Ruth agrees.

Leader: "Ruth, are you clear about what Joan is asking you to do?"

Ruth: "She wants me to remind her to be direct when she needs to be but forgets."
Leader: "Joan, tell Ruth if that's what you want."

At this point, after the agreement is clear, the contract is in place. The leader can invite the members involved to modify or terminate their contract whenever it is unnecessary or when it does not appear to be working. Interpersonal contracting is a very versatile intervention, and leaders should use their imagination to create variations. Interpersonal contracting can be as useful for the support persons as it is for the member or members receiving support because it also maintains their awareness of the behaviors in the contract.

Problematic Member Roles

Members come to groups because of interpersonal difficulties and interact with other group members using the interpersonal behaviors that express these difficulties. Eventually, the way in which a group member interacts with other members can become problematic for the entire group. These problems usually involve group members expending an excessive amount of energy in trying to change the behaviors of the "problematic" group member. Often, these problems arise when a member fails to meet the expectations "that they should be respectful of others, cooperative, responsive, grateful for help, and do what they say they will do" (Kottler, 1994, p. 4). Problematic members are often described as resistant (Kline, 1990) and defined in terms of specific roles (I. D. Yalom & Leszcz, 2020). In general, the literature agrees that members assume problematic roles when their interactions appear to block productive interaction and they are assigned responsibility for ineffective group functioning (Kline, 1997).

When confronting a "problematic role," it is important to consider the basic principles of group dynamics (see Chapter 2) along with group counseling and therapy theories (see Chapter 3). In terms of group dynamics, roles are a structural property of a group's social system—that is, each group member enacts a role because of the expectations of all the other group members and, occasionally, the inadvertent expectations of the group leader. Thus, to change a member's role, interventions must address the expectations of the other group members.

Theory conceptualizations are similar. From the perspective of focal conflict theory, problematic roles are deviant-enabling or deviant-restrictive members who demonstrate habitual personal solutions that cause other members considerable anxiety. Systems theory regards a problematic role as a structural part of a group's social system. Both these theoretical perspectives recognize problematic roles as functionally related to the interactions of all group members.

It is important to remember that members come to groups because of difficulties in their interpersonal relationships. Frequently, these difficulties cause problems for other members and leaders. In addition, individuals who are not appropriate for group membership cause problems in group interaction. Realistically, even the most brilliant sequence of leader interventions may not have a meaningful impact on the interactions of an individual who is inappropriate for group membership. On the other hand, members who are appropriate for group membership can benefit from thoughtful interventions. The objective for conceptualizing interventions, however, is not to always think specifically of helping a member who is causing problems to change their behaviors. Rather, the objective is to think in terms of identifying and helping the members who can benefit from intervention. Usually, this means first looking at the issues being experienced by other group members.

Conceptualizing Problematic Roles

Focal conflict theory provides a framework for conceptualizing problematic member roles and identifying leaders' intervention targets. One intervention scenario surfaces in the case of a deviant member who represents a restrictive solution. A deviant-restrictive member uses a habitual personal solution that interferes with a group-developed enabling solution. For example, a deviant member who fears interpersonal intimacy will react strongly or withdraw from interaction when other members have begun to share their feelings about each other. At other times, the deviant-restrictive member may attempt to persuade other members to discontinue their sharing. Either the withdrawing or the convincing reactions of the deviant-restrictive member can be problematic for the other members because other group members will begin to direct their attention to involving the restrictive member or convincing the restrictive member to participate in the group's enabling solution. By focusing on the deviant-restrictive member, group members deprive themselves of opportunities to participate in more productive interactions. This situation is also problematic for the deviant-restrictive member because of the pressure and the frequent anger that other members direct toward them. The deviant-restrictive member risks becoming a scapegoat if leaders are not sensitive to members building criticisms of this member.

Another intervention scenario involves a deviant member who represents an enabling solution. The deviant-enabling member threatens other group members because their interactive behaviors often frustrate the successful use of the restrictive solution members have developed to avoid anxiety. For example, in a group where members have decided that it is important to avoid the expression of anger, a member who persists in expressing their anger will become a problem for the other members. In this case, other members will attempt to convince the deviant-enabling member to cease their expressions of anger or try to ignore the deviant-enabling member's expressions of anger. These responses slow the progress of the entire group because of the time and energy members devote to changing or ignoring the behaviors of the deviant-enabling member. In reality, the interpersonal behaviors of the deviant-enabling member represent an enabling solution, and the efforts of the other group members are inconsistent with group progress.

Intervening With Problematic Roles

An important first step in intervening with problematic roles is to recognize what is occurring. A role problem usually occurs when members appear to be investing considerable energy in convincing a member to act correctly (i.e., go along with a group-developed enabling or restrictive solution). More pronounced and serious role problems occur when members openly criticize another member for how that member participates. For example, a group has spent 25 minutes trying to encourage a member to stop sharing their feelings. Another example occurs in a group that has tried repeatedly to involve a member who has withdrawn from participation. By conceptualizing role problems in focal conflict terms and by seeing role problems as group problems, leaders can involve group members in potentially productive interaction.

In the case of a deviant-restrictive member, leaders will observe group members trying to influence the deviant-restrictive member to engage in interactions that are more productive. An example of this situation occurs during feedback exchange processes. Leaders will notice a member who does not seem receptive to feedback about a behavior that is legitimately problematic. Usually, this member refuses, rejects, deflects, or ignores other members' efforts to offer feedback. Other examples of role problems with a deviant-restrictive member include members attempting to convince the deviant-restrictive member to share their feelings, or members trying to persuade a deviant-restrictive member to stop criticizing others. In these cases, leaders need to think how they can support the enabling behaviors of other group members and not focus on the behaviors of the deviant-restrictive member.

To initiate role interventions with deviant-restrictive members, leaders must first assess what is occurring in group interactions. For example, a group may persistently use feedback and argument to pressure a deviant-restrictive member to engage in a group-developed enabling solution, or the group may invest considerable energy in attempting to persuade a member to share their emotions or participate more actively. It weighs in favor of intervention if the group is investing so much time and energy in attempting to convince a member to engage in their enabling interactions that they avoid participation that takes advantage of these enabling interactions. For example, a group that spends time trying to encourage a member to be more involved in feedback exchange is unlikely to spend much time involved in feedback exchange.

In some such cases, leaders may find that members are using the deviant-restrictive member as a way to avoid participating in an enabling solution—that is, by investing time and energy in attempting to change the deviant-restrictive member, members avoid more anxiety-provoking interaction. For example, members trying to convince a member to share their feelings are often avoiding sharing their feelings with each other.

When leaders see members using a deviant-restrictive member to avoid anxiety or participation in their enabling solution, leaders should intervene:

Leader: "The longer you all try to talk Bob into hearing your feedback, the longer you avoid exchanging feedback that can help you learn. Steve, you've been responding to something Sylvia is doing. Perhaps you can give her some feedback."

Leader: "Let's change what we're doing. We've spent some time talking to Bruce about what he needs to do differently here. Now it's time to move on. Jim, what would you like to do to improve your relationship with other group members?"

Leader: "You all seem to be spending lots of time working on making Elizabeth be the way you all want her to be instead of doing what you need to do to learn here. Randy, maybe you can tell Rita what you want from her."

Interventions that focus on deviant-restrictive members should focus on the other group members when it is clear that the deviant-restrictive member is not receptive to feedback. The objective is to support the enabling solutions of the other group members. By focusing on enabling solutions, leaders put pressure on the deviant-restrictive member indirectly, without a high risk of scapegoating that member. The deviant-restrictive member will then face increasingly high levels of anxiety produced by attending a group that does not support their use of a restrictive habitual personal solution.

Often, when a group begins to invest energy attempting to influence a deviant-enabling member, it will appear that the group is responding to a threat. This threat frequently appears when members confront or challenge a deviant-enabling member for doing something that is unacceptable in the group. In the case of a deviant-enabling member, the members' efforts usually are to censor that member's enactment of an enabling solution. For example, leaders will commonly observe members attempting to shut down a member's efforts to exchange feedback, express emotions, or share intimate connections with other members. Attempts to shut down a deviant-enabling member often include comments that communicate "You need to keep those feelings to yourself," "Why do you have to be so angry?" or "You're not fitting in, you need to stay positive."

When intervening, leaders need to support the deviant-enabling member. Interventions should focus on supporting the enabling behaviors of the deviant member, protecting the deviant member from pressure to use the group's restrictive behaviors, and helping group members look at the fears associated with the deviant-enabling member's behaviors. The following examples depict leader interventions that accomplish these objectives. The first few demonstrate supporting the enabling behaviors of a deviant member:

Leader: "Karim, I really like the way you spontaneously share your feelings."

Leader: "Jerry, perhaps you can give some of the other members some ideas about how you build up the courage to be direct and honest."

Leader: "You know, Dot, other members seem to have difficulty with you wanting more openness in your relationships with them. I want to support you in achieving that here. Anything I can do to help you out?"

These demonstrate protecting the deviant-enabling member from group pressure:

> *Leader*: "Jeff, I'd like you to talk about what it would be like for you to share your feelings in here before you try to talk Jack out of doing it."
>
> *Leader*: "Jerry's honesty and directness has really upset you, Phyllis. Can you share what makes this so frightening for you?"
>
> *Leader*: "Linda, you really want Dot to back off getting closer to you. What do you have to lose?"

These demonstrate directing the group to explore their reactions to the enabling behaviors of a deviant member:

> *Leader*: "You folks really react each time Karim puts his emotions out there. Dean, what's going on in you when Karim shares his feelings?"
>
> *Leader*: "Most of the group seems to be having some trouble dealing with Jerry's directness. Let's take a look at what makes this so scary for you. Jesse, you are having some noticeable reactions. What's so scary for you?"
>
> *Leader*: "It really seems that Dot hits a nerve in all of you when she asks for more sharing. What's so scary about that? John, you start."

The interventions directed toward the behaviors of a deviant-enabling member are designed to frustrate a group's restrictive solutions. Members who are courageous enough to use enabling behaviors should receive support, and other group members should be guided to examine their surfacing fears. The only exception to this strategy is when a member's enabling behaviors may be so threatening that they cause the group overwhelming anxiety. This requires leaders' best judgment. In this circumstance, the deviant-enabling member should receive feedback about their choices of when to use their enabling behaviors. These members need to examine how to know when it is the best time to use their enabling behaviors and examine how to be more sensitive to when others are ready. Typical examples of members who are ineffective in their use of enabling behaviors are those who disclose intensely personal information before they have developed relationships with other members and members who use self-disclosures to distance themselves from others.

Leader Precautions When Intervening With Problem Roles

Problematic member behaviors include the behaviors of a member who is inappropriate for group membership and the behaviors of a member who threatens other group members. Clearly, the first problem shows the need for careful group composition decisions. In the case of the second problem, leaders need to be aware of several serious pitfalls.

When groups deal with members who do not go along with group-developed enabling or restrictive solutions, leaders can be easily seduced into aligning with group members' perspectives. For example, when groups pressure deviant-restrictive members to use a more enabling solution, such as being less critical, their actions are consistent with leaders' goals and easy for the leader to support. Conversely, when members pressure deviant-enabling members to "back off" their enabling behaviors, leaders may support members' actions inadvertently because the enabling behaviors might also be threatening to the leaders. For example, leaders who are tentative about sharing emotions in their relationships can easily align with group members' efforts to censor the emotional expressions of another member. Similarly, leaders who have not examined their identity and are insensitive to racial, gender, and sexual orientation concerns may align with members who trivialize the value of such social identities and their impact on individual member choices for participation within the group. Thus, leaders must be sensitive to and very aware of their own values, beliefs, and reactions to deviant members and to the potential to scapegoat deviant members.

To monitor the extent to which leaders' personal issues intrude in their interventions with problem members, leaders should assess the intensity of their emotional reactions. Intense emotional reactions may indicate that leaders' personal issues are interfering with their interventions. Leaders should confirm their reactions with observations they make about group interactions. Then, just as in feedback exchange, leaders should identify the words and behaviors problem members are using. Finally, leaders should frankly consider whether they can make an intervention that is not judgmental or excessively influenced by their own personal issues (Kline, 1990).

Considering the removal of a member from the group is the final option when dealing with a problem member. This option is appropriate for members whose needs cannot be met in the group. Other members who are appropriate for membership, however, can also be candidates for removal. After direct feedback and group-focused interventions have proven ineffective, leaders should determine whether the problem member's behaviors will be an ongoing obstacle to the learning of other members. If the member does not respond to interventions and significantly distracts members from productive interaction, leaders should remove the member. In these cases, removal is the absolute last option. Leaders are ethically bound to refer members they remove from their groups to more appropriate treatment options. As a final note, leaders who have experienced the process of responsibly removing a member from their groups are very strong advocates for careful member screening.

Confronting Social Issues

Counseling and therapy groups exist within and cannot escape the influences of broader social and cultural systems. This is especially true when counseling and therapy groups have external boundaries that allow necessary information to flow between the group and its external environment, so that changes members make in group can be transferred to members' relationships outside the group. All groups, to be relevant to the lives of their members, must have external boundaries that do not totally isolate them from the world in which they exist. One important implication of these boundaries is that the social issues occurring in the social environment also occur in counseling and therapy groups.

The Nature of Social Issues in the Group Context

From a systems perspective, all parts of a social system have isomorphic qualities. This means that group interaction inevitably demonstrates the social issues present in the group's social context. Thus, issues related to ageism, racism, sexism, ableism, different religions, cultures, and sexual orientations emerge in some form during group interaction.

Many group leaders can probably describe instances in which they believe diversity issues did not emerge or, if they did, were not relevant to group interaction. These descriptions are understandable but are not defensible. They are understandable because members and leaders often want to avoid the anxiety involved in confronting diversity and identity issues. Such avoidance is common when leaders and members prefer avoiding conflict, confronting their own biases, and dealing with the fears they associate with owning their own prejudices. Such descriptions are not defensible because diversity issues are always present in counseling and therapy groups, just as they are in the broader social context.

When the diversity issues present in a group are not blatant, members and leaders tend to ignore them. From the focal conflict perspective, confronting diversity issues in most counseling and therapy groups is a disturbing motive that leaders and members alike would rather avoid. The reactive motive is fear that conflict will emerge, and individuals will have to admit and confront their own biases and prejudices. Commonly, the focal conflict associated with these fears operates subtly and is undetected or ignored. Thus, diversity issues become a secret in most groups that members and leaders covertly agree to keep. Diversity issues often stay out of awareness unless leaders bring these issues to the attention of group members.

Identifying and confronting diversity, marginalization, and oppression is an important responsibility of group leaders. Fulfilling this responsibility requires commitment and the courage to be proactive. This means that group leaders find time during the life of their group to direct members to confront the biases, fears, pain, and trauma related to being citizens of a world populated by diverse individuals and groups. Being courageous means bringing up and sustaining a discussion of a focal conflict that is difficult to confront.

Confronting Diversity Issues in the Group Context

Leaders can use a reactive approach to confronting diversity issues by confronting these issues whenever they emerge during group interaction. However, it is better to assume a proactive stance by identifying and confronting diversity issues before they emerge. Although either a reactive or a proactive approach can be effective, the pitfall associated with a reactive approach is that leaders might never find the "right time" to address diversity issues. The most important principle is that leaders involve all members in exploring the diversity issues that impact their lives and their relationships with others. This includes broaching subjects to do with racism, sexism, ableism, and so on, and encouraging members to disclose and discuss how their identities and experiences related to those identities impact their engagement within the group. Ideally, leaders should be able to say that they have addressed diversity issues in all the groups they have led.

Confronting diversity issues as they emerge in the immediate group environment is a proactive process that reflects leaders' commitment to confronting biases that limit and harm persons. The process of linking group interaction to diversity issues is one that requires careful timing, and premature introduction of diversity considerations is a possibility. The following scenario illustrates a relatively common group issue and a premature leader intervention:

> Jean has been talking about how the male members of the group have been treating her like the group mascot. She perceives that the male members placate, patronize, and dismiss the importance of her contributions. Her interactions with the male members are intense and emotional. As Jean becomes increasingly clear about her boundaries and her emotional expressions become clearer, the group leader interrupts. "It seems that Jean is talking about some really important issues. What gender issues are you all seeing?"

In this scenario, the group leader is premature in directing members to discuss gender issues. This direction is premature because it preempts interactions that are likely to be extremely productive. Leaders should be careful to allow members to confront the diversity issues that operate in the group at a personal level before introducing the risk of leading the group to a disconnected intellectual conversation. The more personal and emotionally connected the confrontation of diversity issues is to the here and now of group interaction, the more powerful it is. Consider the following example with different leader intervention timing.

> Jean has been talking about how the male members of the group have been treating her like the group mascot. She perceives that the male members placate, patronize, and dismiss the importance of her contributions. Her interactions with the male members are intense and emotional. As Jean becomes increasingly clear about her boundaries and her emotional expressions become clearer, the group leader encourages Jean to give the male members some specific feedback about her reactions to the way they are treating her. As the feedback exchange nears completion, the leader involves the other women in the group by stating, "As Jean has been sharing her experiences, I've noticed the other women in the group reacting intensely to what's been going on. I want to hear your reactions." After their sharing, the leader involves the male members in processing their reactions

> with the goal of increasing their awareness of how they relate to the women in the group. Then the leader states, "You all know that what we're dealing with in here limits the quality of our lives outside of the group as well. Let's talk for a moment about how we can use what we've become aware of in here and outside of group."

In the described scenario, the leader uses group process to complete the emotionally charged relationship work that is necessary for the group to operate effectively. Then, using this energy, the leader involves all the members in conversation that increases awareness and identifies different ways of interaction, both in and outside of the group. This process is the most meaningful for members and does not save members from confronting the biases present in their immediate relationships in the group. Although this scenario deals with gender issues, the process described is equally relevant to other diversity issues that might emerge.

Leaders who are sensitive to diversity, equity, and inclusion issues can also use their observations of group interaction to confront difficult issues. These observations, as described previously, should be connected to members' relationships in the group and not to an intellectualized discussion of "issues out there." Following is an example of how a leader could do this:

> *Leader*: "Don, I've noticed that there seems to be something different about the way group members relate to you. They seem to be careful how they talk to you; they seem to be walking on eggshells. Is this something that happens often to you as an African American male?"
>
> *Don*: "Sometimes it's not as noticeable as it is in this group."
>
> *Leader*: "Don, tell the other members how you feel about this and how you'd like them to interact with you."
>
> *After Don has shared, the leader continues.*
>
> *Leader*: "What's going on? It looks like most of you are feeling sad and ashamed. We need to talk about this."

Using the process described in this scenario, the leader attempts to keep the issue connected with the interactions and emotional experiences of the group members in the here and now. Opportunities like the one in this scenario are opportunities for powerful learning experiences. Although educational input can be productive, it should occur as a follow-up to members' immediate interactions.

Conclusion

When successful, intervention strategies can change a group's culture, including the way members relate to each other. These interventions are often difficult and complicated but at the same time are critical. The first priority of leaders is to shape group interaction so members can learn from one another. Group cultures that do not support feedback exchange, meaningful interaction, and the confrontation of social issues that impair members' relationships are unlikely to provide members with meaningful experiences. Most importantly, groups that develop obstructive norms that block experimentation with new behavior, constructive feedback exchange processes, meaningful intercultural interactions, and connections will hinder interpersonal growth and learning within groups. Leaders have a responsibility—especially in the formative stages of the group—to disrupt obstructive norms and to help members develop new ground rules for functioning in the group. This includes directly discussing the obstacles to members' growth, learning, and change in the group as well as the choices members have to change how they function in the group in order to meet their group membership goals.

Part IV

Real-World INTERACTIVE Group LEADERSHIP

Chapter 12

Ethical Practice of Group Work

Outcomes

Level 1 Outcomes

After reading this chapter, entry-level students and practitioners should be able to:

1. Define ethics and articulate the four primary ethical principles relevant to helping professions and group work.
2. Identify several sets of professional ethics relevant to group work.
3. Describe the unique ethical challenges of group work.
4. Articulate at least one ethical decision-making model.
5. Discuss practices that address the ethical challenges of group work.

Level 2 Outcomes

After reading this chapter, advanced-level students and practitioners should also be able to:

1. Evaluate the ethical standards of several helping professions for their application to group work.
2. Analyze group work scenarios and cases and identify ethical dilemmas.
3. Create and describe scenarios illustrating each of the unique ethical challenges of group work.
4. Apply practices that address the ethical challenges of group work to planning a group.
5. Apply practices that address the ethical challenges of group work to group process.

Effective group work practice and leadership does not rest solely on the foundation of the social context of groups, the unique group environment, group development, and knowledge of group leadership theories and skills. The core value of group work is to help group members achieve their goals. At its most basic level, this value requires that group leaders practice ethically. Group leaders must set up their groups to promote ethical experiences and then embody ethics in their interactions with the group.

The same ethical principles that apply to the practices of individual counseling and therapy apply to group work. However, groups present several unique issues that differentiate their ethical situation from those of other helping modalities. The unique ethical situation presented by group work is grounded in the same structural and process characteristics that make group work an effective helping modality. When group leaders learn now to influence these group structures and processes, they take on an incredible responsibility and must engage throughout the leadership process to act ethically.

It is useful to think of potential ethical issues in group work as involving one or more of three general factors: structural, process, or leadership issues. The primary *structural* issues affecting ethical practice include the planning and screening of the group and the presence of multiple stakeholders within the group setting. The foremost *process* issues affecting ethical group work are the social influence that is part of group work's unique helping power, heightened emotional activation, the encouragement of increasingly intimate self-disclosure, and the existence of the social microcosm within groups. *Leadership* issues that may impact ethical practice are the group leader's power; the group leader's knowledge and training, or lack thereof; and the group leader's self-awareness of values, bias, and personal needs.

This chapter reviews the basic ethical principles relevant to helping and to group work, discusses the utility of ethical decision-making models, introduces the ethical codes of relevant professional organizations, and elaborates on the ethical concerns of group work and their relationship to the framework of interactive group leadership.

Basic Ethical Principles

At the broadest level, *ethics* has been defined as the philosophical study of morals and moral action (Varkey, 2021). Ethics has become a real concern and an important part of practice in the helping professions because inherent power differentials can result in intentional or unintentional harm to those being helped. Such harm is more likely to occur when the helpers, who have more power, are not aware of ethics and do not mindfully incorporate ethics into their practice. Thus, professional ethics serve as an important foundation for helping professions such as medicine, psychology, social work, marriage and family therapy, and counseling.

Although the study of ethics at the philosophical level is complex and nuanced, the helping professions in many cases rely on only four principles to inform their ethical code of practice. These principles are beneficence, nonmaleficence, autonomy, and justice (Varkey, 2021).

The principle of *beneficence* is the directive to benefit others. Beneficence includes the moral imperatives to advocate for the rights of others, to prevent harm when possible, to attempt to stop harm, to assist others who are less able to help themselves, and to assist those who are in danger (Varkey, 2021).

Conversely, the principle of *nonmaleficence* is the directive to do no harm to others (Varkey, 2021). Nonmaleficence is evident in common social messages to not kill others, to refrain from causing pain, to not offend without good reason, and to not deprive others of available resources. For example, nonmaleficence means medical doctors must balance the benefits of interventions and treatments against the negative consequences. In the spirit of nonmaleficence, they must reject those interventions or treatments that are disproportionately harmful to the patient while choosing the best course of action. This balancing may be applied similarly to other helping situations.

The principle of *autonomy* is the directive to promote the freedom and autonomy of others (Varkey, 2021). Autonomy is a person's ability to make substantive choices and direct their own life. Underlying the principle of autonomy is the belief that all people have intrinsic value and should be empowered to make informed and value-consistent choices in the pursuit of self-determination. In helping relationships, promoting autonomy must be weighed against the potential impact of autonomous actions on others and also against individuals' capacity to make autonomous choices. The issue of capacity is particularly contentious because although determinations of competence may be used to keep individuals safe, they can also be used to silence, control, and oppress.

The ethical principle of *justice* is concerned with each person or group receiving what they are due. The idea of justice is related to ideas such as fairness, equality, and need. Different types of justice exist, and, like other ethical principles, these can be culturally and situationally dependent. For example, distributive justice refers to the fair distribution of resources, with fairness being determined by cultural or community social norms. Depending on context, just distribution of resources can be based on equal sharing, need, effort, investment or contribution, merit, and monetary transaction.

Although each principle is important, in practice their different directions may conflict. This is what makes real-life application of ethics both challenging and interesting. When ethical principles provide conflicting guidance, professionals must make determinations based on context, balancing the potential needs of different stakeholders, and the potential for harm and good for each option. This can be a challenging process, making ethical decision-making models useful.

Ethical Decision-Making and Models

Because real-life ethical dilemmas are unpredictable and complex, the ethical codes and standards of helping professions can be insufficient to support the decision-making of group leaders, particularly novice group leaders. Research indicates that use of an established ethical decision-making model improves professionals' decision-making (Varkey, 2021). However, there is no single, endorsed "best" ethical decision-making model. Group workers are strongly encouraged to adopt an ethical decision-making model to help them navigate the multiple institutional, group, relational, and personal contexts that may present during group work (Brabender, 2006).

Kitchener's (1984) model of decision-making, as described by Urofsky et al. (2009), is based on the use of basic ethical principles, or *principle ethics*. This model consists of two levels of moral and ethical reasoning. The first, the *intuitive* level, relies upon an individual's innate or gut response to the ethical dilemma. This response may be based on internalized knowledge of ethics and professional standards, personal moral rules, culture and worldview, and past professional and personal experience. The second, the *critical-evaluative* level, becomes active when the first level alone does not provide adequate guidance. This second level entails applying increasingly abstract moral codes until adequate discernment of the ethical action required is achieved. For example, a group leader might in the moment rely upon their intuitive sense of an ethical dilemma for guidance. If they have a sense of intuition being inadequate, consultation with and close reading of the professional ethical standard is warranted. If the ethical standard is inadequate for guiding action, they might further work through the dilemma by analyzing it using the basic ethical principles.

Kitchener's model defined and illustrated the basic ethical principles in the context of counseling, argued for their primary validity in ethical decision-making in counseling, and supported upholding the ethical principles as an obligation of counseling professionals unless a stronger obligation existed within the circumstance (Urofsky et al., 2009). This ran counter to a tendency in the profession to rank or prioritize the principles or to present them as absolutes, regardless of context. Kitchener's model, however, did not provide process guidance for unclear ethical situations in which group workers must navigate and balance the sometimes competing obligations of ethics in real-life practice. This relative weakness gave rise to several process-oriented models of ethical decision-making, including Haas and Malouf's (2002) model and Welfel's (2013) model.

Haas and Malouf's (2002) framework includes five steps group leaders can follow when encountering ethical dilemmas:

1. Define the ethical issue.
2. Gather information about stakeholders and relevant standards related to the dilemma.

3. Identify an array of potential actions to resolve the dilemma.
4. Evaluate options and implement the best action.
5. Assess the results.

Welfel's (2013) model includes more detail. Steps are as follows:

1. Develop ethical sensitivity.
2. Identify relevant facts and stakeholders.
3. Define central issues in the dilemma and available options.
4. Examine relevant ethical standards, laws, and regulations.
5. Search out ethics scholarship.
6. Apply ethical principles to the situation.
7. Consult with supervisors and respected colleagues.
8. Deliberate and decide.

Becoming familiar with professional ethical standards is an important step in both models.

Professional Organizations and Ethical Standards

While this chapter will not describe in detail each set of professional standards applicable to group work, it aims to provide a starting place for leaders, or other group workers, to locate and familiarize themselves with what is available. All professional organizations that govern helping professions have published ethical standards. The helping professions most often associated with group work are counseling, psychology, social work, and psychiatry, including the American Counseling Association (ACA), the American Psychological Association (APA), and three group-specific organizations: the Association for Specialists in Group Work (ASGW), the Society for Group Psychology and Group Psychotherapy (APA Division 49), and the American Group Psychotherapy Association (AGPA).

The ethical standards of each profession are subject to the cultural context in which they arose and in which they are currently operating. All of these professions have additional sets of best practices or practice guidelines that provide information about the context of the profession and how the organization interprets the application of ethics in the field. Additionally, scholars within each profession and within the domain of group work often write to elaborate and apply these ethics and best practice guidelines to specific populations and specific situations. Interactive group leaders should familiarize themselves with the ethical standards, best practice guidelines, and scholarship that elaborates on ethics within specific settings and with specific populations.

The *ACA Code of Ethics* (ACA, 2014) references group work specifically in three standards: Standard A.9.a. on screening clients for group work, Standard A.9.b. on protecting group members from physical or mental harm, and Standard B.4.a. on communicating the importance and limitations of confidentiality. ASGW is an ACA division that serves group workers across disciplines. Although ASGW does not have a separate code of ethics for group work, it has issued guiding documents that address ethics. McCarthy et al. (2021) collaborated to update and integrate past guiding documents into ASGW's guiding principles for group work. The updated guidance presents as foundational "the belief that group work has unique ethical considerations across training, practice, supervision, evaluation, and research domains" (McCarthy et al., 2021, p. 12) and reinforces that group worker training must include the study of ethics. The importance of diversity, equity, and inclusion as a value of ASGW and part of ethical practice is also integrated throughout the document. The ASGW guidelines do not supplant the *ACA Code of Ethics* (McCarthy et al., 2021).

APA's (2017) ethical principles for psychologists address group work in one brief statement: "When psychologists provide services to several persons in a group setting, they describe at the outset the roles and responsibilities of all parties and the limits of confidentiality" (Standard 10.03). APA Division 49 does not provide any additional guidelines for those conducting group work.

AGPA is a cross-disciplinary organization devoted to promoting group psychotherapy. AGPA's (2002) guidelines for group psychotherapy practice consist of two parts: a description of group therapists' responsibilities to clients and a description of professional standards. Responsibilities include respecting group members' dignity, uniqueness, rights, and autonomy; protecting the privacy and confidentiality of each group member; and protecting group members and the public from unethical, dangerous, or unqualified practice by any group therapist (AGPA, 2002). The professional standards are oriented toward preserving the integrity of the practice of group therapy and emphasize the importance of group therapists engaging in continued education and supervision, participating in group research either as a participant or researcher, and being proactive when they become aware of unethical group therapy taking place.

In addition to this guidance, AGPA also publishes the *International Journal of Group Psychotherapy* (*IJGP*), which provides a wealth of scholarship on group therapy ethics. Examples of ethics topics published in *IJGP* include the ethical imperative of diversity (Debiak, 2007), the ethics of termination (Mangione et al., 2007), confidentiality and privileged communication (Lasky & Riva, 2006), and the ethics of combined individual and group therapy (Brabender & Fallon, 2009). Novice and experienced group workers are encouraged to develop a broad familiarity with the standards of their specific profession, develop in-depth knowledge of published practice guidelines for group work, as well as explore and engage with the scholarship that details the application of ethics and professional ethical codes to specific situations.

Group Ethical Concerns

Several authors have written about the unique challenges presented by the group work environment that affect ethical practice, including Kottler (1994), who outlined a wide variety of issues unique to groups that could become ethical dilemmas. These include the following:

- Verbal hostility is more likely to occur in groups than in individual counseling and affects not only group leaders but other group members.
- Group leaders exert less control over group member behavior in and out of group than in other helping modalities.
- Although group leaders have power that can benefit group members, this power can also harm group members.
- In the absence of competent leadership, there may be a greater potential for members to become dependent on the leader, other group members, and the group.
- Confidentiality in the group setting cannot be guaranteed.
- The likelihood of inadequate training and specific supervision is higher for group work than for individual helping.
- The intensity of group work can make participation more risky psychologically than participation in individual counseling or therapy.
- Poor screening and selection and involuntary participation have different and potentially more destructive consequences in group work than in individual therapy.
- Reentry issues or issues experienced by members once group is over present unique problems.

G. Corey et al. (1995) also addressed the issues affecting ethical practice of group work, breaking them down into seven domains: (a) the rights of group members, (b) psychological risks, (c) maintaining professional relationships with group members, (d) the impact of leader values on the group, (e) the use and misuse of group techniques, (f) ethical issues of termination and follow-up, and (g) legal liability and malpractice. Although these domains overlap and impact each other, they provide a useful way to describe the gamut of ethical issues inherent in groups.

The Rights of Group Members

Group leaders, like other helping professionals, should be knowledgeable about their clients' rights. The rights of group members intersect with and can potentially either support or contradict several of the unique ethical situations of groups. G. Corey et al. (1995) conceptualized these as rights outright, as responsibilities of the group leader, and as situations where group member rights are at risk of infringement. They discussed group members' rights to informed consent, orientation, and screening. These are the responsibility of the group leader, and more information on this can be found in Chapter 15.

G. Corey et al. (1995) also highlighted the dilemma of group members' rights when membership in the group is involuntary. In such cases, group leaders should make every effort to empower involuntary members by providing them with information about the goals and process of the group, the rights they do have within the group, and the implications of group membership outside of the group.

Other rights described by G. Corey et al. (1995) include the right to freedom from coercion and undue pressure, the right to equitable treatment, and the right to confidentiality and privacy (see Chapter 15). With respect to freedom from coercion and undue pressure, group leaders must be able to distinguish between therapeutic and damaging levels of social pressure. They will also benefit their group members by instructing group members on how to resist social pressure and by checking in frequently with the group and group members when feedback giving is active.

Leadership that promotes equitable treatment, or access to the helping power of the group, can be thought of as primarily a function of group leader self-awareness and solid interactive leadership skills. Group leaders need to be self-aware such that they avoid preferential or discriminatory treatment of group members based on social identity characteristics, personality (e.g., introversion vs.

extroversion), or presenting issues. Interactive group leadership skills that elicit participation from all members, support group membership skills and group member interaction, and promote member autonomy will all promote equitable treatment.

Psychological Risks

Both novice and experienced group leaders may forget that although groups can provide great benefits, there is also the potential for psychological harm. Groups can be psychologically risky for many of the same reasons they are beneficial. Groups capitalize on the social influence not only of an authority figure but also of peers. This influence is used to create the conditions for change (e.g., encourage self-disclosure) and to directly change behavior (e.g., encourage clear communication of needs). But sometimes change itself can bring forms of harm—for example, if a group member tries out a newly learned assertiveness skill in an unsafe out-of-group situation. G. Corey et al. (1995) indicated that psychological harm in groups may take the form of feeling pressured to engage in ways that are counter to the group members' needs or wants, losing a sense of privacy after overdisclosing, becoming the target of unwarranted hostility, feeling injured by a breach of confidentiality, and experiencing distress as a result of poorly planned activities.

Maintaining Professional Relationships With Group Members

The foundation of helping is the formation of safe and clearly boundaried relationships between helper and helpee. Within professional helping, these relationships are informed and governed by policies and guidelines created by helping professions organizations.

In these relationships, the primary orientation of the helper is toward meeting the learning, growth, and change needs of the helpee through a set of supportable professional behaviors. A primary threat to this helping orientation within group work is dual relationships where other personal and professional relationships between the group leader and any group member can cloud the perception, intent, and action of the relationship. A secondary threat to the professional relationship is the group leader not being able to provide the ascribed professional behaviors because of a lack of knowledge or skill.

Within groups, the clarity of relationships and boundaries becomes more significant on account of the increased emotional vulnerability of members and the potential comparative aspect of multiple "clients" within one setting. Group leaders should be aware of potential dual relationships with group members via other personal or professional connections they may have with them and minimize these if possible.

The Impact of Leader Values on the Group

The ethical practice of group work relies on group leaders being able to provide equitable and competent treatment to all group members. Group members have the right to form their own goals and determine their own course within the group with the assistance of the group leader and other group members. This right is threatened when group leaders have strong values, biases, or personal reactions that run counter to group member goals and the group leader is unaware of the impact of these values, biases, and reactions.

It is always wrong for the implicit purpose of the group to be to promote the group leader's worldview or meet the group leader's personal needs at the expense of group members. If a group leader cannot adequately identify and work with their own values in conjunction with the values of group members, then they should not work with those group members. Similarly, if group leaders are unable to adequately identify and manage their personal reactions and needs, they must address these issues through supervision or therapy. In either case, a referral to an appropriate resource may be the proper course of action.

Use and Misuse of Group Techniques

As previously described, competent group work relies upon a cohesive way of understanding facilitative group environments and group interaction. To ensure that techniques used within a group are helpful, it is important to conceptualize the group environment and interaction in a way that suggests interventions for maintaining a positive environment and promoting useful interaction among members. This understanding can prevent harmful outcomes.

Interactive group leadership emphasizes the connections between group members' requirements for safety and change and the leader's actions to promote the conditions for that change within the group. As described here, the tenets of interactive group leadership, by identifying beneficial conditions, make it possible for group leaders to identify detrimental conditions and intervene before harm is done to the group as a whole or group members. Interventions used within interactive groups must connect to the interactive purposes.

It is tempting in the challenging environment of groups, where especially novice group leaders can feel vulnerable, for leaders to rely upon techniques that they have observed or heard of eliciting change in other settings. It can be a much less vulnerable position for a leader to rely upon a "canned" activity or technique rather than attempt to use their skills in facilitating interaction, becoming emotionally engaged in the group, and potentially drawing frustration from group members to themselves. The danger of such activities is their disconnection from the immediate needs of the group or group members and the long-term needs of the facilitative group environment. Activities and techniques should be evaluated for their social and cultural appropriateness and their ability to promote a facilitative environment, to meet group members' growth and change needs, and to avoid psychological or physical harm.

Ethical Issues of Termination and Follow-Up

G. Corey et al. (1995) highlighted the vulnerability of group members at termination as a potential ethical issue. Termination from group work has been characterized as a time when learning and growth related to endings can occur, when confusion can come from unconsolidated internal and external changes, and when group members need additional support and framing to realize good outcomes and minimize potential negative impacts (Kline, 2003).

With the potential for emotional stimulation and change that is inherent in group work, it is important for leaders to ethically attend to termination. Group members benefit greatly from the following:

- Being able to make sense of the end of their group experience in ways that are beneficial to them
- Honoring the relationships they have formed within the group
- Honoring their own hard work, risk taking, and change
- Understanding how to best apply what they have learned in group to their life outside of group

Chapter 15 describes how interactive group leaders can set up the conditions for and work toward these termination outcomes throughout their groups.

Legal Liability and Malpractice

Ethics, ethical codes, and laws are related but different. Whereas ethics are aspirational moral codes related to philosophical principles, ethical codes are those aspirational moral codes translated and applied to professional practice. Laws are more specific and overlap with ethics in several ways. Laws are governed by the state or federal government and prohibit certain behaviors while mandating others. Laws that are of particular concern are laws related to professional liability, negligence, and malpractice. Group leaders who are counselors, psychologists, or social workers are held to the standards of their parent professional organizations as well as those of their licensing body—which is almost always at the state level—as they provide services. Furthermore, states have additional laws that define professional liability and malpractice and delineate their consequences.

If harm to a group member can be connected to the group leader not providing care that adheres to their professional standards and the state licensing body, the leader may be considered negligent, as having committed malpractice, and liable for damages. G. Corey et al. (1995) defined the types of injury that group members may experience as a result of negligence as worsening of presenting symptoms or emergence of new symptoms; overextending themselves to failure as a result of misuse or abuse of group techniques; complying with directives and suffering loss of relationships or jobs; self-harm or harm to others; and loss of rights, privileges, or privacy.

To avoid negligence, malpractice, and liability, group leaders must be aware of the laws of their state as well as the standards of practice for their professional organization and group work in general. Additionally, many of the practices already discussed in the context of interactive group work will assist group leaders in practicing in an ethically and legally sound way. As stated previously, skills, interventions, and techniques used by the group leader should be defensible through research and theory and clearly connected to the goals of the group and the individual members. Group members should be well informed about the purpose and process of the groups in which they are participating. Screening, orientation, and informed consent are not only the rights of group members but key tools for leaders in avoiding negligence and malpractice. Woods and Ruzek (2018) also highlighted the diligent documentation of groups and continued assessment of both the group and its individual members as critical to avoiding negligence, malpractice, and liability. These important group leader responsibilities are discussed in depth in Chapter 15.

Ethics and Interactive Group Leadership

Previous literature has addressed the unique ethical issues of group work from a general perspective with some focus on specific techniques and approaches that might pose more risk. This raises the question of whether there are specific ethical issues that might be elevated when group leaders follow an interactive group leadership perspective.

The key principles of interactive group work have an impact on ethical practice. These key principles include creating an environment that balances safety and challenge, encouraging interaction between group members to enable interpersonal learning, and emphasizing increasing group member responsibility for the group rather than solely relying on the group leader.

Additionally, the interactive group leadership functions of norm setting, structuring, boundary management, instruction, regard, languaging, and administration each play a role in ethical interactive group work. Each of these interactive group work principles can assist in upholding the ethical principles of beneficence, nonmaleficence, autonomy, and justice or, in their absence or ill use, result in ethical issues.

Interactive Group Work and Autonomy

Interactive group workers value autonomy. However, interactive group work shares and capitalizes on the social influence that is inherent to all group work. This social influence is what both enables growth and change and also can make operating autonomously within the group difficult for some group members. The emphasis on group member interaction fosters trust and intimacy that makes the group and other group members matter more to an individual within the group. Group members in an interactive group have rich experiential opportunities to practice choosing their relationship behaviors to act autonomously while maintaining connection. Effectively enacting all the interactive group leadership functions supports group member autonomy. Failing to adequately perform any one of the interactive leadership functions may result in group member autonomy being threatened or remaining underdeveloped.

For example, when a group member is receiving feedback from several other group members and feels pressured to immediately change a behavior, the group leader can structure the interaction. The leader can slow the interaction by asking the feedback receiver what they are hearing, highlighting their choices in the moment, and encouraging them to make sense of the feedback in their own time. Additionally, the interactive leader can enact the boundary management function, which is based on the principle of autonomy, to encourage group members to consider their own needs and the needs of others before making choices about what information to share or take in. Prior use of the instruction function by the group leader to assist group members in learning clear communication and good listening skills will also contribute to group member autonomy. Group member autonomy is threatened when group leaders abdicate their role in establishing interactive norms, encouraging here-and-now interaction, structuring interaction, and instructing members in membership skills.

Interactive Group Work and Beneficence

In terms of beneficence, interactive group work and leadership are focused on group members gaining the benefit of interpersonal learning and support within the group. This, however, relies on leader competence, enactment of interactive leadership functions, and commitment to developing an interactive group environment. Group members benefit from an environment that balances safety and challenges and that encourages clear communication of needs, feedback, and boundaries in the here and now. One challenge to this occurring is when group leaders do not understand group interaction well enough to intervene effectively. Ethical group leaders must have a cohesive and useful group leadership framework such as focal conflict, systems, or interpersonal theory to structure their observations, identify effective and ineffective interaction, and suggest interventions.

Another challenge to beneficence through the creation of change and growth is group leaders' personal needs interfering with the empathy, boundaries, emotional regulation, and courage needed to intervene effectively. The authoritative and individuation stages of group development and frustrating group members' restrictive solutions routinely draw frustration or hostility toward group leaders. Anxiety can threaten to overwhelm both group members and group leaders during change-producing feedback exchanges. Group leaders need to be able to emotionally weather these and other trying times to observe and intervene in ways that will ultimately benefit group members by maintaining the interactive group environment.

Interactive Group Work and Nonmaleficence

In terms of nonmaleficence, interactive group leaders are focused on protecting group members from harm. Harm can occur in the ways discussed earlier in this chapter, such as group members feeling pressure to interact in ways that may be psychologically harmful to them or becoming the target of unwarranted and persistent hostility.

Interactive group leaders are knowledgeable and facilitate the conditions that prevent harm through the administrative function by conducting adequate screening, preparing group members, informing them of the purpose and process of the group, and clarifying the limits of confidentiality. They monitor the group for effective interaction and intervene when group interaction is ineffective. Their interventions are strongly connected to group leadership theory and research process goals. Interactive group leaders also structure interactions sufficiently to promote balanced and productive interaction, which lowers the likelihood of harm. They also monitor individual group members, taking note of their level of involvement and the type of interactions in which they are involved.

Interactive group leaders also prevent harm by being self-aware and addressing their interpersonal needs outside of the groups they lead through personal relationships, supervision, individual therapy, and group membership. They prevent harm by being aware of their personal reactions, worldview, values, and sociocultural positionality. Similarly, they are aware of their power within the group and understand the potential it poses for harming group members.

Interactive Group Work and Justice

In terms of justice, interactive group leaders prioritize planning groups, screening potential members, and preparing group members so they can gain equitable benefit from their groups. Group members who are prepared can make informed choices about interacting and will, if they have been adequately instructed about membership skills and supported, engage in the group process productively. Interactive group leaders will monitor group interaction, much like they do to prevent harm, to assess whether group members are interacting in ways that allow them to benefit from the group and intervene if they are not. If they observe dynamics within the group that seem to persistently inhibit the productive participation of one or more members, they also intervene. They also regularly solicit feedback from group members to find out if they believe they are benefiting from group, and if not, why.

Interactive group leaders persistently examine interaction within their groups knowing that societal inequities and their own preference will inevitably emerge and pose a threat to equitable benefit. They are aware of their power, privilege, and social identities and understand that group members may perceive them differently than they wish to be perceived. They understand that group members may see them as insensitive, unsafe, or oppressors and that they may have to actively process and counter those perceptions with actions to encourage those group members to interact productively. Interactive group leaders take seriously their role as social justice advocates and actively seek out systemic barriers that may keep marginalized populations from accessing high-quality group work. They are particularly concerned about developing their own self-awareness, cross-cultural group work skills, and knowledge of alternative forms of group that may suit some group members better.

Conclusion

The ethical practice of interactive group work relies on group leader knowledge, self-awareness, and commitment to interactive group work principles. Group members have a right to competent group leadership. Interactive group leaders must have a deep understanding of foundational ethical principles, their elaboration in professional ethical codes, and their operationalization in real-world group work situations. Group work is ethically unique on account of its multistakeholder nature, unique structural properties, and heightened social influence. Because of this, the administrative leadership function in the form of adequate screening, group member preparation, and informed consent is essential to ethical interactive leadership. To truly act to promote autonomy, beneficence, nonmaleficence, and justice, interactive group leaders need to not only be knowledgeable and skilled but also be aware of how their own personal needs, boundaries, preferences, biases, privilege, and power affect their leadership.

Chapter 13

Contemporary Group Research

Outcomes

Level 1 Outcomes

After reading this chapter, entry-level students and practitioners should be able to:

1. Provide an overview of contemporary group work research.
2. Discuss research that links process and outcome.
3. Discuss research that addresses group work with diverse populations and practice in diverse contexts.
4. Discuss research that links group modality and outcome.

Level 2 Outcomes

After reading this chapter, advanced-level students and practitioners should also be able to:

1. Discuss research that explores the efficacy of groups for specific populations and issues, with a focus on different developmental stages and contexts.
2. Discuss important components of group work research on inclusive practice and implications for the application of skills to diverse populations in different contexts.

Research in group work has evolved over the last 100 years. This evolution has been influenced by the emergence of a scientist-practitioner model of practice in the field of counseling based on the premise "that research coming out of the field should be reflective of the practice taking place within that field, and practice that is occurring should be researched" (Okech et al., 2022, p. 1). Much of the evidence for practice in the field has been gleaned from individual counseling practice and the experience of seasoned group counselors and scholars of practice, such as Irvin D. Yalom, whose individual works and collaborations with Molyn Leszcz continue to have a significant impact on the conceptualization of groups and group therapy practice. However, as the field has grown, so has the research on the practice of group work, with new researchers expanding the work of I. D. Yalom and his collaborators and extending research and scholarship into practice in diverse contexts, with diverse populations and utilizing online mediums.

This chapter guides readers through specific areas of research on group work. These areas have been selected because of their significance in group counseling practice and the authors' perspectives based on decades of experience teaching and supervising group work and researching and writing about group. This chapter will focus on five main areas: (a) research on the application of select group theories and skills, (b) research that links group process and outcome, (c) research that explores the efficacy of groups for specific populations and issues, (d) research on intercultural and inclusive practice in group work, and (e) research that links treatment modality and outcome. Readers are left with general guidelines, specific suggestions, and resources to draw upon when later planning and implementing groups in diverse settings.

Research on the Application of Select Group Theories and Skills

Contemporary group work practice is driven by the ethical mandate that requires counselors providing services to "use techniques/procedures/modalities that are grounded in theory and/or have an empirical or scientific foundation" (American Counseling Association, 2014, Standard C.7.a.). This ethical mandate has created challenges and opportunities for new research exploring aspects of group work practice that are not soundly grounded in past research.

Newer research is examining modalities of practice that have long been assumed to be effective based on practitioner experience. For example, Agazarian (2012), in a study of systems-centered practice, used an inpatient group to examine how systems form, including how subgrouping and role formation and hierarchies emerge within the first few sessions of a group. Validating what practitioners have long observed, Agazarian's findings further emphasized the significance of leaders paying attention to the isomorphic nature of groups and the hierarchies that form within them among members, as well as the implications for members' interpersonal interactions and group outcome. These findings are particularly significant given that over the last 20 years, group systems theory has become one of the most widely used theoretical approaches to group work (Connors & Caple, 2005; Kivlighan & Kivlighan, 2014; Kline, 2003; Sung & Skovholt, 2019).

In a study of master's-level counseling students' group conceptualization skills, Sung and Skovholt (2019) identified two large domains with 12 categories of group conceptualization: group functioning and individual member functioning. These domains are closely aligned with the constructs of group systems theory (e.g., individual, interpersonal, group as a whole; see Chapter 5) and interpersonal approaches to counseling (see Chapter 6). Sung and Skovholt's findings "underscore all three levels" (p. 132) of group systems theory as integral to neophyte group counselors' group conceptualization and intervention levels. These findings were aligned with those of Kivlighan and Kivlighan (2014), who encouraged researchers to simultaneously examine individual and group-as-a-whole experiences because of the inextricable nature of the two experiences for individual members in groups. It is important to point out that the sample in the Sung and Skovholt study had limited racial and cultural diversity, which is an important consideration for all group leaders using traditional theories with samples largely normed on White practitioners.

Perhaps the most researched group counseling theory is the interpersonal approach (Chouliara et al., 2020; Van Nieuwenhove et al., 2020; I. D. Yalom & Leszcz, 2020). I. D. Yalom's past (e.g., 1970, 1975, 1995) and more recent (I. D. Yalom & Leszcz, 2020) work all encompasses the highly referenced 11 therapeutic factors—namely, instillation of hope, universality, imparting of information, altruism, the corrective recapitulation of the primary family group, development of socializing techniques, imitative behavior, interpersonal learning, group cohesiveness, catharsis, and existential factors. Kivlighan and Kivlighan (2014) provided a comprehensive review of research on I. D. Yalom's therapeutic factors and encouraged group work researchers to continue examining the relationship between therapeutic factors, other group processes, and outcome "while paying theoretical and statistical attention to the relational aspects of individual group members and the other group members" (p. 46). Their call is vital given how deeply entrenched the therapeutic factors are in the training, clinical supervision, and practice of group counseling and psychotherapy. The studies they reviewed affirm the intersection and interrelated nature of catharsis and interpersonal learning therapeutic factors: group cohesion and interpersonal learning. The research findings that Kivlighan and Kivlighan (2014) examined support the interpersonal approach conceptual framework that states that a group member's perceptions of "self-disclosure, acceptance, altruism, guidance, vicarious learning, and instillation of hope are all related" (p. 51) to their perception of the depth of the session. Finally, their research showed that the therapeutic experiences group members have are directly correlated to a group leader's style. Leaders who are experienced as caring and responsive, as exercising their executive function when needed and also stimulating emotion appropriately, are likely to stimulate the development of therapeutic factors of instillation of hope, universality, altruism, group cohesiveness, imparting of information, imitative behavior, and existential factors. Furthermore, if such leaders also respond to conflict in the here and now and courageously support members in acknowledging and addressing complex identity and social-cultural experiences, they are likely to help group members sustain those therapeutic factors to their benefit both in and outside the group (Kivlighan & Kivlighan, 2014; I. D. Yalom & Leszcz, 2020).

Although systems theory and interpersonal theory are the group-centered theories most often researched, other theories used to run groups, such as variations of cognitive behavior therapy (CBT), have also been extensively researched (Morgan et al., 2014). However, CBT is not a modality that centers group process or dynamics of groups. Rather, it is focused more on techniques and conceptualization of individual functioning based on principles of individual counseling.

Research Linking Group Process and Outcome

Contemporary group work research also supports the long-held theoretical link between group process and outcome (Burlingame et al., 2014; Gullo et al., 2015; J. Johnson et al., 2005; Kivlighan et al., 2020; Lerardi et al., 2022).

Gullo et al. (2015) examined how a member's attachment dimensions related to their perception of relationship in group. Participants were 91 female- and 21 male-identifying Italian graduate students attending six interpersonal growth groups. No racial or ethnic demographic information was provided, which constrains discussion about cross-cultural application of their findings. Although the implications may speak more to the experiences of White Italian female graduate students, the study yields outcomes that are beneficial to practitioners leading similar groups that have more males and members of underrepresented groups. Gullo et al.'s (2015) findings suggested that the attachment pattern (anxiety and avoidance) of group members was unrelated to their perceptions of "group climate" (p. 18). For practitioners, this gives more agency to the focus on developing a group climate that facilitates relationship building and interactions that can help members meet their group goals. The group process and climate have more agency in facilitating member growth, development, and engagement than do any preconceived notions members have of what their experience might be like.

However, leaders should be cognizant of the modality of counseling they are using as they facilitate the development of group climate and process that can yield positive outcomes. Lerardi et al. (2022) in a comparative study of online and face-to-face counseling found that group members exhibited more anxiety and avoidant behavior in face-to-face groups than they did in remote groups. Accounting for enhanced interpersonal fears in face-to-face settings and muted interpersonal fears in online settings, for some populations, becomes a critical consideration for leaders who want to help members work on more authentic reflections on their own intrapersonal and interpersonal patterns of engagement, especially in groups.

Recent research also provides evidence that supports the intersection between interpersonal learning and positive group outcomes (Burlingame & Jensen, 2017). Interpersonal learning can be defined as lessons on effective interactions or collaborations with others as demonstrated through interpersonal skills. Interpersonal skills are ways and means of interacting with others that demonstrate an ability to engage in effective communication and relationships with others. Interpersonal skills also include the intrapersonal process that one engages in while navigating interactions with others. Interpersonal learning is one of I. D. Yalom's therapeutic factors (I. D. Yalom & Leszcz, 2020). Group members who are open to learning and are able to learn and acquire new interpersonal skills tend to meet their group goals and have positive outcomes in groups (Burlingame & Jensen, 2017; Burlingame et al., 2018).

Recent research also provides evidence that supports the intersection between group cohesion and positive group outcomes (Burlingame & Jensen, 2017; Burlingame et al., 2011b; I. D. Yalom & Leszcz, 2020) "across clinical settings (inpatient and outpatient) and diagnostic classifications" (Burlingame et al., 2018, p. 394). Group cohesion is essentially the therapeutic bond that members experience within their group with each other when they have developed trust and can engage in self-disclosure in the group, are willing to be vulnerable and take risks with each other (e.g., feedback exchange), and experience a sense of acceptance and belonging with each other (I. D. Yalom & Leszcz, 2020). Group cohesion is also directly linked to the therapeutic bond that is associated with a group leader's effective and consistent attending behavior (Burlingame et al., 2018). Group cohesion is more easily defined by how it looks in action than theoretically. Groups that advance through various stages of development to develop cohesion tend to have more positive outcomes (Burlingame et al., 2018). Leaders must pay attention to the role they play in helping members develop group cohesion. This process, which begins at planning and recruitment, requires leaders to center strong meaningful interactions with and among members. If members experience the group and leader as safe—that is, as consistent, authentic, predictable, reliable, and invested in their well-being—the group will advance toward cohesion and positive group outcomes (Alldredge et al., 2021).

Other studies have identified factors that enhance group cohesion and group outcomes. Burlingame and Jensen's (2017) meta-analytic study identified factors that included the leader's theoretical orientation, with interpersonal approaches scoring the highest; the group's size, with five to nine members deemed best for promoting positive relationships among members; the number of sessions, with more than 12 sessions providing members with the best opportunity to develop strong relational bonds; and having younger group members, with youth being correlated with positive group outcomes. These findings do not reveal much about the impact of diversity of group members or the impact of social-cultural contexts on the development of cohesion and group outcomes (Burlingame et al., 2018). However, they do highlight factors to consider when developing long-term groups, such as the importance of group size and length in allowing members to engage in in-depth sharing of experiences and to develop meaningful relationships with each other; the value of an interpersonal theory–centered theoretical orientation; and, perhaps, the importance of group leaders initiating and facilitating intercultural learning opportunities. Such opportunities support members in transcending barriers to intercultural relationships, which emerge when leaders use culturally neutral approaches to leading groups. Finally, group composition also plays a critical role in group process and outcome (see Chapter 15).

Research on the Efficacy of Groups for Specific Populations

Contemporary group work research has been engaged in extensive exploration of treatment processes and outcomes for specific populations over the years (Burlingame et al., 2004, 2014; Janis et al., 2021; I. D. Yalom & Leszcz, 2020). Burlingame et al. (2004) examined the role group therapy plays in the treatment outcome of clients with a specific diagnosis. They found that group members with homogeneous presentation because of their diagnosis tended to have positive treatment outcomes. For example, individuals in the same group who are diagnosed with social phobia, panic disorders, or obsessive-compulsive disorders tend to have positive group therapy outcomes due to the homogeneity of their presentation. Such homogeneity of presentation makes it easier for practitioners to plan for the group's content and process; to predict possible group behavior, challenges, and outcomes; and to strategically plan how to intervene with the group. What remains important for group researchers to explore is the intersection between a specific presentation or medical diagnosis and the social location or social-cultural identity of a group member and its implications for their experience of group climate and process (which research says is critical to positive treatment outcomes). This remains a gap in group counseling research that needs additional studies.

A special population worth considering is that of offenders, who may be incarcerated, and mandated clients, who may be on probation or similarly required supervision programs. Group work is often used with this population; however, Morgan et al. (2014) described how offender groups present problems not typical of therapy groups in other settings, such as a perceived lack of institutional support, confidentiality and client safety issues, and a lack of appropriate group leader supervision. These factors make work with this population even more challenging and limited to a small group of group practitioners even though research presents evidence supporting the utility of the group therapy approach with these populations and its effectiveness being similar to that of individual counseling (Morgan et al., 2014).

Morgan et al. (2014) described several techniques that research shows are effective with the offender and mandated client population. The here-and-now interventions that provide clients with agency and focus on the possibility of changing their current life and influencing their future experiences are particularly effective. Another technique identified by Morgan et al. is psychoeducation, which is critical to expanding this population's self-awareness, their perceptions of self and how others perceive them, the dynamics of their mental health condition, and how to communicate about it. Psychoeducation may also address treatment modalities that might work for them and how to engage with them, as well as socializing skills and techniques that can enhance their integration into society.

Based on an extensive review of literature and experience working with offender and mandated clients, Morgan et al. (2014) also recommended specific strategies for their group work, including (a) risk-need-responsivity, which requires that the intensity of the therapy group (e.g., frequency, duration) be matched to the risk of the offender (i.e., high-risk offenders receive high-intensity services); (b) CBT, which can reduce recidivism and improve mental health outcomes; (c) structured rather than unstructured (e.g., psychodynamic) programs; and (d) homework, which can improve outcomes for offenders and possibly for mandated group members as well. Morgan et al. encouraged practitioners not to neglect the interpersonal counseling approach in their work with the offender and mandated client population. Although structured CBT group approaches yield positive results, alone they cannot provide the foundation for socializing skills development and interpersonal learning that is achieved when they are combined with the interpersonal group counseling approach. In fact, the incorporation of an interpersonal approach can play a critical role in mitigating the recurrence of criminal-associated behavior, such as poor interpersonal functioning, avoidance of responsibilities, and avoidance of prosocial expectations (Morgan et al., 2014).

The research and literature reviewed by Burlingame et al. (2014) highlighted research trends showing that group outcomes continued to be linked to populations served. For example, Burlingame et al. (2014) found 28 additional studies affirming CBT group therapy effects on social phobia symptoms and comorbid depression; 28 more studies showing reliable improvements in emotional distress, coping, and improving life adjustment; and 16 studies in which groups for substance abuse showed positive effects for adolescents and adults, with minor differences in effectiveness between protocols. These studies also affirm long-held beliefs and values about group work practice, such as the importance of intentionality and focus on group dynamics and group culture, the importance of group cohesion as indicated through the dynamics of group interpersonal interactions and its influence on positive group outcomes, and the critical role that therapeutic relationships play in group outcomes (Burlingame et al., 2011a, 2011b; Janis et al., 2021; Kline, 2003; I. D. Yalom & Leszcz, 2020).

Burlingame et al.'s (2014) clarification of the definition of therapeutic relationships (i.e., alliance, cohesion, empathy, and climate) provides practitioners with specific aspects of group work practice to pay attention to during the preparation phase of the group and in the early stages of group development. These are aspects of the therapeutic relationship that research shows work in groups and would benefit from being prioritized by leaders of counseling and psychotherapy groups.

Research on Diversity and Inclusive Group Practice

Contemporary group work research has been engaged in exploring the evidence foundation of the application of widely used group counseling skills in multicultural contexts and with historically underrepresented populations (Alldredge et al., 2021; Chen et al., 2008; Okech & Rubel, 2007; Sue et al., 2019). Almost all foundational theories in the field of group counseling were developed by Western, White, Eurocentric males, and many contemporary studies of group work were normed on predominantly White populations. It is also evident from the best group theories that the individual construct for examining experiences is centralized in the examination of group dynamics and the factors that influence the process of growth and change for individuals (see focal conflict theory, general systems theory, and interpersonal theory in Chapters 4, 5, and 6, respectively). It is even more important to explore how evidence-based practices in the field (Alldredge et al., 2021; Chen et al., 2008) can be applied to work with racial minorities and other underrepresented groups (Okech & Rubel, 2007; Okech et al., 2015, 2016; Sue et al., 2019) in the practice of group work, training, and supervision approaches. As defined by the American Psychological Association (2008), "Evidence-based practice is the integration of the best available research with clinical expertise in the context of patient characteristics, culture and preferences" (para. 1). Evidence-based practice is particularly critical in group work because it ensures that approaches to group conceptualization, interventions, and assessment are grounded in empirically supported principles.

Chen et al. (2008) offered insights from studies such as Burlingame et al. (2004) that can help enhance cross-cultural group counseling that is also grounded on evidence-based interventions. Chen et al. suggested that providing structure and paying attention to group composition, such as recruiting racial minorities into a group to increase voice, are critical cross-cultural interventions. The principles that underscore these strategies are aligned with the expansive works of I. D. Yalom and Leszcz (2020), Okech and Rubel (2007), Rubel (2006), Rubel and Okech (2010, 2018) and Kline (2003). Additionally, Chen et al. (2008) recommended that leaders use an expanded understanding of self-disclosure, a process that allows underrepresented group members opportunities to progressively develop trust and confidence in a group and progressively disclose more aspects of their personal lives in a group (see Chapter 9). This requires that leaders engage in careful member selection and preparation processes (as discussed in Chapter 15) and that they pay attention to group composition that is likely to yield a positive group climate, process, and outcome (Kline, 2003;

I. D. Yalom & Leszcz, 2020). Finally, Chen et al.'s (2008) suggestion that leaders facilitate broaching conversations that include explicit acknowledgement of difference in race and ethnicity and other cultural variables is consistent with scholarship on group regarding diversity competent group work (Rubel, 2006; Rubel & Okech, 2010, 2018). This level of self-disclosure, however, does require a safe environment in the group that can enhance personal disclosures and discussion about identity and experiences of vulnerability, marginalization, and oppression by group members who identify with underrepresented groups. At the same time, the group leader needs to be skilled in holding the space for White majority group members who might be prepared to engage in these conversations or who might get defensive; feel guilty about their White privilege, history, and identity; or check out of the group's discussion. The development of these skills takes time and commitment to serving groups made up of members of diverse backgrounds, identities, and experiences and who are underrepresented in service provision by group counselors. Ultimately, researchers have found that group leaders who understand the value of the therapeutic alliance and invest in strengthening their relationship with group members are likely to see positive outcomes in their groups irrespective of the racial or ethnic backgrounds of group members and the group leader (Alldredge et al., 2021; Walling et al., 2012). These findings underscore the value of focusing on developing interpersonal dynamics in groups that yield meaningful relationships and trust among members.

A critical interpersonal dynamic in groups is a group's interaction with conflict and group leader cultural competence in managing intercultural conflict. Okech et al. (2015, 2016) in their examination of the dynamics of intercultural communication and intercultural conflict in groups highlighted the significance of leader cultural competence through leader personal knowledge, awareness, and experiences of cultures and relationships across cultural groups and contexts. More than 2 decades ago, Spencer-Rodgers and McGovern (2002) were advocating for attention to intercultural communication in groups and the critical role that intentional attention to a multicultural group's communication patterns plays in the group's climate, process, and outcomes. Evidence-based recommendations for facilitating intercultural communication in groups include verbal tracking, paraphrasing content, asking about cultural meanings ascribed to phrases, using visual aids, asking probing questions, restating for clarity, requesting feedback on member experiences of communication facilitation, and so on (Okech et al., 2015; Ting-Toomey & Chung, 2005). These strategies work in groups that are multicultural and multilingual and have been associated with more positive group outcomes.

Additionally, group leaders have a responsibility to respond to conflict when it emerges within their groups and, when possible, to facilitate a resolution among members (Kivlighan & Kivlighan, 2014; Okech et al., 2016; Singh et al., 2012). Research shows that age, gender, and cultural background influence how group members approach and engage in conflict (Gbadamosi et al., 2014; Havenga, 2008; Sogra, 2014). Additionally, research supports "conflict resolution in the here and now" (Kivlighan & Kivlighan, 2014, p. 51) as being the most effective strategy for addressing interpersonal conflicts in groups. Delayed response to conflict only results in greater disruption to individual member group experience and progression toward group cohesiveness. Leaders with knowledge of the value of timely intervention with group conflict, as well as awareness of the importance of these demographic and cultural factors in conflictual interactions, can ask specific questions and offer guidance that is grounded in an understanding of the complex foundations that influence how different group members may approach and react to conflict within the group. Okech et al. (2016) expanded group leader awareness to include skills such as leader broaching behaviors, contextualizing conflict for group members (including explaining its purpose and value for the group), demonstrating recognition of and respect for individual differences and commonalities in human experience, and engaging in "protective confrontation" (p. 362) when a member is unfairly targeted.

In summary, intercultural conflict or contentious diverse perspectives will emerge in groups around issues of racial identity, ethnic identity, and other forms of underrepresented identities. It is important to address these situations as they arise, especially where members of underrepresented populations may be targeted within a group. Sue et al.'s (2019) microintervention strategies offer helpful solutions. These include the leader's responsibility to bring attention to the issue, diffuse any microaggressions, educate the person responsible, and seek outside assistance or support. In groups, seeking external reinforcement or support may include seeking supervision or consultation on the matter so that the leader can strengthen their microintervention approach. Finally, the leader can help empower group members so that they can confront oppressive microaggressions in the group and speak up for themselves. Sue et al. defined *microinterventions* as words and deeds that communicate to targets of microaggressions "(a) validation of their experiential reality, (b) value as a person, (c) affirmation of their racial or group identity, (d) support and encouragement, and (e) reassurance that they are not alone" (p. 134).

Research Linking Treatment Modality and Outcome

Contemporary group work research also examines the link between treatment modalities and outcomes. Overall, research findings are mixed on whether there is any significant difference in outcomes between face-to-face versus online modalities; however, recent studies show with more certainty that, especially for some populations, online groups are as or more effective (see Chapter 14).

In the emerging endemic phase of COVID-19, practitioners and researchers of group work have continued to examine the impact the quick change to online and remote therapy modalities has had on the outcome of groups. Lleras de Frutos et al. (2020) in a study of distressed cancer survivors in either videoconference or face-to-face group therapy found no significant difference in the outcomes of the treatment modalities. G. H. Chan (2020) in a comparative analysis of online, offline, and integrated counseling of Hong Kong youth found that a mixed/hybrid model and online modality were more effective than face-to-face therapy; however, the face-to-face group had the more positive outcomes. This finding is consistent with that of Lerardi et al. (2022) in a study of the effectiveness of online and remote counseling modalities during the COVID-19 pandemic. However, Kozlowski and Holmes (2014) in a pre-COVID-19 phase study examining experiences in online process groups found that participants raised concerns about the linear nature of the environment, a hyper-awareness of the environment, an artificial feel to the environment, role confusion within the group, superficial engagement within the group, feeling "disconnected from one another" (p. 291), and experiencing the group as "unsafe and mistrusting" (p. 292). Similarly, Male et al. (2017) in a study of the experiences of facilitators of professional online support groups in Canada also found that while many people were attracted to online groups because of unique benefits such as anonymity and convenience, the modality also presented significant concerns, such as challenges to participation, including lack of visual cues, disjointed text communication, and rapid pace.

Additionally, Holmes and Kozlowski (2015) in a comparative study of online versus face-to-face process groups in the United States found that "overall participants assessed face-to-face groups as superior on measures of presence, cohesiveness, safety, and delivery method" (p. 241). In summary, research literature from diverse contexts has shown that although college students are attracted to online groups or hybrid groups, and such context causes them less anxiety, the face-to-face group modality still yields more positive impacts and is particularly effective for group cohesion and social connectedness, which research over the years has shown to be critical to positive group outcomes (G. H. Chan, 2020; Kozlowski & Holmes, 2014; Lerardi et al., 2022; Steen et al., 2014).

These research findings show that while online group counseling is growing and has been boosted by the COVID-19 pandemic effect, in both the pre-COVID-19 and endemic eras some group members have reservations about the modality, and group leaders should attend to their concerns in order to obtain positive outcomes in their groups. These studies offer information critical for group leaders who are invested in more positive outcomes for their groups and point to considerations to make in determining their group modality and processes to pay attention to if they choose to run online or hybrid groups. Most importantly, it seems like the key to effective online modality lies with populations served.

What Works in Groups: A Reflective Exercise

Although this reflective exercise was developed for postsession reflections, the questions can also assist group leaders with their group leadership preparation process.

Discuss what has led to your most productive group sessions.

1. What did you (the group leader) do that helped make the session productive?
    - How would you describe your leadership style and how it promoted a productive session?
    - What role did you play in conceptualizing the group's developmental stage?
    - What role did you play in helping highlight the diverse identities and cultural perspectives represented in the group?
    - What role did you play in supporting the group's progression through its different developmental stages?

- Are you consistently using your group counseling theoretical orientation to conceptualize the group's interactions and to make decisions about appropriate and timely interventions with the group?
- Are you consistently relying on evidence-based and innovative, culturally responsive approaches to ground your interventions with your group?
- What role did you play in teaching feedback models, encouraging feedback exchange, and facilitating feedback exchange effectively?
- If you have a coleader, what is the nature of your interactions within the group?
- Are you supporting and enhancing each other's interventions and interactions with group members?
- How are you working cooperatively to enhance your objectives for the group and the group's progress toward its objectives?

2. What role did you play in enhancing interpersonal communication within your group?
    - What role did you play in enhancing intercultural communication within your group?
    - What role did you play in enhancing multilingual communication within your group?
    - What role did you play to enhance feedback exchange among group members?
    - How quickly did you conceptualize and respond to conflict within the group?
3. What did the members do to help make the session productive?
    - What kind of norms of communication have group members developed?
    - What kinds of intercultural norms of engagement have members developed in the group?
    - How do members interact when issues of diverse racial, ethnic, gender, sexual orientation, or other identity-specific and cultural perspectives and experiences emerge within the group?
    - How did members interact with each other during moments of conflict?
    - How did members respond to your efforts to help them address and resolve the conflict within the group?
    - How do members react to each other when experiencing vulnerability?

- How would you describe members' engagement in self-disclosure and interpersonal risks?

4. What occurred in the group that convinced you that the session was productive?
    - Consider feedback exchange initiation, process, and closure loops.
    - Consider the nature and depth of discussions around social-cultural identities and experiences.
    - Consider the nature of interpersonal connections, including the nature, depth, and frequency of self-disclosure among members.
    - Consider the nature of interaction around interpersonal conflict and whether members are able to remain engaged and resolve or reach an agreement around such conflicts.
    - Consider the progress that members are making toward meeting the group's objectives and their individual interpersonal and intrapersonal group goals.

Conclusion

Group practice assessment is key to the success of groups and can be divided into three components: the evaluation of group creation procedures and protocol (i.e., member selection, group composition, and member preparation for groups), group processes (e.g., interpersonal norms, feedback exchange process, and emotional and experience processing within the group), and the assessment of group member experiences (e.g., achievement of personal interpersonal and intrapersonal goals). These three components are critical to the success of groups, irrespective of the type of group (described in Chapter 14). The development of group process and member experience assessment and evaluation protocols ensures that group objectives are being advanced, the needs of group members are being met, and the group leader is meeting their ethical and leadership obligations. It is critical for leaders to know which approaches and interventions are effective for the type of group they lead and the populations they serve and, most importantly, that the procedures, protocols, interventions, and strategies that they use are evidence-based and will work with the populations they serve.

Additionally, it is critical for group leaders to stay abreast of the research and innovative practices in the field so that they can practice what works in groups. The successful use of appropriate evidence-based intervention strategies can change a group's culture and outcome. Changes in a group's culture change the way members relate to each other and can create a climate that supports open discussion about member social locations, cultural identity, the vulnerability of group members, group member self-disclosure, risk-taking, and commitment to personal growth and change. These conditions make groups work and lead to positive outcomes for group members. The interventions that create these conditions (see Chapter 11) are often challenging and complicated, but at the same time they are critical. They include challenging obstructing norms, experimenting with new norms, intervening by facilitating interpersonal contacts and contracts (see Chapter 6) when members' interpersonal boundaries are impeding movement toward group objectives, observing and intervening with problematic member roles, naming and confronting social and cultural issues as they emerge within the group, and so on.

Furthermore, research shows that group leaders' first priority is to shape group interaction so members can get to know each other, learn from one another, and form relationships that can also facilitate productive interactions around their presenting concerns, intersecting social-cultural identities, and group goals. Group cultures and climates that do not support self-disclosure, vulnerability, feedback exchange, meaningful interaction, and the confrontation of social-cultural issues that impair members' relationships are unlikely to provide members with meaningful experiences and a positive group outcome.

Chapter 14

Introduction to Group Types and Settings

Outcomes

Level 1 Outcomes

After reading this chapter, entry-level students and practitioners should be able to:

1. Name the major group types and describe their characteristics.
2. Describe the different settings in which group work may occur and discuss group types that may be offered in each setting.
3. Discuss the relationship of individual theoretical orientation to group leadership.
4. Identify the benefits and drawbacks of manualized group work.
5. Articulate key issues related to conducting group work online.
6. Discuss the relevance of interactive group work to diverse group work types and settings.
7. Identify and discuss the multicultural and diversity issues that may be significant in each group type and setting.

Level 2 Outcomes

After reading this chapter, advanced-level students and practitioners should also be able to:

1. Apply interactive group leadership functions and basic leadership skills to case examples for each of the major group types.
2. Analyze group interaction scenarios from different group types using a leadership theory and generate interventions.
3. Evaluate an online group case from an interactive group leadership perspective.
4. Critique a manualized group treatment protocol from an interactive group leadership perspective.

One reality of group work is that group structures, such as norms and roles, group development, therapeutic factors, leadership functions, and leadership skills, are shared across all groups. However, the type of group and the setting in which it occurs affect how these group structures appear, how the leader must work with them, and how the interactive group works. This chapter reviews interactive group therapeutic factors and leadership functions, describes the four main group types and discusses their relationship to interactive group leadership, introduces major settings in which group work occurs, and describes the implications of interactive group leadership across these groups and settings. Additionally, this chapter discusses online groups, manualized groups, and their relationship to interactive group work.

The four group types identified by the Association for Specialists in Group Work (ASGW) are (a) task or work groups, (b) psychoeducational groups, (d) counseling groups, and (d) therapy groups (see Figure 14.1). The types of groups serve different purposes and, because of their different goals, require different consideration by the group leader during the planning, administration, and operation of the group (Gladding, 2019; McCarthy et al., 2021). However, all groups can and should be interactive and have common structures that affect the group environment, interaction, and work toward group and individual goals. As such, the knowledge and skills of interactive group leaders are transferrable across group types. A

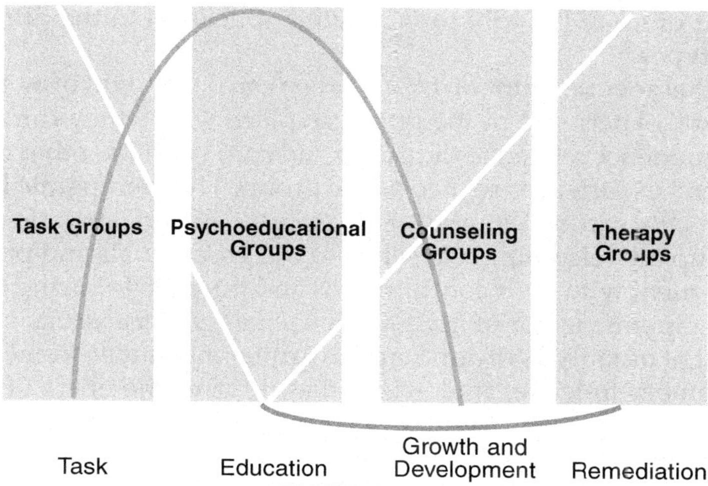

FIGURE 14.1

Group Types and Objectives

Note. Circular lines indicate the groups' shared focus on achieving goals, teaching new skills, and facilitating growth and development. Task = specific goal; Education = knowledge to prevent negative behavior; Growth and Development = interpersonal growth and development; Remediation = use of interpersonal action or a particular approach such as dialectical behavior therapy to address deep-seated distress-related patterns.

useful way to think about the group structures and how they affect interactive group leadership across group types is to examine how interactive therapeutic factors apply across the group types. When group leaders understand which therapeutic factors should be developed and maintained in a particular group, they can determine which interactive leadership functions to emphasize while leading that group.

Interactive Therapeutic Factors and Leadership Functions

The interactive group environment prioritizes interpersonal learning; member-to-member interaction; and member, rather than leader, contributions to meeting group and individual goals. Thus, the four primary interactive therapeutic factors leaders attend to are (a) self-disclosure, (b) acceptance, (c) learning through interpersonal action, and (d) insight. Leaders who work toward developing these factors in group will enable productive group processes to occur in all four group types. The interactive therapeutic factors are discussed in depth in Chapter 7, but they can be thought of more broadly to facilitate application to the different group types.

The therapeutic factor of *self-disclosure* can be thought of as group members' experience of the group as place where they can voice their experience related to the group and come to know other group members' experiences related to the group. The therapeutic factor of *acceptance* can be thought of as group members' experience of the group as welcoming and safe and the group goals and process as congruent with their contributions and purpose for being there. The therapeutic factor of *learning though interpersonal action* can be thought of broadly as the presence in group of member-to-member and member-to-leader interaction that informs members of their functioning and impact within the group process and toward accomplishing goals. The therapeutic factor of *insight* can be thought of as group members' experience of gaining personal understanding of their role within and relationship to the group and, ultimately, their relationship to the desired group outcomes.

Across group types, the development of therapeutic factors happens when leaders perform critical functions. Interactive group leaders use theory to inform leadership functions in that theory influences group conceptualization, which informs leadership objectives. Then, these objectives are served by the leadership functions. The interactive group leader or facilitator uses skills, interventions, and strategies to perform the desired function to meet its objective. Interactive group leadership functions work to create a group environment in which group members learn from each other or work together in the service of group and individual goals. The seven interactive leadership functions are norm setting, boundary management, structuring, instruction, regard, languaging, and administration, as described in Chapter 7.

Group Types

Although helping professionals typically envision group work as group counseling or group psychotherapy, group work also includes other group types. The definitions of group types overlap, but they can be distinguished, to a great degree, by their purposes and processes. ASGW (2000) defined four main group types: task or work groups, psychoeducational groups, counseling groups, and psychotherapy groups. Another commonly encountered group type is the support group, which bears some features of other group types but has a distinct purpose and process.

Task and Work Groups

Task groups and work groups are likely the most common type of group work that laypeople (i.e., those not in the helping professions) experience. Almost everyone can and will be a part of a task or work group at some point in their lives.

As defined by McCarthy et al. (2021), task groups "promote efficient and effective accomplishment of tasks by a group of people typically assembled to achieve a specific and time-limited goal" (p. 12). ASGW (2000) defined the specialization in task and work group facilitation as

> the application of principles of normal human development and functioning through group based educational, developmental, and systemic strategies applied in the context of here-and-now interaction that promote efficient and effective accomplishment of group tasks among people who are gathered to accomplish group task goals. (Definitions section)

People experience work groups within their families, communities, organizations, schools, and jobs. Gladding (2019) described task groups as including such far-flung groups as teams, volunteer groups, school learning groups, scientific task forces, and high-performing business divisions. The purpose of a task group might be for a family to prepare a house for sale, for a charitable organization to put on a community fundraiser, for a professional organization to revise their best practice guidelines, for a middle school group to complete a research project, or for a company's marketing team to create a marketing plan for a new product.

Gladding (2019) distinguished between work groups and teams. He characterized work teams as less collaborative, more focused on individual productivity, and more likely to have a formal leader. He characterized teams as more interdependent, as focused on group products, and as having shared leadership responsibilities. Gladding (2019) also indicated that while work groups may be larger, teams should be kept to 10 or fewer members to avoid subgrouping.

Hulse-Killacky et al. (2001) described assumptions that must be met for task groups to be successful. These assumptions can be summarized as follows:

- The purpose of the group is evident to all members.
- A group culture is developed and maintained that emphasizes collaboration, respect, and acknowledgment of individuals, subgroups, and the group as a whole.

- Although content is often very important in task groups, here-and-now process is regularly attended to by the leader and members to address conflict, to provide feedback, and to make sense of the process.
- Although the leader must have the skills necessary to help group members relate to one another and complete tasks, group members must be empowered and active participants in the process.

Interactive therapeutic factors in task groups. Task and work groups may not be perceived by many as needing interactive leadership. Because task and work groups have goals that are primarily external to group members, the various therapeutic factors and leadership functions are enacted differently than in other types of groups. However, task and work groups still require an environment conducive to clear and open communication and collaboration. Although task and work group members are not in the group to grow, change, and heal, they should expect to feel safe, valued, and motivated (Gladding, 2019). The combination of interactive therapeutic factors forms a picture of the environment of the functioning task group, and it is evident how the factors are mutually influential:

- *Self-disclosure* in task and work groups takes the form of members sharing their ideas and reactions to others' ideas. Members self-disclose emotional reactions that are relevant to working relationships and task completion. Examples of this are when a task group member shares that a responsibility is not something they can reasonably do or that they are frustrated that a colleague is consistently late to work meetings.
- *Acceptance* in task and work groups takes the form of members' comfort sharing ideas and reactions in a noncritical environment. Acceptance also appears as members' clear commitment to accomplishing the group's task. Examples of this are when a group member shares an idea knowing their team may provide feedback but will not be harshly critical or when a group member works an extra hour on a project because they feel valued and know others are committed also.
- *Learning through interpersonal action* is evident in task and work groups when members exchange feedback about performance and working relationships. This may also take the shape of members sharing information helpful to task completion with each other. Examples of this include a group member giving

feedback to a colleague that their persistent lateness is perceived as not caring or sharing that the research a colleague is using is outdated and providing more current information.
- *Insight* in task and work groups occurs when members learn how their work behaviors are perceived and gain awareness of their relationship to the task and the group itself. An example of this is when a member receives feedback that their lateness is perceived as not caring about the task and they realize their motivation is low because they do not feel safe or valued in the group.

Psychoeducational Groups

Within the helping professions, psychoeducational groups are likely the most common form of group encountered (see Figure 14.2). Almost everyone can benefit from some sort of psychoeducational group.

As described by McCarthy et al. (2021), psychoeducational groups "promote personal and interpersonal growth and development [and] often work to prevent future difficulties and enhance personal attributes and abilities" (p. 12). ASGW (2000) defined specialization in psychoeducational group leadership as

> the application of principles of normal human development and functioning through group based educational and developmental strategies applied in the context of here-and-now interaction that promote personal and interpersonal growth and development and the prevention of future difficulties among people who may be at risk for the development of personal or interpersonal problems or who seek enhancement of personal qualities and abilities. (Definitions section)

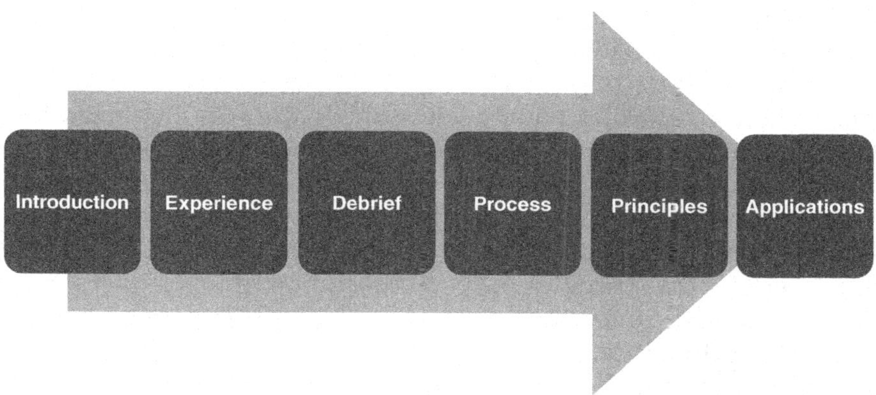

FIGURE 14.2
Psychoeducational Groups and Structured Experiences

Note. A process for structured experiences (experiential learning design structure).

People may encounter psychoeducational groups in educational, counseling, psychological, medical, corrections, or public health settings. A key feature of psychoeducational groups is the balance of educational content with group process, with an emphasis on developmental or psychological content aimed at promoting healthy development and preventing distress. Often the learning process is augmented by activities that highlight or allow group members to apply key concepts. Because of their educational nature, psychoeducational groups are often viewed by participants with less suspicion or stigma than groups that are more process oriented. Examples of psychoeducational groups include those designed to help members gain life skills, cope with divorce, manage anger, or adapt to chronic illness. Gladding (2019) recommended that adult psychoeducational groups include no more than 12 members and that children's groups include fewer. Additionally, most psychoeducational groups are short-term or time-limited groups of 8 to 10 weeks duration.

Furr (2000) described a process for developing sound psychoeducational groups. This process includes identifying an overarching purpose, creating intermediate goals to achieve the purpose, setting attainable goal-oriented objectives for group sessions, selecting activities that meet those objectives and are complementary to group development, then evaluating if the objectives, goals, and purpose have been met. Furr's focus on designing or selecting group activities that complement group development is consistent with the challenge of balancing content and process in psychoeducational groups.

While psychoeducational groups are characterized by the growth-oriented educational content they purvey, it is generally accepted that content and group process must be balanced (Champe & Rubel, 2012; Furr, 2000). Champe and Rubel (2012) characterized the dilemma of the psychoeducational group leader as follows: "Too much focus on group process risks veering into the territory of therapy groups, while too much focus on the content and conceptual learning risks merely teaching to people sitting in a circle" (p. 74). They related the struggles psychoeducational group leaders may have balancing content and process to the highly planned nature of most psychoeducational groups, which leaves little time for real group process, and the difficulty novice or untrained group leaders may have in distinguishing between content and process.

Champe and Rubel (2012) proposed a three-pronged way of viewing psychoeducational group content and learning to clarify where group leaders can intervene to correct or encourage group process. They contended that psychoeducational group leaders should strive to (a) create and maintain a group environment that is safe, emotionally stimulating, and sensitive to emotions because this is necessary for optimal learning; (b) work in the here and now to encourage interpersonal learning because group members will learn content best in the context of the group session with each other; and (c) explore group members' reactions to content during the group because they will have potentially shared productive reactions that can be reinforced and nonproductive reactions that should be voiced and processed.

Interactive therapeutic factors in psychoeducational groups. Psychoeducational groups are very popular and often led by less trained or untrained group leaders who do not balance content and process well. Such groups can be perceived to be more like a class that would not benefit from interactive group leadership. However, because psychoeducational groups promote growth and change through education and developmental strategies in the context of group interaction, interactive therapeutic factors are demonstrated somewhat differently than they are in other types of groups. Although they are often moderately to highly structured, psychoeducational groups also rely on interaction within the group, such as activities, discussion, sharing of experiences, and interpersonal feedback, to help group members understand the content, apply it within the group, and then apply it in their lives. Psychoeducational groups are most effective when they are safe, emotionally stimulating, and interactive. Therefore, attending to interactive therapeutic factors is important:

- *Self-disclosure* is evident in psychoeducational groups when members share experiences, ideas, and emotional reactions relevant to the topic. Helpful self-disclosure occurs when members share their reactions with other group members that affect their learning process. Examples of this include a member sharing that they felt deeply saddened by a guided imagery exercise or a member sharing that another member's story about being successfully assertive with a doctor was inspiring.
- *Acceptance* is conspicuous in psychoeducational groups when members experience a nonjudgmental environment, understand a common need for participation, and feel valued for their contributions. Examples of this are when a group member feels

safe enough to share that they do not understand a concept or when a group member tries to connect with another member during an activity because they believe it will help the other member and the group.

- *Learning through interpersonal action* is apparent in psychoeducational groups when members learn about the group topic or alternative behaviors from the sharing of others. It is also apparent when group members try to apply their new knowledge in the group and receive feedback on how well it worked. Examples of this include when a group member hears how another member interprets the meaning of a helpful concept and understands it better as a result or when a group member receives feedback that they have not applied their newly learned listening skills fully.
- *Insight* is seen in psychoeducational groups when members apply group content to their group experiences and their life and gain awareness of their behaviors and choices in and out of the group. An example of this is when a member of an academic success group learns about the dynamics of procrastination from group content and discussion, then they understand how this self-defeating behavior has damaged both their self-esteem and academic progress.

Counseling Groups

In contrast to psychoeducational groups, counseling groups may have some educational content but rely more heavily on group processes to spur growth and change within the group. According to Gladding (2019), counseling groups are meant for people who are experiencing developmental struggles that cannot be fully addressed with information alone. ASGW indicates that "counseling groups strive to alleviate personal and interpersonal problems of living. Counseling groups promote personal and interpersonal growth and address the needs of those experiencing challenging life transitions" (McCarthy et al., 2021, p. 13). ASGW (2000) defined specialization in group counseling as

> the application of principles of normal human development and functioning through group based cognitive, affective, behavioral, or systemic intervention strategies applied in the context of here-and-now interaction that address personal and interpersonal problems of living and promote personal and interpersonal growth and development among people who may be experiencing transitory

> maladjustment, who are at risk for the development of personal or interpersonal problems, or who seek enhancement of personal qualities and abilities. (Definitions section)

Covering the life span, counseling groups are commonly used in situations such as adjusting to divorce, coping with chronic illness, developing assertive communication skills, and dealing with school adjustment. Such groups could reasonably be administered as psychoeducational groups. However, counseling groups focus less on learning helpful content and more on engaging in support, interaction, and practice of skills within the group. Counseling groups are typically time limited but do rely heavily on group member interaction, feedback, and interpersonal learning to accomplish their goals (Gladding, 2019). Thus, counseling group leaders should attend to creating a group environment that facilitates these conditions.

Counseling groups are well suited to interactive group leadership because they rely on member interaction, feedback, and interpersonal learning to accomplish their developmental and preventive goals. Counseling groups may be brief or time limited, which may limit the development of the group and the growth of members. Consequently, it is even more important that group leaders capitalize on creating a facilitative environment that emphasizes member interactions in the here and now, feedback, and interactive therapeutic factors:

- *Self-disclosure* is observable as a therapeutic factor in counseling groups when members share personal information about their here-and-now reactions and emotions. These reactions and emotions may be related to the group's purpose or process. An example of this is when a member of a social anxiety group shares that they feel left out of the group process when they do not interact or when the same member might share that they feel envious or deficient when they see other group members verbally connecting.
- *Acceptance* is evident as a therapeutic factor in counseling groups when members perceive that other members care about, understand, and accept them and that the group has an important role in their lives. An example of this is when a group member who is normally mistrustful of others takes a risk to discuss a difficult life occurrence with the group. They do this because they believe, from past group interaction, that others in the group will listen and try to be helpful.

- *Learning through interpersonal action* is apparent in counseling groups when members receive feedback and learn how their behaviors impact others. They may experiment with behaviors based on feedback exchange and observation. An example of this is when a group member receives feedback that if they do not interact in the group and frown when others are vulnerable, they are perceived as intimidating or judgmental. They then try to respond supportively when others are vulnerable.
- *Insight* is noticeable in counseling groups when members, after getting feedback and experimenting with new behaviors, come to understand the reasons for their past behaviors. An example of this is if the group member who is learning to respond to others more supportively comes to understand that they did not previously believe that they could be helpful to others and therefore did not try to be supportive.

Therapy Groups

The term *therapy group* may bring up the classic image of a serious therapist who meets over a span of years with an array of group members. The group members in this scenario are experiencing profound struggles in their lives and engaging in deep exploration within the groups.

Commonly encountered psychotherapy groups may include groups designed to address a specific diagnosis, such as depression, anxiety, or posttraumatic stress disorder. These groups could also be offered as counseling groups. However, the distinguishing feature of psychotherapy groups is the depth of the work and length of the group. Gladding (2019) indicated that therapy group members may have experienced long-term distress and may have mental health diagnoses. With that, the goals of therapy groups are often to remediate deep-seated intrapsychic and interpersonal patterns that are connected to group members' distress. This remediation may take place solely through the interpersonal action and learning of the group but may also rely on a particular approach, such as dialectical behavior therapy (DBT; e.g., Gill et al., 2018), or a theoretical orientation, such as psychodynamic (e.g., Lorentzen et al., 2018).

Like counseling groups, therapy groups are well suited for interactive group leadership and maybe even more so. Because of their remediative goals and focus on long-standing intrapsychic and interpersonal patterns, therapy groups are seen as treatment and tend to be longer in duration than psychoeducational or counseling groups. The more in-depth goals and intensive processes of therapy groups require higher levels of trust, vulnerability, and interaction from group members. Focusing on interactive therapeutic factors enables this trust, vulnerability, and interaction as follows:

- *Self-disclosure* is observable in therapy groups much as it is in counseling groups. The therapeutic factor of self-disclosure appears as group members disclose their feelings about and reactions to here-and-now group interaction and the group's purposes. They may also share emotions related to previous experiences. In a DBT therapy group for emotion dysregulation an example of this might be a group member sharing how difficult it is to not harshly judge the intense emotions they are having in group.
- *Acceptance* is demonstrated in therapy groups, like counseling groups, when members perceive that other members care for, understand, and accept them and that the group fills an important role in their lives. An example of this is when the above group member has an angry outburst during one session but returns the next week despite feeling intense shame because they value the group and believe the other group members understand and care.
- *Learning through interpersonal action* is evident in therapy groups when members learn about their behaviors and experiment with new ones based on feedback exchange and observation. An example of this is the above group member receiving feedback that others feel very sad when hearing them treating their shameful feelings like facts. The next time they feel intense shame they ask the group to help them use some of the skills they are learning in group.
- *Insight* is occurring in therapy groups when members learn how they are perceived by others and understand their thoughts, feelings, and behaviors better. They also develop understanding of the reasons for and origins of their behaviors. An example of this is when the above group member, after repeatedly feeling ashamed and reaching out to the group for help, begins to understand that as painful as the shame was it was less painful than relying on their childhood caregivers.

Group Settings

Group work is used in many different settings because it is both effective and efficient for a wide variety of purposes, issues, and populations. The major settings in which groups are offered include behavioral and mental health settings, schools, colleges and universities, rehabilitation settings, and addictions treatment. Each setting poses challenges and offers benefits. The practice of manualized group work and the use of online groups both cut across settings and group types.

Behavioral and Mental Health Settings

A major category of settings that routinely utilize group work is behavioral health and mental health settings. While some view behavioral health as dealing only with the psychological impacts of medical conditions, the term *mental health* is often used interchangeably with *behavioral health*. The two realms overlap substantially but can be differentiated by behavioral health's broader scope and inclusion of physical conditions as precursors and sequelae. Mental health is more accurately used as a subset of behavioral health that deals only with the psychological and social consequences of emotions, cognitions, and behavior. For example, the focus of behavioral health might be the effect of diabetes on a person's depression as well as the effect of depression on their physical condition. Mental health would focus more narrowly on the depression.

The Substance Abuse and Mental Health Services Administration (SAMHSA; n.d.) has defined behavioral health as "the promotion of mental health, resilience and wellbeing; the treatment of mental and substance use disorders; and the support of those who experience and/or are in recovery from these conditions, along with their families and communities" (p. 1). Many authors also include addictions treatment and settings within the domain of behavioral and mental health. Indeed, SAMHSA (n.d.) includes treatment and prevention of addictions, substance abuse disorders, and dual diagnoses as integral to its behavioral health integration initiatives. Consistent with SAMHSA's initiative, a focus on behavioral health is becoming predominant across the helping professions as the link between social and psychological factors and physical health gains increasing acceptance in the powerful medical community (Kalodner & Hanus, 2010). A term related to behavioral and mental health is *community mental health*. Briggs et al. (2019) indicated that community mental health is mental health services provided in the local setting of the individual rather than in an institution. Considerations for all four of these domains are introduced in the following sections.

Nature of Behavioral and Mental Health Settings

Behavioral and mental health settings for group work are numerous and diverse in focus and structure. However, they tend to share some common characteristics and structures. Behavioral and mental health settings may operate within hierarchical, multilevel systems run by federal, state, and local governments, as well as for-profit and nonprofit organizations. Examples of these are Veteran's Affairs (VA) hospitals or clinics (federal), state psychiatric hospitals (state), and community mental health centers (local; Kalodner & Hanus, 2010). An example of a for-profit behavioral or mental health setting is a mental health division of a for-profit medical center or a for-profit addictions treatment facility, whereas examples of nonprofit behavioral or mental health settings are grant-funded local agencies specializing in treating survivors of childhood sexual abuse or adults with dual diagnoses (substance abuse and mental health diagnoses). Regardless, behavioral and mental health settings tend to be busy, understaffed, concerned with productivity and accountability, reliant on external funding (e.g., Medicare, Medicaid, health insurance, grant funding), and increasingly incorporating evidence-based practices (Kalodner & Hanus, 2010; Macgowan & Hanbridge, 2014). Although there are exceptions, because they are outgrowths of the larger political system and culture, behavioral and mental health settings also tend to mirror and propagate the wide variety of oppressions, including ageism, classism, racism, ethnocentrism, sexism, heterosexism, religious or spiritual oppression, and ableism, affecting those with physical, cognitive, or psychiatric disabilities.

Challenges to Group Work in Behavioral and Mental Health Settings

Groups in behavioral and mental health settings address a wide array of critical psychosocial and medical needs for an increasingly large number of people of diverse ages and identities. But these settings pose several common challenges to implementing effective group work. Some challenges are inherent to almost all group work but might be uniquely demonstrated in these settings. For example, while group work is viewed as efficient, cost-sparing, and effective, it may be difficult to form groups in these settings. Finding sufficient appropriate referrals for groups is an understudied and often difficult element of group work in behavior and mental health systems (H. Bernard et al., 2008). Even within a large community or organization, filling a specific need, for example the need for a group for female-identifying adolescents with depression and anxiety, may be particularly difficult. The effect of group work conducted with poorly attended or poorly screened groups as well as the added stress and workload of recruiting, screening, and administering groups are clearly challenges.

Training and supervision of group leaders in behavioral and mental health settings may also be a challenge. Although some settings, such as for veterans (Kalodner & Hanus, 2010) or for addictions treatment (Faragher & Soberay, 2014), are more group oriented, groups may be seen as a secondary service in other behavioral and mental health settings. This may result in hiring practices oriented more toward practitioners specializing in individual treatment who may not have the knowledge, inclination, confidence, or emotional preparation to run effective groups meant to treat difficult issues. This is in addition to the marginalization of group-specific training in mental health professional preparation programs (H. Bernard et al., 2008). Group workers in medical settings may need additional knowledge about the medical issues of their group members. Rath & Conchie (2009) emphasized the need for trained group leaders to run higher acuity groups in behavioral health settings, such as psychotherapy groups, and cautioned that the lack of well-trained group leaders may result in groups that maintain or promote unhealthy behavior. Training is especially critical to fully realize the cultural responsiveness and social justice competency that group leaders should have.

Examples of Groups Offered in Behavioral and Mental Health Settings

All four types of groups (task, psychoeducational, counseling, and therapy groups) are appropriate for and may be offered in behavioral and mental health settings including addictions settings. Examples of psychoeducational groups that may be offered in behavioral and mental health settings include groups on the effects of addiction on families, accessing community support services, and self-help strategies (Faragher & Soberay, 2014) as well as health promotion through weight loss or smoking cessation (Greene et al., 2014). Examples of counseling groups that may be offered in behavioral and mental health settings include groups for women working on depression or posttraumatic stress disorder (PTSD), multicouple groups for improving relationships, and multifamily group eating disorder treatment (Briggs et al., 2019). Finally, examples of therapy groups that may be offered in behavioral and mental health settings include dual-diagnosis groups, cognitive behavioral therapy groups as a part of substance abuse day-treatment programs, or DBT groups for emotion regulation (Kalodner & Hanus, 2010).

School Settings

Schools make use of group work in many shapes and forms. Groups may involve different stakeholders, including students, families, staff, and administrators, though the goal of a vast majority of the groups is improving the educational and psychosocial experience of students. School settings include public and private K–12 schools. Although K–12 schools are traditionally thought of as brick-and-mortar institutions, they are increasingly offered as online education and as collaborations with community colleges, trade schools, and universities. K–12 schools may be staffed by paraprofessional helpers and include internal mental health clinics or services to address the increasingly acute mental health needs of children and adolescents (American Academy of Pediatrics, n.d.).

Falco and Bauman (2014) found group work to be an effective approach for addressing many diverse issues experienced by children and adolescents in the school setting. They characterized group work as not only effective and efficient but developmentally suited for school-age children who prioritize peer relationships. They also indicated that the school setting has distinctive characteristics that affect the use of groups.

Nature of School Settings

A predominant feature of the school setting is the age range and developmental level of the students who are potential group members (Falco & Bauman, 2014). Students may be as young as 4 years or as old as 18 years or more. This broad range of developmental level means that the educational system accommodates students who range from being totally dependent to being nearly independent. It is also mandated by the Individuals with Disabilities Education Act (2004) that a free public education and related services be provided to qualified students with physical, cognitive/learning, and emotional disabilities. Funding issues and limited resources mean many schools face overcrowding, large class sizes, and limited ability to provide accommodations, which results in stress for both students and staff.

The combination of these factors with adult-centric staff and administrative structures that can be hierarchical, political, and bureaucratic often results in oppressive experiences for children and adolescents who are struggling in the school system and for their allies within the system. In addition to these forms of ageism and ableism, schools, as outgrowths of the larger political system and culture, also tend to mirror and propagate all other forms of oppression unless counselors, teachers, staff, and administrators actively work to counter them. The workload of teachers, staff, and administrators is often overwhelming, leading to burnout. They have to balance the challenge of genuinely caring for children and adolescents while working within a system that is meant to help them but often ends up harming the most vulnerable.

Group Work Challenges in School Settings

Despite the uniqueness of the school setting for group work, some challenges parallel the challenges of behavioral and mental health systems. Although group work is touted as an efficient way to meet student needs, forming groups may be a challenge. This results less from the referral and access issue of behavioral and mental health settings and more from structural issues that provide little time and flexibility for students to attend groups. Creative school counselors who value group work use several strategies to form groups, such as using off-blocks, lunch times, and after school to conduct groups or using whole class periods to provide guidance group experiences around topics all students can benefit from. However, most school counselors have overly high student-to-counselor ratios and only use a small amount of their time for direct student contact. School counselors must be very motivated to form and provide groups in the school setting.

Another parallel issue is the problematic training and supervision of school counselors for group work. Falco and Bauman (2014) indicated that graduate training for group work for school counselors is generally sparse and not focused on the needs of children and adolescents and the demands of the school system. They indicated that a minority of school counselor trainees will have even observed a group conducted in a school before they graduate and, more often than not, trainees will feel unprepared to run groups. Additionally, research on school counselors' post-master's degree professional development indicates that few school counselors receive essential skills-oriented supervision after graduation, and often professional development opportunities, particularly ones offered onsite, are not counseling oriented. This clearly poses a challenge to offering effective groups in schools and may explain Hoag and Burlingame's (1997) finding that while school counseling groups are effective at meeting childrens' and adolescents' needs, groups in mental health settings tend to be more effective.

A final challenge to effective group work in schools is the large and complex social and professional milieu of schools. Not only are students classmates, but they may also be friends, bullies, victims, or romantic partners. Adults in the setting may have multiple roles with students, including counselor, teacher, coach, mentor, disciplinarian, and authority figure. Confidentiality and privacy can be an issue in this setting, where group members may have dual relationships with other members and the school counselor. Counselors who run groups in schools should be prepared both to continually reinforce and promote the idea of confidentiality to their student group members and to advocate with teachers, staff, and administrators to respect the privacy of students whenever possible.

Types of Groups Offered in School Settings

A unique feature of school settings is that they rarely offer mental health treatment. Students who experience more acute or severe social or psychological distress are most often referred to behavioral or mental health resources in the community. Thus, therapy groups are rarely if ever offered within school settings (Falco & Bauman, 2014). However, task groups, psychoeducational groups, and counseling groups are common in schools.

Examples of task groups that may involve students are groups to plan student service projects or form clubs. Falco and Bauman (2014) also indicated that while task groups are product-oriented they provide students with the opportunity to grow and develop useful personal and relational skills. Task groups in schools may also involve counselors, teachers, staff, parents, and administrators as they engage in student support teams. Psychoeducational groups are probably the most common school-based groups. Some typical psychoeducational groups are friendship groups, academic skills groups, and career exploration groups. These groups focus on providing students with knowledge and skills critical for participating effectively in the learning environment and opportunities to integrate and practice what they have learned. Counseling groups in the schools may include groups to address stress, social problems, divorce, or grief experienced by students.

College and University Settings

College and university settings are sometimes thought of as natural extensions of K–12 education. Students arriving on college and university campuses may be as young as 17, but in reality, they do not have an upper age limit. For younger students, going to college may be their first foray into independence and the first time they manage their own money, keep their own sleep schedules, and take responsibility for their own schoolwork. For older students it may represent a major life or career change, a huge stressor on top of work and family obligations, or the realization of a dream. Some students may be undergraduates taking courses without a specific goal and focusing on their social life, while others may be highly focused on demanding degrees or fulfilling the competitive prerequisites for medical school, law school, or another graduate degree. Some students may be attending college in their hometown, while others may be living across the country from their families or have come from overseas for education. Racial and ethnic diversity is also increasing on college and university campuses (Whittingham, 2014). And while colleges and universities are often seen as leaders in diversity and equity initiatives, they are still products of discriminatory political, bureaucratic, and cultural systems that may perpetuate racism, classism, sexism, heterosexism, religious and spiritual oppression, ageism, and ableism.

Nature of College and University Settings

Colleges and universities differ significantly in their internal culture and in the characteristics of their students. Kalodner and Hanus (2010) maintained that students at smaller, privately run religious institutions may differ greatly from those at large public institutions. Byrd and McKinney (2012) indicated that institutional factors, such as campus climate and students' satisfaction with the institution, are related to students' mental health. Specifically, students who experienced the campus climate more negatively, for example perceiving the campus climate as racially tense, had a higher likelihood of poor mental health. Institutional satisfaction was associated with better mental health. Whittingham (2014) suggested that "centers may best be characterized as dealing with the same issues as they always have but in greater numbers, with more diversity, and with an increasingly severe population being added to their center caseload" (p. 329). Regardless, counseling centers must tailor their operations and approaches to their student body's needs.

A common characteristic of college and university counseling centers is that they are often underfunded. This puts stress on staff and the students they serve. Additionally, the demand for counseling center services and the acuity of college students' psychological issues have increased dramatically in recent years. Xiao et al. (2017) summarized the extant literature as indicating that many students are entering college with a history of psychological treatment and that common issues brought to college and university counseling centers include grief, depression, medical issues, personality disorders, suicidality, sexual assault, stress and anxiety, academic skills, and family or relationship issues. Xiao et al. further found that most college and university counseling center directors believe that workloads are too high, and more staff are needed. Such a lack of resources might result in coping strategies such as referring out to the community, limiting sessions, and using waitlists. Within this pressured system, Whittingham (2014) wrote that groups have long been a part of college and university counseling center offerings. Although their focus has changed over time—moving from a preventive, personal growth focus to a time-limited, topic-driven orientation and process-oriented psychotherapy focus—groups remain a popular choice for treatment.

Group Work Challenges in College and University Settings

Whittingham (2014) contended that a dedicated group coordinator is an essential part of the college and university counseling center staff and a quality group work program. Challenges to conducting group work in college and university settings are numerous. These challenges include inadequate referrals, ineffective screening procedures for groups, and group leader training and practice issues (Whittingham, 2014). Groups may be needed but not filled because of a lack of referrals, therapist and client skepticism about the effectiveness of groups, or therapist and client discomfort with the increased emotional activation and vulnerability that groups may pose for both.

Some of this may be linked to inadequate training experiences for psychologists, social workers, and counselors working in these centers. They may not understand the powerful benefits well-run groups may offer and may not understand the importance of skilled screening, pregroup preparation, and group leadership to effective groups. Whittingham (2014) suggested that a group coordinator can and should familiarize staff with current group work research, hold trainings on group work for staff, and strive to create a culture of "Why not group?" where staff assume that all students may benefit from group unless there is a strong contraindication.

A final challenge identified by Whittingham (2014) is the generally brief nature of college and university counseling center groups. This is attributed to the seasonal nature of college and university activity and the quarter- or semester-bound academic cycle that may affect the length, timing, and feasibility of groups. The brief nature of these groups requires competent screening to avoid destructive or restrictive dynamics as well as clear goals, a strong group-long focus on those goals, and skillful process and here-and-now focused leadership to prosper. Whittingham (2014) also indicated that critical exploration of multicultural and social identity dynamics in these groups is essential because of the previously mentioned supersystem issues (Rubel & Okech, 2006).

Types of Groups Offered in College and University Settings

College and university counseling centers take advantage mainly of psychoeducational, counseling, and therapy groups. Psychoeducational groups are frequently offered because they allow students and clients to learn and practice helpful skills, and they fit the goal-oriented and time-limited needs of the system (Whittingham, 2014). Examples of psychoeducational groups suited for college and university settings are knowledge- and skills-oriented stress management, substance dependency, depression management, or academic support groups (Kalodner & Hanus, 2010; Whittingham, 2014). Examples of counseling groups that may be offered in college and university counseling centers are grief or bereavement groups, relationship issue groups, identity exploration groups, and career exploration groups that take a developmental and process-oriented stance (Kalodner & Hanus, 2010). Therapy groups held within college and university counseling centers might include groups for anxiety, depression, PTSD, or issues related to personality disorders. Students attending these groups may be more distressed, and the groups may have a strong process and interpersonal orientation and focus (Kalodner & Hanus, 2010). However, Whittingham (2014) cautioned that groups serving more acute student mental health needs using a strong process orientation require critical evaluation of their appropriateness based on student/client culture and social identity, competent screening, and leadership that is skilled in forming working alliances and utilizing interpersonal processes in a brief format. He summarized that these groups require a great deal from group leaders in terms of theoretical knowledge and technical skill.

Rehabilitation Settings

Rehabilitation counseling focuses on the personal, social, and environmental impact of disabilities on people's lives (Patterson et al., 2005). F. Chan et al. (2004) described rehabilitation counseling as an endeavor

> where the counselor works collaboratively with the client to understand existing problems, barriers and potentials in order to facilitate the client's effective use of personal and environmental resources for career, personal, social and community adjustment following disability. (p. 3)

Rehabilitation counselors assist, work with, and empower people with disabilities for the purpose of improving their lives. They may also provide advocacy to counter widespread ableism that is ingrained in society and is a barrier to people with disabilities' full participation in society. Helping others in this way requires rehabilitation counselors to acquire and maintain knowledge and skills necessary to accomplish these tasks. Leahy et al. (2009) described seven functions and six knowledge areas that are part of the rehabilitation counselor's job. The job functions include vocational counseling and consultation, counseling intervention, community-based rehabilitation service activities, case management, applied research, assessment, and professional advocacy. The six knowledge domains include assessment and consultation related to career counseling, techniques and application of counseling theories, rehabilitation services and resources, case and caseload management, health care and disability systems, and the medical/functional/environmental implications of disability. This list gives some sense of the breadth and depth of rehabilitation counselors' work and training.

According to F. Chan et al. (2004), rehabilitation counselors traditionally worked in federal or state vocational rehabilitation organizations with people with physical and mental disabilities. More recently, rehabilitation counselors have gained more employment options on account of the widening scope of who qualifies for services and may work in proprietary rehabilitation companies, private practice, private nonprofit rehabilitation facilities/organizations, insurance companies, medical centers or general hospitals, and businesses/corporations. Rehabilitation counselors may hold the certified rehabilitation counselor credential and may also hold the licensed professional counselor credential.

Nature of Rehabilitation Settings

Rehabilitation settings are varied in size, funding, breadth and focus of clientele served, and breadth and focus of services offered. However, all rehabilitation settings provide services to people with disabilities. Disabilities can be described as physical, cognitive, or psychological impairments that significantly limit at least one major life activity. These life activities include but are not limited to things such as seeing, hearing, eating, sleeping, walking, standing, lifting, bending, speaking, breathing, learning, reading, concentrating, thinking, communicating, caring for oneself, completing manual tasks, and working (Ellis et al., 2014). Disabilities can be divided broadly into physical, cognitive/intellectual, and mental health disabilities as well as into visible and invisible disability categories. Rehabilitation counselors must be aware that disabilities affect clients' health, financial status, social life, and identity. Work in rehabilitation settings often involves being knowledgeable about or interacting with assistive technologies, federal mandates affecting people with disabilities, medical professionals, educators, potential employers, financial support sources, disability lawyers, and more (F. Chan et al., 2004).

Group Work Challenges in Rehabilitation Settings

Groups are an effective, efficient, and flexible treatment in the rehabilitation setting (Ellis et al., 2014). Groups offer people with disabilities mutual support, connection, and empowerment with others who share some aspect of lived experience. However, the challenges to running effective groups in rehabilitation settings are as diverse as the clienteles' needs, the varied roles rehabilitation counselors fill, and the varied nature of the settings. The broad and intense nature of the needs of rehabilitation counseling clients calls for rehabilitation counselors who wish to run effective groups to learn a challenging amount of information about, among other things, specific disabilities and medical needs, the psychosocial needs of group members, designing groups to meet those needs, and providing accommodations for members. A small example that provides a glimpse of some of these challenges is a rehabilitation counselor running a psychodrama identity exploration group for clients with physical disabilities. The counselor needs to make sure, at the least, that the group space is physically accessible, that all activities are accessible to all group members, that all group materials are accessible (e.g., braille handouts, screen readers, audiotaped information), and that an American Sign Language interpreter is available if needed.

Another challenge to running groups in rehabilitation settings is the training and professional and personal development of the group leader. F. Chan et al. (2004) indicated that because of rehabilitation counseling's broadly varied roles and stakeholder needs, overall training might be inadequate to fill those roles and meet the needs. While group counseling theory and skills was identified as one of three subdomains of the counseling interventions domain, it is realistic to be skeptical that preparation to run groups is adequate. Additionally, because of the highly marginalized nature of disability identities and ubiquitous stereotypes, bias, and prejudices related to disability, counselors leading groups in rehabilitation settings must have well-developed awareness of their personal experiences with and beliefs about disability, privilege, and externalized or internalized oppression. Without this, they risk perpetuating oppressive societal dynamics in and out of their groups.

Types of Groups Offered in Rehabilitation Settings

All four types of group work may be implemented in rehabilitation settings. The varied needs of service consumers and resources available in settings mean that task groups, psychoeducational groups, counseling groups, and therapy groups may be of value. Some examples of task groups that might be found in rehabilitation settings include advocacy groups and case management groups. Psychoeducational groups are valuable because of the empowering nature of information, education, and learning. Examples of psychoeducational groups that may be offered in rehabilitation settings include employment groups (Harley & Kim, 2019) or groups meant to provide information on and practice opportunities for self-advocacy skills. Examples of counseling groups can include grief groups for those with recently acquired disabilities and disability identity development groups. Examples of therapy groups that may occur in rehabilitation settings include groups for PTSD caused by medical trauma and group treatment for people with a psychiatric disability, such as bipolar disorder.

Ellis et al. (2014) suggested that regardless of the group type or focus, group leaders should follow seven principles when working with people with disabilities: (a) center the person, (b) treat disability as a cultural factor, (c) acknowledge and foster identity development, (d) counter stigma and accommodate, (e) nurture belonging, (f) adapt for ability level, and (g) envision options.

Group Work Online

Technology has been used in helping processes for quite some time. Early versions of technology-assisted counseling and therapy utilized telephones, emails, or online chats and texting. Psychiatrists and psychologists have used older, cumbersome versions of teleconferencing to serve rural communities for at least 2 decades (Weinberg, 2021). The development of more streamlined versions of videoconferencing technology (VCT), such as Skype, Adobe Connect, and Zoom, spurred increased use of synchronous online technology for individual counseling, therapy, and supervision, and even for groups.

However, use of VCT for individual therapy was stigmatized and marginalized despite promising preliminary evidence. Its use for groups was met with even greater skepticism. That was before the COVID-19 pandemic (Weinberg, 2021). The pandemic drove a mass exodus of counselors and therapy from in-person modes of helping (including group work) to VCT. Some would say this occurred recklessly given the emphasis in professional codes of ethics on adequate training, supervision, and practicing within one's scope of competence (Weinberg, 2021). Reckless or not, the swift and large-scale shift to VCT exposed many, many skeptical counselors and therapists and their clients to online therapy and online group work. And the face of counseling, therapy, and group work is likely permanently changed (I. D. Yalom & Leszcz, 2020).

While prior to the pandemic research on online counseling, therapy, and group work was occurring at a slow pace, the pandemic has motivated researchers to focus more attention on the process and efficacy of online counseling, therapy, and group work. Research to this point is showing that, in general with a few exceptions, both online individual and online group therapy are as effective or nearly as effective as their face-to-face counterparts (Gentry et al., 2019; Weinberg, 2020, I. D. Yalom & Leszcz, 2020). A review by Gentry et al. (2019) identified a somewhat lower level of cohesion in online groups than in face-to-face groups but without significant loss of effectiveness. A study comparing online groups and treatment-as-usual face-to-face groups for veterans showed increased enrollment, attendance, cohesion, and peer support for the online groups (Fortier et al., 2022). This result highlights the potential benefits of the online setting in terms of increased accessibility to all types of group work for some populations.

Challenges of Online Group Work

Weinberg (2021) characterized some of the primary concerns about the online setting for groups as well as some considerations for addressing these concerns. He noted that although there are clear differences between online groups and face-to-face groups, these differences are not necessarily disadvantages. He characterized some of the differences as losses that may always be considered deficits in online groups and others as losses that can be worked through as a part of the group process. Below, these differences and concerns are detailed and discussed in terms of other scholarship on online groups. They include changes in the setting, disembodied therapeutic relationships, changed therapist presence, a changed and more transparent backdrop, differential benefits for group members, and resistance to online groups (Weinberg, 2021).

Changes in the setting. Weinberg (2021) described the material changes to the group environment that occur when groups move online. Traditionally, importance has been given to a stable and carefully crafted group setting characterized by firm time and space boundaries, including the setup of the group room. The setting and boundaries are intended to promote psychological safety, including the safety offered by promoting, if not guaranteeing, confidentiality. The online environment is much less under the group leader's control. Group members are in their own environments and expose other group members to those environments also. This can lower group members' perceptions of psychological safety. Weinberg (2021) suggested that group leaders can compensate for this shift by providing group members with firm guidelines and suggestions for controlling the environment from which they participate in online groups, processing perceived lack of safety, and reinforcing the concept of and processes that support confidentiality.

Weinberg (2021) placed potential unreliability of technology in the same category, indicating that lagging video or audio or members unintentionally leaving the group can also affect safety and cause anxiety or frustration. He proposed a similar approach to ameliorating this effect by providing guidelines for members' hardware, software, and internet service as well as working through any resulting relational or emotional difficulties as a part of the group process.

Disembodied therapeutic relationships. Weinberg (2021) described the issue of the perceived lack of an embodied presence in online groups. He characterized this as a concern that other scholars share, that while faces are visible in online groups, *body language* is not as readily seen and experienced. He indicated that this concern is supported by interpersonal neurobiological conceptualizations that link body-to-body interaction to affect regulation. However, he countered this concern with two points. One is that faces, which are part of body-to-body interaction, are often actually *more* visible in online group work. Additionally, he indicated that while body-to-body interaction is less likely online, the individual group members and group leader still have their own embodied experience. Some anecdotal evidence exists that group leaders can compensate via both facial expression and body language by exaggerating and making both more visible.

Changed therapist presence. Weinberg (2021) suggested that group leaders working online may struggle with a sense that they have lost their *therapeutic presence*. Engaging the whole self with the client and being present in the moment for the sake of the client are both parts of therapeutic presence. It also can include the group leader's attention, curiosity, emotions, and spontaneity. In face-to-face work, this therapeutic presence is intentional but part of a more familiar process. In the less familiar online environment, Weinberg (2021) suggested, increased intention can compensate for the lack of familiarity and perceived deficits. Group leaders working online should consider carefully increasing self-disclosure, increasing their own vulnerability and spontaneity, and encouraging group members to use their imagination.

Transformed and more transparent backdrop. Several group scholars (Weinberg, 2021; I. D. Yalom & Leszcz, 2020) have suggested that leading online groups is more difficult, in part, because it requires more focus and discipline to avoid becoming distracted by activity in the leader's and members' environments. Because of this tendency on the part of both leaders and members of online groups, group leaders must put increased energy and focus into assisting group members to stay engaged, connect with each other, and benefit from the group.

Weinberg (2020) observed that group leaders and members may overlook activity in other group members' environment, seemingly pretending that nothing untoward is happening. He suggests that group leaders attend to group members' background environments and process significant events as if they occurred *in the group*. It is important that this be done without punishing the group member at the center of the interaction. Similarly, he suggested that how group members *show up* to online group work should be addressed just as it would be in face-to-face groups. For example, if a group member who is normally quite put together and has a tidy office in their background shows up unkempt with an unfamiliar and chaotic backdrop, the group leader either should address this or should encourage other group members to share their reactions or concern. Again, this should be done with care to avoid shaming.

Differential benefits for group members. Weinberg (2021) observed through his experience that some group members appeared to be able to participate more productively in online groups than in face-to-face groups. He characterized these group members as those who were uncomfortable with close relationships and seemed anxious, intimidated, and prone to withdrawing from face-to-face group interaction. Theoretically, he found support in Marmarosh et al.'s (2013) work on attachment in group psychotherapy. They theorized that dismissive-avoidant group members will tend to discount and emotionally distance themselves from the emotional intensity connections of the face-to-face group. Weinberg (2021) contended that when these group members moved online the lowered emotional intensity allowed them to participate and engage more fully in the group process. This may be supported by Fortier et al.'s (2022) findings that veterans with higher levels of distress and psychiatric burden appeared to find it easier to participate, give feedback, and receive feedback in online groups than in face-to-face groups. Weinberg (2021) indicated, however, that other subpopulations of group members, such as those with relational trauma, may feel less safe in online group formats.

Resistance to online groups. Resistance on the part of both the therapist and client to online therapy and group work is a common theme in the literature (Weinberg, 2020, 2021; I. D. Yalom & Leszcz, 2020). With the material changes and challenges that occur in the shift from face-to-face to online group work, it is easy for both group leaders and group members to excuse lack of interaction, lack of emotional intimacy in the group, or feeling disconnected based on the online format. As Weinberg (2021) stated, this type of resistance forms, according to leaders and members, because "the online group feels less 'real'" (p. 87). He attributed this not necessarily to the actual environmental challenges of online groups but to a fear and avoidance of intimacy in the group. This would be like the focal conflict conceptualization (see Chapter 4) of group members and the group leader colluding to support a restrictive solution to lower anxiety. That is, both the members and leader may be blaming the online format for struggling to stay engaged as a way to avoid the anxiety of wanting intimacy but being afraid to attempt to attain it within the group. Weinberg indicated that group leaders should differentiate between actual barriers to online communication and those that are minor and used to avoid the hard but productive work of groups.

Ethical and legal issues. Weinberg (2020) highlighted the ethical and legal issues that are exacerbated by online group work, focusing on four key issues: limitations on client confidentiality, the need for an informed consent process specifically addressing the risks and benefits of online counseling, limitations to therapist practice across state borders, and license portability. Confidentiality and privacy are affected using online technologies for group work, and Weinberg (2020) suggested researching videoconferencing software and applications carefully for their security and for compliance with the Health Insurance Portability and Accountability Act of 1996.

Counselor and therapist ability to work with clients in other states is another key issue. Most but not all state licensing bodies restrict their licensees from working with clients (thus, group members) who are in other states where they are unlicensed. Weinberg recommended that group leaders carefully research state regulations to determine in which state they can accept and work with group members. Additionally, group leaders should make sure their informed consent documents spell out the benefits and risks of online groups. And, finally, even being in the same state, group leaders may not be able to respond quickly enough to a group member crisis. To be ready for crisis situations, group leaders should collect physical addresses and phone numbers for all group members.

Manualized Group Work

The evolution of counseling and therapy resulted in and benefited from an increasing emphasis on evidence of and accountability for positive outcomes (Macgowan & Hanbridge, 2014; Strupp & Anderson, 1997). Related to this push for evidence and accountability, therapy manuals became popular because they allowed promising treatments to be described specifically, facilitated standardization of treatment approaches, and helped clinicians become proficient at using these approaches. These factors facilitated research that identified valid treatment approaches that were reliably effective. As Strupp and Anderson (1997) contended, "Manuals have aided researchers in arriving at improved specifications of the 'independent variable' in therapy" (p. 76).

The use of treatment manuals appears to have a dual purpose: to substantiate effective therapeutic approaches and to assist therapists in accurately and effectively using these approaches to help clients. Over time, use of evidence-based practices and therapy manuals has evolved and been refined to the point that researchers and experienced practitioners commonly understand that treatment manuals are not intended to rigidly control therapist behavior. Rather, they are tools for therapists to start a journey toward effective work with clients (Strupp & Anderson, 1997). This, however, becomes an issue when therapists are not given adequate instruction, time, practice, and supervision to master the complex task of building effective work with clients *around* the armature of the treatment manual. This is all too common in the resource-poor and hurried world of training programs and practice in the helping professions. As Strupp and Anderson (1997) indicated, some clinicians are simply more inclined to be rigid and less effective in how they use treatment manuals.

This leads to the question "How does this apply to group work?" It applies to group work because group workers are under the same pressure to substantiate the effectiveness of their groups using evidence and to effectively use evidence-based practice to help members achieve their goals (Macgowan & Hanbridge, 2014). Group workers may be required to use group treatment manuals at their place of employment or to apply for grant funding (A. D. Galinsky et al., 2006). However, if using treatment manuals to research and guide individual therapy is complex, then using treatment manuals to research and guide group work is even more complex.

Challenges of Manualized Group Work

The challenge of this complexity can be seen if one thinks about how the core interactive group work principles might interact with a rigidly interpreted group work treatment manual. Interactive group work is reliant on a facilitative group environment and effective group member interaction skills, both of which depend on group leaders' efforts. Group leaders must establish facilitative norms and teach members how to effectively disclose personal information, exchange interpersonal feedback, and engage collaboratively to learn and grow. Interactive group environments are characterized by members interacting openly and honestly. To do this, groups must have norms and roles that encourage members to accept personal responsibility, believe in active participation, commit to collaborative learning, and value risk-taking. Each of these steps and outcomes is intricately interdependent on the others and relies on group leaders responding sensitively to group process in the moment to challenge ineffective interaction and structures and encourage more effective group interaction. This cannot be accomplished through a linearly designed manual that includes topics and activities and little or no guidance on process.

A. D. Galinsky et al. (2006) argued that group treatment manuals should neither be rejected on the basis that group leaders need absolute freedom to run their groups intuitively and spontaneously nor be accepted part and parcel as a cookbook for excellent groups. Rather, A. D. Galinsky et al. suggested an artful balance of guidance from the treatment manual blending with the group leader's knowledge of group process. A. D. Galinsky et al. offered four general principles for designing group treatment manuals that connect well with interactive group work: (a) use of current research to inform the manual, (b) consultation with practitioners and consumers to test ideas, (c) inclusion of guidance about group processes, and (d) consideration of diversity and guidance on ways to accommodate different ways of being. A. D. Galinsky et al. also offered four principles for group leaders: (a) careful researching and choosing of manuals, (b) use of group leadership theory and other group structural and process concepts to conceptualize interaction, (c) adaptation and adjustment of content and process to respond to interaction, and (d) commitment to learning how to optimally use the chosen manual.

Paquin (2017) took a similar approach to balancing and integrating the content of a group treatment manual and the principles of effective group work. She suggested five principles that will serve as the answers to the following challenges of using manualized group treatments.

Ignoring group development to move forward with content. Group development happens! To ignore group development phases is to ignore the relational needs and issues of the members within the group. A poorly designed manual is out of step with the relational stages that group members need to experience to work together toward the group's goals. Paquin (2017) suggested that group leaders be aware of group development models, analyze group interaction regularly to determine what development issues the group is working through, and incorporate interventions that have the goal of moving the group through a developmental phase if the group seems stuck.

Prioritizing content and planned structure at the expense of process. Groups that rely solely on content and planned structure can begin to feel like a bad classroom. Group members become demoralized because their emotions and experience of the group do not seem to matter to the leader. Process issues are not dealt with, and the group becomes ineffective. Paquin (2017) suggested attending to both content and process. This requires the group leader to be sensitive to the emotions of group members, to be aware of their interactions, and to bring these to the attention of the group if they indicate a process issue or an opportunity for the manual content to be illustrated or reinforced in the group interaction.

Allowing the group to become too there and then. Groups that are "there and then" are at times interesting but quickly become stagnant. They rarely accomplish the goal of the group even if the members' there-and-then sharing is related to the treatment manual content. Paquin (2017) suggested that group leaders take opportunities to pull such interaction into the here and now. The here-and-now experience is emotionally stimulating and allows group members to practice relevant concepts from the manual, providing the manual is well designed. If a member is sharing about a there-and-then application of a topic, the leader can ask, "How is that happening right now in here?" "How would you feel if that happened right now?" "Is there someone in here who is doing that in the group right now?" or "Who would be most likely to do that or have the hardest time doing that?" Group leaders should try to work feedback exchange into the here-and-now process of the group.

The underemotional or toxically emotional group. Underemotional and toxically overemotional groups suffer from the same fatal flaw in the end: Group members are unable to connect emotionally. When group members do not connect emotionally, trust and cohesion do not build, and the group stagnates. Paquin (2017) suggested that group leaders facilitate group members' corrective emotional experiences even as the treatment manual is being enacted. This requires that group leaders actively norm the group to be emotionally expressive; teach and reinforce membership skills, especially how to share emotions and how to effectively listen; take opportunities to connect group members through bridging and feedback loops; and model caring and responding supportively when group members are vulnerable.

Disadvantaging diverse group members by focusing on preset structure. The social microcosm sneaks into every group. This means that group members who have reactions, values, or lived experiences that are marginalized may have a difficult time self-disclosing. When they express a difference, most of the group will try to shut them down—subtly or loudly. Especially during early group development phases, many group members would secretly like everyone in the group to think and feel the same as they do. Unfortunately, this may result in the perpetuation of societal oppression, particularly in groups where a focus on structure may deemphasize attention to process. Paquin (2017) suggested that group leaders counter this by being aware of their own power and positionality and how these may be represented in the group composition. This may occur in part during screening and preparation, but group leaders should also encourage norms that enable conversation about how cultural, identity, and lived-experience differences affect participation, process, and equal benefit.

Application to other structured group approaches. The beauty of considering how to optimally balance content and process in manualized group treatment is that this consideration can inform group leadership with other structured group approaches from classroom guidance groups, psychoeducational groups of all types, and focused group treatments such as cognitive behavioral groups for depression or DBT groups for emotional dysregulation. The processes, leadership functions, and goals of interactive group work are woven through the structures of these groups in ways that appropriately advance group development, encourage facilitative norms, prioritize group member interaction, draw interaction into the here and now when appropriate, and identify and challenge process problems that are potentially stalling the group or making it unsafe. To do this, group leaders need to have a firm grasp of the objectives of the structured group and also the objectives of interactive group work. These objectives should interact, not compete, to forward the group and benefit the group members.

Conclusion

This chapter described and defined the different types of groups readers may encounter in different settings and described how the differences in structure and purpose may affect group leadership. Readers were introduced to task and work groups, psychoeducational groups, counseling groups, and therapy groups and each type's relationship to the interactive therapeutic factors. The settings in which these groups are most often offered (i.e., behavioral and mental health, school, college, and rehabilitation settings) were described, and the unique needs of the settings were highlighted. Finally, online and manualized group formats were discussed and described. Each group format presents unique considerations for the interactive group leader as they build a facilitative, interactive environment for interpersonal learning.

Chapter 15

Organization and Operation

Outcomes

Level 1 Outcomes

After reading this chapter, entry-level students and practitioners should be able to:

1. Outline planning decisions and discuss the implications that the various types of counseling and therapy groups have for these decisions.
2. Explain how to recruit, screen, and prepare group members; the importance of group composition; and the implications of serving groups and clients of diverse backgrounds.
3. Describe essential group operating guidelines and how to implement them across homogeneous and heterogeneous groups.
4. Discuss how to manage groups (e.g., open, closed).
5. Explain the benefits and issues associated with coleading and leading solo, as well as how to work effectively with a coleader.

Level 2 Outcomes

After reading this chapter, advanced-level students and practitioners should also be able to:

1. Discuss research that explores the efficacy of coleadership and solo leadership and the implications for group members' experiences.
2. Discuss research that explores the implications of strategic group recruitment, screening, and member preparation processes for the experiences of diverse groups and group outcomes in general.

Leaders perform tasks related to the organization and operation of their groups. Such tasks include planning the group, recruiting and selecting members, composing the group, using essential group guidelines, managing open groups, maintaining productive coleader relationships, and terminating groups and members. By carefully performing these organizational and operational tasks, leaders can form groups that function with minimal distractions. Groups function more effectively when leaders and members do not have to deal with the annoyances created by oversights that occurred in planning, errors in selecting members and composing the group, and problems that emerge because of unstated policies.

Planning

Planning is the first step in developing a productive group. When leaders or coleaders decide to form groups, the decisions they make about group type, size, duration, and composition set the tone for what will follow.

Planning Decisions

When planning groups, leaders should carefully decide on the type, size, member composition, duration, and session length of the group they will offer. These decisions, all of which can influence each other, may require an assessment of the resources (i.e., time, space, technology) the leader has available.

Ultimately, decisions made during planning determine the potential effectiveness of the prospective group. As an example, a time-limited group that is scheduled to last only eight sessions will not function effectively if it is unstructured, remains open to new members, and includes a heterogeneous membership of 12 or more. That group is most likely to be effective if it is moderately structured, has a theme focus, has a homogeneous membership, and is closed to new members once it commences. A *homogeneous* membership means that members share characteristics such as presenting concerns or demographic profiles. For example, an 8-week group with 10 adults who have difficulty expressing anger would provide members with didactic input and assertiveness skill building to help them learn how to effectively communicate their needs and preferences.

When assessing their resources, leaders should consider scheduling, space availability, and the length of time they can commit to the proposed group. Limited time and conflicting scheduling demands should cause leaders to question the wisdom of committing to a long-term or open-ended group. Leaders who decide that they can make a long-term commitment to in-person groups also need to guarantee the availability of a suitable physical space. For online synchronous groups, leaders should carefully consider the confidentiality and privacy of clients as they plan the physical location where they will be situated as they facilitate the group. Leaders are ready to make decisions about the modality, type, and size of their group once they have made time and scheduling decisions, determined that they have space availability, and addressed privacy concerns.

Leaders with limited time should consider shorter, more structured groups with members who are more homogeneous. This does not mean that members cannot be from diverse backgrounds. The principle is that groups should become more theme-focused and structured as time becomes more limited. Groups planned for 6 to 8 weeks, for example, are most likely to be effective if they include some structured experience and instruction and they are designed to serve a specific population of potential members with a specific need. As available time increases, progressively less structured, less heterogeneous, and more process focused groups become better options.

When planning groups, leaders should be aware of alternative group types and formats. Besides ranging in duration, groups vary in terms of structure, openness to adding members, and membership size.

Duration

With respect to duration, most groups are time limited, meaning that they have a predetermined concluding date. Long-term *time-limited groups* commonly last from 30 to 40 sessions. *Open-ended groups*, or ongoing groups, have no predetermined conclusion and occur more commonly in settings such as treatment facilities that have groups scheduled on a regular basis. Occasionally, open-ended groups operate in outpatient or private practice settings.

Both long-term time-limited and open-ended groups tend to emphasize group process and interpersonal learning, to be unstructured, and to have heterogeneous memberships. Ideally, heterogeneous membership groups have members whose characteristics mirror those of the population of the community in which the group convenes. By mirroring the population, these groups enact the social microcosm (I. D. Yalom & Leszcz, 2020). In both types of groups, members terminate when they meet their treatment goals. Consequently, these groups are commonly open to new members.

When time-limited groups convene for 20 to 30 weeks, leaders need to make careful decisions regarding group structure, group size, policy regarding openness to new members, and group composition, including diversity of membership. Although groups of this duration function effectively without a great deal of structure, leaders who form 20- to 30-week-long unstructured groups will be more successful with a homogeneous membership. Examples of time-limited homogeneous groups that can be highly successful include unstructured process groups for college students dealing with relationship concerns or midlife women considering a major lifestyle change. These groups are more likely to be effective when closed to new members.

Leaders of time-limited groups lasting 20 to 30 weeks may consider the addition of new members during initial group meetings, but only if the group is unstructured. Conversely, structured groups that feature a sequence of lessons or structured activities have a great deal of difficulty accommodating new members because new members will have missed interaction and content provided in missed sessions. This problem magnifies new members' feelings of being "outsiders," especially if new members identify with marginalized and underrepresented groups within the context of the group. When considering the addition of new members, leaders should consider the interpersonal style of the potential members. Potential members who are reticent and highly anxious in interpersonal situations are not appropriate additions after initial sessions, given the time constraints of these groups.

Short-term groups lasting from 10 to 20 sessions require homogeneous memberships. Groups with homogeneous memberships are usually theme focused, meaning that a common characteristic of the group's members is the group's intervention objective. For example, a grief group designed to help members deal with grief issues includes members who are grieving, a social skills group designed to improve social skills is composed of members who have problems with social skills, an experience of race and racism group is designed for members examining their racial identity and struggling with experiences of racism in society. Because of the short duration of these groups, it is essential that they remain closed to new members.

Brief groups last from six to 10 sessions and use learning activities and direct instruction to achieve group goals.

Structure

Leaders of short-term groups with specific learning objectives should consider the use of structure. Structured groups, as mentioned earlier, feature a planned sequence of lessons and structured activities, such as role plays, group exercises designed to meet specific learning objectives, and clear evaluation procedures. Structure should be balanced with time for here-and-now interpersonal feedback exchange and exploration of identity development and diverse experiences of group members.

Even in short-term structured groups with specific objectives, there are opportunities for intercultural and interpersonal learning. For example, leaders of a brief group that has the objective of improving its members' relationships will plan to share specific information and use role play to practice skills. Because of the group's time limitations, leaders should close these groups to new members once they begin and work only with members with shared concerns (see Table 15.1).

The more leaders want to take advantage of interpersonal learning and its benefits, the more they should emphasize a process focus and aim to use ongoing or longer time-limited groups with heterogeneous memberships, which can be open to new members. If less time is available, process-focused groups should be closed to new members and have homogeneous memberships. As available time increases, the need to close groups to new members and serve homogeneous memberships diminishes.

Size and Openness

Leaders' decisions about the size of their proposed group depend on their previous decisions regarding resources and group type. In

TABLE 15.1
Group Types and Formats

Duration	Structure	Openness to New Members	Membership
Long term, open ended	Low	Open	Heterogeneous
Long term, time limited (30–40 minutes)	Low	Open	Heterogeneous
Time limited			
20–30 sessions	Moderate	Closed or open initially to select members	Homogeneous
10–20 sessions	Moderate	Closed	Homogeneous
Short term (10–20 sessions)	The longer the duration, the lower the structure (depending on goals)	Closed	Homogeneous
Brief (6–8 weeks)	Moderate	Closed	Homogeneous

general, the literature recommends a range of five to 10 members for therapy groups (MacKenzie, 1990; I. D. Yalom & Leszcz, 2020).

Specific recommendations have varied. Gladding (2019) indicated that counseling groups are most effective when membership ranges from five to nine members. I. D. Yalom and Leszcz (2020) considered the ideal group size to be seven or eight members. MacKenzie (1990) and Kline (2003) considered the ideal membership to be five or seven members because groups that have an odd number of members are less likely to experience the polarizing effects of subgrouping.

When making decisions about group size, leaders should also carefully consider their group's objectives and duration. In groups that have fewer than five members, leaders become increasingly involved in order to encourage interaction. As time passes, because of leaders' increased levels of activity, interaction in groups with fewer than five members begins to resemble interaction in individual counseling or therapy (MacKenzie, 1990; I. D. Yalom & Leszcz, 2020). When membership becomes larger than 10, members lack sufficient time to work on individual concerns (I. D. Yalom & Leszcz, 2020). MacKenzie (1990) stated that when group membership falls into the range of 15 to 20 members, leaders are unable to attend to individual needs, and the group develops a leader-centered format that closely resembles a classroom setting.

Brief groups that have specific objectives and include direct instruction can include as many as 10 to 15 members. This is because these groups will be leader centered (i.e., leaders provide information and directions) and do not depend heavily on interpersonal learning to meet group goals. Brief groups designed to include a focus on interpersonal learning are more effective when they include a membership that falls into the ideal range of five to eight members. Brief groups that become less leader centered are effective only with smaller group memberships.

Long-term, time-limited closed groups function well with eight to 10 members. Starting with a group of 10 is a good strategy if leaders anticipate members dropping out of the group and want to avoid assimilating new members. Table 15.2 offers some general guidelines for leaders to consider as they plan groups. It illustrates how group type, duration, and structure influence decisions to accept or close the group to new members and suggests the number of members a group can effectively serve. These considerations are critical aspects of planning for a group and preparing members for their experience.

Session Length

Another planning consideration is the length of group sessions. In general, group sessions last from 1 to 2 hours, with 1.5 hours probably being the most common length. When planning the length of a group's session, leaders should consider structure and objectives. Leaders also need to remember that members need time to transition from their daily interactions to the group environment. Groups that last only 1 hour seem to end prematurely, whereas some groups lasting 2 or more hours seem to be excessively demanding on members. It is therefore critical to consider prospective members' presenting concerns and reported interpersonal functioning levels in groups when determining which group assignment is appropriate (Piper et al., 2007).

A final consideration regarding the length of group sessions and size of a proposed group relates to the ages and special needs of group members. When, for example, composing a group for children, leaders must consider their needs and developmental level (Geroski et al., 2021). Think in terms of less, less not in process but in group size and duration. Gladding (2019) suggested that groups that last for 20 minutes may be very appropriate for members who

TABLE 15.2
General Group Planning Guidelines

Group Type, Duration, and Application	Structure	Open or Closed	Members[a]
Long term			
Open ended			
Inpatient therapy group	Low (meeting goals terminate)	Open (to selected new members)	5–8
Time limited (30–40 weeks)			
Counseling or therapy group for a heterogeneous membership	Low	Closed (after initial session)[b]	5–8
Counseling or therapy group addressing eating disorders with an educational component	Moderate	Closed (after initial session)[b]	8–10
Time limited (20–30 weeks)			
Counseling or therapy group for members diagnosed with depression with an educational component	Moderate	Closed (after initial session)[b]	8–10
A process-focused counseling or therapy group for people addressing relationship issues	Low	Closed (after initial session)[b]	5–8
Short term			
Time limited (10–12 weeks)			
Counseling group for adolescents dealing with parents' divorce	Moderate	Closed	6–10
Time limited (12–20 weeks)			
A cognitive-behavioral group for depression	High	Closed	8–10
A process focused counseling group for members dealing with the loss of a partner	Low	Closed	5–8
Brief			
Time limited (6–10 weeks)			
Solution-focused group for members with relationship problems	High	Closed	10–15

[a]These are suggestions for adult members. Make adjustments for differing age groups and population characteristics. [b]Leaders should carefully screen members for inclusion after the group has commenced. Admission of new members needs to recognize group development issues.

are 5 or 6 years old. When planning groups for children and members with special needs, leaders need to consider evidence-based literature regarding group objectives, appropriate group size, and the duration of a group's sessions.

Recruiting Group Members

The decisions leaders make about the type, size, duration, and objectives of the group they are planning establish whom to recruit for group membership. As stated previously, theme-focused and short-term groups serve a homogeneous membership predetermined by group objectives. Open-ended and longer time-limited groups, on the other hand, benefit from a more heterogeneous membership. Even so, in recruiting members for a long-term group, leaders should articulate a general description of the clientele most appropriate for group membership. For example, leaders recruiting members for a long-term group may state that adults who are nearing termination of individual counseling and want to improve the quality of their relationships are most likely to benefit from participation.

Leaders can use a variety of methods for announcing their groups and recruiting members. Whether leaders use their referral networks, advertisements, or clients already receiving services in their agencies, they should state the group's objectives and characteristics of appropriate members, including racial, ethnic, and gender identity–related demographic information. Leaders interested in serving culturally diverse group members should be more explicit about that objective in their recruitment material in order to attract members of underrepresented populations to their groups. In addition, leaders should state that they will interview prospective members before the onset of the group to ensure that the group is the most appropriate form of service. When announcing a group, leaders should also include information about scheduling, fee structure, and the duration of the group and information that describes the nature of the procedures to be used, the leaders' experience and commitment to leading culturally inclusive groups, and the expectations for member participation.

Member Selection, Group Composition, and Member Preparation

Member selection and group composition are critical determinants of group effectiveness (Geroski et al., 2021; Kline, 2003; I. D. Yalom & Leszcz, 2020). Invariably, however, group leaders working in educational and social service agencies comment on how they are required to include anyone referred to their groups. These leaders protest that they are unable to screen out individuals who are unsuitable for group membership. In contrast to this practice, group literature strongly insists that careful member selection and group composition decisions are both ethically necessary and critical to group effectiveness (American Counseling Association [ACA], 2014; Association for Specialists in Group Work [ASGW], 2021). Poorly composed groups will experience group development issues significant enough to negate their potential effectiveness.

Dies (1993), an early scholar on group composition and membership, made an important distinction between member selection and group composition. Group composition refers to the composite of the choices leaders make about members to be included in their groups. Member selection, on the other hand, involves a series of individually focused decisions. By focusing too heavily on individual decisions, leaders will make group composition errors. As leaders select members, they should be clear about the "big picture," or composite, of their decisions. For example, a leader who selects members for a group designed to improve relationships is likely to have problems if all the members chosen are withdrawn. Instead, this leader needs to be sure to include a mixture of withdrawn and outgoing members. In essence, homogeneous groups can have heterogeneous member composition; the key is consistency in the nature of the presenting concern that brings the members into the group.

As leaders develop a plan for selecting members and composing their groups, they should carefully construct procedures to prepare members for group participation. Pregroup preparation is an educational intervention that explains what individuals should expect from group membership. It is widely recognized as instrumental to effective group functioning, especially in the early stages of group development. In addition, pregroup preparation is an ethical responsibility for group leaders (ASGW, 2021; see Chapter 12).

Member Selection Criteria

To comply with ethical standards and standards of practice, leaders must screen potential group members to determine their appropriateness for the group being offered (ACA, 2014; ASGW, 2021). Defining who is an appropriate member for a group is not a major issue in theme-focused short-term groups because the theme generally defines the membership. In longer groups that stress interpersonal learning with a relatively heterogeneous membership, leaders should consider selection criteria carefully. Leaders also need to understand that some individuals are clearly not appropriate for group counseling and therapy. Selection criteria for a group thus include qualifications for inclusion and exclusion.

Member selection studies have changed emphasis from diagnostic interviews to assessment procedures that stress the prospective members' ability to function and learn in an interpersonal environment (Dies, 1993). According to Dies (1993), the ultimate aim of pregroup assessment is "establishing the optimal therapeutic 'fit' among the patient, the therapist(s), and the group system" (p. 487). Dies noted that although research has not developed highly reliable techniques for predicting success, it has offered a number of useful guidelines for the inclusion of potential members. Dies discussed six assessment tasks for member selection: (a) intrapersonal diagnosis, (b) interpersonal assessment, (c) motivational appraisal, (d) goal setting, (e) evaluation of expectancies, and (f) initiation of the therapeutic alliance. In essence, Dies suggested that pregroup assessment should evaluate prospective members in terms of their ability to interact and benefit from interaction with others, their motivation for and expectations of treatment, and their ability to be helpful to others. Dies also maintained that member selection ultimately rests on leaders' clinical judgment.

I. D. Yalom and Leszcz (2020) also stressed the role of leaders' clinical judgment in the screening process. They cautioned against accepting members who are deeply resistant to joining the group or who do not see its potential benefit to them. I. D. Yalom and Leszcz also described a number of criteria that suggest a person's appropriateness for group membership. First, it is essential to establish that the potential member's concern is interpersonal in nature. Clients who require treatment that involves here-and-now interaction, interpersonal learning processes, emotional immediacy, spontaneity, some level of interest in intercultural interactiont, commitment to improving relationships, and relationship-focused work are well suited for group therapy.

Criteria for excluding persons from group membership are irrelevant if leaders have developed adequate criteria for inclusion. Leaders, however, should consider a number of criteria for excluding members for greater specificity in their screening procedures. Exclusion criteria include difficulty managing stimulating environments, acute agitation, persistent hypervigilance and suspiciousness, inflexible denial, antisocial or sociopathic personality features, a schizoid interpersonal style, and pathology that requires intensive long-term treatment (MacKenzie, 1990). In essence, individuals who demonstrate pathology that precludes interpersonal treatment are unsuitable for inclusion in most group applications. Again, the best guide will be the clinical judgment of group leaders.

Conducting the screening interview. Screening interviews provide the means for leaders to gather the information necessary to make decisions about potential members and group composition

(ACA, 2014; ASGW, 2021; Couch, 1995; Geroski et al., 2021). These interviews are also the initial step in developing therapeutic relationships and preparing members for group work. Couch (1995), one of the pioneer scholars on the importance of screening group members, identified four basic steps for conducting the screening interview: identifying needs, expectations, and commitment; challenging myths and misconceptions; conveying information; and screening. These steps organize screening assessment and initiate the member preparation process.

The first step involves interviewing prospective members about their needs for treatment, expectations about group process, and commitment to and motivation for change. This stage helps prospective members clarify their concerns and treatment goals (Couch, 1995). From the leader's perspective, the most important aspect of this phase is to evaluate prospective members' commitment to change. Assessing commitment to change involves questioning prospective members about their motivation and acceptance of responsibility. Ideal candidates for group treatment are self-motivated, as opposed to being coerced by others to seek treatment; believe that their participation will be productive; and believe that their participation and progress are their responsibility.

The second step identifies prospective members' assumptions about group participation. Couch (1995) maintained that individuals who do not have experience as group members tend to have misconceptions about what being a group member involves. Thus, leaders should listen for erroneous ideas about group participation when they conduct screening interviews. Once leaders identify erroneous assumptions, their goal is to correct these assumptions by offering accurate information. By doing so, leaders initiate the member preparation process and thus ensure their success.

Leaders provide prospective members with essential information in the third step of the screening interview. Essential information includes expectations for maintaining confidentiality, leaders' ethical obligations for breaking confidentiality (e.g., the requirement to inform authorities about child abuse), and the knowledge that it is impossible to guarantee confidentiality. Finally, leaders must provide informed consent in a developmentally appropriate way (ASGW, 2021; Geroski et al., 2021). ASGW's Best Practice Guidelines (R. V. Thomas & Pender, 2008, Section A.7) define informed consent as follows:

> Group workers provide in oral and written form to prospective members (when appropriate to group type): the professional disclosure statement; group purpose and goals; group participation expectations including voluntary and involuntary membership;

> role expectations of members and leader(s); policies related to entering and exiting the group; policies governing substance use; policies and procedures governing mandated groups (where relevant); documentation requirements; disclosure of information to others; implications of out-of-group contact or involvement among members; procedures for consultation between group leader(s) and group member(s); fees and time parameters; and potential impacts of group participation. (p. 114)

In guiding principles for group work, ASGW (2021) echoed these best practice guidelines and cautioned leaders against describing information shared in a group as being *privileged information*, unless that term is defined by the state in which the group is situated.

After providing prospective members with essential information, leaders should obtain written consent from the prospective member or, if the prospective member is a minor, from the parent or guardian. Leaders must clearly convey informed consent and confidentiality information, taking into consideration developmental (e.g., age, cognitive functioning) and cultural (e g., language, family involvement in the consent process) factors, and being certain that prospective members understand this information and consent or offer assent (in the case of minors) before their admission to group.

The final step of the screening interview involves assessing prospective members' suitability for group membership. Much of the information necessary to decide about a prospective member is the result of observation and questioning during the previous phases of the screening interview. However, leaders should not hesitate to ask the questions necessary to make informed decisions.

As leaders conclude screening interviews, prospective members should be informed if the group is not suitable for their needs and treatment goals. If another form of service is more appropriate, leaders should be prepared to provide necessary referral information, especially to members of underrepresented groups who may have a more difficult experience finding another option (ASGW, 2021; Shin et al., 2016). Members who are appropriate for the group and meet the leaders' needs for group composition should be given the necessary scheduling and location information. Members who are appropriate for the group but do not meet leaders' group composition needs should have several choices, including other forms of treatment, volunteering for a waitlist (either for the next group or for admission after the group begins), or referral.

Group Composition

In general, the more short term and issue focused a group is, the more homogeneous the group membership should be (Salvendy, 1993; I. D. Yalom & Leszcz, 2020). In other words, members should have shared concerns and, when possible, demographic factors should be taken into consideration. It is critical, however, that the desire for homogeneity in a group does not result in the exclusion of people who identify with underrepresented groups (e.g., racial and gender minorities, non-English-speaking recent immigrants). Group composition becomes less important when members share a common issue and the group is more structured (Salvendy, 1993; I. D. Yalom & Leszcz, 2020). In contrast, long-term groups that depend on members' interaction and have an insight orientation are best composed with a more heterogeneous membership. In the case of longer term interactively focused groups, composition becomes a critical concern for leaders (I. D. Yalom & Leszcz, 2020).

MacKenzie (1990) offered some specific recommendations for the composition of closed time-limited groups that have withstood the test of time. MacKenzie maintained that homogeneity is essential for a time-limited group, because members who share common concerns are able to develop group cohesion rapidly. However, in groups relying on interaction as the primary learning modality, homogeneity of common concerns is insufficient for composition decisions (MacKenzie, 1990). When members' interaction becomes important, leaders must also attend to "interactional variety" (MacKenzie, 1990, p. 100), in which case the need to balance members across several interactional types is emphasized. MacKenzie suggested selecting members according to their role types to ensure that there is a balance of sociable, structural, and divergent members (see Chapter 2). Schutz's (1966) and Bennis and Shepard's (1956) group development theories provide alternative conceptualizations of personality types that also can be used to guide group composition decisions (see Chapter 3). It is also critical to consider cultural diversity and the importance of inclusive groups and inclusive leadership, so that group members have the opportunity to experience well-facilitated and inclusive intercultural communication.

A final tenet of group composition is the "Noah's Ark principle" (MacKenzie, 1990, p. 100). This principle holds that there should be no fewer than two people of any identity description. Thus, there should be at least two members of any race, gender, ethnic origin, age group, sexual preference, or religion. The principle behind this recommendation is the importance of taking preemptive measures to avoid group member isolation and scapegoating that might occur when a member has no one else in the group with whom they share similar backgrounds, life experiences, or physical traits.

Salvendy (1993) offered several additional broad principles for composing time-limited groups that have also withstood the test of time. First, group members should have a common tolerance for anxiety because members who vary in their tolerance for vulnerability, for example, will be continuously conflicted over how personal to be during group interaction. Second, group leaders should consider several compatibility issues, one of which is the fit between member and leader styles. Members who demand structure and indicate the need for intensive instruction are not a good match for leaders who use less structured, interactive approaches. Leaders should also consider members' compatibility. Groups composed of members who range widely in their "psychological mindedness," or motivation for treatment, are not likely to interact effectively. Note that none of these factors recommend the exclusion of members of underrepresented groups who have traditionally experienced exclusion from service in the counseling profession (Shin et al., 2016).

Group composition decisions, when made thoughtfully, can accelerate the development and the effectiveness of groups. Authors do vary, however, in their opinions about how to compose groups and even how concerned to be about group composition. I. D. Yalom and Leszcz (2020) stated that when selecting members, leaders should use only the most general principles of balancing age and gender along with how energetically members might participate in group. Their recommendation was informed by years of experience in the field and the knowledge that rigid selection procedures can lead to the exclusion of vulnerable populations and people who are culturally and linguistically diverse. Whitaker and Lieberman (1964), the foundational theorists of group interpersonal learning, maintained that it is crucial to select members who can tolerate similar levels of anxiety and vulnerability. Group development theorists (Bennis & Shepard, 1956; Schutz, 1966) have contended that personality styles and how successfully members have confronted developmental issues are essential to making sound composition choices. There is no divergence, however, in authors' opinions that it is unacceptable to include members whose participation may exacerbate their situation or cause harm to other group members.

Member Preparation

Group counseling and therapy texts consistently advocate pregroup member preparation. However, research on the effectiveness of member preparation is not definitive. Foundational research in the field describing the effects of member preparation on group outcome is not persuasive (Kline, 2003; I. D. Yalom & Leszcz, 2020). However, research from 30 years ago (Dies, 1993; Piper, 1994) established that pregroup preparation has several important effects on member participation during initial sessions. These effects include improved attendance, reduced dropout rates, increased motivation, enhanced feedback exchange, and increased self-disclosure. Other early scholars, such as Sklare et al. (1990), pointed out that pregroup preparation reduces new members' anxiety during initial sessions, improves participation, and increases group cohesion and interaction.

When preparing members for group participation, leaders can use a variety of educational and experiential approaches to orient members to group membership, including addressing issues of cultural and linguistic diversity. Steps toward inclusivity may include the use of interpreters or process observers to enhance inclusive leadership practices (Okech, 2023). The information to be provided to members in pregroup preparation includes expectations of group members, the role of group leaders, the group therapy process, group development issues, essential group norms, inclusive leadership practices, and how to get the most from group participation (Geroski et al., 2021; Kline, 2003; I. D. Yalom & Leszcz, 2020). In performing preparation tasks, leaders should be careful not to initiate therapeutic work before the group commences.

Pregroup preparation should address fears about group participation (e.g., rejection, isolation, discrimination, silencing, breach of confidentiality; Levine, 1991; Okech & Rubel, 2007). By encouraging members to share their apprehensions about group membership and then addressing these fears, leaders help members lower their anxiety about becoming group members. Perhaps the most common fear is that confidentiality will be broken. To address these fears, leaders must acknowledge that although they cannot guarantee confidentiality, it is seldom a problem because members can choose what they disclose. This means that members make their choices about what to disclose on the basis of a growing mutual trust among members.

Other typical fears for new group members might include being embarrassed by disclosing why they are joining the group and the feelings they are experiencing. In addition, fears of rejection and being intimate with others are common. Members of underrepresented groups, who also tend to be minorities in groups, harbor valid fears of rejection and marginalization within the group. To address these fears, leaders should reassure new members that most new members share these fears and that they will deal with these fears as the group develops. Leaders should focus on instilling hope regarding the group experiences, and they can do so by assuring members of their commitment to inclusive leadership. They can be sure to reference their screening and member preparation procedures that lay the foundation for discussion of issues of diversity, discrimination, and marginalization and their impact on member relationships and their lives in and outside the group.

When leaders integrate pregroup preparation into their individual screening sessions, they should keep three primary objectives in mind. First, they need to provide information about group counseling or therapy and describe what members should expect from group participation. Along with their verbal descriptions, leaders can provide printed materials designed to educate members about group counseling and therapy and the procedures used to help members change (e.g., interpersonal feedback, experimentation with new behaviors, consensual validation). Leaders should repeat this information freely during initial sessions to ensure members understand the experience to which they are committing (MacKenzie, 1990). Second, leaders should elicit and address fears members may have about group participation (Geroski et al., 2021; Okech & Rubel, 2007). Third, potential members should be oriented to interpersonal learning, or, as MacKenzie (1994) put it, members need to be primed for an interpersonal focus. Members are *primed* when leaders, during preparation, direct members to reflect on their significant relationships and describe the impact of these relationships on their lives. Leaders then point out how group process successfully addresses the impact of these relationships and elicits change.

Leaders who use group meetings for pregroup preparation have the same goals (see Chapter 14) as those who use individual screening sessions. However, group preparation sessions can use experiential methods along with the instruction used to orient members in individual pregroup preparation sessions. MacKenzie (1990) suggested using structured experiences during pregroup meetings in which members first introduce themselves to orient members to what it will be like to self-disclose during initial sessions. Then, leaders ask members to express interpersonal goals (e.g., ask members to share one way that they would like to improve their interpersonal relationships) to orient members to interpersonal learning (Kline, 2003). Leaders process these experiences by initiating discussion of what these experiences were like for members and by describing how these experiences are similar to group interaction.

With either group or individual approaches, leaders need to ensure that new members clearly understand what to expect from group membership. It is critical that new members know how groups help members and how interpersonal learning processes provide this help. Finally, pregroup preparation should address the fears that individuals have about becoming group members and prime new members for interpersonal learning. The reassurance leaders provide reduces new members' anxieties and develops positive expectations about group participation.

Essential Operating Guidelines

There are several essential guidelines that leaders should implement as they begin their groups: prohibition of physical or psychological harm, confidentiality, limits on out-of-group socializing, and boundaries for leaders' relationships with members. These guidelines should be included in the ground rules presented during a group's initial meeting and the information discussed during screening and pregroup preparation meetings.

Prohibition of Physical or Psychological Harm

Group leaders should be extremely clear that members shall not harm each other. Leaders must unambiguously specify absolute prohibitions against verbal abuse and physical assault. Leaders also must clearly state that they will remove members immediately who harm others.

The prohibition of psychological harm is often an issue with members who lack the interpersonal and self-management skills necessary to express their anger appropriately. Leaders should be careful in selecting these individuals for group membership. When these individuals become verbally abusive, leaders must decide whether they should discontinue these members' participation in the group. Clearly, leaders should remove these members if they do not respond to feedback and instruction about more appropriate interpersonal behaviors and continue to be verbally abusive.

Confidentiality

Prospective members must understand the importance of confidentiality and the impossibility of guaranteeing it. During pregroup meetings, leaders also should inform members of the circumstances in which leaders are ethically and legally obligated to break confidentiality.

Once the group begins, leaders must reiterate confidentiality policies and ensure that members understand these policies. Confidentiality is essential for the development of a group's external boundaries and members' trust in each other. Leaders should encourage members to build trust incrementally, and members need to recognize that trust grows on the basis of their observations of others' reactions to disclosures that are progressively intimate.

The discussion in Chapter 9 of self-disclosure as a membership skill provides useful suggestions for how leaders can present the idea of disclosing progressively intimate material to build trust. Once members trust each other, the issue of confidentiality subsides. In addition, the risk of members breaking confidentiality diminishes as members deepen their trust in each other and as group cohesion builds.

When presenting the requirement for maintaining confidentiality, leaders should state a confidentiality policy. This policy should clearly define what happens if a member breaks confidentiality. A policy stating that members will be immediately terminated from the group if they break confidentiality is recommended. By deciding on a policy before the group begins, stating and reiterating this policy in pregroup meetings and the initial group session, and upholding this policy, leaders establish a clear boundary. Leaders should understand, however, that even in the case of clearly stated boundaries, circumstances can make these policies feel ambiguous.

In contrast to a specific policy, some leaders, on hearing of a breach of confidentiality, will share that confidentiality has been broken with the group. They will then leave the matter up to the group, allowing members to decide the fate of the offending member. This approach places excessive pressure on the group and can be punishing for the member who has broken the group's confidence. Members, if given the responsibility for making this decision, confront their own concerns about exclusion and acceptability, causing the group to resurrect early group development issues. If members decide to allow the offending member to remain in the group, trust issues will emerge that can stall group progress. Leaders must take responsibility for dealing with a member who has broken confidentiality and must communicate their expectations and consequences of violation to group members.

Limits on Out-of-Group Socializing

Clear boundaries must also be set for *extra-group* socializing, which occurs when members meet outside of group meeting times. Leaders, while acknowledging that they cannot prevent extra-group socializing, should discuss the effects that such socializing has on group functioning. Extra-group socializing has two prominent negative influences on group functioning. First, when members discuss their group experience outside the group, they avoid discussing issues in group that can be productive learning experiences for the entire membership. This takes energy from group interaction and may resolve issues in a nonproductive manner. For example, Jack has a strong reaction to Phyllis and discusses this reaction outside the group with Jane. If this discussion results in Jack being convinced by Jane to not share this reaction in the group (e.g., "Oh, her. Everyone has the same reaction"), Phyllis does not receive potentially valuable feedback, and Jack is deprived of an opportunity to confront one of his own concerns.

Second, extra-group socializing becomes a group issue when members develop relationships with each other outside the group and form a subgroup around a group issue. This form of subgrouping appears when members protect each other or present a unified stand on a group issue. An illustration is when two members meet outside the group because they share a similar reaction to having to share emotions in group. These members attempt to rescue each other from having to share emotions and unite to confront group pressure to share emotions.

Leaders should realize that extra-group socializing is inevitable, especially in longer term groups. Despite this, leaders should present the boundary that extra-group socializing is not acceptable, arguing that it reduces members' learning opportunities, lessens the energy of group interaction, and slows group progress.

Boundaries for Leaders' Relationships With Members

For ethical reasons, leaders must not have social relations with group members. However, rules for other interactions are not as clear cut. Leaders should set relationship boundaries with members for between-session processing, concurrent individual therapeutic relationships, and discussing members' conflicts with other members. Whenever leaders interact with members between group meetings, there is potential to interfere with group interaction and progress.

Between-group processing occurs when members initiate conversation or pose seemingly harmless questions to leaders about what occurred in a group session. Statements such as "Well, that was certainly an amazing session" or questions such as "How do you think I handled the way she attacked me?" can lead to counterproductive interaction. Interaction with members between sessions is counterproductive whenever it allows members to discuss any concern that can be handled in group. Because it is easy to become engaged in counterproductive conversation, leaders need to be clear about their boundaries and what interactions are most appropriate for the group. Conversations in which a member addresses an issue that concerns group interactions, other members, or interpersonal concerns are most appropriate for group sessions.

Concurrent individual therapeutic relationships with group members can be appropriate. However, leaders should be clear that these relationships usually complicate their relationships with members and have several negative group outcomes. Members frequently view members who have individual sessions out of the group with leaders as having special relationships with leaders. Here, feelings of resentment and beliefs that those seeing leaders are receiving special treatment emerge. Members seen as having a special relationship with leaders often find themselves in the difficult position of having to defend the extra time they have with leaders. Leaders are also in a difficult position, having to justify seeing a member outside group and to explain that seeing a member outside group is not offering that member special treatment. To add to these complications, leaders have to avoid sharing individual session material in group. Having to be careful not to share information that has emerged in individual sessions in group interferes with leaders' spontaneity and choice of interventions. In addition, members seeing leaders outside group will invariably discuss their group experiences. Such discussion in individual sessions creates two problems: a blurring of the boundaries between the complicated member/leader and client/counselor dual relationships, and the potential for resolving group issues outside the group. Because of these complications, leaders and members are better off not seeing each other in concurrent individual sessions.

Leaders should specifically state that they will not discuss what has occurred in group when outside group. Often members are motivated to discuss their concerns with leaders outside of group because they find the anxiety of directly addressing these concerns in group overwhelming. By discussing members' concerns outside of group, leaders collude with members to avoid potentially powerful learning experiences. Leaders should understand the consequences of interacting with members outside of group and avoid doing so unless dictated by circumstances such as frank suicidal ideation or threats of psychological or physical harm from other members.

Managing Open Groups

Groups open to new members present difficult challenges to group leaders and members. The addition of new members causes initial group development issues to recycle and negates leaders' efforts to establish functional external boundaries. The frequent addition of new members challenges ongoing members because they revisit issues related to developing trust and defining their role in the group. Because members revisit early group development issues, they are much less likely to face crucial group development issues that tend to surface during later stages of development. Most practitioners agree that short-term groups should be closed to new members once they have commenced.

Leaders of groups face difficulties when unfortunate realities such as agency policies or a rapidly changing patient census do not permit closing their groups to new members. Groups in settings that require the inclusion of new members are likely to experience the cyclic problem of including new members followed by group dropouts followed by more new members. These cyclic problems lead to groups that never seem to develop the cohesion necessary for productive interpersonal work.

Group Development Issues

When members' concerns about belonging and trust recycle, their opportunities to learn from interactions in a more highly developed group evaporate. This means that members will address issues related to belonging, trust, and depth of involvement when the group begins and will address these issues again each time a new member joins the group.

Occasionally, members will become frustrated with their slow progress and angrily confront leaders for not making the group a place safe enough to express their concerns. In more structured groups, members will develop a sense of frustration about having to review information from previous sessions to bring new members "up to speed." Developmentally, groups that regularly accept new members die of arrested growth in initial stages.

Coping With Open Groups: Realistic Goals

Open groups are a major challenge for group leaders. The challenge is how to help members learn in a context that recycles early group development concerns. Unfortunately, the best answer, closing groups to new members, is unacceptable in some settings. To deal with members not being able to resolve and move beyond initial stage issues, leaders need to utilize a structured group approach and lower their expectations for what the group can accomplish.

A necessary compromise might be a structured approach that uses group activities and instruction in which each session's content and skills are independent of the content or skills developed in other sessions. These independent sessions are thematically related stand-alone "workshops." For example, a leader may develop a series of structured activities designed to enhance members' relationship skills. Sessions could include experiential exercises in clear communication, giving feedback, sharing feelings, communicating assertively, using responsible language, and other related activities.

Leaders who conduct groups that accept new members on a frequent basis need to lower their expectations for the depth of member involvement and the impact of interpersonal learning. Leaders must identify meaningful and realistic goals that offer members significant help in spite of the limitations of their group's open format. In addition, leaders should not abandon paying attention to process, identifying members' relationship issues, encouraging the use of interpersonal feedback, and providing opportunities to process members' interactions.

Ideally, leaders should not consider the inclusion of a new member when a group is dealing with critical developmental issues, such as a crisis in trust or the definition of external boundaries. In addition, leaders should consider the suitability of potential new members in terms of their treatment needs and interpersonal style. A potential member who struggles with being open with others and is not minded toward psychology is not an appropriate candidate, especially for a short-term group nearing its conclusion or a time-limited group in its final 10 weeks.

Coleadership

Coleadership involves two group leaders in a supportive yet challenging relationship. Most authors maintain that effective coleader relationships have a powerful impact on group members and are an important tool for leadership training (Okech, 2008; Okech & Kline, 2005, 2006; I. D. Yalom, 1995). The literature reflects authors' preferences, as there is little evidence to support the efficacy of coleadership relative to solo leadership. Most authors prefer coleading to leading solo and encourage the use of group coleadership.

In general, the literature highlights the benefits of coleadership while also warning group leaders to be cognizant of the issues and the added demands associated with coleadership. Individuals considering coleading a group should not jump to the conclusion that coleadership is "easier," and they should make an informed decision about coleading. Included in this decision should be awareness of the benefits and challenges of coleading and what is required to develop and maintain a highly effective coleader relationship (Okech, 2008; Okech & Kline, 2005, 2006). When considering a coleadership relationship, leaders also need to be clear about the impact of coleader relationship dynamics on group process (Okech, 2008; I. D. Yalom & Leszcz, 2020).

Okech and Kline (2005, 2006) and Okech (2008) described benefits and issues encountered by group leaders-in-training who work with coleaders. When working with experienced leaders, leaders-in-training benefit from immediate feedback and the modeling of experienced leaders. At the same time, leaders-in-training invariably encounter feelings that they cannot possibly measure up to the competence of more experienced coleaders (Okech & Kline, 2006). In contrast, when coleaders-in-training lead with each other, they experience mutual support that diffuses some of the anxiety of learning to lead groups (Okech, 2008).

Coleadership Benefits

In general, the literature agrees that coleadership offers specific benefits to both beginning and experienced practitioners (Okech & Kline, 2005; Roller & Nelson, 1993; I. D. Yalom & Leszcz, 2020). One benefit is the ongoing learning opportunity provided by coleader peer supervision (Okech, 2008; Roller & Nelson, 1993; I. D. Yalom & Leszcz, 2020). Another advantage is that coleaders have separate points of view that help them generate more intervention possibilities for difficult group issues, thus increasing the chances of success (I. D. Yalom & Leszcz, 2020). An effective coleader relationship also offers coleaders mutual support that includes acknowledgment for effective work. Acknowledgment leads to increased job satisfaction, provides emotional support, prevents burnout, and prevents feelings of isolation (Okech, 2008; Roller & Nelson, 1993; I. D. Yalom, 1995). Coleaders have the advantage of being able to perform complementary roles during group sessions. For example, while one leader intervenes, the other can monitor group reactions. In addition, coleaders can help each other examine reactions to group members that interfere with their effectiveness and ability to maintain objectivity (Roller & Nelson, 1993) or respond appropriately to group members (Okech, 2008).

Coleadership provides several benefits to group members as well. When coleaders have a well-functioning, egalitarian relationship, their work together is a model for members who struggle in their relationships (Roller & Nelson, 1993; I. D. Yalom & Leszcz, 2020). In addition, having both female and male coleaders allows members to address family-of-origin issues and confront authority issues with people of the opposite sex (MacKenzie, 1990; Roller & Nelson, 1993), whereas having coleaders of different racial and cultural backgrounds allows members to examine issues of implicit bias and race-based dynamics regarding authority and who should wield it.

Coleadership Issues

Issues surfacing in coleader relationships have a negative effect on group functioning. One of the most common issues is competition between coleaders (Okech & Kline, 2005, 2006; I. D. Yalom & Leszcz, 2020). Competition between coleaders surfaces in a variety of ways. Some examples are competition over who is the most "gifted" leader, who is most liked by members, who is "right," and who should "be in charge." When coleaders compete with each other, their groups often polarize, splitting into factions and aligning themselves with one of the coleaders (Okech & Kline, 2006). Polarization around coleaders becomes a thorny issue when leaders disagree and members take sides.

Another issue related to coleader competition emerges when coleaders have conflicting theoretical orientations (Roller & Nelson, 1993; I. D. Yalom & Leszcz, 2020). Conflicting theoretical orientations create problems during group sessions when coleaders conceptualize interactions and necessary interventions differently. Between sessions, conflicting theoretical orientations make it difficult to plan for subsequent sessions, because the leaders have different objectives. Before agreeing to form a coleader relationship, prospective coleaders should understand the need to use a compatible theory to conceptualize group interactions and interventions. Coleaders who adhere to different theories will have to work very hard to develop a shared description of what is occurring in group and reach agreement on intervention objectives and strategies.

Closely related to conflicting theoretical orientations is confusion and poor communication during and between group sessions (Okech,

2008; Roller & Nelson, 1993; I. D. Yalom & Leszcz, 2020). Often, confusion and poor communication are evidence of disagreement over how to conceptualize group interaction and interventions. During a session, this often results in leaders using conflicting interventions that are confusing to members, who have to shift topics abruptly and follow different lines of exploration. Between sessions, poor communication leads to conflict and misunderstandings that when not related to conflicting perspectives are usually the result of coleaders not expending sufficient energy to communicate their perspectives clearly.

To maintain a collaborative relationship, coleaders must have clear relationship boundaries. Issues emerge when the coleaders have confusing, diffuse, or impermeable relationship boundaries (Roller & Nelson, 1993; I. D. Yalom, 1995). Coleaders with overly diffuse boundaries are reluctant to be honest for fear of offending each other. When their boundaries are too diffuse, coleaders also will be reluctant to confront group issues that resemble the issues experienced in the coleaders' relationship (MacKenzie, 1990; Okech, 2008). Impermeable boundaries in coleader relationships are also unproductive, making effective communication highly unlikely and preventing issues that adversely influence the coleader relationship from being addressed.

Coleading requires effective communication and coordination of efforts. These demands require coleaders to attend to their relationship. If the coleader relationship is not sound, coleaders will spend excessive energy attending to their relationship during group sessions. For example, coleaders who compete over whose conceptualization of group dynamics is most correct will focus on proving who is right during the group session (Okech & Kline, 2006). The result is that coleaders, at one time or another, miss important group issues or do not support each other's interventions to the detriment of group members. An effective coleader relationship is critical if group interaction, not the coleader relationship, is to be the focus of the coleaders' attention during group sessions (Okech, 2008). The literature maintains that only effective coleader relationships have a positive effect on groups (Haziza, 2018; Luke & Hackney, 2007; Okech, 2008).

Coleader Relationships and Group Issues

Groups led by coleaders experience the benefits of coleadership and the complications of the coleaders' relationship dynamics. Coleaders must acknowledge potential complications when they plan their groups. In particular, they should discuss how they want learning to occur. When coleaders discuss how they want learning to occur in their group, they should discuss how members should be involved in group interaction. Coleaders who emphasize interpersonal learning as opposed to direct instruction as the primary learning modality will most likely agree that the quality of members' interactions essentially determines what is to be learned in their group. Coleaders who agree that members' interactions are essential need to evaluate how they are willing to communicate in their relationship (Okech, 2008).

In supervision, coleaders are often surprised when asked how the issues they describe in group interaction are transpiring in their relationship (Haziza, 2018; Okech, 2008). Invariably, if the coleaders are honest, they will identify similar if not identical issues in their relationship. For example, coleaders who complain that members persistently avoid sharing emotions will acknowledge that they have avoided sharing emotions in their coleader relationship. Coleaders are commonly unable to help group members confront issues that they are unwilling to confront in their relationship (Okech, 2008).

Developing a coleader relationship requires a great deal of energy. First, each coleader must invest the energy necessary to ensure clear and complete communication. Second, coleaders should seriously commit to offering and receiving honest feedback. To do so, each coleader must be willing to approach difficult issues, such as one coleader's perception that the other is dominating interaction, is excessively judgmental, or is not open to hearing a different perspective. Third, effective coleader relationships require emotional honesty and openness. Each leader must be willing to develop a highly effective interpersonal relationship and encounter the emotions and awkward situations that this involves.

Working Together In and Outside of Group

When coleaders begin working together, they should develop a clear understanding of their working relationship in and outside of group. Roller and Nelson (1993) contended that coleaders should explicitly address a number of factors as they initiate the process of developing their relationship, including the following:

- Theoretical orientation
- Preferred activity level
- Leadership style
- Leadership strengths and weaknesses

- Relationship issues that may potentially interfere
- How they should communicate in group
- How they should support each other's interventions

More recently, Okech (2008) described the value of coleaders agreeing on out-of-group working relationship factors, including the following:

- Time for postgroup processing
- Planning time
- Supervision time
- A commitment to dealing with coleader relationship issues

Postgroup Processing

One of the greatest advantages of coleadership is the opportunity for postgroup processing. Ideally, coleaders will spend time discussing their experiences during a group session immediately after the conclusion of the session (Okech, 2008). Postgroup processing involves coleaders discussing their experiences and perceptions of members' interactions and their work together. This time also should include the exchange of coleader feedback.

Coleaders should develop and agree on a process for postgroup processing and session recording review when possible. If leaders have time, they can experiment with using the process during a single meeting. If time is limited, coleaders should process immediately after the session.

Coleaders should set clear boundaries regarding feedback exchange during postgroup meetings but should not set limits that restrict feedback that can help develop their relationship. To be effective, coleaders need to process personal reactions to group events and each other. For example, a coleader who is angry with their partnering coleader because the partner controls interactions will feel controlled and may withdraw unless able to process that reaction with the partnering coleader. Coleaders using the ORAL feedback model discussed in Chapter 9 have a format that allows them to address personal reactions in a productive fashion. If coleaders elect to preclude personal reactions from postgroup sessions, they ignore issues that significantly influence their work together.

When coleaders plan postgroup processing sessions, they should discuss how they will use theory. A recommended process involves four steps:

1. Each coleader describes their perception of what occurred in group interaction.
2. Coleaders reach an agreement about the most significant events in group interaction.
3. Coleaders define these events in terms of the theory they are using.
4. Coleaders assess the impact of their social and cultural identity on their coleader dynamics and the impact it has on their groups.

Once coleaders have conceptualized interactions according to their theory, they should agree on some general goals for the next session.

Planning Time

Planning involves making a number of decisions before the group convenes for the first meeting and making decisions between sessions about the following session. Planning interventions and strategies requires coleader agreement on what needs to happen for the group to function most effectively. Examples of goals for the next session can be as simple as working harder to direct members to address group focal conflicts or as complicated as developing a strategy to help members develop role flexibility. After coleaders agree on possible interventions and strategies, they should agree on plans for working together in the next session.

Planning time can be included in supervision, postgroup processing, or coleader video review sessions. Coleaders should recognize the need to make plans and, at the same time, understand the need to be flexible enough to respond to changes in group interaction that dictate acting differently.

Supervision and Consultation

Coleaders should seriously consider their needs for supervision. Some coleaders choose to obtain supervision, while others choose to review video recordings of their sessions, obtain occasional consultation, or depend solely on postsession processing. Whatever the choice or choices, coleaders should be aware of the advantages and limitations of each option.

Coleaders who choose supervision have several important advantages over coleaders who do not. First, supervision offers coleaders feedback about relationship issues of which they may be unaware. For example, coleaders may not be aware that they avoid confronting certain issues in their relationship or that one coleader defers to the other. Second, a supervisor offers coleaders conceptualizations of group interaction and interventions from the perspective of a person who is not involved in the group or in the coleadership relationship.

The competence and courage of the supervisor are critical if coleaders are to benefit from supervision. Supervision from a supervisor who is unwilling to confront coleaders' relationship issues or who is not sufficiently knowledgeable about group theory and dynamics is likely to waste coleaders' time. Coleaders will not profit from work with a supervisor who has limited knowledge of group work because the supervisor will also have limited ability to help coleaders diagnose group issues, apply theory, and develop interventions. Conversely, supervision from a supervisor who is an experienced leader willing to confront coleader relationship issues and is expert in applying group theory and dynamics principles can be extremely productive for coleaders.

Coleaders who are unable to receive ongoing supervision should consider consultation in combination with postgroup processing and reviews of their recorded sessions. Coleaders should use consultation when they reach an impasse in the groups they lead or become aware that they are having coleader relationship issues they cannot resolve. This can contribute significantly to coleader development.

The next best option to receiving competent supervision is reviewing group video recordings. Coleaders who meet to process their group experiences and review the recording of a session shortly after the conclusion of the session can find this process productive. Prior to beginning the review, coleaders should agree on the process of their review sessions. This agreement should specify what feedback to exchange, which theory to use to conceptualize group interactions, how to use session video recordings, and some form of session closure.

In addition, coleaders should consider the content of their video review sessions. Possible content includes emotional reactions, perceptions, significant group events, the coleaders' working relationship, and impressions of members and their relationships. Agreeing to content and process avoids confusion and establishes a plan that ensures the sharing and processing of important information.

Resolving Relationship Issues

Effective coleader relationships require commitment to resolving relationship issues because issues that remain unresolved in the coleader relationship invariably surface in group interaction. For example, coleaders who hesitate to exchange honest feedback invariably communicate, in some indirect way, this issue to group members (Okech, 2008). The result is that group interaction will begin to mirror the coleaders' issues (Okech & Kline, 2006).

An illustration of how coleaders' relationship issues influence group interaction occurred during a supervision session when coleaders complained how their group seemed to be stalled in its development and that members seemed to avoid exchanging "difficult but beneficial" feedback. The supervisor then asked the coleaders to share the "difficult but beneficial" feedback they had offered each other. The coleaders paused, then began to share some of the feedback they had been exchanging. The supervisor commented that it seemed that this feedback sounded safe and mostly complimentary. The supervisor then asked the coleaders to share the feedback they had thought about sharing but chose not to share. This conversation led to a discussion of the coleaders' fears about harming their relationship and being regarded as incompetent by the other coleader. Over the next several group sessions, after the coleaders began exchanging more frank and challenging feedback, group interaction became progressively more intense, and feedback became more difficult and beneficial.

Because of the isomorphic connection between coleader relationship issues and group issues, coleaders need to explore their relationship frankly to determine how their issues play out in group interaction. Coleaders should also pay attention to group issues to see whether these issues are present in their relationship, including their social location and cultural identity. Once such issues are identified, coleaders need to work diligently to address and resolve them. Coleaders will find that addressing and resolving relationship issues ultimately leads to the discussion and resolution of that issue in group interaction.

Leading Solo

Leading without a coleader avoids coleadership issues and allows the fullest expression of a leader's personal style. Leading solo also means that the supportive processes available to coleaders are not immediately available. Without the support of a coleader, leaders are under greater pressure to define and understand group issues and intervene effectively. Solo leaders must also manage the challenges and occasional attacks of group members without the support of a coleader. Thus, leaders who lead alone must attain higher levels of competence and self-confidence, which result from support, supervision, and experience.

Support Versus Supervision

Supportive relationships that encourage the exploration of emotional reactions and perceptions help leaders develop confidence in their ability to lead alone. In addition, leaders benefit from supervision when it includes exploration of personal reactions to group interaction and input designed to develop the skills and the conceptual abilities necessary to operate independently.

Colleagues who are experienced group leaders can offer developing leaders important support. Support differs from supervision in that support provides a nonevaluative mentoring relationship in which the goals are to listen, offer suggestions, and provide encouragement to the developing leader. Receiving support from colleagues is especially critical when supervision is not available. Developing leaders benefit from discussing their impressions and emotional reactions to the groups they lead and from hearing the encouragement of an experienced and trusted colleague. Supervision, on the other hand, is a formal hierarchical relationship that establishes roles and expectations for the supervisor and the group leader. Supervision is most commonly a regularly scheduled meeting in which a leader shows a group session video recording. During this meeting, the leader presents an overview of important interactions, a theoretical explanation of the interactions, a description and rationale for interventions, and specific requests for feedback and suggestions.

Supervision provides the supportive mechanism of helping leaders process their emotional reactions and perceptions and makes an active contribution to improving leaders' effectiveness. By watching recordings and listening to how leaders conceptualize group interaction and interventions, supervisors can identify developmental needs for skills and theory application along with personal issues that interfere with leaders' effectiveness. Supervision should also help leaders identify what they do well and reinforce their progress. When supervision is culturally responsive and grounded in the understanding that the social microcosmic nature of groups implies that groups also encounter similar social-cultural factors as experienced in society, it becomes a transforming force for a group leader or coleaders' group leadership experience (Okech & Kline, 2006).

Starting and Ending Group Sessions

Starting Sessions

Starting and ending group sessions involves leaders helping members make transitions. At the start of a session, leaders should help members transition from their customary modes of social interaction to the intensive reflection and interaction of group. Effective transitioning sets the stage for the work members do in the session. At the end of a session, leaders should help members achieve "reentry" to life outside of group, so they can capture their learning and become reoriented to social interactions. Starting and ending sessions on time communicates clear leadership boundaries and signifies specific boundaries for starting and ending members' work.

The procedures for starting unstructured and structured groups are very different. In structured groups with specific learning objectives, leaders can begin simply by summarizing what was covered in the previous session and then describing what will be covered in the current session. In unstructured groups, leaders have to help members make the more difficult transition to here-and-now interaction.

Beginning any group's first session is simple because specific procedures are necessary. Here, leaders review the group's purposes, procedures, and ground rules that were described in pregroup preparation and begin with a comment regarding members getting to know each other. At this point, leaders can elect to use a structured approach that directs members to introduce themselves or use an activity that involves more specific instructions. These beginning procedures should also be performed whenever a new member is added to the group.

Later sessions in unstructured groups are different because there is no specific content to cover other than reminding members about some of the preliminary comments made in the first session. As a session begins, leaders may elect to make a starting comment or simply observe how members interact. Making comments about beginning is probably more useful in helping members transition, setting the stage for interpersonal work, and initiating interaction. Leaders can experiment with various opening statements to see what works best for the group they are leading. Several examples follow.

Leader: "There seems to be some discomfort here and some uneasiness about how to get the group started tonight." (*Observation*)

Leader: "John, it looks like you're really uncomfortable right now. Tell the group what's going on with you." (*Observation and directive*)

Leader: "Who would like to start tonight?" (*Question to start the basic facilitation sequence*)

Leader: "How many of you are feeling scared about sharing what's going on with you? Talking about what scares you in here will be helpful." (*Question and directive*)

Asking members to review a previous session or to discuss how they have applied what they learned in a previous session can also work, but these approaches are risky for several reasons. First, members can avoid here-and-now interaction by engaging in a historical review of the previous meeting. Second, members can shift to an out-of-group focus. Finally, members frequently respond to requests for reviewing previous sessions or discussing the application of group learning by staring blankly at the group leader; this is seldom helpful.

Ending Sessions

When ending a group session, leaders must remain aware of what is occurring in group interaction and the amount of time remaining in the session. Jacobs et al. (2012) indicated that as a session approaches its end, all members should have the opportunity to share reactions to what has occurred during the group. This promotes cohesiveness. Also helpful is a process in which members are instructed to talk about what they have learned or what they have experienced during the session (e.g., predominant feelings, personal reaction to interaction) and not to interact with each other. This procedure provides a process that marks the end of interpersonal work and transitions members to out-of-group interaction. Depending on the length of the session and the number of members, this process should take from 5 to 10 minutes. Whatever way leaders choose to end group sessions, they should track the amount of time remaining and help members transition from interpersonal work to ending the session.

In transitioning from intensive interpersonal interaction to concluding a group session, leaders should let members know how much time they have left to work. For example, a leader might say, "You need to think about reaching some conclusion to your work. There's about 10 minutes left before we have to wrap up." An alternative procedure is for leaders to take charge of interaction in order to complete members' work, stating, for example, "We have 20 minutes left. Ahmed, you were having a strong reaction to what Steve just said to you. Share your reaction with him in the form of feedback."

When interaction prior to a group's ending does not involve members in intense interaction, transitioning to the closing of the session is much easier. In this case, leaders might say something like, "We've got about 15 minutes left, so there's time to clarify impressions any of you might have about what happened tonight." This statement transitions to ending and attempts to keep members engaged in potentially useful interactions. With limited time remaining (i.e., 5 to 10 minutes), leaders should be careful not to initiate exchanges that might require more substantial interaction, such as initiating feedback requests and experimenting with new behaviors.

Termination

Termination in some form is inevitable in all groups. Termination problems occur when members terminate prematurely or when a group ends before its objectives have been met. Termination also signifies the end of the group or means that a member will not be returning. These endings have special significance for all members and leaders.

Premature Termination

Rice (1996) provided a useful context for understanding premature termination. When members join groups, they agree to continue as group members until they meet their counseling or therapy goals; this agreement is a treatment contract. Thus, members who leave a group before they meet their treatment goals or a short-term group before its conclusion break their treatment contract. Breaking a treatment contract signifies premature termination. The term *premature termination* can also identify a group that ends before its designated ending.

Most often, premature termination means that members choose to discontinue their membership because they perceive that the group is not meeting their needs. This perception is often associated with ineffective member preparation—that is, members feeling threatened by the emotional demands of group membership or believing that participation is not helpful. Rice (1996) noted a variety of reasons members drop out of groups. Some members drop out when they have unexpressed anger toward leaders and when they feel unfairly attacked. In other cases, members fear their own anger, intimacy, or the anger of others and may terminate prematurely because of their reluctance to deal with their group's ending.

Whatever the members' reasons, premature termination represents a treatment failure. To reduce the probability of premature termination, leaders need to stress the demands and commitments necessary to be successful as a group member during pregroup preparation. Preparation alone does not guarantee that members will choose not to leave groups prematurely. In addition, leaders should take steps to prevent premature termination and to make premature termination a therapeutic experience for the remaining and departing members when it occurs.

Rice (1996) suggested a strategy for preventing premature termination. In time-limited groups, leaders should predict premature termination about four sessions before the group's end. When asked whether they have considered leaving before the end, members have the opportunity to discuss premature termination as a group issue. This allows members to share their fears of ending the group and to deal with issues related to being abandoned by significant people. Most important, discussing termination allows members to approach the issues and feelings associated with termination together.

Many group members contemplate leaving groups prematurely because they perceive that they are misunderstood or believe that they are not receiving sufficient attention. When leaders convey the attitude that understanding why a member wants to leave is important and ask that member to share their feelings and thoughts about leaving, that member often chooses not to leave the group (Rice, 1996).

Gladding (2021) discussed two other approaches for dealing with premature termination that limit the impact it has on the group. The first approach is useful when leaders become aware that they will have to leave the group before its termination. In this case, leaders should inform group members as soon as possible so that they can prepare for termination and have sufficient opportunity to express their immediate reactions. The second approach describes what leaders can do when they learn that a member plans to terminate prematurely. In this case, leaders invite the member to discuss their feelings in group. Gladding (2021) echoed Rice in his observation that these members frequently choose not to leave the group if they use the opportunity to discuss their feelings completely.

Gladding (2021) described another premature termination scenario—a member leaving the group unannounced. When possible, leaders should ask the member to return to the group to share his or her reasons for leaving without exerting undue pressure. This meeting helps remaining members understand the departing member's reasons for leaving. Whether or not the member returns to share why they decided to leave the group, members need to deal with their feelings about the loss of a member. Leaders should listen for members blaming themselves for a member choosing to leave along with expressions of sadness over the loss. It is critical that members address these feelings fully.

Rice (1996) stated that premature termination makes careful pregroup member preparation necessary. He also pointed out that predictors of members continuing in the group include members having recently terminated individual therapy and/or participation in concurrent individual therapy. Careful member selection and preparation and leaders' clinical judgment of who the best candidates are for group membership ultimately provide the most essential factors for dealing with premature termination.

Termination of a Group Member

When members meet their goals in an open-ended or a long-term group, it is time for them to terminate. This event has significance for the members who are leaving and for the members and the leaders who remain. I. D. Yalom and Leszcz (2020) noted that as a member nears termination, other members may attempt to influence the member to stay. Occasionally, the terminating member attempts to make leaving easier by making their presence uncomfortable for others or by suggesting a way to stay connected to the members they are leaving behind. In each of these scenarios, members are attempting to avoid the termination issues of loss and abandonment. When leaders inadvertently support members' attempts to avoid dealing with the termination of a member, they collude with members to avoid termination issues.

Klein (1996) described seven tasks that leaders should perform when a member terminates in an open-ended or long-term group:

1. Encourage terminating members to discuss their thoughts about terminating in the group.
2. Help members review what they have accomplished and what treatment goals they have yet to accomplish.

3. Help the terminating member discuss what it has been like to be a member of the group and what it will be like to leave the group.
4. Encourage the terminating member to say good-bye to each remaining member and to the entire group.
5. Provide potentially useful referrals and help the terminating member make plans for what they will do after leaving the group.
6. Help remaining members explore their feelings about the meaning and experience of having another member leave the group.
7. Introduce, when appropriate, the prospect of including a new member.

When completing the tasks suggested by Klein, leaders should remain aware that terminating a member has significance for the remaining members. It is easy to forget that remaining members and leaders need to face difficult termination issues before they resume work. By resuming work as if nothing has happened, leaders and members avoid dealing with difficult feelings that are important to their development as persons. To address termination feelings adequately, leaders should allow members time to grieve the loss of an important person. It is also crucial that leaders of established groups ensure that members have dealt with their loss before a new member is included.

The Process of Ending a Time-Limited Group

Leaders initiate the termination of a time-limited group when prospective members have their initial contact with group leaders and leaders inform prospective members of the group's date of termination. Although termination and the realities of limited time are always present in these groups, members seem to lose awareness of the approaching ending. The group literature (e.g., Gladding, 2021) describes members' losing awareness of their group's ending as avoidance.

Avoidance of termination issues is common for members in groups that face ending or the loss of a member. Members avoid acknowledging the ending of their group for various reasons. I. D. Yalom and Leszcz (2020) described members' avoidance as an attempt to manage the pain of separation, a view that is consistent with the bulk of the group literature, which characterizes members as experiencing concerns connected to loss, abandonment, and grief. Termination issues in time-limited groups vary slightly from those faced in ongoing groups (MacKenzie, 1994). Leaders should view termination as a tool that can accelerate members' progress in time-limited groups. Leaders of time-limited groups should carefully consider the strategy described by MacKenzie (1994). To take advantage of this strategy, leaders should make certain that they maintain a closed group.

MacKenzie (1994) encouraged leaders to initiate discussion of termination in their pregroup contact with potential members. During pregroup contacts, leaders should emphasize the time limitations of the group and that members will have to "get to work" early in the group if they are seriously concerned about meeting their goals. Leaders continue to remind members about the group's time limitations whenever the group meets, until the fourth session before the end of the group.

The fourth session from the end marks the time when many members terminate prematurely because they want to avoid termination concerns (MacKenzie, 1994). During this session, leaders should ask members whether they are considering leaving the group before it ends. This discussion allows members to air their concerns about termination. Issues that commonly surface during this discussion include the idea that there is insufficient time, fears about separation, feelings about abandonment, and resentment about the group having to end. MacKenzie (1994) observed that as members discuss leaving, they often experience feeling closer to each other. As this discussion continues, leaders need to remind members that while time is running out, there is still time to reach goals. Group literature (Gladding, 2021; I. D. Yalom & Leszcz, 2020) has described leaders offering an invitation to members to address any "unfinished business" or interpersonal issues they have not completely dealt with before the group terminates.

Termination Sessions

In a group's final session, leaders need to accomplish a number of important goals. Leaders should conduct the final session as the culmination of a group termination process that was initiated at least four sessions prior to the ending. The termination process emphasizes the ending of the group and encourages members to meet their goals and to finish interpersonal work with other members.

The goals of the final session are to deal with the emotions members have about the termination of their relationships with one another, to review and summarize what members have learned, and to say good-bye. To meet these goals, leaders should develop a plan to structure the final group session in a way that helps members move from being highly engaged to increasingly separate as the session progresses.

The final session can begin with leaders asking members to share feelings about terminating the group and their relationships with each other. Exchanging feedback during this phase involves the clear understanding that feedback will not initiate interpersonal work. Feedback during the final group session is a mechanism for sharing reactions and memorable impressions with each other.

Next, leaders become progressively more structured in their instructions as the session continues and direct members to share what they have learned and how they have applied this learning in their relationships outside the group. This phase is a "go-around" in which members take turns sharing but not interacting. Finally, members say their good-byes. This phase can include symbolic structured activities, such as exchanging symbolic gifts. In planning and conducting termination sessions, leaders need to be conscious of the time they have to accomplish termination goals.

Termination is an emotionally intense time for all members and the leader. The expression and sharing of emotions are heartfelt and significant for all. Termination signifies the end of meaningful relationships and, thus, is a sad time, but it is also a time for celebration.

Conclusion

The organization and operation of counseling and therapy groups involves careful planning and the use of procedures that increase the chances that a group will operate smoothly. Leaders who carefully plan, select, and prepare group members will minimize the potential problems that logistical issues or inappropriate or ill-prepared members will cause as the group progresses. Leaders who work to optimize the effectiveness of their coleader relationship or who seek needed support as solo leaders will ultimately have more satisfying leadership experiences and lead more productive groups. Finally, leaders who use procedures that recognize the needs of group members to start, conclude, and terminate members and groups are most likely to meet the needs of group members as they transition in and out of their group experience.

Chapter 16

Becoming a Group Leader

Outcomes

Level 1 Outcomes

After reading this chapter, entry-level students and practitioners should be able to:

1. Describe how leaders' interpersonal functioning impacts their leadership ability.
2. Explain how group leaders' knowledge of group development, group dynamics, leadership theory, and interventions impacts their group leadership ability.
3. Articulate the importance of group membership experiences to group leader development.
4. Describe the importance of and ways to gain supervised group leadership experience.

Level 2 Outcomes

After reading this chapter, advanced-level students and practitioners should also be able to:

1. Evaluate and improve their own process for gaining the personal, relational, and sociocultural awareness necessary for effective and just group leadership.
2. In consultation or supervision, assess their own knowledge of group development, group dynamics, leadership theory, and interventions and create a plan for future learning.
3. As a client or group leader, articulate the essential components of group work supervision.
4. Integrate their own personal awareness, knowledge, and group leadership experiences to articulate an emerging personally congruent leadership style.

Throughout their careers, group leaders are confronted with the emotional and intellectual challenges of leading groups. They will continue to experience the challenges related to apprehensions about their abilities and the emotions connected to their own relational concerns playing out in group interaction. In addition, all leaders will experience the intellectual and emotional challenges of conceptualizing individual and interpersonal concerns, defining themes in group interaction, and developing appropriate interventions—all as group interaction swirls around them. Groups are complex and emotionally stimulating. They are filled with the sometimes competing wants and needs of group members and the group leader. Thus, becoming and being a leader is filled with emotional and intellectual challenges.

Becoming an effective group leader means acquiring knowledge and experience as a group leader and as a group member. It also means participating actively in one's own ongoing personal and professional development. A critical part of foundational group leadership preparation is having a meaningful growth experience as a group member. Beyond personal growth, group leaders must understand, at a minimum, group development theory, group leadership theory, and group dynamics principles and their intersection with the intercultural contexts of their groups and/or the unique characteristics and experiences of the populations they serve. From all this knowledge, they must develop an array of personally congruent skills, interventions, and personal awareness. Gaining leadership experience with different coleaders and with diverse members in groups with a variety of purposes and in various settings will also enhance group leaders' development. Leaders should take advantage of as many opportunities as possible to interact with other group leaders and group work supervisors. Finally, because leading groups is both highly rewarding and personally demanding, leaders must attend to their own physical and emotional well-being.

Emotional Challenges

During their initial experiences, group leaders may be surprised by the intensity of their emotional reactions. Beginning leaders in particular may be anxious about intervening competently, hearing the emotion-laden concerns of members, and being able to manage their own emotional reactions to group interactions. While awareness of the potential emotional intensity is important, group leaders should not expect awareness to be a panacea. It is important that group leaders lead groups without the erroneous assumption that they should be or could be immune to emotional reactions. Instead, leaders should be clear that "therapists are entitled to the same range of human emotions and reactions as anyone else" (Levine, 1991, p. 55).

Group leaders' emotional reactions to group interactions are normal. In fact, leaders' emotional reactions are an important window into what members are experiencing and are essential for leaders to genuinely engage members. Before they can use their emotions as a group leadership asset, developing leaders must accept and tolerate their own emotional reactions. Leaders who accept and tolerate their emotional reactions can then learn to use these emotions to meaningfully connect with the experiences of group members. Leaders who are comfortable with their own emotional reactions can reflect on those reactions to understand members' experiences more fully. Thus, when a leader is aware that they are sad about a group interaction, they can intervene, for example by saying "I'm sensing sadness in the group about what Chandra just said. Who would like to share their sadness with Chandra?"

Leaders who reflect on their emotions to initiate emotion-stimulating interventions can help members who struggle to make emotional connections. At times, interventions based on leaders' reflections of their own emotional reactions can help the group move from disconnected cognitive discussion toward members making more emotional and intimate connections. These interventions, where leaders tune into their own emotions to facilitate members' connections with each other, can provide the building blocks for deep understanding between members.

Weiner (1993) reinforced the importance of leaders developing comfort with their emotions and the emotions of group members. Weiner indicated that to lead groups that stress members' interaction effectively, leaders must be sensitive to their groups' "emotional undercurrents" (p. 86). Weiner went on to state that "the interpersonal group leader also needs to tolerate and to deal with intense emotions and emotional interchanges that result from dealing with here-and-now interpersonal relationships" (p. 86).

Group leaders who shut off or deny awareness of their own emotional experiences also deny themselves a valuable way to understand members' experiences. They limit their ability to help members make meaningful contact with each other. Eventually, group members will not trust leaders who attempt to deny their own emotions because members will perceive these leaders as emotionally distant and aloof. Shutting off or denying awareness of emotions is a protective strategy used by leaders who view their own emotions as unacceptable. Generally, these leaders fear that their emotions will overwhelm them, cause them to lose control, and ultimately cause them to be judged or rejected as leaders.

Inevitably, the fears of leaders who deny or shut off their emotions become their reality. These leaders eventually witness several unfortunate outcomes. Some experience overwhelming emotions when intense group interactions overcome their attempt to shut down or deny emotions. These leaders become overwhelmed because their requirement for maintaining emotional control is unattainable and because their fear of losing emotional control is coming true. Leaders who have an especially rigid requirement for emotional control that do not allow for even small amounts of anxiety may have particularly frightening experiences leading groups.

Leaders who fear their own emotions and the emotions of others will inevitably direct members' interactions away from emotional and potentially productive topics. These leaders lead members away from issues that elicit their own emotions because the emotions elicited by the discussion make the leader feel vulnerable. Because of this vulnerability, leaders who cannot accept or tolerate their own emotions will deprive their group members of meaningful opportunities to confront difficult issues. Individuals who rigidly suppress their own emotions or who fear others' emotions are not appropriate candidates for the role of group leader. They will require individual or group therapy to develop sufficient tolerance for their own and others' emotions before being able to fill this role.

Leaders who cannot accept or tolerate their own emotions often attempt to deny and hide their emotional reactions. This is usually not successful because members are very sensitive to the emotional tone of leaders' nonverbal communication, reactions, and interventions. Invariably, leaders who try to suppress their emotional reactions end up communicating their emotions to group members. When members sense that leaders are attempting to hide their emotions, they will question the leaders' sincerity. In addition, members interpret group leaders' attempts to hide emotions as a message that expressing emotions is inappropriate. Finally, group members may become angry if leaders deny and attempt to hide their emotions while concurrently encouraging members to express their emotions. Leaders who attempt to mask their own emotional reactions eventually lose their credibility and hurt the interactive environment by sending the message that emotions should be denied. Ultimately, leaders cheat members when they attempt to hide or deny their emotions.

The leadership role does not require leaders to be an emotional "blank slate." Rather, the role requires leaders to be guides who help members find, develop awareness of, and understand their emotional worlds. To fill this role, leaders must be tuned into members' emotions while being emotionally congruent themselves. Wright (2000) contended that leaders must develop thoughtful awareness and tolerance of affective states and "clarify what is the essence and deep structure [of] what we inevitably communicate" (p. 195).

Another important aspect of leaders' emotional experiences during group sessions is being clear about their motivations as they intervene by maintaining awareness of their own emotions. Supporting this, Shapiro et al. (1998) argued that individuals, group leaders included, commonly act on their emotions rather than on their thoughts. Because emotions powerfully initiate action, group leaders' interventions can be an indication of their emotional reactions to interaction rather than their studied assessment of interaction. Thus, leaders who are not fully aware of their emotions will be more likely to make emotionally motivated interventions that are not based on a clear understanding of what is happening in the group.

In addition to supporting group leader emotional awareness, Shapiro et al. (1998) described two leader attitudes that benefit leaders who are emotionally aware: "1. My feelings are an accurate and in-depth index of group process. 2. Whatever I feel is a result of something that is going on in the group" (p. 140). Leaders who acknowledge and develop comfort with their emotions are most likely to maintain awareness of their emotional reactions during group sessions, and emotional awareness helps leaders understand group interaction and connect with members' experiences.

Leaders' Personal Issues

A significant leadership problem occurs when leaders do not understand how their personal reactions to group interaction influence their interventions. When unrecognized, leaders' personal issues and beliefs related to culture, social identities, and personal and sexual relationships could have an unintentional but profoundly adverse influence on their interpretation of group interaction and their interventions. Group leaders must maintain awareness of their issues and beliefs related to culture, social identities, and personal and sexual relationships if they intend to respond to issues in group interaction instead of their personal biases and interpersonal issues.

Because leaders are not immune to personal concerns, they must have a continuous awareness of how their personal concerns could influence how they understand group interaction and how they form interventions. This awareness is critical because group interaction can powerfully evoke relationship concerns for group members and group leaders. Levine (1991) described six personal characteristics that reflect developmental issues and interpersonal needs that could affect group leaders. Thus, these characteristics should be of concern to developing group leaders. These characteristics are (a) self-reliance and dependency needs, (b) comfort with authority, (c) acceptance needs, (d) comfort with others' emotional expression and the leader's own emotions, (e) comfort with intimacy and capacity for intimacy in the leader's own relationships, and (f) comfort with separation. Levine believed that group leaders' characteristics in these areas are derived from their relationships and families of origin. When group leaders are not aware of and have not achieved some resolution of their developmental issues, they are likely to try to meet these needs as they lead groups. In addition, leaders who have not adequately resolved these issues will tend to direct members away from important interactions that resemble these concerns. This is because group leaders who have not resolved their issues will experience discomfort as these issues surface.

Rosenberg (1993) discussed the necessary qualities of a group therapist and presented ideas similar to Levine (1991). Rosenberg focused on the complexity of group leaders' relationships with members and how leader countertransference can affect the group process adversely. From Rosenberg's perspective, leaders must be aware of their emotional reactions and their needs for expressing emotion and experiencing intimacy. Rosenberg also stressed that leaders must develop understanding of their needs in the areas of control, dependence, love, and sex. To develop awareness of and to monitor these needs, leaders commonly need therapeutic experiences as clients.

Horwitz (2000) also described how group leaders' needs may adversely affect group members' progress. Horwitz believed that individuals who lead groups for the purpose of maintaining or enhancing their self-esteem are likely to slow members' therapeutic progress and may damage members. For example, leaders who use their interactions with members to bolster their self-image as highly effective and caring therapists will rarely risk intervening in ways that lead to negative reactions or criticism. These leaders are likely to give preferential treatment to group members who are complimentary and may intervene in a punishing way with members who are not. In extreme cases, group leaders who attempt to satisfy narcissistic needs may encourage members to be complimentary about their skills and insights. When group leaders intervene in ways designed to maintain their self-esteem, they avoid interventions that are challenging and gravitate toward interventions that may initially seem impressive to members. The use of interventions aimed at personal glorification is a clear indication that the leader is using groups unethically to meet their own needs. As stated by Shapiro et al. (1998), "Unless the leader is self-aware, there is an ever-present danger that her personal conflicts, inadequacies, and needs, instead of those of the members, will guide group interventions" (p. 118). To guard against this danger, leaders must maintain a high level of self-awareness and participate in experiences that deepen their self-understanding throughout their careers.

Knowledge

In addition to the emotional and personal challenges of group leadership, leaders face intellectual demands. Group leaders must acquire the knowledge necessary to conceptualize group interactions and develop interventions that benefit group members. However, it is insufficient to only obtain the knowledge necessary to conceptualize group interaction. Leaders must systematically integrate their theoretical knowledge and personal perspectives into their practice (Bascue, 1978). This type of integration of knowledge into practice requires group leaders to be open to change by examining their own beliefs and allowing themselves to evolve rather than simply ingesting a group theory and performing it while leading a group.

Group leaders must develop an adequate knowledge base to understand group interaction and define objectives to promote an effective group environment and group member interactions. At a minimum, this knowledge includes an understanding of group counseling, therapy theory, and group dynamics principles. Leaders who understand theory and group dynamics principles can apply them to prioritize and conceptualize group interaction. Once they have conceptualized interaction, they can develop and use interventions that lead to meaningful changes in members. Additionally, with experience and reflection, leaders should be able to articulate personally congruent theory, skills, and interventions.

Group leaders must also have a basic understanding of group dynamics. Understanding how norms and roles develop as a product of group interactions is critical. This understanding guides interventions meant to develop group environments that support risk-taking, experimentation, and interpersonal learning. Leaders who do not comprehend these basic principles will not be able to identify productive or counterproductive patterns that emerge in members' interactions. If they cannot identify patterns, they will be unable to structure interventions aimed at modifying blocking norms or deal with role problems.

Group leaders also need to develop a working knowledge of an appropriate group counseling or therapy theory. This is essential. Without an appropriate theory (see Chapter 3 for the characteristics of an appropriate theory), leaders will find the complexity of group interaction overwhelming. Leaders who use a theory designed for individual counseling or therapy will suffer a serious disadvantage. Those without a theory will suffer a similar fate. Without an appropriate group counseling or therapy theory, these leaders have nothing to guide them in identifying important interactions, no concepts that can help them understand interactions, and no model to guide interventions (Shapiro et al., 1998).

Experience

An underemphasized area within counseling accreditation standards and therapy certification criteria is the requirement for leaders to have a formative group membership. Although counseling training standards (Council for Accreditation of Counseling and Related Educational Programs, 2024) require a group experience for counseling trainees, they offer no guidelines for the type, quality, or intensity of these experiences. In the area of group psychotherapy, the American Group Psychotherapy Association (see www.agpa.org) does not require experiences as group members for entry into the organization's clinical membership status. In addition, the more stringent standards for certification as a certified group psychotherapist do not stipulate experience as a group member. This is also true for the entry-level national certified counselor and the advanced-level certified clinical mental health counselor certifications.

Despite vague, absent, or minimal certification and accreditation requirements, most scholars in the field of group counseling and psychotherapy strongly emphasize the need for developing group leaders to have group member experience as a part of their training. These authors (e.g., Forsyth, 2011; Glass & Benshoff, 1999; I. D. Yalom & Leszcz, 2020) agree that formative experiences as group members are necessary for trainees to become competent practitioners. I. D. Yalom and Leszcz (2020) described the indispensable benefits of group participation for leaders-in-training:

> They experience the power of the group—the power to wound and to heal. They learn how important it is to be accepted by the group; what self-disclosure really entails; how difficult it is to reveal your secret world, your fantasies, feelings of vulnerability, hostility, and tenderness. They learn to appreciate their own strengths as well as their weaknesses. They learn about their own preferred role in the group . . . Perhaps most striking of all, they learn about the role of the leader by becoming aware of their own dependency and their own often unrealistic appraisal of the leader's power and knowledge. (pp. 654–655)

Shapiro et al. (1998) also addressed the need for leaders-in-training to have experiences as members. They indicated that group leaders can begin to understand the powerful effects of group membership only when they have had experiences as group members, and these powerful effects include the intense social pressure and anxiety about participation. Shapiro et al. also indicated that group leaders must understand the group members' experience emotionally and at a sensory level to be optimally effective.

Leaders who have experienced meaningful growth as group members likely have an advantage over leaders who have not. They will understand the experience of change from the perspective of a group member and will likely have a deeper belief in the power of group interaction to produce meaningful change. Leaders who have not had productive experiences as group members may struggle to congruently advocate for members' participation and may not be able to interact with members with the same conviction as leaders who have had productive experiences. Developing leaders should reflect on the following questions, which are answerable only from the perspective of experience: Can I fully understand what it is like to be a member? Do I have a deep well of group membership experience that allows me to connect emotionally with group members' experiences of the group process? Can I congruently encourage members to participate in a process in which I have chosen not to participate? Have I encountered the impact of my acculturation and social identities in a group setting and worked through their personal and leadership implications?

In addition to participating as a group member, group leaders-in-training should take advantage of opportunities to lead groups in a variety of settings with a variety of members. Leaders who have a broad range of experiences leading will have encountered a variety of group dynamics, issues in interaction, member characteristics, and member concerns, improving their ability to adapt to ever-changing group dynamics. Varied experiences also encourage leaders to develop a more flexible style and be more open to understanding individual differences and unique group interaction issues. Leaders who gather most of their leadership experiences in one environment may develop a narrow set of expectations for group dynamics and member concerns. Leaders who have a narrow range of experiences are also not likely to develop a full range of group conceptualization skills and interventions. Consequently, leaders with a limited range of experiences may develop a limited set of beliefs about what members need and what group development issues may emerge. Over time, these limited beliefs may cause leaders to miss important group content and be less able to adjust their intervention and conceptualization skills to diverse memberships and issues.

Leading with different coleaders broadens leaders' experiences in a way that is similar to leading groups in different settings with different members. Leaders benefit from opportunities to work with different coleaders for several reasons. First, leading with a variety of coleaders demands that leaders clarify their relationship concerns with each other. This reclarification process helps leaders maintain awareness of how their relationship concerns influence their interactions with group members. Second, it provides leaders with an opportunity to observe alternative interventions and leadership styles. Finally, it offers leaders the opportunity to process group events, receive immediate feedback, and reality-test reactions to group members with different leaders operating from a variety of perspectives. Work with coleaders also prevents isolation.

As leaders gain experience, they will eventually encounter the problem of isolation. When leaders have no one with whom to process their leadership experiences, reality-test their impressions, or explore the effectiveness of their interventions, they experience isolation. When isolation persists, leaders become stagnant in their development—they do not hear new ideas, varying perspectives, or the challenges posed by others that may sharpen their conceptualization or diagnostic skills. Isolated leaders operate on untested assumptions about their style and effectiveness. Although group leaders can partially compensate for isolation by reading, attending workshops, and reflecting on their practice, they are still isolated. Interaction with other group leaders and supervisors about their perceptions of group, the effects of their personal concerns on their leadership, and the effectiveness of their style and interventions is critical for leaders' ongoing development.

In addition to monitoring the safety, need, and progress of group members, supervision of group work should emphasize both the content knowledge that is essential to competent group leadership and the within-supervision interpersonal processes that are supportive of learning. This combined focus attends to the supervisory working alliance, emphasizes the essential differences between individual therapy and group work, and brings to life important knowledge within the supervision process. Supervision models such as Rubel and Okech's (2006) supervision of group work model draw attention to the individual, interpersonal, and group-as-a-whole levels of supervisees' groups. The model also includes the supervision foci of and supervisory roles of J. M. Bernard's (1979) individual supervision-oriented discrimination model of supervision. Okech and Rubel (2007) extended Bernard's model to attend to critical diversity and multicultural content and process. To enable direct learning from the supervision process, group supervision of group work remains the most theoretically sound modality for providing group work supervision (Riva, 2014). Supervision of group processes should mirror the processes of the groups led by supervisees and emphasize the creation of an interactive environment, interactions among supervision group members, and feedback originating from within the group. See Figure 16.1 for a supervision of group work model.

Personal Development

It is extremely important that group leaders attend to their personal development. This is especially important in terms of their own relationship needs. As described earlier in this chapter, leaders' relationship needs may adversely influence the decisions they make about interventions. The most problematic form of this is

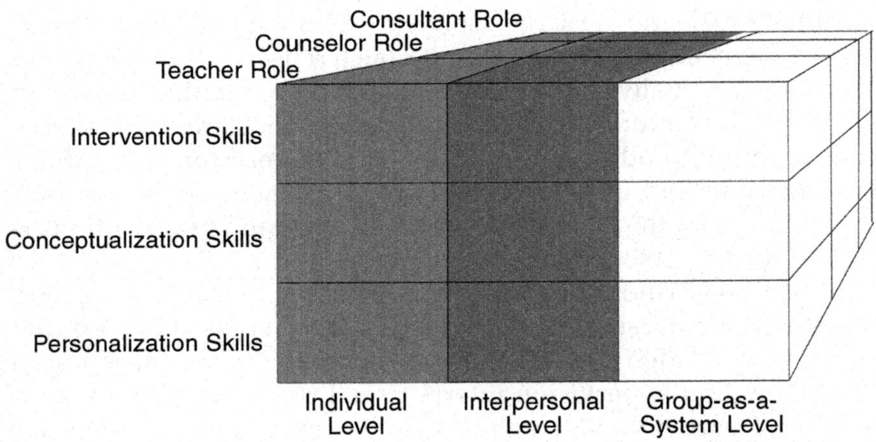

FIGURE 16.1
Supervision of Group Work Model

Note. Reprinted with permission from Rubel, D., & Okech, J. E. A. (2006). The supervision of group work model: Adapting the discrimination model for supervision of group workers. *The Journal for Specialists in Group Work, 31*(2), p. 116. Copyright 2006 by Taylor & Francis.

when leaders who are unaware of problems in their relationships use group interaction to meet their own relationship needs. Leaders must maintain awareness of their own relationship needs as they lead and should take necessary measures to attend to problems they experience in their relationships. Day (1993), Horwitz (2000), Levine (1991), Rosenberg (1993), Shapiro et al. (1998), Weiner (1993), and I. D. Yalom (1995) strongly suggested that leaders and leaders-in-training attend to their own relationship needs either in therapy groups, in peer supervision groups, or in individual therapy.

Because of the emotional and relational demands of group leadership, leaders should allow themselves adequate time to reflect on their own life, social and cultural context, and practice. Group leadership can be exhilarating and gratifying. It can also be frustrating, and it demands considerable physical and emotional energy. Leaders should be aware of the physical and emotional demands of leadership and attend to these needs.

Possibly the most effective way for group leaders to understand their interpersonal boundaries, become aware of their emotions and interpersonal behaviors, develop social and cultural self-awareness, and clarify their beliefs about relationships and the experiences of others is to participate as members of peer supervision or therapy groups. The group therapy literature repeatedly emphasizes ongoing peer supervision groups as a means for group therapists to maintain and further develop awareness of their own countertransference and narcissistic issues (e.g., Borders, 1991; Pager et al., 2018; Valentino et al., 2016). For example, Horwitz (2000) described the benefits of effective peer supervision groups: "When functioning optimally, such groups provide the opportunity to expose one's anxieties and self-doubts to a few trusted fellow professionals" (p. 233). Other avenues for maintaining awareness of personal boundaries and clarifying relationship concerns are in counseling and therapy groups led by master practitioners.

Personal Leadership Style

Shapiro et al. (1998) described an additional personal objective in the process of becoming an effective group leader. They indicated that as leaders gain experience and competence, their ongoing development should include development of a personally congruent leadership style. Furthermore, Shapiro et al. indicated that leaders and their groups benefit from the leader using a method that reflects their personal values and nature. A personally congruent leadership style is ultimately the most effective. Leaders who mimic others' leadership style, use programmed skills, or depend on structured or rigid techniques abandon the power of personal contact and isolate themselves from the lives of their groups' members. This has the consequence of depriving both the leader and member of the enjoyment and benefits of group work.

Acquisition of at least one relevant leadership theory is required to support the development of a leader's personal leadership style. Group leaders who engage in thoughtful and reflective practice eventually develop a theoretical perspective that represents their assumptions about group interaction and accommodates their leadership style. Acquiring theory relevant to group work is the first critical step.

Personal Boundaries of the Group Leader

Group leaders' personal boundaries define how they participate in groups as leaders and as people. These boundaries vary from leader to leader, depending on personal style. However, some parameters hold true for all group leaders. First, group leaders must interact with group members in a way that helps members learn. Second, leaders must not prioritize their personal needs over the needs of group members. Two other leader boundary concerns also require specific discussion. These concerns require reflection and are not as easily defined as the first two boundary concerns. One boundary concern involves leaders' views about the use and limits of power, authority, and responsibility in the leadership role. The other concern centers on leaders' awareness of and actions related to their own personal biases related to gender, race, religion, and culture.

Power, Authority, and Responsibility

An important boundary concern is the product of leaders' beliefs about the limits and extent of their power to influence what occurs during group sessions (Whitaker, 1985). Whitaker (1985) commented that leaders often possess unrealistic assumptions about their real power to influence group members. Whitaker (1985) also discussed how leaders' beliefs about their power can lead to frustration and even to a desire to abandon the power they actually have to influence group members.

Occasionally, leaders develop the belief that they influence members too easily and wish that they did not have the power they think they have. However, Whitaker (1985) contended that group leaders have the responsibility to use what power they have to further their purposes in the group, and thus group leaders must be aware of and accept responsibility for their power. Realistically, much of the power leaders have within groups is a function of their role. Role-related power involves convening groups and establishing and maintaining group membership. In addition, leaders have power because the leadership role requires them to be "in charge" of directing interaction. In the group room, leaders' power derives from their ability and success in directing group interaction in a way that influences member change.

Coupled with directing interaction, leaders also have power because of their knowledge and ability to observe the group from a different, more informed perspective than members. By sharing observations and using observations to formulate interventions, leaders can bring awareness to issues members want to avoid. This means that leaders become influential because their knowledge allows them to identify disturbing and reactive motives. By intervening in a way that causes members to confront disturbing and reactive motives, leaders have the power to regulate the amount of anxiety present in the group room.

The power group leaders possess is largely limited to role-associated parameters: the power to direct interaction, the power to form and convene the group, the power to include and exclude members, the power to use their knowledge and observational perspective to identify issues, and the power to regulate anxiety. Beyond these parameters, the power leaders have to influence members to change is limited.

Whitaker (1985) maintained that group leaders have the power to control only their own behavior in groups. Leaders have the power to choose the content of their interventions, to confront or ignore issues, and to collude with or frustrate restrictive solutions. Leaders do not have the power to change members; they have the power only to increase the chances that members will choose to change. Thus, leaders who become disappointed or frustrated because they have not successfully changed how members interact are acting on an erroneous assumption about the extent of their power. In general, any power that leaders have should be used to encourage members to make decisions that can lead to positive changes.

Whitaker (1985) further maintained that group leaders have an obligation to work diligently with the resources they have, including power, to utilize the group to benefit group members. Given that leaders are responsible for meeting the ethical standards of practice, they should examine the realities of group practice as they define the boundaries of their responsibilities. Although they have the power to influence their groups, they do not have the power to determine group outcomes.

Whitaker (1985) further asserted that leaders' interaction within their groups is only one factor that determines the outcome of the group. In terms of leader responsibility, this means that leaders are obligated to behave in ways that are consistent with supporting facilitative group environments and positive group outcomes. This also means that leaders are obligated to refrain from acting in ways that make the group environment unhelpful or harmful to members. Group leaders do have the power to harm group members and have an ethical and moral responsibility to avoid this.

Leaders must carefully examine their beliefs about the realistic boundaries of their power and responsibility. Leaders who believe that they have the power and the responsibility to change others should reevaluate these beliefs. Leaders who believe they can change others are likely to view members who do not change in the desired ways as noncompliant or resistant and to regard themselves as having failed at leadership.

Leaders who have the belief that they can change others often need to see progress to validate this belief; they may also begin to overinflate perceptions of their importance in members' lives (Wright, 2000). Members of the groups led by leaders with these needs and beliefs are likely to experience leaders' frustration and rejection if they do not respond in the ways the leaders wish. Leaders who function with these needs and beliefs lead ineffectively and will eventually harm members.

Cultural, Social Identity, and Intersectionality Issues

The need for social and cultural awareness and an emphasis on culturally responsive leadership have been discussed throughout this book. These imperatives have had a place in group work for decades. Rosenberg (1993) wrote about leaders' boundaries as an issue of cultural awareness: "Group therapists must also be aware of their social ideals and religious values, so that they can realistically set boundaries of their own behavior and respect the boundaries of the group members" (p. 652). Clearly, leaders' awareness of their own positionality, culture, and life experiences must be sufficient such that they are aware of their power and are able to see group members as individuals who have different positionalities, cultures, and life experiences than their own. When they can do this, they can avoid harming group members by denying members' experiences and reenacting harmful societal dynamics. Leaders are ethically and morally obligated to examine and confront their own personal biases, privilege, and experiences as oppressors and the oppressed.

Many authors believe that the first step a counselor or therapist should take when working with socially and culturally diverse clients or group members is to gain clarity about their own life experiences, beliefs, feelings, and assumptions. C. C. Lee (1991) stressed that counselors should be fully aware of their own heritage as well as the biases they have that might interfere with how effectively they can help others. Yu and Gregg (1993) emphasized that the process of developing awareness demands that counselors uncover potential "blind spots" relative to diverse clientele:

> Counselors should recognize they may unknowingly harbor biases and prejudices toward members of specific ethnic groups. They need to be willing to work through these issues before true therapeutic work can begin. If they cannot do so, a referral may be necessary. (p. 91)

It goes without saying that the deleterious effects of unexamined therapist bias and prejudice extend not only to ethnicity and race but to age, gender, sexual orientation, ability status, class, and religion and spirituality. D'Andrea and Daniels (1997) extended this conversation to group leaders, stating that competent group leaders must

> examine their own assumptions, biases, and feelings concerning diverse cultural-racial groups . . . consider the way these assumptions/biases/feelings might affect their interactions with group members . . . [and] be aware of the ways in which the group members' assumptions, biases, and feelings about culturally-different persons may influence the group process. (p. 106)

The Association for Specialists in Group Work articulated essential attitudes about working with diverse group members in its guiding principles for group work (McCarthy et al., 2021). This document contains important statements regarding the attitudes leaders should maintain as they develop an understanding of their beliefs, values, and biases relative to serving diverse group members effectively. Leadership attitudes should include an awareness of one's own race, ethnicity, cultural heritage, gender, socioeconomic status, sexual orientation, abilities, religion, and spiritual beliefs, as well as respect for differences. Leaders should also understand how their personal experiences and histories affect group dynamics (McCarthy et al., 2021). Perhaps most important, group leaders should be aware of and avoid stereotypes and focus on developing an understanding of each individual in the context of group interaction (McRae, 1994).

Lazerson and Zilbach (1993) made critical points about the need to develop awareness of culturally supported stereotypes relative to gender. They emphasized that group leaders can inadvertently intervene in a way that supports stereotypes or intentionally intervene in a way that challenges stereotypes. Group leaders who are aware of the gender stereotypes that operate in their groups can have an impact on members' interpersonal issues and social and political awareness. Group leaders who confront cultural gender stereotypes confront issues that greatly influence members' relationship attitudes and self-esteem concerns. Unfortunately, many group leaders remain oblivious to their gender biases and do not understand how their perceptions and interventions may inadvertently support stereotypes that limit or damage group members.

Being an Anarchist and Orchestrator

As groups evolve, leaders should encourage members to take risks in their relationships within the group and, ultimately, in their relationships outside the group. Leaders will find that interventions are necessary to help members extend their customary and habitual boundaries of safety (see Battilana & Kimsey, 2017). The leader-anarchist intervenes to challenge these familiar and potentially detrimental boundaries, disrupt comfortable interaction patterns, say what members will not say, and confront issues that members collude to avoid. Being a leader-anarchist requires courage and a commitment that prioritizes helping members change over the leader's own comfort.

At other times, leaders will find that the group process engages members in productive interaction without needing much, if any, leader participation. Some leaders struggle with this independence, believing that members should require or need their input and direction. However, leaders need to orchestrate interaction only to ensure that members have equal opportunities to participate. The role of leader-orchestrator will not satisfy an ego that demands being the center of attention. Rather, filling this role means that the leader values the importance of members making meaningful emotional connections and learning from one another. Filling this role signifies that members have learned how to become self-reliant interpersonal learners.

Conclusion

Both novice and experienced leaders benefit from creating an ongoing development plan. This plan should include experiences that broaden leaders' understanding of group members' characteristics and issues and prioritize gaining information that deepens understanding of theory and interventions. This plan should also incorporate time devoted to personal growth, including exploration of personal culture, values, social positionality, and privilege.

The pathway to learning everything there is to learn about leading groups and becoming a person who can effectively and optimally lead groups is endless but enriching and enjoyable. Reading group-related research and theory, attending conferences and workshops throughout their careers, and engaging in leading a variety of groups with supervision allows leaders to broaden and deepen their understanding of group leadership in ways that can directly benefit group members. Regardless of the form of learning, leaders should regard their ongoing learning as an important way to maintain their interest and enthusiasm. Ongoing development requires continuous self-examination, change, and professional growth. Leaders who choose to discontinue their development and stop challenging themselves could be at risk of becoming stagnant, boring, and ineffective as professionals and as people.

Leaders should also stay keenly aware that they are part of a broader social context. Because leaders understand how groups work, they also understand how society functions, how its various subgroups interact, and how this can be to the detriment of people's welfare. Group leaders should carefully consider how to use their knowledge to confront social issues in their groups, in their professional organizations, and in society. Although leaders may debate their obligation to become social activists, they must understand their obligation to confront the social issues that oppress the members of their groups.

Developing and growing as a group leader is both an intellectual and a personal process. Leaders should attend to their personal and spiritual growth and to their physical well-being. Ongoing personal growth should incorporate experiences that challenge comfortable personal boundaries. These experiences can include joining a therapy or a peer supervision group, attending personal growth workshops, or traveling in countries with diverse cultures. Leaders should also consider their own spiritual development, which is a matter of personal preference and can include participating in religious organizations, learning to meditate, spending time alone in the wilderness, and devoting time for quiet reflection. Finally, it is critically essential that leaders attend to their physical well-being. This is necessary if group leaders are to deal effectively with the stress of leading groups and maintaining the emotional balance necessary to operate at their highest level of awareness and energy.

References

Agazarian, Y. M. (1997). *Systems-centered therapy for groups*. Guilford Press.

Agazarian, Y. M. (2012). Systems-centered group psychotherapy: Putting theory into practice. *International Journal of Group Psychotherapy, 62*(2), 171–195. https://doi.org/10.1521/ijgp.2012.62.2.171

Alldredge, C. T., Burlingame, G. M., Yang, C., & Rosendahl, J. (2021). Alliance in group therapy: A meta-analysis. *Group Dynamics: Theory, Research, and Practice, 25*(1), 13–28. https://doi.org/10.1037/gdn0000135

American Academy of Pediatrics. (n.d.). *AAP-AACAP-CHA declaration of a national emergency in child and adolescent mental health*. https://www.aap.org/en/advocacy/child-and-adolescent-healthy-mental-development/aap-aacap-cha-declaration-of-a-national-emergency-in-child-and-adolescent-mental-health/

American Counseling Association. (2014). *ACA code of ethics*. https://www.counseling.org/resources/aca-code-of-ethics.pdf

American Group Psychotherapy Association. (2002). *AGPA and IBCGP guidelines for ethics*. https://www.agpa.org/home/practice-resources/ethics-in-group-therapy

American Psychological Association. (2008). *Evidence-based practice in psychology*. https://www.apa.org/practice/resources/evidence

American Psychological Association. (2017). *Ethical principles of psychologists and code of conduct* (2002, amended effective June 1, 2010, and January 1, 2017). https://www.apa.org/ethics/code/

Association for Specialists in Group Work. (2000). Association for Specialists in Group Work professional standards for the training of group workers. *The Journal for Specialists in Group Work, 25*, 327–342.

Association for Specialists in Group Work. (2012). *Multicultural and social justice competence principles for group workers*. https://asgw.org/wp-content/uploads/2020/06/ASGW_MC_SJ_Priniciples_final_ASGW_Website_04_17_12.pdf

Association for Specialists in Group Work. (2021). *ASGW guiding principles for group work*. https://asgw.org/wp-content/uploads/2021/07/ASGW-Guiding-Principles-May-2021.pdf

Barker, P. (1992). *Basic family therapy*. Oxford University Press.

Bascue, L. O. (1978). A conceptual model for training group therapists. *International Journal of Group Psychotherapy, 28*(4), 445–452. https://doi.org/10.1080/00207284.1978.11491636

Battilana, J., & Kimsey, M. (2017, September 18). Should you agitate, innovate, or orchestrate? *Stanford Social Innovation Review*. https://doi.org/10.48558/3YGB-3M56

Becvar, D. S., & Becvar, R. J. (1996). *Family therapy: A systemic integration* (3rd ed.). Allyn & Bacon.

Becvar, R. J., Canfield, B. S., & Becvar, D. S. (1997). *Group work: Cybernetic, constructivist, and social constructionist perspectives*. Love Publishing Company.

Bemak, F., & Chung, R. C.-Y. (2004). Teaching multicultural group counseling: Perspectives for a new era. *The Journal for Specialists in Group Work, 29*(1), 31–41. https://www.tandfonline.com/doi/full/10.1080/01933920490275349

Benne, K. D., & Sheats, P. (1948). Functional roles of group members. *Journal of Social Issues, 2*, 42–47.

Bennis, W. G., & Shepard, H. A. (1956). A theory of group development. *Human Relations, 9*(4), 415–437. https://doi.org/10.1177/001872675600900403

Bernard, H., Burlingame, G., Flores, P., Greene, L., Joyce, A., Kobos, J. C., Leszcz, M., MacNair-Semands, R. R., Piper, W. E., McEneaney, A. M. S., & Feirman, D. (2008). Clinical practice guidelines for group psychotherapy. *International Journal of Group Psychotherapy, 58*(4), 455–542. https://doi.org/10.1521/ijgp.2008.58.4.455

Bernard, H. S., & MacKenzie, K. R. (Eds.). (1994). *Basics of group psychotherapy*. Guilford Press.

Bernard, J. M. (1979). Supervisor training: A discrimination model. *Counselor Education and Supervision, 19*(1), 60–68.

Bion, W. R. (1961). *Experiences in groups*. Basic Books.

Bloch, S., & Crouch, E. (1985). *Therapeutic factors in group psychotherapy*. Oxford University Press.

Borders, L. D. (1991). A systematic approach to peer group supervision. *Journal of Counseling & Development, 69*(3), 248–252. https://doi.org/10.1002/j.1556-6676.1991.tb01497.x

Bowen, M. (1966). The use of family theory in clinical practice. *Comprehensive Psychiatry, 7*(5), 345–374.

Brabender, V. (2006). The ethical group psychotherapist. *International Journal of Group Psychotherapy, 56*(4), 395–414. https://doi.org/10.1521/ijgp.2006.56.4.395

Brabender, V. M., & Fallon, A. (2009). Ethical hot spots of combined individual and group therapy: Applying four ethical systems. *International Journal of Group Psychotherapy, 59*(1), 127–147. https://doi.org/10.1521/ijgp.2009.59.1.127

Briggs, C. A., Foster, L. H., & Moore, M. (2019). Groups with individuals, couples, and families in mental health settings. In D. Cappuzzi & M. Stauffer, *Foundations of group counseling* (pp. 261–280). Pearson.

Bugental, J. F. T. (1965). *The search for authenticity: An existential-analytic approach to psychotherapy*. Holt, Rinehart and Winston.

Burlingame, G. M., Fuhriman, A. J., & Johnson, J. (2004). Process and outcome in group counseling and psychotherapy: A perspective. In J. L. DeLucia-Waack, D. A. Gerrity, C. R. Kalodner, & M. T. Riva (Eds.), *Handbook of group counseling and psychotherapy* (pp. 49–61). Sage Publications. https://doi.org/10.4135/9781452229683.n4

Burlingame, G. M., & Jensen, J. L. (2017). Small group process and outcome research highlights: A 25-year perspective. *International Journal of Group Psychotherapy, 67*(1), S194–S218. http://doi.org/10.1080/00207284.2016.1218287

Burlingame, G. M., McClendon, D., & Alonso, J. (2011a). Cohesion in group psychotherapy. In J. C. Norcross (Ed.), *A guide to psychotherapy relationships that work* (2nd ed., pp. 110–131). Oxford University.

Burlingame, G. M., McClendon, D. T., & Alonso, J. (2011b). Cohesion in group therapy. *Psychotherapy, 48*(1), 34–42. https://psycnet.apa.org/doi/10.1037/a0022063

Burlingame, G. M., McClendon, D. T., & Yang, C. (2018). Cohesion in group therapy: A meta-analysis. *Psychotherapy, 55*(4), 384–398. https://psycnet.apa.org/doi/10.1037/pst0000173

Burlingame, G. M., Strauss, B., & Joyce, A. (2013). Change mechanisms and effectiveness of small group treatments. In M. J. Lambert (Ed.), *Bergin & Garfield's handbook of psychotherapy and behavior change* (6th ed., pp. 640–689). Wiley & Sons.

Burlingame, G. M., Whitcomb, K., & Woodland, S. (2014). Process and outcome in group counseling and psychotherapy perspective. In J. L. DeLucia-Waack, C. R. Kalodner, & M. T. Riva (Eds.), *Handbook of group counseling and psychotherapy* (2nd ed., pp. 55–70). Sage Publications. http://doi.org/10.4135/9781544308555.n5

Burrow, T. (1928). The basis of group-analysis, or the analysis of the reactions of normal and neurotic individuals. *British Journal of Medical Psychology, 8*, 198–206. https://doi.org/10.1111/j.2044-8341.1928.tb00686.x

Byrd, D., & McKinney, K. J. (2012). Individual, interpersonal, and institutional level factors associated with the mental health of college students. *Journal of American College Health, 60*(3), 185–193. http://doi.org/10.1080/07448481.2011.584334

Carroll, M., Bates, M., & Johnson, C. (1997). *Group leadership: Strategies for group counseling leaders* (3rd ed.). Love.

Champe, J., Okech, J. E. A., & Rubel, D. (2013). Emotion regulation: Processes, strategies, and applications for group work training and supervision. *The Journal for Specialists in Group Work, 38*(4), 349–368. http://doi.org/10.1080/01933922.2013.834403

Champe, J., & Rubel, D. J. (2012). Application of focal conflict theory to psychoeducational groups: Implications for process, content, and leadership. *The Journal for Specialists in Group Work, 37*(1), 71–90. https://doi.org/10.1080/01933922.2011.632811

Chan, F., Chronister, J., Catalana, D., Chase, A., & Eun-Jeong, L. (2004). Foundations of rehabilitation counseling. *Directions of Rehabilitation Counseling, 15*, 1–11.

Chan, G. H. (2020). A comparative analysis of online, offline, and integrated counseling among hidden youth in Hong Kong. *Children and Youth Services Review, 114*, Article 105042. https://doi.org/10.1016/j.childyouth.2020.105042

Chen, E. C., Kakkad, D., & Balzano, J. (2008). Multicultural competence and evidence-based practice in group therapy. *Journal of Clinical Psychology, 64*(11), 1261–1278. http://doi.org/10.1002/jclp.20533

Chouliara, Z., Karatzias, T., Gullone, A., Ferguson, S., Cosgrove, K., & Draucker, C. B. (2020). Therapeutic change in group therapy for interpersonal trauma: A relational framework for research and clinical practice. *Journal of Interpersonal Violence, 35*(15-16), 2897–2916. http://doi.org/10.1177/0886260517696860

Cialdini, R. B., Kallgren, C. A., & Reno, R. R. (1991). A focus theory of normative conduct: A theoretical refinement and reevaluation of the role of norms in human behavior. *Advances in Experimental Social Psychology, 24*, 201–234. https://doi.org/10.1016/S0065-2601(08)60330-5

Connors, J. V., & Caple, R. B. (2005). A review of group systems theory. *The Journal for Specialists in Group Work, 30*(2), 93–110. http://doi.org/10.1080/01933920590925940

Corey, G., Williams, G. T., & Moline, M. E. (1995). Ethical and legal issues in group counseling. *Ethics & Behavior, 5*(2), 161–183. https://doi.org/10.1207/s15327019eb0502_4

Corey, M. S., Corey, G., & Corey, C. (2017). *Groups: Process and practice* (10th ed.). Cengage Learning.

Corsini, R., & Rosenberg, B. (1955). Mechanisms of group psychotherapy: Processes and dynamics. *The Journal of Abnormal and Social Psychology, 51*(3), 406–411. https://doi.org/10.1037/h0048439

Couch, R. D. (1995). Four steps for conducting a pregroup screening interview. *The Journal for Specialists in Group Work, 20*(1), 18–25. https://doi.org/10.1080/01933929508411321

Council for Accreditation of Counseling and Related Educational Programs. (2024). *2024 CACREP standards.* https://www.cacrep.org/wp-content/uploads/2023/06/2024-Standards-Combined-Version-6.27.23.pdf

D'Andrea, M., & Daniels, J. (1997). Multicultural group counseling. In S. T. Gladding (Ed.), *New developments in group counseling* (ED404610)(pp. 105–110). ERIC. https://files.eric.ed.gov/fulltext/ED404610.pdf

Davis, M. H., & Franzoi, S. L. (1987). Private self-consciousness and self-disclosure. In V. J. Derlega & J. H. Berg (Eds.), *Self-disclosure: Theory, research, and therapy.* Plenum.

Day, M. (1993). Training and supervision in group psychotherapy. In H. I. Kaplan & B. J. Saddock (Eds.), *Comprehensive group psychotherapy* (3rd ed., pp. 656–668). Williams & Wilkins.

Debiak, D. (2007). Attending to diversity in group psychotherapy: An ethical imperative. *International Journal of Group Psychotherapy, 57*(1), 1–12. https://doi.org/10.1521/ijgp.2007.57.1.1

Dies, R. R. (1993). Research on group psychotherapy: Overview and clinical applications. In A. Alonso & H. I. Swiller (Eds.), *Group therapy in clinical practice* (pp. 473–518). American Psychiatric Press.

Donigian, J., & Hulse-Killacky, D. (1999). *Critical incidents in group therapy* (2nd ed.). Brooks/Cole.

Donigian, J., & Malnati, R. (1997). *Systemic group therapy: A triadic model.* Brooks/Cole.

Durkin, H. E. (1981). Group therapies and general systems theory as an integrative structure. In J. E. Durkin (Ed.), *Living groups: Group psychotherapy and general systems theory* (pp. 5–23). Brunner/Mazel.

Durkin, J. E. (Ed.). (1981). *Living groups: Group psychotherapy and general systems theory*. Brunner/Mazel.

Ellis, S. K., Simpson, C. G., Rose, C. A., & Plotner, A. J. (2014). Group work with persons with disabilities. In J. L. DeLucia-Waack, C. R. Kalodner, & A. T. Riva (Eds.), *Handbook of group counseling and psychotherapy* (2nd ed., pp. 264–275). Sage.

Ettin, M. F., Cohen, B. D., & Fidler, J. W. (1997). Group-as-a-whole theory viewed in its 20th-century context. *Group Dynamics: Theory, Research, and Practice, 1*(4), 329–340.

Falco, L. D., & Bauman, S. (2014). Group work in schools. In J. L. DeLucia-Waack, C. R. Kalodner, & A. T. Riva (Eds.), *Handbook of group counseling and psychotherapy* (2nd ed., pp. 318–328). Sage.

Faragher, J. M., & Soberay, A. (2014). Group approaches for addictive behaviors. In J. L. DeLucia-Waack, C. R. Kalodner, & A. T. Riva (Eds.), *Handbook of group counseling and psychotherapy* (2nd ed., pp. 410–420). Sage.

Fenster, A., & Fenster, J. (1998). Diagnosing deficits in "basic trust" in multiracial and multicultural groups: Individual or social psychopathology? *Group, 22*(2), 81–93. https://doi.org/10.1023/A:1022175412817

Forsyth, D. R. (1999). *Group dynamics* (3rd ed.). Brooks/Cole–Wadsworth.

Forsyth, D. (2011). Group dynamics. In R. Miller, E. Balcetis, S. Burns, D. Daniel, B. Saville, & W. Woody (Eds.), *Promoting student engagement: Vol. 2. Activities, exercises and demonstrations for psychology courses* (pp. 28–32). Society for the Teaching of Psychology, American Psychological Association.

Fortier, C. B., Currao, A., Kenna, A., Kim, S., Beck, B. M., Katz, D., Hursh, C., & Fonda, J. R. (2022). Online telehealth delivery of group mental health treatment is safe, feasible, and increases enrollment and attendance in post-9/11 U.S. veterans. *Behavior Therapy, 53*(3), 469–480. https://doi.org/10.1016/j.beth.2021.11.004

Freud, S. (1948). *Group psychology and the analysis of the ego*. Hogarth. (Original work published 1921)

Fulmer, R. (2018). The evolution of the psychodynamic approach and system. *International Journal of Psychological Studies, 10*(3), 1–6. https://doi.org/10.5539/ijps.v10n3p1

Furr, S. R. (2000). Structuring the group experience: A format for designing psychoeducational groups. *The Journal for Specialists in Group Work, 25*(1), 29–49. https://doi.org/10.1080/01933920008411450

Galinsky, A. D., Magee, J. C., Inesi, M. E., & Gruenfeld, D. H. (2006). Power and perspectives not taken. *Psychological Science, 17*(12), 1068–1074. https://doi.org/10.1111/j.1467-9280.2006.01824.x

Galinsky, M. J., Terzian, M. A., & Fraser, M. W. (2008). The art of group work practice with manualized curricula. *Social Work With Groups, 29*(1), 11–26. http://doi.org/10.1300/J009v29n01_03

Gbadamosi, O., Baghestan, A. G., & Al-Mabrouk, K. (2014). Gender, age and nationality: Assessing their impact on conflict resolution styles. *Journal of Management Development, 33*(3), 245–257. http://doi.org/10.1108/JMD-02-2011-0024

Gentry, M. T., Lapid, M. I., Clark, M. M., & Rummans, T. A. (2019). Evidence for telehealth group-based treatment: A systematic review. *Journal of Telemedicine and Telecare, 25*(6), 327–342. http://doi.org/10.1177/1357633X18775855

Geroski, A., Okech, J. E. A., & Krauss, K. (2021). *Group work in schools: Preparing, leading, responding*. Cognella.

Gibb, J. R. (1961). Defensive communication. *Journal of Communication, 11*(3), 141–148. https://doi.org/10.1111/j.1460-2466.1961.tb00344.x

Gibbard, G. S., Hartman, J. J., & Mann, R. D. (Eds.). (1974). *Analysis of groups*. Jossey-Bass.

Gill, D., Warburton, W., Simes, D., & Sweller, N. (2018). Group therapy for emotional dysregulation: Treatment for adolescents and their parents. *Child and Adolescent Social Work, 35*, 169–180. https://doi.org/10.1007/s10560-017-0510-8

Gladding, S. T. (1995). *Group work: A counseling specialty* (2nd ed.). Merrill.
Gladding, S. T. (1999). *Group work: A counseling specialty* (3rd ed.). Merrill.
Gladding, S. T. (2019). *Groups: A counseling specialty* (8th ed.). Pearson.
Gladding, S. (2021). *Counseling and psychotherapy: Theories and interventions*. Wiley.
Glass, J. S., & Benshoff, J. M. (1999). PARS: A processing model for beginning group leaders. *The Journal for Specialists in Group Work, 24*, 15–26.
Goldenberg, I., & Goldenberg, H. (1991). *Family therapy: An overview* (3rd ed.). Brooks/Cole.
Gray, W. (1981). The evolution of emotional-cognitive and system precursor theory. In J. E. Durkin (Ed.), *Living groups: Group psychotherapy and general systems theory* (pp. 5–23). Brunner/Mazel.
Greene, J., Sacks, R. M., & McMenamin, S. B. (2014). The impact of tobacco dependence treatment coverage and copayments in Medicaid. *American Journal of Preventive Medicine, 46*(4), 331–336.
Griffin, P. (1997). Introductory module for the single issue courses. In M. Adams, L.A. Bell, and P. Griffin (Eds.), *Teaching for Diversity and Social Justice: A Sourcebook* (pp.61–81). New York: Routledge.
Gullo, S., Lo Coco, G., Di Fratello, C., Giannone, F., Mannino, G., & Burlingame, G. (2015). Group climate, cohesion and curative climate. A study on the common factors in group process and their relation with members attachment dimensions. *Research in Psychotherapy: Psychopathology, Process and Outcome, 18*(1), 10–20. https://doi.org/10.4081/ripppo.2015.160
Haas, L. J., & Malouf, J. L. (2002). *Keeping up the good work: A practitioner's guide to mental health ethics* (3rd ed.). Professional Resource Press/Professional Resource Exchange.
Han, A., & Vasquez, M. (2000). Group intervention and treatment with ethnic minorities. In J. Aponte & J. Wold (Eds.), *Psychological intervention and cultural diversity* (2nd ed., pp. 110–130). Allyn & Bacon.
Hansen, J. C., Warner, R. W., & Smith, E. J. (1980). *Group counseling: Theory and process* (2nd ed.). Rand McNally.
Harley, D. A., & Kim, B. J. (2019). Groups in rehabilitation settings. In D. Cappuzzi & M. Stauffer, *Foundations of group counseling* (pp. 261–280). Pearson.
Havenga, W. (2008). Gender and age differences in conflict management within small businesses. *South African Journal of Human Resource Management, 6*(1), 22–28. http://doi.org/10.4102/sajhrm.v6i1.143
Haziza, N. (2018). Co-leadership and supervision: A group within a group. *Eastern Group Psychotherapy Society, 42*(1), 49–54. http://doi.org//10.13186/group.42.1.0049
Health Insurance Portability and Accountability Act of 1996, Pub. L. No. 104-191, § 264, 110 Stat. 1936 (1996). https://www.hhs.gov/hipaa/for-professionals/privacy/laws-regulations/combined-regulation-text/index.html

Helms, J., & Cook, D. (1999). *Using race and culture in counseling and psychotherapy: Theory and process*. Allyn & Bacon.

Hoag, M. J., & Burlingame, G. M. (1997). Evaluating the effectiveness of child and adolescent group treatment: A meta-analytic review. *Journal of Clinical Child Psychology, 26*(3), 234–246. http://doi.org/10.1207/s15374424jccp2603_2

Hollenbaugh, K. M. H., & Goodrich, K. M. (2021). Assessment and research standards in group work: A call to action for counselors, counselor educators, and researchers. *The Journal for Specialists in Group Work, 46*(3), 235–237. http://doi.org/10.1080/01933922.2021.1944572

Holmes, C. M., & Kozlowski, K. (2015). A preliminary comparison of online and face-to-face process groups. *Journal of Technology in Human Service, 33*(3), 241–262. http://doi.org/10.1080/15228835.2015.1038376

Horwitz, L. (2000). Narcissistic leadership in psychotherapy groups. *International Journal of Group Psychotherapy, 50*(2), 219–235. http://doi.org/10.1080/00207284.2000.11490999

Hulse-Killacky, D., Killacky, J., & Donigian, J. (2001). *Making task groups work in your world*. Merrill Prentice Hall.

Individuals With Disabilities Education Act, 20 U.S.C. § 1400 (2004).

Ivey, A. E. (1994). *Intentional interviewing and counseling: Facilitating client development in a multicultural society* (3rd ed.). Brooks/Cole.

Ivey, A. E., D'Andrea, M. J., & Ivey, M. B. (2011). *Theories of counseling and psychotherapy: A multicultural perspective* (7th ed.). Allyn & Bacon.

Jacobs, E. E., Schimmel, C. J., & Masson, R. L., & Harvill, R. L. (2012). *Group counseling: Strategies and skills* (8th ed.). Brooks/Cole

Janis, R. A., Burlingame, G. M., Svien, H., Jensen, J., & Lundgreen, R. (2021). Group therapy for mood disorders: A meta-analysis. *Psychotherapy Research, 31*(3), 342–358. https://doi.org/10.1080/10503307.2020.1817603

Johnson, D. W., & Johnson, F. P. (2000). *Joining together: Group theory and group skills* (7th ed.). Allyn & Bacon.

Johnson, J., Burlingame, G. M., Olsen, J. A., & Davies, D. R. (2005). Group climate, cohesion, alliance, and empathy in group psychotherapy: Multilevel structural equation models. *Journal of Counseling Psychology, 52*, 310–321. https://doi.org/10.1037/0022-0167.52.3.310

Jourard, S. M. (1964). *The transparent self*. Van Nostrand.

Kalodner, C. R., & Hanus, A. E. (2010). Groups across settings. In R. K. Conyne (Ed.), *The Oxford handbook of group counseling* (pp. 399–415). Oxford Library of Psychology.

Kernberg, O. (1976). *Object relations theory and clinical psychoanalysis*. Aronson.

Kerr, M. E. (1981). Family systems theory and therapy. In A. S. Gurman & D. P. Kniskern (Eds.), *Handbook of family therapy* (pp. 226–266). Brunner/Mazel.

Kivlighan, D. M., Jr., Gullo, S., Giordano, C., Di Blasi, M., Giannone, F., & Lo Coco, G. (2021). Group as a social microcosm: The reciprocal relationship between intersession intimate behaviors and in-session intimate behaviors. *Journal of Counseling Psychology, 68*(2), 208–218. https://psycnet.apa.org/doi/10.1037/cou0000495

Kivlighan, D. M., Jr., & Kivlighan, D. M., III. (2014). Therapeutic factors: Current theory and research. In J. L. DeLucia-Waack, C. R. Kalodner, & M. T. Riva (Eds.), *Handbook of group counseling and psychotherapy* (pp. 46–54). Sage Publications.

Kivlighan, D. M., III, Adams, M. C., Drinane, J. M., Tao, K. W., & Owen, J. (2019). Construction and validation of the multicultural orientation inventory—group version. *Journal of Counseling Psychology, 66*, 45–55. https://doi.org/10.1037/cou0000294

Kivlighan, D. M., III, Aloe, A. M., Adams, M. C., Garrison, Y. L., Obrecht, A., Ho, Y. C. S., Kim, J. Y. C., Hooley, I. W., Chan, L., & Deng, K. (2020). Does the group in group psychotherapy matter? A meta-analysis of the intraclass correlation coefficient in group treatment research. *Journal of Consulting and Clinical Psychology, 88*(4), 322–337. https://doi.org/10.1037/ccp0000474

Klein, R. H. (1996). Introduction to special section on termination and group therapy. *International Journal of Group Psychotherapy, 46*(1), 1–4. https://doi.org/10.1080/00207284.1996.11491480

Kline, W. B. (1986). Working through the risks: A structured experience to facilitate self-disclosure. *The Journal for Specialists in Group Work, 11*(4), 209–212. https://doi.org/10.1080/01933928608411858

Kline, W. B. (1990). Responding to "problem" members. *The Journal for Specialists in Group Work, 15*(4), 195–200. https://doi.org/10.1080/01933929008412227

Kline, W. B. (1997). Group as a whole dynamics and the "problem" member: Conceptualization and intervention. In S. T. Gladding (Ed.), *New developments in group counseling* (ED404610) (pp. 93–95). ERIC. https://files.eric.ed.gov/fulltext/ED404610.pdf

Kline, W. B. (2003). *Interactive group counseling and therapy*. Merrill Prentice Hall.

Kottler, J. A. (1994). Working with difficult group members. *The Journal for Specialists in Group Work, 19*(1), 3–10. https://doi.org/10.1080/01933929408413757

Kozlowski, K. A., & Holmes, C. M. (2014). Experiences in online process groups: A qualitative study. *The Journal for Specialists in Group Work, 39*(4), 276–300. http://doi.org/10.1080/01933922.2014.948235

Lasky, G. B., & Riva, M. T. (2006). Confidentiality and privileged communication in group psychotherapy. *International Journal of Group Psychotherapy, 56*(4), 455–476. https://doi.org/10.1521/ijgp.2006.56.4.455

Lazerson, J. S., & Zilbach, J. J. (1993). Gender issues in group psychotherapy. In H. I. Kaplan & B. J. Saddock (Eds.), *Comprehensive group psychotherapy* (3rd ed., pp. 682–692). Williams & Wilkins.

Leahy, M. J., Muenzen, P., Saunders, J. L., & Strauser, D. (2009). Essential knowledge domains underlying effective rehabilitation counseling practice. *Rehabilitation Counseling Bulletin, 52*(2), 95–106. https://doi.org/10.1177/0034355208323646

Lee, C. C. (1991). New approaches to diversity: Implications for multicultural counselor training and research. In C. C. Lee & B. L. Richardson (Eds.), *Multicultural issues in counseling: New approaches to diversity.* American Association for Counseling and Development.

Lee, R. M., & Robbins, S. B. (2000). Understanding social connectedness in college women and men. *Journal of Counseling & Development, 78*(4), 484–495. http://doi.org/10.1002/j.1556-6676.2000.tb01932.x

Lerardi, E., Bottini, M., & Crugnola, C. R. (2022). Effectiveness of an online versus face-to-face psychodynamic counseling intervention for university students before and during the COVID-19 period. *BMC Psychology, 10*, Article 35, 1–10. https://doi.org/10.1186/s40359-022-00742-7

Leszcz, M. (1992). The interpersonal approach to group psychotherapy. *International Journal of Group Psychotherapy, 42*(1), 37–62. https://doi.org/10.1080/00207284.1992.11732579

Levine, B. (1991). *Group psychotherapy: Practice and development*. Waveland Press.

Lewin, K. (1944). The dynamics of group action. *Educational Leadership, 1*, 195–200.

Lieberman, M. (2013). *Social: Why our brains are wired to connect*. Crown Publishers.

Lieberman, M., Yalom, I., & Miles, M. (1973). *Encounter groups: First facts.* Basic Books.

Lindbloom, G., Ten Eyck, T., & Gallon, S. (2005). *Clinical supervision I: Building chemical dependency counseling skills* (3rd ed.). Northwest Frontier Addiction Technology Transfer Center.

Lleras de Frutos, M., Medina, J. C., Vives, J., Casellas-Grau, A., Marzo, J. L., Borràs, J. M., & Ochoa-Arnedo, C. (2020). Video conference vs face-to-face group psychotherapy for distressed cancer survivors: A randomized controlled trial. *Psycho-Oncology, 29*(12), 1995–2003. https://doi.org/10.1002/pon.5457

Lorentzen, S., Strauss, B., & Altmann, U. (2018). Process-outcome relationships in short- and long-term psychodynamic group psychotherapy: Results from a randomized clinical trial. *Group Dynamics: Theory, Research, and Practice, 22*(2), 93–107. https://doi.org/10.1037/gdn0000084

Luke, M., & Hackney, H. (2007). Group coleadership: A critical review. *Counselor Education and Supervision, 46*(4), 280–293. https://doi.org/10.1002/j.1556-6978.2007.tb00032.x

Macgowan, M. J., & Hanbridge, A. S. (2014). Advancing evidence-based group work in community mental health settings: Methods, challenges, and opportunities. In J. L. DeLucia-Waack, C. R. Kalodner, & A. T. Riva (Eds.), *Handbook of group counseling and psychotherapy* (2nd ed., pp. 303–317). Sage.

MacKenzie, K. R. (1990). *Introduction to time-limited group psychotherapy*. American Psychiatric Press.

MacKenzie, K. R. (1992). *Classics in group psychotherapy*. Guilford Press.

MacKenzie, K. R. (1994). The developing structure of the therapy group system. In H. S. Bernard & K. R. MacKenzie (Eds.), *Basics of group psychotherapy* (pp. 35–59). Guilford Press.

Male, D. A., Fergus, K. D., & Stephen, J. E. (2017). Professional online support group facilitators: Guarantors of maximal group utility. *International Journal of Group Psychotherapy, 67*(3), 314–336. http://doi.org/10.1080/00207284.2016.1240587

Mangione, L., Forti, R., & Iacuzzi, C. M. (2007). Ethics and endings in group psychotherapy: Saying good-bye and saying it well. *International Journal of Group Psychotherapy, 57*(1), 25–40. https://doi.org/10.1521/ijgp.2007.57.1.25

Marmarosh, C. L., Markin, R. D., & Spiegel, E. B. (2013). *Attachment in group psychotherapy*. American Psychological Association.

Maslow, A. H. (1970). *Motivation and personality* (2nd ed.). Harper & Row.

McCarthy, C. J., Bauman, S., Choudhuri, D. D., Coker, A., Justice, C., Kraus, K. L., Luke, M., Rubel, D., & Shaw, L. (2021). Association for Specialists in Group Work guiding principles for group work. *The Journal for Specialists in Group Work, 47*(1), 10–21. https://doi.org/10.1080/01933922.2021.1950882

McRae, M. B. (1994). Interracial group dynamics: A new perspective. *The Journal for Specialists in Group Work, 19*(3), 168–174. https://doi.org/10.1080/01933929408414361

Mead, W. R. (1977). Feedback: A "how to" primer for t-group participants. In R. T. Golembiewski & A. Blumberg (Eds.), *Sensitivity training and the laboratory approach: Readings about concepts and applications* (3rd ed., pp. 92–109). Peacock.

Miles, J. R., Anders, C., Kivlighan, D. M., III, & Belcher Platt, A. A. (2021). Cultural ruptures: Addressing microaggressions in group therapy. *Group Dynamics: Theory, Research, and Practice, 25*(1), 74–88. https://doi.org/10.1037/gdn0000149

Miles, J. R., & Paquin, J. D. (2013). Best practices in group counseling and psychotherapy research. In J. DeLucia-Waack, C. Kalodner, & M. Riva (Eds.), *Handbook of group counseling and psychotherapy* (2nd ed., pp. 178–192). Sage Publications.

Mind Tools Content Team. (n.d.). *Self-disclosure: Connecting with honest and personal communication*. https://www.mindtools.com/pages/article/self-disclosure.htm

Minuchin, S. (1974). *Families and family therapy*. Harvard University Press.

Morgan, R. D., Romani, C. J., & Gross, N. R. (2014). Group work with offenders and mandated clients. In J. L. DeLucia-Waack, C. R. Kalodner, & M. T. Riva (Eds.), *Handbook of group counseling and psychotherapy* (pp. 441–449). Sage Publications.

Muskat, B., Mishna, F., Farnia, F., & Wiener, J. (2010). "We may not like it, but we guess we have to do it": Bringing agency-based staff on board with evidence-based group work. *Social Work With Groups, 33*(2-3), 229–247. http://doi.org/10.1080/01609510903366228

Namburi, N., & Tadi, P. (2021). *Managed care economics.* StatPearls Publishing.

Okech, J. E. A. (2008). Reflective practice in group co-leadership. *The Journal for Specialists in Group Work, 33*(3), 245–266. https://doi.org/10.1080/01933920802196138

Okech, J. E. A. (2015). The ORAL model for feedback exchange. In M. Luke & K. Goodrich (Eds.), *Group work experts share their favorite supervision activities: Vol. 2* (pp. 162–167). Association for Specialists in Group Work.

Okech, J. E. A. (2023). Effective observation: Skills of process observation. In D. Choudhuri & C. J. McCarthy (Eds.), *Fundamentals of group process observation* (pp. 19–30). Taylor & Francis.

Okech, J. E. A., & Kline, W. B. (2005). A qualitative exploration of group co-leader relationships. *The Journal for Specialists in Group Work, 30*(2), 173–190. http://doi.org/10.1080/01933920590926048

Okech, J. E. A., & Kline, W. B. (2006). Competency concerns in group co-leader relationships. *The Journal for Specialists in Group Work, 31*(2), 165–180. http://doi.org/10.1080/01933920500493829

Okech, J. E. A., Ort, J., Steen, S., & Goodrich, K. (2022). New group work practice manuscripts: Recommendations for manuscript development [Editorial]. *The Journal for Specialists in Group Work, 47*(1), 1–9. http://doi.org/10.1080/01933922.2022.2014744

Okech, J. E. A., Pimpleton, A. M., Vannata, R., & Champe, J. (2015). Intercultural communication: An application to group work. *The Journal for Specialists in Group Work, 40*(3), 268–293. http://doi.org/10.1080/01933922.2015.1056568

Okech, J. E. A., Pimpleton-Gray, A. M., Vannata, R., & Champe, J. (2016). Intercultural conflict in groups. *The Journal for Specialists in Group Work, 41*(4), 350–369. http://doi.org/10.1080/01933922.2016.1232769

Okech, J. E. A., & Rubel, D. (2007). Diversity competent group work supervision: An application of the supervision of group work model (SGW). *The Journal for Specialists in Group Work, 32*(3), 245–266. http://doi.org/10.1080/01933920701431651

Okech, J. E. A., Rubel, J. D., Jamaleddine, M., Hutchinson, C., & Redmond, L. (2023). Applying the principles of anti-oppression to group work supervision. *The Journal for Specialists in Group Work, 48*(2), 90–108. https://doi.org/10.1080/01933922.2023.2190775

Ormont, L. (1990). The craft of bridging. *International Journal of Group Psychotherapy, 40*(1), 3–17. http://doi.org/10.1080/00207284.1990.11490580

Pager, S. C., Kuipers, P., Bell, K., & Hall, F. (2018). Evaluation of a peer group model of supervision for the Allied Health Workforce in Queensland: A descriptive overview. *The Internet Journal of Allied Health Sciences and Practice, 16*(2), 1–8.

Paquin, J. C. (2017). Delivering the treatment so that the therapy occurs: Enhancing the effectiveness of time-limited, manualized group treatments. *International Journal of Group Psychotherapy, 67*(sup1), S141–S153. https://doi.org/10.1080/00207284.2016.1218771

Patterson, J. B., Szymanski, E. M., & Parker, R. M. (2005). Rehabilitation counseling: The profession. In R. M. Parker, E. M. Szymanski, & J. B. Patterson (Eds.), *Rehabilitation counseling: Basics and beyond* (pp. 1–25). PRO-ED.

Piper, W. E. (1993). The use of transference interpretation. *American Journal of Psychotherapy, 47*(4), 477–478. https://doi.10.1176/appi.psychotherapy.1993.47.4.477

Piper, W. E. (1994). Client variables. In A. Fuhriman & G. M. Burlingame (Eds.), *Handbook of group psychotherapy* (pp. 83–113). John Wiley and Sons.

Piper, W. E., Joyce, A. S., McCallum, M., & Azim, H. F. (1998). Interpretive and supportive forms of psychotherapy and patient personality variables. *Journal of Consulting and Clinical Psychology, 66*(3), 558–567. https://doi.org/10.1037/0022-006X.66.3.558

Piper, W. E., Ogrodniczuk, J. S., Joyce, A. S., Weideman, R., & Rosie, J. S. (2007). Group composition and group therapy for complicated grief. *Journal of Consulting and Clinical Psychology, 75*(1), 116–125. http://doi.org/10.1037/0022-006X.75.1.116

Pollio, D. E., & Macgowan, M. J. (2010). The andragogy of evidence-based group work: An integrated educational model. *Social Work With Groups, 33*(2-3), 195–209. http://doi.org/10.1080/01609510903498617

Porter, L. M., & Mohr, B. (1982). Conditions for laboratory learning. In L. M. Porter & B. Mohr (Eds.), *Readings book for human relations training* (7th ed., p. 10). National Training Laboratory Institute.

Pratt, J. H. (1906). The home sanitorium treatment of consumption. *Boston Medical and Surgical Journal, 17*(154), 210–216.

Rath, T. & Conchie, B. (2009). *Strengths based leadership: Great leaders, teams, and why people follow*. Gallup Press.

Raven, B. H., & French, J. R. P., Jr. (1965). Social influence and power. In I. D. Steiner & M. Fishbein (Eds.), *Current studies in social psychology* (pp. 371–382). Holt, Rinehart and Winston.

Rice, C. A. (1996). Premature termination of group therapy: A clinical perspective. *International Journal of Group Psychotherapy, 46*(1), 5–23. http://doi.org/10.1080/00207284.1996.11491481

Rioch, M. J. (1975). The work of Wilfred Bion on groups. In A. D. Colman & W. H. Bexton (Eds.), *Group relations reader* (pp. 21–23). GREX.

Riva, M. T. (2014). Supervision of group leaders. In J. L. DeLucia-Waack, C. R. Kalodner, & M. T. Riva (Eds.), *Handbook of group counseling and psychotherapy* (pp. 146–158). Sage Publications. https://doi.org/10.4135/9781544308555.n12

Rogers, C. R. (1961). *On becoming a person*. Houghton Mifflin.

Rogers, C. R. (1970). *Carl Rogers on encounter groups*. Harper & Row.

Roller, B., & Nelson, V. (1993). Cotherapy. In H. I. Kaplan & B. J. Saddock (Eds.), *Comprehensive group psychotherapy* (3rd ed., pp. 304–312). Williams & Wilkins.

Rosenberg, P. P. (1993). Qualities of the group psychotherapist. In H. I. Kaplan & B. J. Saddock (Eds.), *Comprehensive group psychotherapy* (3rd ed., pp. 648–656). Williams & Wilkins.

Rubel, D. (2006). Diversity issues in group work. In D. Capuzzi, D. Gross, & M. Stauffer (Eds.), *Introduction to group work* (4th ed., pp. 213–238). Love Publishing.

Rubel, D., & Okech, J. E. A. (2006). The supervision of group work model: Adapting the discrimination model for supervision of group workers. *The Journal for Specialists in Group Work, 31*(2), 113–134. http://doi.org/10.1080/01933920500493597

Rubel, D., & Okech, J. E. A. (2010). Diversity issues in group work. In D. Capuzzi, D. Gross, & M. Stauffer (Eds.), *Introduction to group work* (5th ed., pp. 219–247). Love.

Rubel, D., & Okech, J. E. A. (2018). Diversity and multicultural group counseling. In D. Capuzzi & M. Stauffer (Eds.), *Foundations of group counseling* (pp. 111–131). Pearson.

Rutan, J. S. (1993). Preface. In A. Alonso & H. I. Swiller (Eds.), *Group therapy in clinical practice* (pp. xxi–xxix). American Psychiatric Press.

Salvendy, J. T. (1993). Selection and preparation of patients and organization of the group. In H. I. Kaplan & B. J. Saddock (Eds.), *Comprehensive group psychotherapy* (3rd ed., pp. 73–79). Williams & Wilkins.

Scheidlinger, S. (1993). History of group psychotherapy. In H. I. Saddock & B. J. Kaplan (Eds.), *Comprehensive group psychotherapy* (3rd ed., pp. 1–24). Williams & Wilkins.

Schutz, W. C. (1966). *The interpersonal underworld*. Science and Behavior Books.

Schutz, W. C. (1973). *Elements of encounter*. Joy Press.

Shapiro, J. L., Peltz, L. S., & Bernadette-Shapiro, S. (1998). *Brief group treatment: Practical training for therapists and counselors*. Brooks/Cole.

Sharf, R. S. (1996). *Theories of psychotherapy and counseling: Concepts and cases*. Brooks/Cole.

Sherif, M. (1936). *The psychology of social norms*. Harper & Row.

Shin, R. Q., Smith, L. C., Welch, J. C., & Ezeofor, I. (2016). Is Allison more likely than Lakisha to receive a callback from counseling professionals? A racism audit study. *The Counseling Psychologist, 44*(8), 1187–1211. https://doi.org/10.1177/0011000016668

Simon, G. M. (2015). Structural couple therapy. In A. S. Gurman, J. L. Lebow, & D. K. Snyder (Eds.), *Clinical handbook of couple therapy* (5th ed., pp. 358–384). Guilford Press.

Singh, A. A., Merchant, N., Skudrzyk, B., & Ingene, D. (2012). Association for Specialists in Group Work: Multicultural and social justice competence principles for group workers. *The Journal for Specialists in Group Work, 37*(4), 312–325. http://doi.org/10.1080/01933922.2012.721482

Sklare, G., Keener, R., & Mas, C. (1990). Preparing members for "here-and-now" group counseling. *The Journal for Specialists in Group Work, 15*(3), 141–148. https://doi.org/10.1080/01933929008411924

Sogra, K. J. (2014). *The impact of gender differences on the conflict management styles of managers in Bangladesh: An analysis.* Cambridge Scholars Publishing.

Spencer-Rodgers, J., & McGovern, T. (2002). Attitudes toward the culturally different: The role of intercultural communication barriers, affective responses, consensual stereotypes, and perceived threat. *International Journal of Intercultural Relations, 26*(6), 609–631. http://doi.org/10.1016/S0147-1767(02)00038-X

Stapley, L. F. (2006). *Individuals, groups, and organizations beneath the surface.* H. Karnac.

Steen, S., Vasserman-Stokes, E., & Vannatta, R. (2014). Group cohesion in experiential growth groups. *The Journal for Specialists in Group Work, 39*(3), 236–256. http://doi.org/10.1080/01933922.2014.924343

Stock, D., & Lieberman, M. A. (1962). Methodological issues in the assessment of total-group phenomena in group therapy. *International Journal of Group Psychotherapy, 12*(3), 312–325. https://doi.org/10.1080/00207284.1962.11508279

Stock, D., Whitman, R. M., & Lieberman, M. A. (1958). The deviant member in therapy groups. *Human Relations, 11*, 341–372.

Strupp, H. H., & Anderson, T. (1997). On the limitations of therapy manuals. *Clinical Psychology: Science and Practice, 4*(1), 76–82. https://doi.org/10.1111/j.1468-2850.1997.tb00101.x

Substance Abuse and Mental Health Services Administration. (n.d.). *SAMHSA—Behavioral health integration.* https://www.samhsa.gov/sites/default/files/samhsa-behavioral-health-integration.pdf

Sue, D. W., Alsaidi, S., Awad, M. N., Glaeser, E., Calle, C. Z., & Mendez, N. (2019). Disarming racial microaggressions: Micro intervention strategies for targets, White allies and bystanders. *American Psychologist, 74*, 128–142. https://doi.org/10.1037/amp0000296

Sue, D. W., & Sue, D. D. (2003). *Counseling the culturally diverse: Theory and practice* (4th ed.). John Wiley & Sons.

Sullivan, H. S. (1953). *The interpersonal theory of psychiatry.* Norton.

Sullivan, H. S. (1955). *Conceptions of modern psychiatry.* Tavistock.

Sung, Y., & Skovholt, T. M. (2019). Master group counselors' case conceptualizations. *The Journal for Specialists in Group Work, 44*(2), 118–137. http://doi.org/10.1080/01933922.2019.1599479

Thomas, N., Pilecki, B., & McKay, D. (2015). Contemporary cognitive therapy: A review of theory, history, and evidence. *Psychodynamic Psychiatry, 43*(3), 423–461. http://doi.org/10.1521/pdps.2015.43.3.423

Thomas, R. V., & Pender, D. A. (2008). Association for Specialists in Group Work: Best practice guidelines 2007 revisions. *The Journal for Specialists in Group Work, 33*(2), 111–117.

Ting-Toomey, S., & Chung, L. C. (2005). *Understanding intercultural communication*. Oxford University Press.

Tubbs, S. L. (1992). *A systems approach to small group interaction* (4th ed.). McGraw-Hill.

Tubbs, S. L., & Carter, R. M. (Eds.). (2020). *Shared experiences in human communication*. Routledge. https://doi.org/10.4324/9781351306560

Tuckman, B. W. (1965). Developmental sequences in small groups. *Psychological Bulletin, 63*, 384–399.

Tuckman, B. W., & Jensen, M. A. C. (1977). Stages of small group development revisited. *Group and Organizational Studies, 2*(4), 419–427. http://doi.org/10.1177/105960117700200404

Urofsky, R. I., Engels, D. W., & Engebretson, K. (2008). Kitchener's principle ethics: Implications for counseling practice and research. *Counseling and Values, 53*(1), 67–78. https://doi.org/10.1002/j.2161-007X.2009.tb00114.x

Valentino, A. L., LeBlanc, L. A., & Sellers, T. P. (2016). The benefits of group supervision and a recommended structure for implementation. *Behavior Analysis in Practice, 9*(4), 320–328. https://doi.org/10.1007/s40617-016-0138-8

Vander Kolk, C. J. (1985). *Introduction to group counseling and psychotherapy*. Merrill.

Van Nieuwenhove, K., Truijens, F., Meganck, R., Cornelis, S., & Desmet, M. (2020). Working through childhood trauma-related interpersonal patterns in psychodynamic treatment: An evidence-based case study. *Psychological Trauma, 12*(1), 64–74. http://doi.org/10.1037/tra0000438

Varkey, B. (2021). Principles of clinical ethics and their application to practice. *Medical Principles and Practice, 30*, 17–28. http://doi.org/10.1159/000509119

Vinogradov, S., & Yalom, I. D. (1990). Self-disclosure in group psychotherapy. In G. Stricker & M. Fisher (Eds.), *Self-disclosure in the therapeutic relationship* (pp. 191–204). Plenum Press. https://doi.org/10.1007/978-1-4899-3582-3_13

Walling, S. M., Suvak, M. K., Howard, J. M., Taft, C. T., & Murphy, C. M. (2012). Race/ethnicity as a predictor of change in working alliance during cognitive behavioral therapy for intimate partner violence perpetrators. *Psychotherapy, 49*(2), 180–189. http://doi.org/10.1037/a0025751

Watzlawick, P., Weakland, J., & Fisch, R. (1974). *Change: Principles of problem formation and problem resolution*. Norton.

Weinberg, H. (2020). Online group psychotherapy: Challenges and possibilities during COVID-19—A practice review. *Group Dynamics, 24*(3), 201–211. https://doi.org/10.1037/gdn0000140

Weinberg, H. (2021). Obstacles, challenges, and benefits of online group psychotherapy. *American Journal of Psychotherapy, 74*(2), 83–88. https://doi.org/10.1176/appi.psychotherapy.20200034

Weiner, M. (1993). Role of the leader in group psychotherapy. In H. I. Saddock & B. J. Sadock (Eds.), *Comprehensive group psychotherapy* (3rd ed., pp. 85–93). Williams & Wilkins

Welfel, E. (2013). *Ethics in counselling and psychotherapy: Standards, research and emerging issues* (5th ed.). Brooks/Cole.

Wender, L. (1936). The dynamics of group psychotherapy and its application. *Journal of Nervous and Mental Disease, 84*(1), 54–60. https://doi.org/10.1097/00005053-193607000-00005

Wheelan, S. A. (1994). *Group processes: A developmental approach.* Allyn & Bacon.

Whitaker, D. S. (1985). *Using groups to help people*. Routledge.

Whitaker, D. S. (1989). Group focal conflict theory: Description, illustration and evaluation. *Group, 13*, 225–251. https://doi.org/10.1007/bf01473154

Whitaker, D. S., & Lieberman, M. A. (1964). *Psychotherapy through the group process*. Atherton Press.

Whittingham, M. (2014). Group work in colleges and university counseling centers. In J. L. DeLucia-Waack, C. R. Kalodner, & A. T. Riva (Eds.), *Handbook of group counseling and psychotherapy* (2nd ed., pp. 329–339). Sage.

Woods, J., & Ruzek, N. (2018). Ethics in group psychotherapy. In M. D. Ribeiro, J. M. Gross, & M. M. Turner (Eds.), *The college counselor's guide to group psychotherapy* (pp. 83–100). Routledge/Taylor & Francis Group. https://doi.org/10.4324/9781315545455-9

Wright, F. (2000). The use of self in group leadership: A relational perspective. *International Journal of Group Psychotherapy, 50*(2), 181–198. https://doi.org/10.1080/00207284.2000.11490997

Xiao, H., Carney, D. M., Youn, S. J., Janis, R. A., Castonguay, L. G., Hayes, J. A., & Locke, B. D. (2017). Are we in crisis? National mental health and treatment trends in college counseling centers. *Psychological Services, 14*(4), 407–415. https://doi.org/10.1037/ser0000130

Yalom, I. D. (1970). *The theory and practice of group psychotherapy*. Basic Books.

Yalom, I. D. (1975). *The theory and practice of group psychotherapy* (2nd ed.). Basic Books.

Yalom, I. D. (1995). *The theory and practice of group psychotherapy* (4th ed.). Basic Books.

Yalom, I. D., & Leszcz, M. (2005). *The theory and practice of group psychotherapy* (5th ed.). Basic Books.

Yalom, I. D., & Leszcz, M. (2020). *The theory and practice of group psychotherapy* (6th ed.). Basic Books.

Yalom, V. J., & Vinogradov, S. (1993). Interpersonal group psychotherapy. In H. I. Kaplan & B. J. Saddock (Eds.), *Comprehensive group psychotherapy* (3rd ed., pp. 185–195). Williams & Wilkins.

Young, M. E. (1992). *Counseling methods and techniques: An eclectic approach.* Merrill.

Yu, A., & Gregg, C. H. (1993). Asians in groups: More than a matter of cultural awareness. *The Journal for Specialists in Group Work, 18*(2), 86–93. https://doi.org/10.1080/01933929308413741

Index

Figures and tables are indicated by "f" and "t" following the page numbers.

A

(Continued)

B

(Continued)

(Continued)

G

(Continued)

J

K

L

Q

R

(Continued)

T

U

V